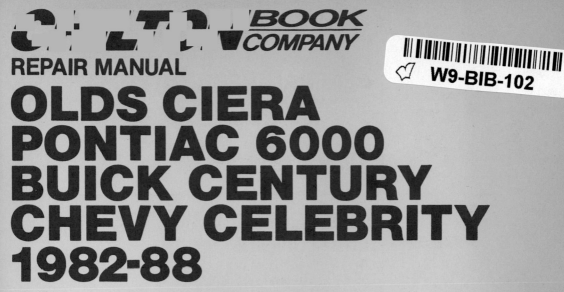

**CHILTON BOOK COMPANY**

# REPAIR MANUAL

# OLDS CIERA
# PONTIAC 6000
# BUICK CENTURY
# CHEVY CELEBRITY
# 1982-88

## All U.S. and Canadian front wheel drive models

W9-BIB-102

President GARY R. INGERSOLL
Senior Vice President, Book Publishing and Research RONALD A. HOXTER
Publisher KERRY A. FREEMAN, S.A.E.
Editor-in-Chief DEAN F. MORGANTINI, S.A.E.
Senior Editor RICHARD J. RIVELE, S.A.E.


CHILTON BOOK COMPANY
Radnor, Pennsylvania
19089

# CONTENTS

## SAFETY NOTICE

Proper service and repair procedures are vital to the safe, reliable operation of all motor vehicles, as well as the personal safety of those performing repairs. This book outlines procedures for servicing and repairing vehicles using safe, effective methods. The procedures contain many NOTES, CAUTIONS and WARNINGS which should be followed along with standard safety procedures to eliminate the possibility of personal injury or improper service which could damage the vehicle or compromise its safety.

It is important to note that repair procedures and techniques, tools and parts for servicing motor vehicles, as well as the skill and experience of the individual performing the work vary widely. It is not possible to anticipate all of the conceivable ways or conditions under which vehicles may be serviced, or to provide cautions as to all of the possible hazards that may result. Standard and accepted safety precautions and equipment should be used when handling toxic or flammable fluids, and safety goggles or other protection should be used during cutting, grinding, chiseling, prying, or any other process that can cause material removal or projectiles.

Some procedures require the use of tools specially designed for a specific purpose. Before substituting another tool or procedure, you must be completely satisfied that neither your personal safety, nor the performance of the vehicle will be endangered.

Although information in this guide is based on industry sources and is as complete as possible at the time of publication, the possibility exists that the manufacturer made later changes which could not be included here. While striving for total accuracy, Chilton Book Company cannot assume responsibility for any errors, changes, or omissions that may occur in the compilation of this data.

## PART NUMBERS

Part numbers listed in this reference are not recommendations by Chilton for any product by brand name. They are references that can be used with interchange manuals and aftermarket supplier catalogs to locate each brand supplier's discrete part number.

## SPECIAL TOOLS

Special tools are recommended by the vehicle manufacturer to perform their specific job. Use has been kept to a minimum, but where absolutely necessary, they are referred to in the text by the part number of the tool manufacturer. These tools can be purchased, under the appropriate part number, from the Service Tool Division, Kent-Moore Corporation, 1501 South Jackson Street, Jackson, MI 49203, or an equivalent tool can be purchased locally from a tool supplier or parts outlet. Before substituting any tool for the one recommended, read the SAFETY NOTICE at the top of this page.

## ACKNOWLEDGMENTS

The Chilton Book Company Expresses its appreciation to the General Motors Corporation, Detroit, Michigan for their generous assistance.

Information has been selected from shop manuals, owners manuals, service bulletins and technical training manuals.

Manufactured in the United States of America
    67890        7654321

Chilton's Repair Manual: Olds Cutlas Ciera/Pontiac 6000/Buick Century/Chevrolet Celebrity 1982–88
ISBN 0-8019-7848-3 pbk.
Library of Congress Catalog Card No. 87-47927

# General Information and Maintenance

**1**

## HOW TO USE THIS BOOK

Chilton's Repair and Tune-Up Guide for GM A-Body cars is designed to teach you some of the operating principles of your car, and guide you through maintenance and repair operations. You can perform many repairs yourself, as long as you have the time, initiative, patience, and an assortment of basic tools.

A secondary purpose of this book is a reference for owners who want to understand their car and/or their mechanics better. In this case, no tools at all are required.

Chapters 1 and 2 will probably be the most frequently used in the book. The first chapter contains all the information that may be required at a moment's notice—information such as the location of the various serial numbers and the proper towing instructions. It also contains all the information on basic day-to-day maintenance that you will need to ensure good performance and long component life. Chapter 2 covers tune-up procedures which will assist you not only in keeping the engine running properly and at peak performance levels, but also in restoring some of the more delicate components to operating condition in the event of a failure. Chapters 3 through 10 cover repairs (rather than maintenance) for various portions of the car, with each chapter covering either one system or two related systems. The appendix then lists general information which may be useful in rebuilding the engine or performing some other operation on any car.

In using the Table of Contents, refer to the bold listings for the beginning of the chapter. See the smaller listings or the index for information on a particular component or specifications.

Before removing any bolts, read through the entire procedure. This will give you the overall view of what tools and supplies will be required. There is nothing more frustrating than having to walk to the bus stop on Monday morning because you were short one bolt on Sunday afternoon. So read ahead and plan ahead. Each operation should be approached logically and all procedures thoroughly understood before attempting any work.

Cautions and notes will be provided where appropriate to help prevent you from injuring yourself or damaging your car. Therefore, you should read through the entire procedure before beginning the work, and make sure that you are aware of the warnings. Since no number of warnings could cover every possible situation, you should work slowly and try to envision what is going to happen in each operation ahead of time.

When it comes to tightening things, there is generally a slim area between too loose to properly seal or resist vibration and so tight as to risk damage or warping. When dealing with major engine parts, or with any aluminum component, it pays to procure a torque wrench and go by the recommended figures.

When reference is made in this book to the right side or left side of the car, it should be understood that the positions are always to be viewed from the front seat. Thus, the left side of the car is always the driver's side and the right side is always the passenger's side, even when facing the car, as when working on the engine.

We have attempted to eliminate the use of special tools whenever possible, substituting more readily available hand tools. However, in some cases the special tools are necessary. These can be purchased from your General Motors dealer, or an automotive parts store.

Always be conscious of the need for safety in your work. Never get under the car unless it is firmly supported by jackstands or ramps. Never smoke near or allow flame to get near the battery or the fuel system. Keep your clothing, hands and hair clear of the fan and pulleys when working near the engine, if it is running.

Most importantly, try to be patient; even in the midst of an argument with a stubborn bolt, reaching for the largest hammer in the garage is usually a cause for later regret and more extensive repair. As you gain confidence and experience, working on your car will become a source of pride and satisfaction.

When repair is not considered practical, we tell you how to remove the part and then how to install the new or rebuilt replacement. In this way, you at least save the labor costs. This book will not explain such things as rebuilding the differential for the simple reason that the expertise required and the investment in special tools make this task uneconomical.

## TOOLS AND EQUIPMENT

It would be impossible to catalog each and every tool that you may need to perform all the operations included in this book. It would also not be wise for the amateur to rush out and buy an expensive set of tools on the theory that he may need one of them at some time. The best approach is to proceed slowly, gathering together a good quality set of those tools that are used most frequently. Don't be misled by the low cost of bargain tools. It is far better to spend a little more for quality, name brand tools. Forged wrenches, 12 point sockets and fine-tooth ratchets are a better investment than their less expensive counterparts. As any good mechanic can tell you, there are few worse experiences than trying to work on a car or truck with bad tools. Your monetary savings will be far outweighed by frustration and mangled knuckles.

Begin accumulating those tools that are used most frequently: those associated with routine maintenance and tune-up. In addition to the normal assortment of screwdrivers and pliers, you should have the following tools for routine maintenance jobs:

1. SAE (or Metric) or SAE/Metric wrenches-sockets and combination open end/box end wrenches in sizes from ⅛" (3 mm) to ¾" (19 mm) and a spark plug socket (⅝").

If possible, buy various length socket drive extensions. One break in this department is that the metric sockets available in the U.S. will all fit the ratchet handles and extensions you may already have (¼", ⅜", and ½" drive);

2. Jackstands for support;
3. Oil filter wrench;
4. Oil filler spout for pouring oil;
5. Grease gun for chassis lubrication;
6. A container for draining oil;
7. Many rags for wiping up the inevitable mess.

In addition to the above items there are several others that are not absolutely necessary, but handy to have around. These include oil dry (oil-absorbent), a transmission funnel and the usual supply of lubricants, antifreeze and fluids, although these can be purchased as needed. This is a basic list for routine maintenance, but only your personal needs and desire can accurately determine your list of tools.

A more advanced set of tools, suitable for tune-up work, can be drawn up easily. While the tools are slightly more sophisticated, they need not be outrageously expensive. The key to these purchases is to make them with an eye towards adaptability and wide range. A basic list of tune-up tools could include:

1. Tachometer;
2. Spark plug gauge and gapping tool;
3. Feeler gauges;
4. Timing light.

The choice of a timing light should be made carefully. A light which works on the DC current supplied by the car battery is the best choice; it should have a xenon tube for brightness. Since all A-Body cars have an electronic ignition system, the timing light should have an inductive pickup which clamps around the No. 1 spark plug cable (the timing light illustrated has one of these pickups).

In addition to these basic tools, there are several other tools and gauges which, though not particularly necessary for basic tune-up work, you may find to be quite useful. These include:

1. A compression gauge. The screw-in type seals easily and eliminates the need for a remote starting switch during compression testing.
2. A manifold vacuum gauge;
3. A 12 VDC test light;
4. A combination volt/ohmmeter;
5. An induction meter, used to determine whether or not there is current flowing through a wire.

Finally, you will find a torque wrench necessary for all but the most basic of work. The beam-type models are perfectly adequate. The newer click-type (breakaway) and digital torque wrenches are more accurate, but are also much more expensive and must be periodically recalibrated.

## Special Tools

Most of the jobs covered in this guide can be accomplished with commonly available hand tools. However, in some cases special tools are required. Your General Motors dealer can probably supply the necessary tools, or they can be ordered from:

Kent-Moore Corporation
1501 South Jackson St.
Jackson, MI. 49203

## SERVICING YOUR CAR SAFELY

It is virtually impossible to anticipate all of the hazards involved with automotive mainte- nance and service, but car and common sense will prevent most accidents.

The rules of safety for mechanics range from "don't smoke around gasoline", to "use the proper tool for the job". The trick to avoiding injuries is to develop safe work habits and take every possible precaution.

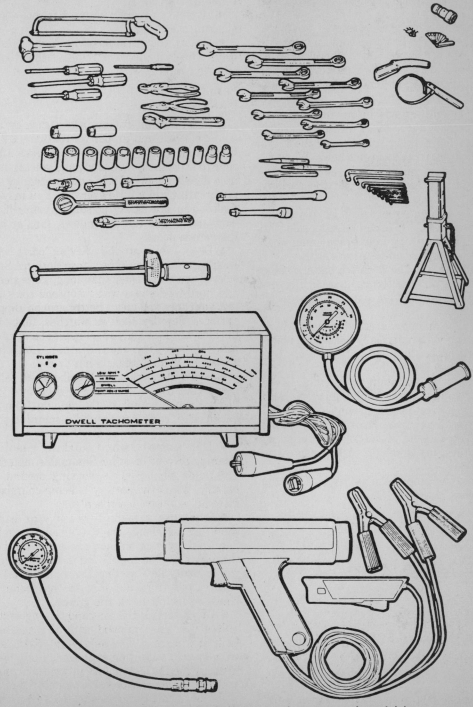

Basic assortment of handtools for most maintenance and repair jobs

## Do's

● Do keep a fire extinguisher and first aid kit within easy reach.

● Do wear safety glasses or goggles when cutting, drilling, grinding or prying, even if you have 20/20 vision. If you wear glasses for the sake of vision, then they should be made of hardened glass that can serve also as safety glasses, or wear safety goggles over your regular glasses.

● Do shield your eyes whenever you work around the battery. Batteries contain sulphuric acid; in case of contact with the eyes or skin, flush the area with water or a mixture of water and baking soda and get medical attention immediately.

● Do use safety stands for any undercar service. Jacks are for raising vehicles; safety stands are for making sure the vehicle stays raised until you want it to come down. Whenever the vehicle is raised, block the wheels remaining on the ground and set the parking brake.

● Do use adequate ventilation when working with any chemicals. Like carbon monoxide, the asbestos dust resulting from brake lining wear can be poisonous in sufficient quantities.

● Do disconnect the negative battery cable when working on the electrical system. The secondary ignition system can contain up to 40,000 volts.

● Do follow manufacturer's directions whenever working with potentially hazardous materials. Both brake fluid and antifreeze are poisonous if taken internally.

● Do properly maintain your tools. Loose hammerheads, mushroomed punches and chisels, frayed or poorly grounded electrical cords, excessively worn screwdrivers, spread wrenches (open end), cracked sockets, slipping ratchets, or faulty droplight sockets can cause accidents.

● Do use the proper size and type of tool for the job being done.

**Always support the car on jackstands when working underneath it**

● Do when possible, pull on a wrench handle rather than push on it, and adjust your stance to prevent a fall.

● Do be sure that adjustable wrenches are tightly adjusted on the nut or bolt and pulled so that the face is on the side of the fixed jaw.

● Do select a wrench or socket that fits the nut or bolt. The wrench or socket should sit straight, not cocked.

● Do strike squarely with a hammer – avoid glancing blows.

● Do set the parking brake and block the drive wheels if the work requires that the engine be running.

## Don't's

● Don't run an engine in a garage or anywhere else without proper ventilation – EVER! Carbon monoxide is poisonous; it takes a long time to leave the human body and you can build up a deadly supply of it in your system by simply breathing in a little ever day. You may not realize you are slowly poisoning yourself. Always use power vents, windows, fans or open the garage doors.

● Don;t work around moving parts while wearing a necktie or other loose clothing. Short sleeves are much safer than long, loose sleeves and hard-toed shoes with neoprene soles protect your toes and give a better grip on slippery surfaces. Jewelry such as watches, fancy belt buckles, beads or body adornment of any king is not safe working around a car. Long hair should be hidden under a hat or cap.

● Don't use pockets for toolboxes. A fall or bump can drive a screwdriver deep into your body. Even a wiping cloth hanging from the back pocket can wrap around a spinning shaft or fan.

● Don't smoke when working gasoline, cleaning solvent or other flammable material.

● Don't smoke when working around the battery. When the battery is being charged, it gives off explosive hydrogen gas.

● Don't use gasoline to wash your hands; there are excellent soaps available. Gasoline may contain lead, an lead can enter the body through a cut, accumulating in the body until you are very ill. Gasoline also removes all the natural oils from the skin so that bone dry hands will suck up oil and grease.

● Don't service the air conditioning system unless you are equipped with the necessary tools and training. The refrigerant, R-12, is extremely cold and when exposed to the air, will instantly freeze any surface it comes in contact with, including your eyes. Although the refrigerant is normally non-toxic, R-12 becomes a deadly poisonous gas in the presence of an open flame. One good whiff of the vapors from burning refrigerant can be fatal.

## SERIAL NUMBER IDENTIFICATION

### Vehicle

The vehicle identification number (V.I.N.) is a seventeen digit alpha/numeric sequence stamped on a plate which is located at the top, left hand side of the instrument panel.
As far as the car owner is concerned, many of the digits in the V.I.N. are of little or no value. At certain times, it may be necessary to refer to the V.I.N. to interpret certain information, such as when ordering replacement parts or determining if your vehicle is involved in a factory service campaign (recall). In either of these instances, the following information may be helpful:

- 1ST DIGIT—Indicates the place of manufacture. A **1** designates the U.S.A.; **2** designates Canada.
- 8TH DIGIT—Indicates the type and the manufacturer of the original engine which was installed in the vehicle (see Engine).
- 10TH DIGIT—Indicates the model year of the vehicle. **C** designates a 1982 model, **D** is for 1983, and so on.
- 11TH DIGIT—Indicates the specific plant at which the vehicle was assembled.
- 12TH-17TH DIGITS—This is the plant sequential number, which identifies the specific number of each vehicle within a production

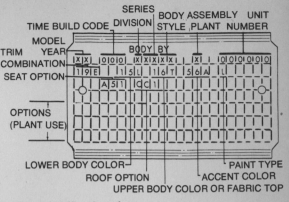

**Body identification plate**

run. In the event of engineering change or a recall involving only a certain quantity of vehicles within a production run, the affected vehicles can be identified.

### Body

An identification plate for body-related items is attached to the front tie bar, just behind the passenger side headlamp. Information on the body identification plate would rarely be useful to the owner. An illustration of the plate is provided.

### Engine

The engine identification code will sometimes be required to order replacement engine

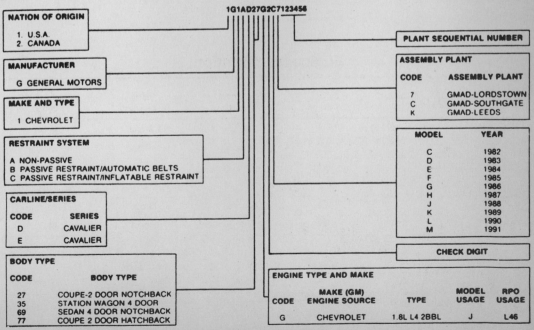

**Vehicle Identification Numbers**

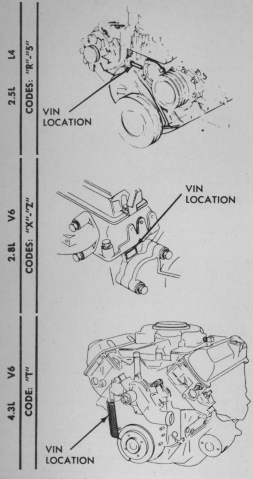

2.5L    L4    CODES: "R"-"5"

2.8L    V6    CODES: "X"-"Z"

4.3L    V6    CODE: "T"

VIN LOCATION

VIN LOCATION

VIN LOCATION

Engine VIN locations

parts. The code is stamped in different locations, depending upon the size of the engine. Refer to the accompanying illustrations to determine the code location for your engine.

## Transaxle

The transaxle code serves the same purpose as the engine identification code. Transaxle code locations may be determined by referring to the accompanying illustration.

## Drive Axle

The drive axle code is stamped onto the axle shaft near the CV boot.

## ROUTINE MAINTENANCE

Proper maintenance of any vehicle is the key to long and trouble-free vehicle life. As a conscientious car owner, set aside a Saturday morning, say once a month, to check or replace items which could cause major problems later. keep your own personal log to jot down which services you performed, how much parts cost you, the date, and the exact odometer reading at the time. Keep all receipts for such items as engine oil and filters, so that they may be referred to in case of related problems or to determine operating expenses. As a do-it-yourselfer, these receipts are the only proof you have that the required maintenance was performed. In the event of a warranty problem, these receipts will be invaluable.

## Engine Identification

| Year | 8th Digit of V.I.N. | Option Code | Engine Displacement Cu. In. (L) | Engine Manufacturer | Fuel Delivery System |
|------|------|------|------|------|------|
| 1982–88 | R | LR8 | 151 (2.5) | Pontiac | T.B.I. |
| 1983–84 | 5 | LW9 | 151 (2.5) | Pontiac | 2 bbl. carb. |
| 1982–86 | X ① | LE2 | 173 (2.8) | Chevrolet | 2 bbl. carb. |
| 1984 | Z ② | LH7 | 173 (2.8) | Chevrolet | 2 bbl. carb. |
| 1982–85 | E | LK9 | 183 (3.0) | Buick | 2 bbl. carb. |
| 1984–85 | 3 | LN3 | 231 (3.8) | Buick | M.F.I. |
| 1986–88 | 3 | LN3 | 231 (3.8) | Buick | S.F.I. |
| 1985–88 | W | LB6 | 173 (2.8) | Chevrolet | M.F.I. |
| 1982–85 | T | LT7 | 263 (4.3) | Oldsmobile | Diesel-F.I. |

① Standard performance engine
② High performance engine
bbl. carb.—barrel carburetor
F.I.—Fuel injection

T.B.I.—Throttle body (fuel injection); Sometimes referred to as E.F.I. (electronic fuel injection).
M.F.I.—Multi Port Fuel Injection
S.F.I.—Single Port Fuel Injection

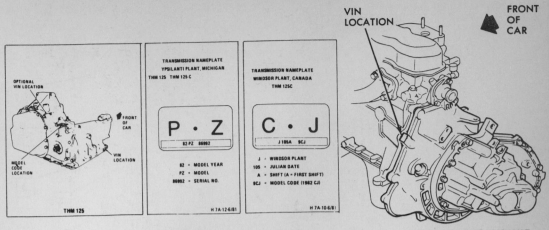

**Transaxle identification number location**

The literature provided with your car when it was originally delivered includes the factory recommended maintenance schedule. If you do not have the factory schedule, we have provided a mirror image of the GM schedule which should be used. No matter which schedule is used, follow it to the letter. Even if your A-Body was previously owned, it is important that the maintenance be performed. The effects of poor maintenance can at least be halted by initiating a regular maintenance program.

## Air Cleaner

Regular air cleaner element replacement is a must, since a partially clogged element will cause a performance loss, decreased fuel mileage, and engine damage if enough dirt gets into the cylinders and contaminates the engine oil.

The air cleaner element must be checked periodically. Replacement of the element is simply a matter of removing the wing nut(s) from the air cleaner lid, lifting off the lid, and removing the old filter element. Wipe the inside of the housing with a damp cloth before placing the new element into the housing. When tightening the wing nut(s), just snug it down with moderate finger pressure. Excessive tightening of the wing nut(s) will damage components.

NOTE: *Never attempt to clean or soak the element in gasoline, oil, or cleaning solvent. The element is designed to be a throw-away item.*

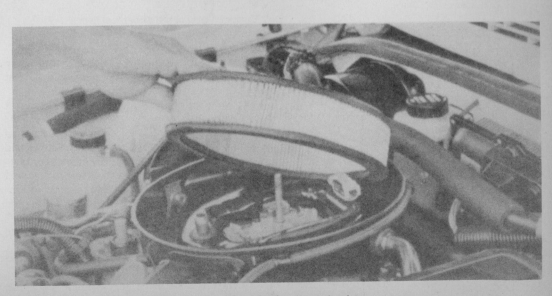

**Lift the old filter element out**

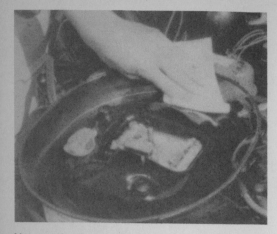

Always wipe out the inside of the housing before installing a new element

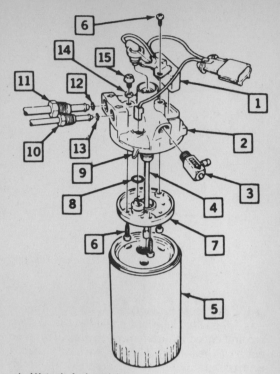

1. Water in fuel module
2. Cover assembly
3. Drain valve—7 N·m (5 lbs. ft.) min.
4. Water in fuel probe (part of No. 2)
5. Filter
6. Fully driven, seated and not stripped
7. Fuel heater (optional)
8. "O" ring
9. Bracket lock tab (part of No. 2)
10. Outlet pipe fitting—23 N·m (17 lbs. ft.)
11. Inlet pipe fitting—27 N·m (20 lbs. ft.)
12. Outlet pipe "O" ring
13. Inlet pipe "O" ring
14. Air bleed seal
15. Air bleed

Exploded view of the diesel fuel filter

## Fuel Filter

### REMOVAL AND INSTALLATION

#### Gasoline Engines

##### INTERNAL

The internal filter is located in the inlet fitting of all carburetors. The elements are spring loaded and are held against the inlet fitting gasket surface.

1. Disconnect the fuel line connection at the fuel inlet filter nut. Remove the inlet filter nut, the filter and the spring.

2. Install a new filter (with the check valve end facing the fuel line), the spring, the gasket and the fuel line nut.

3. Torque the fuel filter nut to 18 ft.lb. (24 Nm.), then install the fuel line and check for leaks.

##### INLINE

The inline filter is found in the fuel system under the hood.

CAUTION: *Before removing the filter, be sure to relieve the pressure in the system. Use a back-up wrench to remove or install the fuel filter. If O-rings are involved, be sure to replace them with new ones. Torque the fittings to 22 ft.lb. (30 Nm.).*

#### Diesel Engines

The fuel filter is located on the left fender front wheel house.

1. Disconnect the fuel lines from the inlet and the outlet ports. Disconnect the drain hose and, if equipped, the electrical connector harness at the filter.

2. Remove the filter assembly clamp-to-bracket bolts and the clamp. Rotate the filter assembly to disengage it from the bracket, then remove the filter assembly.

3. Cover the assembly with a cloth and clamp it in a vise, using the line openings and the flat on the opposite side.

4. Remove the filter and clean the gasket mounting surface.

5. Coat the new filter gasket with engine oil or diesel fuel. Install the filter on the cover and tighten it to ⅔ turn beyond the gasket contact.

6. Place the assembly into the bracket and engage the bracket lock tab into the bracket. Install new O-rings and loosely assemble the fuel lines to the assembly.

7. To complete the installation, reverse the removal procedures.

8. Open the air bleed screw, turn the ignition switch to the Run position (the pump will run) and close the air bleed screw when fuel flows from the opening.

**PCV valve**

9. Start the engine and check for leaks.
NOTE: *The inline filter should be changed when changing the fuel filter.*

## PCV Valve

The Positive Crankcase Ventilation (PCV) valve regulated crankcase ventilation during various engine running conditions. At high vacuum (idle speed and partial load range) it will open slightly and at low vacuum (full throttle) it will open fully. This causes vapors to be drawn from the crankcase by engine vacuum and then sucked into the combustion chamber where they are dissipated.

The PCV valve must be replaced every 30,000 miles. Details on the PCV system, including system tests, are given in Chapter Four.

The valve is located in a rubber grommet in the valve cover, connected to the air cleaner housing by a large diameter rubber hose. To replace the valve:

1. Pull the valve (with the hose attached) from the rubber grommet in the valve cover.
2. Remove the valve from the hose.
3. Install a new valve into the hose.
4. Press the valve back into the rubber grommet in the valve cover.

### PCV FILTER

The PCV filter is located in the air cleaner housing and must be replaced every 50,000 miles.

1. Remove the air cleaner housing lid.
2. Slide back the filter retaining clip and remove the old filter.
3. Install the new filter, replace the retaining clip and replace the housing lid.

## Evaporative Emissions System

Check the fuel vapor lines and the vacuum hoses for proper connections and correct routing, as well as condition. Replace clogged, damaged or deteriorated parts as necessary.

For more details on the evaporative emissions system, please refer to Chapter 4.

## Battery

The single battery used in models equipped with gasoline engines is located at the drivers side front corner of the engine compartment. Because of the added cranking loads, diesel models use two batteries; one in each front corner of the engine compartment. All models use a Delco Freedom II battery. Though this battery is considered to be maintenance free due to the fact that it will never need water added, the battery should be given some attention once in a while.

The major cause of slow engine cranking or a no-start condition is battery terminals which are loose, dirty, or corroded. Every 3 months or so, disconnect the battery and clean the terminals of both the battery and the cables. Cleaning tools for this purpose are available at most any auto parts store. When you buy a cleaning tool, be sure to specify whether you have a top terminal or side terminal battery, as the type of tool differs depending upon the style of battery.

CAUTION: When loosening or tightening the positive battery cable screw(s) at the battery, DO NOT touch the wrench to any metal surface. Personal injury and/or component damage will result.

NOTE: *To use a terminal cleaning tool on*

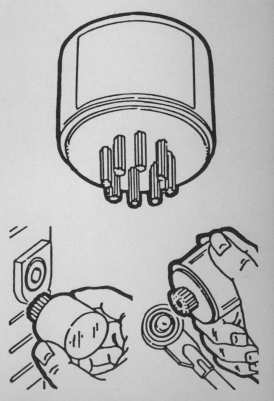

**A special tool is available for cleaning the side terminals and clamps**

*the battery(ies), it will probably be necessary to remove the windshield washer bottle (all models) or the coolant recovery tank (diesel only) to gain the necessary clearance.*

Check the battery cables for signs of wear or chafing. If corrosion is present on the cable or if the cable is visible through the cable jacket, the cable assembly should be replaced. If cable replacement is necessary, it is best to purchase a high quality cable that has the cable jacket sealed to the terminal ends.

Batteries themselves can be cleaned using a solution of baking soda and water. Surface coatings on battery cases can actually conduct electricity which will cause a slight voltage drain, so make sure the battery case is clean. To remove the battery(ies):

1. Raise the hood and remove the front end diagonal brace(s) from above the battery(ies).

2. Disconnect the battery cables from the battery(ies). It may be necessary to use a small box end wrench or a ¼″ drive ratchet to sneak in between the battery and the windshield washer (or coolant recovery) tank. Avoid using an open-end wrench for the cable bolts. See the previous CAUTION.

3. Loosen and remove the battery holddown bolt and block. The use of a long extension which places the ratchet above the battery makes it very easy to get to the holddown bolt.

4. Carefully lift the battery from the engine compartment. It may be necessary to remove the air cleaner intake duct (except 4-cyl.) or the intake resonator (4-cyl. only) for clearance.

5. Clean the battery and the battery tray thoroughly with the baking soda/water solution. Don't allow the solution to get into the small vent holes of the battery.

6. Rinse the battery with clear water and wipe it dry with a couple of clean paper towels. Don't use the towels for anything else—they probably have traces of sulfuric acid on them. Dispose of the paper towels.

7. Thoroughly flush the battery tray and the surrounding area with clear water. Using a wire brush, remove any rust which may be on the tray. Clear away the rust and dry the tray.

8. Coat the battery tray liberally with anti-rust paint. Thoroughly clean the battery and cable terminals BEFORE installing the battery.

9. Install the battery in the reverse of steps 1-4. Tighten the holddown bolt snugly—don't overtighten it.

After you clean the terminals and reconnect the battery, apply a corrosion inhibitor to the terminals. Stay away from using any substance which is not meant specifically for this purpose. Do not apply the corrosion inhibitor to the mating surfaces of the terminals unless specified by the chemical manufacturer.

Any time the engine won't crank, check the color of the battery condition indicator (which is actually a built-in hydrometer). If the indicator is green, the battery is sufficiently charged and in good condition. A complete check of the starter and related wiring should be performed. If the indicator is darkened, the battery is discharged. In this case, the reason for the discharge should be determined (e.g. low alternator output, voltage draw, etc.) then the battery itself should be tested and recharged. If the indicator is light without a green dot visible or if it is yellow in color, the battery must be replaced—DO NOT attempt to test or recharge a battery with this indicator condition. Test the electrical system after the battery has been replaced.

## Drive Belts
### INSPECTION

Every 12 months or 15,000 miles (every 5,000 miles on diesel engines, not dependent upon a period in months), check the drive belts for proper tension. Also look for signs of wear, fraying, separation, glazing and so on, and replace the belts as required.

### ADJUSTMENT

Belt tension should be checked with a gauge made for that purpose. If a gauge is not available, tension can be checked with moderate thumb pressure applied to the belt at its longest span midway between pulleys. If the belt has a free span less than twelve inches, it should deflect approximately ⅛-¼″. If the span is longer than twelve inches, deflection can range between ⅛″ and ⅜″.

NOTE: *Models with diesel engines use a serpentine belt which is automatically adjusted by a spring loaded belt tensioner. Adjustments are not normally required.*

1. Loosen the driven accessory's pivot and mounting bolts.

2. Move the accessory toward or away from the engine until the tension is correct. You can use a wooden hammer handle or a broomstick as a lever, but do not use anything metallic.

3. Tighten the bolts and recheck the tension. If new bolts have been installed, run the engine for a few minutes, then recheck and readjust as necessary.

It is better to have belts too loose than too tight, because overtight belts will lead to bearing failure, particularly in the water pump and alternator. However, loose belts place an extremely high impact load on the driven component due to the whipping action of the belt.

# HOW TO SPOT WORN V-BELTS

V-Belts are vital to efficient engine operation—they drive the fan, water pump and other accessories. They require little maintenance (occasional tightening) but they will not last forever. Slipping or failure of the V-belt will lead to overheating. If your V-belt looks like any of these, it should be replaced.

This belt has deep cracks, which cause it to flex. Too much flexing leads to heat build-up and premature failure. These cracks can be caused by using the belt on a pulley that is too small. Notched belts are available for small diameter pulleys.

**Cracking or weathering**

Oil and grease on a belt can cause the belt's rubber compounds to soften and separate from the reinforcing cords that hold the belt together. The belt will first slip, then finally fail altogether.

**Softening (grease and oil)**

Glazing is caused by a belt that is slipping. A slipping belt can cause a run-down battery, erratic power steering, overheating or poor accessory performance. The more the belt slips, the more glazing will be built up on the surface of the belt. The more the belt is glazed, the more it will slip. If the glazing is light, tighten the belt.

**Glazing**

The cover of this belt is worn off and is peeling away. The reinforcing cords will begin to wear and the belt will shortly break. When the belt cover wears in spots or has a rough jagged appearance, check the pulley grooves for roughness.

**Worn cover**

This belt is on the verge of breaking and leaving you stranded. The layers of the belt are separating and the reinforcing cords are exposed. It's just a matter of time before it breaks completely.

**Separation**

### REMOVAL AND INSTALLATION

1. Loosen the driven accessory's pivot and mounting bolts.

2. Move the accessory toward or away from the engine until there is enough slack in the belt to slip it over the pulley of the driven accessory.

3. Install the new belt and move the accessory toward or away from the engine until the tension is correct. You can use a wooden hammer handle or a broomstick as a lever, but do not use anything metallic.

3. Tighten the bolts and adjust the belt tension as explained above.

## Hoses

The upper and lower radiator hoses and the heater hoses should be checked periodically for deterioration, leaks, and loose clamps. G.M. recommends that this be done every 12 months, or 15,000 miles. For your own peace of mind, it may be wise to check these items at least every spring and fall, since the summer and winter months wreak the most havoc with your cooling system. Expect to replace the hoses about every 24 months or 30,000 miles. To replace the hoses:

### REMOVAL AND INSTALLATION

1. Drain the cooling system.
CAUTION: *When draining the coolant, keep in mind that cats and dogs are attracted by the ethylene glycol antifreeze, and are quite likely to drink any that is left in an uncovered container or in puddles on the ground. This will prove fatal in sufficient quantity. Always drain the coolant into a sealable container. Coolant should be reused unless it is contaminated or several years old.*

2. Loosen the hose clamps at each end of the hose to be removed. If the clamps are of the type which have a screw positioned vertically in relation to the hose, loosen the screw and gently tap the head of the screw towards the hose. Repeat this until the clamp is loose enough. If corrosion on the clamp prevents loosening in this manner, carefully cut the clamp off with cutters and replace the clamp with a new one.

3. Once the clamps are out of the way, grasp the hose and twist it off of the tube connection using only moderate force. If the hose won't break loose, DON'T use excessive force — doing so can easily damage the heater core and/or radiator tubes. Using a razor blade, carefully slit the portion of the hose which covers the connection point, peel the hose off of the connection and disconnect the hose.

4. If so equipped, disconnect the hose routing clamps from the hose.

5. Remove the hose and clean the hose connection points.

6. Slip the (loosened) hose clamps onto the hose ends and install the new hose, being careful to position the hose so that no interference is encountered.

7. Position the clamps at the ends of the hoses, beyond the sealing bead, and centered on the clamping surface. Tighten the hose clamps with a screwdriver — don't use a wrench on the screw heads to tighten them, as overtightening can damage the hose and/or connections points.

8. Refill the cooling system (detailed later) and check for leakage.

## Air Conditioning System
### GENERAL SERVICING PROCEDURES

The most important aspect of air conditioning service is the maintenance of a pure and adequate charge of refrigerant in the system. A refrigeration system cannot function properly if a significant percentage of the charge is lost. Leaks are common because the severe vibration encountered in an automobile can easily cause a sufficient cracking or loosening of the air conditioning fittings; as a result, the extreme operating pressures of the system force refrigerant out.

The problem can be understood by considering what happens to the system as it is operated with a continuous leak. Because the expansion valve regulates the flow of refrigerant to the evaporator, the level of refrigerant there is fairly constant. The receiver/drier stores any excess of refrigerant, and so a loss will first appear there as a reduction in the level of liquid. As this level nears the bottom of the vessel, some refrigerant vapor bubbles will begin to appear in the stream of liquid supplied to the expansion valve. This vapor decreases the capacity of the expansion valve very little as the valve opens to compensate for its presence. As the quantity of liquid in the condenser decreases, the operating pressure will drop there and throughout the high side of the system. As the R-12 continues to be expelled, the pressure available to force the liquid through the expansion valve will continue to decrease, and, eventually, the valve's orifice will prove to be too much of a restriction for adequate flow even with the needle fully withdrawn.

At this point, low side pressure will start to drop, and severe reduction in cooling capacity, marked by freeze-up of the evaporator coil, will result. Eventually, the operating pressure of the evaporator will be lower than the pressure

# HOW TO SPOT BAD HOSES

Both the upper and lower radiator hoses are called upon to perform difficult jobs in an inhospitable environment. They are subject to nearly 18 psi at under hood temperatures often over 280°F., and must circulate nearly 7500 gallons of coolant an hour—3 good reasons to have good hoses.

A good test for any hose is to feel it for soft or spongy spots. Frequently these will appear as swollen areas of the hose. The most likely cause is oil soaking. This hose could burst at any time, when hot or under pressure.

**Swollen hose**

Cracked hoses can usually be seen but feel the hoses to be sure they have not hardened; a prime cause of cracking. This hose has cracked down to the reinforcing cords and could split at any of the cracks.

**Cracked hose**

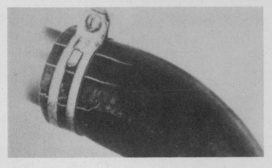

Weakened clamps frequently are the cause of hose and cooling system failure. The connection between the pipe and hose has deteriorated enough to allow coolant to escape when the engine is hot.

**Frayed hose end (due to weak clamp)**

Debris, rust and scale in the cooling system can cause the inside of a hose to weaken. This can usually be felt on the outside of the hose as soft or thinner areas.

**Debris in cooling system**

of the atmosphere surrounding it, and air will be drawn into the system wherever there are leaks in the low side.

Because all atmospheric air contains at least some moisture, water will enter the system and mix with the R-12 and the oil. Trace amounts of moisture will cause sludging of the oil, and corrosion of the system. Saturation and clogging of the filter/drier, and freezing of the expansion valve orifice will eventually result. As air fills the system to a greater and greater extent, it will interfere more and more with the normal flows of refrigerant and heat.

From this description, it should be obvious that much of the repairman's time will be spent detecting leaks, repairing them, and then restoring the purity and quantity of the refrigerant charge. A list of general precautions that should be observed while doing this follows:

1. Keep all tools as clean and dry as possible.

2. Thoroughly purge the service gauges and hoses of air and moisture before connecting them to the system. Keep them capped when not in use.

3. Thoroughly clean any refrigerant fitting before disconnecting it, in order to minimize the entrance of dirt into the system.

4. Plan any operation that requires opening the system beforehand, in order to minimize the length of time it will be exposed to open air. Cap or seal the open ends to minimize the entrance of foreign material.

5. When adding oil, pour it through an extremely clean and dry tube or funnel. Keep the oil capped whenever possible. Do not use oil that has not been kept tightly sealed.

6. Use only refrigerant 12. Purchase refrigerant intended for use in only automatic air conditioning systems. Avoid the use of refrigerant 12 that may be packaged for another use, such as cleaning, or powering a horn, as it is impure.

7. Completely evacuate any system that has been opened to replace a component, or that has leaked sufficiently to draw in moisture and air. This requires evacuating air and moisture with a good vacuum pump for at least one hour.

If a system has been open for a considerable length of time it may be advisable to evacuate the system for up to 12 hours (overnight).

8. Use a wrench on both halves of a fitting that is to be disconnected, so as to avoid placing torque on any of the refrigerant lines.

9. When overhauling a compressor, pour some of the oil into a clean glass and inspect it. If there is evidence of dirt or metal particles, or both, flush all refrigerant components with clean refrigerant before evacuating and recharging the system. In addition, if metal parti-

cles are present, the compressor should be replaced.

10. Schrader valves may leak only when under full operating pressure. Therefore, if leakage is suspected but cannot be located, operate the system with a full charge of refrigerant and look for leaks from all Schrader valves. Replace any faulty valves.

### Additional Preventive Maintenance Checks

#### ANTIFREEZE

In order to prevent heater core freeze-up during A/C operation, it is necessary to maintain permanent type antifreeze protection of +15°F, or lower. A reading of –15°F is ideal since this protection also supplies sufficient corrosion inhibitors for the protection of the engine cooling system.

NOTE: *The same antifreeze should not be used longer than the manufacturer specifies.*

#### RADIATOR CAP

For efficient operation of an air conditioned car's cooling system, the radiator cap should have a holding pressure which meets manufacturer's specifications. A cap which fails to hold these pressures should be replaced.

#### CONDENSER

Any obstruction of or damage to the condenser configuration will restrict the air flow which is essential to its efficient operation. It is therefore a good rule to keep this unit clean and in proper physical shape.

NOTE: *Bug screens are regarded as obstructions.*

#### CONDENSATION DRAIN TUBE

This single molded drain tube expels the condensation, which accumulates on the bottom of the evaporator housing, into the engine compartment. If this tube is obstructed, the air conditioning performance can be restricted and condensation buildup can spill over onto the vehicle's floor.

### SAFETY PRECAUTIONS

Because of the importance of the necessary safety precautions that must be exercised when working with air conditioning systems and R-12 refrigerant, a recap of the safety precautions are outlined.

1. Avoid contact with a charged refrigeration system, even when working on another part of the air conditioning system or vehicle. If a heavy tool comes into contact with a section of copper tubing or a heat exchanger, it can easily cause the relatively soft material to rupture.

2. When it is necessary to apply force to a fit-

ting which contains refrigerant, as when checking that all system couplings are securely tightened, use a wrench on both parts of the fitting involved, if possible. This will avoid putting torque on refrigerant tubing. (It is advisable, when possible, to use tube or line wrenches when tightening these flare nut fittings.)

3. Do not attempt to discharge the system by merely loosening a fitting, or removing the service valve caps and cracking these valves. Precise control is possible only when using the service gauges. Place a rag under the open end of the center charging hose while discharging the system to catch any drops of liquid that might escape. Wear protective gloves when connecting or disconnecting service gauge hoses.

4. Discharge the system only in a well ventilated area, as high concentrations of the gas can exclude oxygen and act as an anaesthetic. When leak testing or soldering, this is particularly important, as toxic gas is formed when R-12 contacts any flame.

5. Never start a system without first verifying that both service valves are back-seated, if equipped, and that all fittings throughout the system are snugly connected.

6. Avoid applying heat to any refrigerant line or storage vessel. Charging may be aided by using water heated to less than 125° to warm the refrigerant container. Never allow a refrigerant storage container to sit out in the sun, or near any other source of heat, such as a radiator.

7. Always wear goggles when working on a system to protect the eyes. If refrigerant contacts the eyes, it is advisable in all cases to see a physician as soon as possible.

8. Frostbite from liquid refrigerant should be treated by first gradually warming the area with cool water, and then gently applying petroleum jelly. A physician should be consulted.

9. Always keep refrigerant drum fittings capped when not in use. Avoid sudden shock to the drum, which might occur from dropping it, or from banging a heavy tool against it. Never carry a drum in the passenger compartment of a car.

10. Always completely discharge the system before painting the vehicle (if the paint is to be baked on), or before welding anywhere near refrigerant lines.

## SYSTEM INSPECTION

The air conditioning system should be checked periodically for worn hoses, loose connections, low refrigerant, leaks, dirt and bugs. If any of these conditions exist, they must be corrected or they will reduce the efficiency of your air conditioning system.

## CHECKING THE SYSTEM FOR LEAKS

Refrigerant leaks show up as oily areas on the various components because the compressor oil is transported around the entire system along with the refrigerant. Look for oily spots on all the hoses and lines, and especially on the hose and tubing connections. If there are oily deposits, the system may have a leak, and you should have it checked by a qualified repairman.

NOTE: *A small area of oil on the front of the compressor is normal and no cause for alarm.*

## KEEP THE CONDENSER CLEAR

Periodically inspect the front of the condenser for bent fins or foreign material (dirt, bugs, leaves, etc.) If any cooling fins are bent, straighten them carefully with needlenosed pliers. You can remove any debris with a stiff bristle brush or hose.

## OPERATE THE A/C SYSTEM PERIODICALLY

A lot of A/C problems can be avoided by simply running the air conditioner at least once a week, regardless of the season. Let the system run for at least 5 minutes a week (even in the winter), and you'll keep the internal parts lubricated as well as preventing the hoses from hardening.

## REFRIGERANT LEVEL CHECK

The factory installed air conditioning unit has no sight glass for system checks. It is recommended that all air conditioning service work be entrusted to a qualified mechanic. The system is a potentially hazardous one.

## GAUGE SETS

Most of the service work performed in air conditioning requires the use of two gauges, one for the high (head) pressure side of the system, the other for the low (suction).

The low side gauge records both pressure and vacuum. Vacuum readings are calibrated from 0 to no less than 60 psi.

The high side gauge measures pressure from 0 to at least 600 psi. Both gauges are threaded into a manifold that contains two hand shut off valves. Proper manipulation of these valves and the use of the attached test hoses allow the user to perform the following services:

1. Test high and low side pressures.
2. Remove air, moisture, and contaminated refrigerant.
3. Purge the system of refrigerant.
4. Charge the system with refrigerant.

The manifold valves are designed so they have no direct effect on gauge readings, but serve only to provide for, or cut off, flow of refrigerant through the manifold. During all testing and hook-up operations, the valves are kept in a closed position to avoid disturbing the refrigeration system. The valves are opened only to purge the system of refrigerant or to charge it. When purging the system, the center hose is uncapped at the lower end, and both valves are cracked open slightly. This allows refrigerant pressure to force the entire contents of the system out through the center hose. During charging, the valve on the high side of the manifold is closed, and the valve on the low side is cracked open. Under these conditions, the low pressure in the evaporator will draw refrigerant from the relatively warm refrigerant storage container into the system.

## DISCHARGING THE SYSTEM

CAUTION: *Perform in a well ventilated area. The compressed refrigerant used in the air conditioning system expands and evaporates into the atmosphere at a temperature of –21.7°F (–29.8°C) or less. This will freeze any surface (including your eyes) that it contacts. In addition, the refrigerant decomposes into a poisonous gas in the presence of flame.*

1. Operate the air conditioner for at least 10 minutes.
2. Attach the gauges, shut off the engine, and the air conditioner.
3. Place a container or rag at the outlet of the center charging hose on the gauge. The refrigerant will be discharged there and this precaution will control its uncontrolled exposure.
4. Open the low side hand valve on the gauge slightly.
5. Open the high side hand valve slightly.
NOTE: *Too rapid a purging process will be identified by the appearance of an oily foam. If this occurs, close the hand valves a little more until this condition stops.*
6. Close both hand valves on the gauge set when the pressures read 0 and all the refrigerant has left the system.
NOTE: *The system should always be discharged before attempting to remove any hoses or component parts of the air conditioning system.*

## EVACUATING THE SYSTEM

Before charging any system it is necessary to purge the refrigerant and draw out the trapped moisture with a suitable vacuum pump. Failure to do so will result in ineffective charging and possible damage to the system.

Use this hook-up for the proper evacuation procedure:
1. Connect both service gauge hoses to the high and low service outlets.

2. Open high and low side hand valves on gauge manifold.
3. Open both service valves a slight amount (from back seated position), allow refrigerant to discharge from system.
4. Install center charging hose of gauge set to vacuum pump.
5. Operate vacuum pump for at least one hour. (If the system has been subjected to open conditions for a prolonged period of time it may be necessary to "pump the system down" overnight. Refer to "System Sweep" procedure.)
NOTE: *If low pressure gauge does not show at least 28 in.Hg within 5 minutes, check the system for a leak or loose gauge connectors.*
6. Close hand valves on gauge manifold.
7. Shut off pump.
8. Observe low pressure gauge to determine if vacuum is holding. A vacuum drop may indicate a leak.

## SYSTEM SWEEP

An efficient vacuum pump can remove all the air contained in a contaminated air conditioning system very quickly, because of its vapor state. Moisture, however, is far more difficult to remove because the vacuum must force the liquid to evaporate before it will be able to remove it from the system. If a system has become severely contaminated, as, for example, it might become after all the charge was lost in conjunction with vehicle accident damage, moisture removal is extremely time consuming. A vacuum pump could remove all of the moisture only if it were operated for 12 hours or more.

Under these conditions, sweeping the system with refrigerant will speed the process of moisture removal considerably. To sweep, follow the following procedure:
1. Connect vacuum pump to gauges, operate it until vacuum ceases to increase, then continue operation for ten more minutes.
2. Charge system with 50% of its rated refrigerant capacity.
3. Operate system at fast idle for ten minutes.
4. Discharge the system.
5. Repeat twice the process of charging to 50% capacity, running the system for ten minutes, and discharging it, for a total of three sweeps.
6. Replace drier.
7. Pump system down as in Step 1.
8. Charge system.

## CHARGING THE SYSTEM

CAUTION: *Never attempt to charge the system by opening the high pressure gauge control while the compressor is operating. The compressor accumulating pressure can burst*

## Troubleshooting Basic Air Conditioning Problems

| Problem | Cause | Solution |
|---|---|---|
| There's little or no air coming from the vents (and you're sure it's on) | • The A/C fuse is blown<br>• Broken or loose wires or connections<br>• The on/off switch is defective | • Check and/or replace fuse<br>• Check and/or repair connections<br><br>• Replace switch |
| The air coming from the vents is not cool enough | • Windows and air vent wings open<br>• The compressor belt is slipping<br>• Heater is on<br>• Condenser is clogged with debris<br>• Refrigerant has escaped through a leak in the system<br>• Receiver/drier is plugged | • Close windows and vent wings<br>• Tighten or replace compressor belt<br>• Shut heater off<br>• Clean the condenser<br>• Check system<br><br>• Service system |
| The air has an odor | • Vacuum system is disrupted<br>• Odor producing substances on the evaporator case<br>• Condensation has collected in the bottom of the evaporator housing | • Have the system checked/repaired<br>• Clean the evaporator case<br><br>• Clean the evaporator housing drains |
| System is noisy or vibrating | • Compressor belt or mountings loose<br>• Air in the system | • Tighten or replace belt; tighten mounting bolts<br>• Have the system serviced |
| Sight glass condition<br>  Constant bubbles, foam or oil streaks<br>  Clear sight glass, but no cold air<br>  Clear sight glass, but air is cold<br>  Clouded with milky fluid | <br>• Undercharged system<br><br>• No refrigerant at all<br>• System is OK<br>• Receiver drier is leaking dessicant | <br>• Charge the system<br><br>• Check and charge the system<br><br>• Have system checked |
| Large difference in temperature of lines | • System undercharged | • Charge and leak test the system |
| Compressor noise | • Broken valves<br>• Overcharged<br><br>• Incorrect oil level<br><br><br>• Piston slap<br>• Broken rings<br>• Drive belt pulley bolts are loose | • Replace the valve plate<br>• Discharge, evacuate and install the correct charge<br>• Isolate the compressor and check the oil level. Correct as necessary.<br>• Replace the compressor<br>• Replace the compressor<br>• Tighten with the correct torque specification |
| Excessive vibration | • Incorrect belt tension<br>• Clutch loose<br>• Overcharged<br><br>• Pulley is misaligned | • Adjust the belt tension<br>• Tighten the clutch<br>• Discharge, evacuate and install the correct charge<br>• Align the pulley |
| Condensation dripping in the passenger compartment | • Drain hose plugged or improperly positioned<br>• Insulation removed or improperly installed | • Clean the drain hose and check for proper installation<br>• Replace the insulation on the expansion valve and hoses |
| Frozen evaporator coil | • Faulty thermostat<br>• Thermostat capillary tube improperly installed<br>• Thermostat not adjusted properly | • Replace the thermostat<br>• Install the capillary tube correctly<br><br>• Adjust the thermostat |
| Low side low—high side low | • System refrigerant is low<br><br>• Expansion valve is restricted | • Evacuate, leak test and charge the system<br>• Replace the expansion valve |
| Low side high—high side low | • Internal leak in the compressor—worn | • Remove the compressor cylinder head and inspect the compressor. Replace the valve plate assembly if necessary. If the compressor pistons, rings or |

## Troubleshooting Basic Air Conditioning Problems (cont.)

| Problem | Cause | Solution |
|---|---|---|
| Low side high—high side low (cont.) | | cylinders are excessively worn or scored replace the compressor |
| | • Cylinder head gasket is leaking | • Install a replacement cylinder head gasket |
| | • Expansion valve is defective | • Replace the expansion valve |
| | • Drive belt slipping | • Adjust the belt tension |
| Low side high—high side high | • Condenser fins obstructed | • Clean the condenser fins |
| | • Air in the system | • Evacuate, leak test and charge the system |
| | • Expansion valve is defective | • Replace the expansion valve |
| | • Loose or worn fan belts | • Adjust or replace the belts as necessary |
| Low side low—high side high | • Expansion valve is defective | • Replace the expansion valve |
| | • Restriction in the refrigerant hose | • Check the hose for kinks—replace if necessary |
| | • Restriction in the receiver/drier | • Replace the receiver/drier |
| | • Restriction in the condenser | • Replace the condenser |
| Low side and high side normal (inadequate cooling) | • Air in the system | • Evacuate, leak test and charge the system |
| | • Moisture in the system | • Evacuate, leak test and charge the system |

*the refrigerant container, causing severe personal injury.*

Refrigerant enters the suction side of the system as a vapor while the compressor is running. Before proceeding, the system should be in a partial vacuum after adequate evacuation. Both hand valves on the gauge manifold should be closed.

1. Attach both test hoses to their respective service valve ports. Mid-position manually operated service valves, if present.

2. Install the dispensing valve (closed position) on the refrigerant container. (Single and multiple refrigerant manifolds are available to accommodate one to four 15 oz. cans.)

3. Attach the center charging hose to the refrigerant container valve.

4. Open dispensing valve on the refrigerant valve.

5. Loosen the center charging hose coupler where it connects to the gauge manifold to allow the escaping refrigerant to purge the hose of contaminants.

6. Tighten the center charging hose connector.

7. Purge the low pressure test hose at the gauge manifold.

8. Start the engine, roll down the windows and adjust the air conditioner to maximum cooling. The engine should be at normal operating temperature before proceeding. The heated environment helps the liquid vaporize more efficiently.

NOTE: *Placing the refrigerant can in a container of warm water (no hotter than 125°F*

*[52°C]) will speed the charging process. Slight agitation of the can is helpful too, but be careful not to turn the can upside down.*

9. Crack open the low side hand valve on the manifold. Manipulate the valve so that the refrigerant that enters the system does not cause the low side pressure to exceed 40 psi. Too sudden a surge may permit the entrance of unwanted liquid to the compressor. Since liquids cannot be compressed, the compressor will suffer damage if compelled to attempt it. If the suction side of the system remains in a vacuum the system is blocked. Locate and correct the condition before proceeding any further.

### Leak Testing the System

There are several methods of detecting leaks in an air conditioning system; among them, the two most popular are (1) halide leak-detection or the "open flame method," and (2) electronic leak-detection.

The halide leak detection is a torch like device which produces a yellow-green color when refrigerant is introduced into the flame at the burner. A purple or violet color indicates the presence of large amounts of refrigerant at the burner.

An electronic leak detector is a small portable electronic device with an extended probe. With the unit activated the probe is passed along those components of the system which contain refrigerant. If a leak is detected, the unit will sound an alarm signal or activate a display signal depending on the manufacturer's design. It is advisable to follow the manufacturer's instructions as the design and function of the detection may vary significantly.

CAUTION: *Care should be taken to operate either type of detector in well ventilated areas, so as to reduce the chance of personal injury, which may result from coming in contact with poisonous gases produced when R-12 is exposed to flame or electric spark.*

## Windshield Wipers

Each exposed windshield wiper is divided basically into four segments:

1. Wiper arm connected to the pivot at the base of the windshield.

2. Wiper blade connected at the opposite end of the wiper arm and hoes the yokes.

3. Wiper yokes hold the element in a manner which distributed the pressure load across the element.

4. Wiper element flexible rubber element which contacts the windshield glass and actually performs the cleaning function.

For maximum effectiveness and longest life, the windshield and wiper elements should be kept clean. Dirt, tree sap, road tar, etc., will cause streaking, smearing, and wiper element deterioration. Hardening of the elements will cause the elements to chatter as they wipe the windshield. Wash the windshield thoroughly with a galss cleaner at least once a month. Wipe off the rubber element with a wet rag afterwards.

Obviously, the item most frequently requiring replacement is the element. It is very rarely necessary to replace the blade or arm unless they become accidentally bent or damaged in some other manner.

Your A-Body can use one of three types of elements: the first type is commonly referred to as the Anco® style; the second type is the Trico® style; and the third is the plastic style which uses a plastic blade assembly. Replacement of any element type is very simple and requires only a few minutes to do.

### REPLACEMENT

#### ANCO® Style Element

1. Locate the red release button at the top of one of the yokes (free yoke), push the button, and separate the free yoke from the blade.

2. Pull the element out of the other yoke (attached yoke).

3. Transfer the free yoke to the new element,

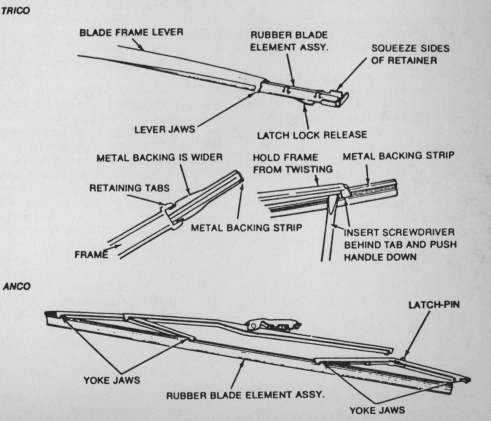

**The rubber element can be changed without replacing the entire blade assembly; your car may have either one of these types of blades**

being sure to engage the element into all of the yoke jaws.

4. Feed the other end of the element into the attached yoke, again being sure that the element is fully engaged.

5. Push the button and snap the free yoke into place on the blade. Release the button and double-check that the element is fully engaged into all of the yoke jaws.

### Trico® Style Element

1. Squeeze the sides of the element retainer (located on only one side of the element) and pull the element out of the blade/yoke assembly.

2. To install the new element, guide the new element into all of the blade/yoke jaws. The element must be positioned in the same manner as the one which was removed. When the retainer comes in contact with the end of the blade, make sure that each side of the retainer is positioned on the inside of the jaws, then snap the element into place.

3. Check that the element is fully engaged to all of the jaws before operating the wipers.

### Plastic

1. Remove the wiper blade and element assembly from the wiper arm.

2. Pull the wiper blade and the element apart, then pull the element downward. This will disengage the element from the retaining tabs.

3. Pull the element out, guide the new element into place, and release the hand pressure on the blade to engage the retaining tabs. Be sure that the element is completely engaged. Snap the wiper blade and element assembly into place on the arm.

Two different wiper blade attachment methods are used. Refer to the accompanying illustration to replace the blades.

Wiper arm replacement is covered in Chapter 6, later in this book.

## Tires and Wheels

### TIRE ROTATION

Tire rotation is recommended every 6,000 miles or so, to obtain maximum tire wear. The pattern you use depends on whether or not your car has a usable spare. Radial tires should not be cross-switched (from one side of the car to the other). They last longer if their direction of rotation is not changed. Snow tires sometimes have directional arrows molded into the side of the carcass. The arrow shows the direction of rotation. They will wear very rapidly if the rotation is reversed. Studded tires will lose

their studs if their rotational direction is reversed.

NOTE: *Mark the wheel position or direction of rotation on radial tires or studded snow tires before removing them.*

### TIRE DESIGN

For maximum satisfaction, tires should be used in sets of five. Mixing of different types (radial, bias-belted, fiberglass belted) should be avoided. Conventional bias tires are constructed so that the cords run bead to bead at an angle. Alternate plies run at an opposite angle. This type of construction gives rigidity to both tread and side wall. Bias belted tires are similar in construction to conventional bias ply tires. Belts run at an angle and also at a $90^0$ angle to the bead, as in radial tires. Tread life is improved considerably over the conventional bias tire. The radial tire differs in construction, but instead of the carcass running at an angle of $90^0$ to each other they run at an angle of $90^0$ to the bead. This gives the tread a great deal of rigidity and the side wall a great deal of flexibility (which accounts for the characteristic bulge associated with radial tires).

### INFLATION PRESSURE

Tire inflation is the most ignored item of auto maintenance. Gasoline mileage can drop as much as 0.8% for every 1 pound per square inch (psi) of under inflation.

Two items should be a permanent fixture in every glove compartment: a tire pressure gauge and a tread depth gauge. Check the tire air pressure (including the spare) regularly with a pocket type gauge. Kicking the tires won't tell you a thing, and the gauge on the service station air hose is notoriously inaccurate.

The tire pressures recommended for your car are usually found on the left door or in the owner's manual. Ideally, inflation pressure should be checked when the tires are cool. When the air becomes heated it expands and the pressure increases. Every 10° rise (or drop) in temperature means a difference of 1 psi, which also explains why the tire appears to lose air on a very cold night. When it is impossible to check the tires cold, allow for pressure build-up due to heat. If the hot pressure exceeds the cold pressure by more than 15 psi, reduce your speed, load or both. Otherwise internal heat is created in the tire. When the heat approaches the temperature at which the tire was cured, during manufacture, the tread can separate from the body.

CAUTION: *Never counteract excessive pressure build-up by bleeding off air pressure (letting some air out). This will only further raise the tire operating temperature.*

Before starting a long trip with lots of luggage, you can add about 2-4 psi to the tires to make them run cooler, but never exceed the maximum inflation pressure on the side of the tire.

### TREAD DEPTH

All tires made since 1968, have 7 built-in tread wear indicator bars that show up as ½" wide smooth bands across the tire when $1/16$" of tread remains. The appearance of tread wear indicators means that the tires should be replaced. In fact, many states have laws prohibiting the use of tires with less than $1/16$" tread.

You can check your own tread depth with an inexpensive gauge or by using a Lincoln head penny. Slip the Lincoln penny into several tread grooves. If you can see the top of Lincoln's head in 2 adjacent grooves, the tires have less than $1/16$" tread left and should be replaced. You can measure snow tires in the same manner by using the tails side of the Lincoln penny. If you can see the top of the Lincoln memorial, it's time to replace the snow tires.

### CARE OF SPECIAL WHEELS

If you have invested money in magnesium, aluminum alloy or sport wheels, special precautions should be taken to make sure your investment is not wasted, and that your special wheels look good for the lifetime of the car.

Special wheels are easily scratched and/or damaged. Occasionally check the rim for cracks, damage or air leaks. If any of these conditions are found, replace the wheel. In order to prevent this type of damage, and the costly replacement of a special wheel, observe the following precautions:

• Take special care not to damage the wheels during removal, installation, balancing etc. After removal of the wheels from the car, place them on a rubber mat or other protective surface.

• While the vehicle is being driven, be careful not to drive over sharp obstacles or allow the wheels to contact the shoulder of the road.

• When washing, use a mild detergent and water. Avoid using cleansers with abrasives, or hard brushes. And a little polish after washing will help your wheels keep that new look.

• If possible, remove your special wheels from the car during the winter months, and replace them with regular steel rims. Salt and sand that is applied to the roadways for snow removal during these months can do severe damage to special wheels.

• Make sure that the recommended lug nut torque is never exceeded, or you may crack your wheels. And never use snow chains with special wheels.

• If you intend to store the wheels, lay them flat on a protective surface and cover them. Do not stack them on top of each other and do not place anything else, except a protective cover, on them.

## Troubleshooting Basic Wheel Problems

| Problem | Cause | Solution |
| --- | --- | --- |
| The car's front end vibrates at high speed | • The wheels are out of balance<br>• Wheels are out of alignment | • Have wheels balanced<br>• Have wheel alignment checked/adjusted |
| Car pulls to either side | • Wheels are out of alignment<br><br>• Unequal tire pressure<br>• Different size tires or wheels | • Have wheel alignment checked/adjusted<br>• Check/adjust tire pressure<br>• Change tires or wheels to same size |
| The car's wheel(s) wobbles | • Loose wheel lug nuts<br>• Wheels out of balance<br>• Damaged wheel<br><br><br>• Wheels are out of alignment<br><br>• Worn or damaged ball joint<br>• Excessive play in the steering linkage (usually due to worn parts)<br>• Defective shock absorber | • Tighten wheel lug nuts<br>• Have tires balanced<br>• Raise car and spin the wheel. If the wheel is bent, it should be replaced<br>• Have wheel alignment checked/adjusted<br>• Check ball joints<br>• Check steering linkage<br><br>• Check shock absorbers |
| Tires wear unevenly or prematurely | • Incorrect wheel size<br><br>• Wheels are out of balance<br>• Wheels are out of alignment | • Check if wheel and tire size are compatible<br>• Have wheels balanced<br>• Have wheel alignment checked/adjusted |

## Troubleshooting Basic Tire Problems

| Problem | Cause | Solution |
|---|---|---|
| The car's front end vibrates at high speeds and the steering wheel shakes | • Wheels out of balance<br>• Front end needs aligning | • Have wheels balanced<br>• Have front end alignment checked |
| The car pulls to one side while cruising | • Unequal tire pressure (car will usually pull to the low side)<br>• Mismatched tires<br><br>• Front end needs aligning | • Check/adjust tire pressure<br><br>• Be sure tires are of the same type and size<br>• Have front end alignment checked |
| Abnormal, excessive or uneven tire wear<br><br>See "How to Read Tire Wear" | • Infrequent tire rotation<br><br>• Improper tire pressure<br><br>• Sudden stops/starts or high speed on curves | • Rotate tires more frequently to equalize wear<br>• Check/adjust pressure<br><br>• Correct driving habits |
| Tire squeals | • Improper tire pressure<br>• Front end needs aligning | • Check/adjust tire pressure<br>• Have front end alignment checked |

## Tire Size Comparison Chart

| "Letter" sizes | | | Inch Sizes | Metric-inch Sizes | | |
|---|---|---|---|---|---|---|
| "60 Series" | "70 Series" | "78 Series" | 1965–77 | "60 Series" | "70 Series" | "80 Series" |
| | | Y78-12 | 5.50-12, 5.60-12<br>6.00-12 | 165/60-12 | 165/70-12 | 155-12 |
| | | W78-13 | 5.20-13 | 165/60-13 | 145/70-13 | 135-13 |
| | | Y78-13 | 5.60-13 | 175/60-13 | 155/70-13 | 145-13 |
| | | | 6.15-13 | 185/60-13 | 165/70-13 | 155-13, P155/80-13 |
| A60-13 | A70-13 | A78-13 | 6.40-13 | 195/60-13 | 175/70-13 | 165-13 |
| B60-13 | B70-13 | B78-13 | 6.70-13 | 205/60-13 | 185/70-13 | 175-13 |
| | | | 6.90-13 | | | |
| C60-13 | C70-13 | C78-13 | 7.00-13 | 215/60-13 | 195/70-13 | 185-13 |
| D60-13 | D70-13 | D78-13 | 7.25-13 | | | |
| E60-13 | E70-13 | E78-13 | 7.75-13 | | | 195-13 |
| | | | 5.20-14 | 165/60-14 | 145/70-14 | 135-14 |
| | | | 5.60-14 | 175/60-14 | 155/70-14 | 145-14 |
| | | | 5.90-14 | | | |
| A60-14 | A70-14 | A78-14 | 6.15-14 | 185/60-14 | 165/70-14 | 155-14 |
| | B70-14 | B78-14 | 6.45-14 | 195/60-14 | 175/70-14 | 165-14 |
| | C70-14 | C78-14 | 6.95-14 | 205/60-14 | 185/70-14 | 175-14 |
| D60-14 | D70-14 | D78-14 | | | | |
| E60-14 | E70-14 | E78-14 | 7.35-14 | 215/60-14 | 195/70-14 | 185-14 |
| F60-14 | F70-14 | F78-14, F83-14 | 7.75-14 | 225/60-14 | 200/70-14 | 195-14 |
| G60-14 | G70-14 | G77-14, G78-14 | 8.25-14 | 235/60-14 | 205/70-14 | 205-14 |
| H60-14 | H70-14 | H78-14 | 8.55-14 | 245/60-14 | 215/70-14 | 215-14 |
| J60-14 | J70-14 | J78-14 | 8.85-14 | 255/60-14 | 225/70-14 | 225-14 |
| L60-14 | L70-14 | | 9.15-14 | 265/60-14 | 235/70-14 | |
| | A70-15 | A78-15 | 5.60-15 | 185/60-15 | 165/70-15 | 155-15 |
| B60-15 | B70-15 | B78-15 | 6.35-15 | 195/60-15 | 175/70-15 | 165-15 |
| C60-15 | C70-15 | C78-15 | 6.85-15 | 205/60-15 | 185/70-15 | 175-15 |
| | D70-15 | D78-15 | | | | |
| E60-15 | E70-15 | E78-15 | 7.35-15 | 215/60-15 | 195/70-15 | 185-15 |
| F60-15 | F70-15 | F78-15 | 7.75-15 | 225/60-15 | 205/70-15 | 195-15 |
| G60-15 | G70-15 | G78-15 | 8.15-15/8.25-15 | 235/60-15 | 215/70-15 | 205-15 |
| H60-15 | H70-15 | H78-15 | 8.45-15/8.55-15 | 245/60-15 | 225/70-15 | 215-15 |
| J60-15 | J70-15 | J78-15 | 8.85-15/8.90-15 | 255/60-15 | 235/70-15 | 225-15 |
| | K70-15 | | 9.00-15 | 265/60-15 | 245/70-15 | 230-15 |
| L60-15 | L70-15 | L78-15, L84-15 | 9.15-15 | | | 235-15 |
| | M70-15 | M78-15 | | | | 255-15 |
| | | N78-15 | | | | |

Note: Every size tire is not listed and many size comparisons are approximate, based on load ratings. Wider tires than those supplied new with the vehicle, should always be checked for clearance.

## STORAGE

Store the tires at the proper inflation pressure if they are mounted on wheels. Keep them in a cool dry place, laid on their sides. If the tires are stored in the garage or basement, do not let them stand on a concrete floor. Set them on strips of wood.

## BUYING NEW TIRES

When buying new tires, give some though to the following points, especially if you are considering a switch to larger tires or a different profile series:

1. All four tires must be of the same construction type. This rule cannot be violated. Radial, bias, and bias-belted tires must not be mixed.

2. The wheels should be the correct width for the tire. Tire dealers have charts of tire and rim compatibility. A mismatch will cause sloppy handling and rapid tire wear. The tread width should match the rim width (inside bead to inside bead) within an inch. For radial tires, the rim width should be 80% or less of the tire (not tread) width.

3. The height (mounted diameter) of the new tires can change speedometer accuracy, engine speed at a given road speed, fuel mileage, acceleration, and ground clearance. Tire manufacturers furnish full measurement specifications.

4. The spare tire should be usable, at least for short distance and low speed operation, with the new tires.

5. There shouldn't be any body interference when loaded, on bumps, or in turns.

## FLUIDS AND LUBRICANTS

## Fuel and Engine Oil Recommendations

### FUEL RECOMMENDATIONS

#### Gasoline

All G.M. A-Body cars must use unleaded fuel. The use of leaded fuel will plug the catalyst rendering it imperative, and will increase the exhaust back pressure to the point where engine output will be severely reduced. The minimum octane for all engines is 87 RON. All unleaded fuels sold in the U.S. are required to meet this minimum octane rating.

Use of a fuel too low in octane (a measurement of anti-knock quality) will result in spark knock. Since many factors affect operating efficiency, such as altitude, terrain, air temperature and humidity, knocking may result even

## Oil Viscosity Selection Chart

| | Anticipated Temperature Range | SAE Viscosity |
|---|---|---|
| Multi-grade | Above 32°F | 10W—40 10W—50 20W—40 20W—50 10W—30 |
| | May be used as low as −10°F | 10W—30 10W—40 |
| | Consistently below 10°F | 5W—20 5W—30 |
| Single-grade | Above 32°F | 30 |
| | Temperature between +32°F and −10°F | 10W |

though the recommended fuel is being sued. If persistent knocking occurs, it may be necessary to switch to a slightly higher grade of unleaded gasoline. Continuous or heavy knocking may result in serious engine damage, for which the manufacturer is not responsible.

NOTE: *Your car's engine fuel requirement can change with time, due to carbon buildup, which changes the compression ratio. If your car's engine knocks, pings, or runs on, switch to a higher grade of fuel, if possible, and check the ignition timing. Sometimes changing brands of gasoline will cure the problem. If it is necessary to retard timing from specifications, don't change it more than a few degrees. Retarded timing will reduce power output and fuel mileage, and will increase engine temperature.*

#### Diesel

WARNING: *Failure to use fuels specified below will result in engine damage for which the manufacturer is not responsible. Use of fuel additives is NOT recommended.*

At any outside temperature above 20°F, Number 2-D diesel fuel should be used, since it will give better fuel economy then Number 1-D. When the outside temperature is below 20°F, use either Number 1-D fuel (preferred if available) or a blended Number 2-D. The blended

## Oil Viscosity Selection Chart 1987–88

| | Anticipated Temperature Range | SAE Viscosity |
|---|---|---|
| Multi-grade | Temperature between +100°F and −20°F | 5W-30 |

Number 2-D has 1-D fuel in it, but will usually be called just Number 2-D. Check with the service station operator to be sure you get the proper fuel.

NOTE: *Diesel fuel may foam during filling, which is normal. The foam may cause the automatic pump nozzle to turn off before the tank is actually filled. The foaming effect can be reduced by slowing the fill rate.*

## OPERATING IN COLD WEATHER

All types of diesel fuel have a certain paraffin content. The paraffin components are high in energy content and help to improve fuel economy. Below about 20°F, the trouble with paraffin begins. At this temperature, the paraffin components begin turning to wax flakes. Depending upon the temperature, the wax flakes can block wither or both of the two fuel filters (tank or engine) and stop fuel from reaching the engine.

Since Number 2-D fuel has more paraffin components than Number 1-D (or blended Number 2-D), Number 2-D would be more apt to cause waxing problems (See Fuel Recommendations).

If the fuel tank filter plugs due to waxing, a check valve inside of the fuel tank will open and allow fuel to flow to the engine. Because of the check valve location, not all of the fuel in the tank can be used if the filter remains clogged (check valve open). About 4 gallons of fuel will remain in the tank when you run out of fuel. When driving in temperatures below 20°F, be sure to keep the tank more than ¼ full to help prevent running out of fuel if the filter plugs.

If equipped, the fuel line heater should be used when temperatures are expected to be below 10°F and you have Number 2-D fuel in the tank.

## WATER IN THE FUEL

Diesel fuel should be purchased from a reputable dealer, since the majority of the water found in a diesel fuel system gets into the system during refueling. Water can cause extensive (and expensive) damage to the diesel fuel system.

The A-Bodies have a water separator system in the fuel tank and a Water-In-Fuel indicator on the instrument panel. The indicator is designed to illuminate when starting the engine (as a bulb check), or when water is detected in the tank. If the light comes on at any other time, there is probably a fault in the detector circuit. If the engine loses power and begins to run rough without the detector light on, there is probably water in the system. Both the fuel system and the detector circuit should be checked.

If the indicator light comes on immediately after refueling, a large amount of water was pumped into the tank—DON'T run the engine; the fuel system must be purged right away.

If the indicator lights after braking, cornering, etc., a moderate amount of water is in the system. In this case, the water should be removed within one or two days.

## PURGING THE FUEL SYSTEM

Please refer to Chapter 5 for this information.

CAUTION: *Use the same safety precautions when working around diesel fuel as you would when working around gasoline (No smoking; No sparks; No trouble lamps in the area, etc.).*

## OIL RECOMMENDATIONS

### Gasoline Engine

Under normal conditions, the engine oil and the filter should be changed at the first 7500 miles or once a year (1982-86 models), or every 3,000 miles or 3 months (1987-88 models) or whichever comes first. G.M. recommends that the oil filter be changed at every other oil change thereafter on the 1982-86 models. On 1987 and later models G.M. recommends that the oil filter be changed at every oil change. For the small price of an oil filter, it's cheap insurance to replace the filter at every oil change on the 1982-86 models as well. One of the larger filter manufacturers points out in its advertisements that not changing the filter leaves one quart of dirty oil in the engine. This claim is true and should be kept in mind when changing your oil.

Under severe conditions, such as: a) driving in dusty areas. b) trailer towing. c) frequent idling or idling for extended periods. or d) frequently driving short distances (4 miles or so) in freezing weather, the engine oil and filter should be changed every 3 months or 3000 miles, whichever comes first. If dust storms are ever encountered in your area, change the oil and filter as soon as possible after the storm.

The A.P.I. (American Petroleum Institute) designation (printed on the oil container) indicates the classification of engine oil for use under certain operating conditions. Oils having an A.P.I. service designation of SF should be used in your A-Body. The SF rating designates the highest quality oil meant for passenger car usage. It is okay to use an SF oil having a combination rating such as SF/CC or SF/CD for gasoline powered engines. In addition, G.M. recommends the use of SF/Energy Conserving oil. Oils labeled, Energy Conserving (or Saving); Fuel (Gas or Gasoline) Saving, etc., are recommended due to their superior lubricating qualities (less friction = easier and more efficient engine operation) and fuel saving characteristics. Use of engine oil additives is not recommended, because if the correct oil is purchased to begin with, the additives will be of no value.

NOTE: *Use of engine oils without an SF rating, or failing to change the oil and filter at the recommended intervals will cause excessive engine wear and could affect your warranty.*

### Diesel Engines

The engine oil requirements for diesel engines are more stringent than those for gasoline engines, since contaminant build-up in the engine oil occurs much faster in the diesel engine. Also, the diesel contaminants are more damaging to the engine oil.

Under normal operating conditions, the engine oil and filter MUST be changed every 5000 miles, regardless of the time period involved.

Under severe operating conditions, such as those mentioned previously under Gasoline Engines, the oil and filter must be changed every 2500 miles or 3 months, whichever comes first.

In the diesel equipped A-Body, ONLY an engine oil having one of the two following A.P.I. desingations should be used: SF/CC or SF/CD. Period! Don't use any other type of oil.

CAUTION: *Failure to use an SF/CC or SF/CD oil will result in excessive engine wear and will probably void the engine warranty. Failure to change the oil and filter at the recommended intervals will have the same results.*

In diesel engines, the use of oil in regard to its viscosity is limited. With a diesel, you only have three choices: 10W-30, 15W-40, or straight 30W. Refer to the accompanying chart to choose the engine oil viscosity according to the expected outside air temperature.

### CHECKING THE OIL LEVEL

The engine oil level may be checked either when the engine is cold or warm, though the latter is preferred. If you check the level while the engine is cold, DO NOT start the engine first, since the cold oil won't drain back to the

Oil dipstick location—typical

engine oil pan fast enough to give an accurate reading. Even when the engine is warm, wait a couple of minutes after turning it off to let the oil drain back to the pan.

1. Raise the hood, pull the dipstick out and wipe it clean.

2. Reinsert the dipstick, being sure that you push it back in completely.

3. Pull the dipstick back out, hold it horizontally, and check the level at the end of the dipstick. Some dipsticks are marked with **ADD** and **FULL** lines, others with **ADD 1 QT** and **OPERATING RANGE**. In either case, the level must be above the **ADD** line. Reinsert the dipstick completely.

4. If oil must be added, it can be poured in through the rocker (valve) cover after removing the filler cap on the cover. Recheck the level a few minutes after adding oil.

5. Be sure that the dipstick and oil filler cap are installed before closing the hood.

### CHANGING THE ENGINE OIL AND FILTER

1. Drive the car until the engine is at normal operating temperature. A run to the parts store for oil and a filter should accomplish this. If the engine is not hot when the oil is changed, most of the acids and contaminants will remain inside the engine.

2. Shut off the engine, and slide a pan of at least six quarts capacity under the oil pan.

3. Remove the drain plug from the engine oil pan, after wiping the plug area clean. The drain plug is the bolt inserted at an angle into the lowest point of the oil pan.

4. The oil from the engine will be HOT. It will probably not be possible to hold onto the drain plug. You may have to let it fall into the pan and fish it out later. Allow all the oil to drain completely. This will take a few minutes.

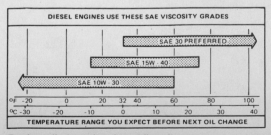

Engine oil viscosity chart (diesel)

5. Wipe off the drain plug, removing any traces of metal particles. Check the condition of the plastic drain plug gasket. If it is cracked or distorted in any way, replace it. Reinstall the drain plug and gasket. Tighten the drain plug snugly.

6. The oil filter for the V6 gasoline engine is right up front, just behind the radiator. The four cylinder oil filter is at the back of the engine. It is impossible to reach from above, and almost as inaccessible from below. It may be easiest to remove the right front wheel and reach through the fender opening to get at the four cylinder oil filter. The oil filter of the diesel V6 engine is located on the passenger side face of the engine block. Use an oil strap wrench to loosen the oil filter; these are available at auto parts stores. It is recommended that you purchase one with as thin a strap as possible, to get into tight areas. Place the drain pan on the ground, under the filter. Unscrew and discard the old filter. It will be VERY HOT, so be careful.

7. If the oil filter is on so tightly that it collapses under pressure from the wrench, drive a long punch or a nail through it, across the diameter and as close to the base as possible, and use this as a lever to unscrew it. Make sure you are turning it counterclockwise.

8. Clean off the oil filter mounting surface with a rag. Apply a thin film of clean engine oil to the filter gasket.

9. Screw the filter on by hand until the gasket makes contact. Then tighten it by hand an additional ½ to ¾ of a turn. Do not overtighten.

10. Remove the filler cap on the rocker (valve) cover, after wiping the area clean.

11. Add the correct number of quarts of oil specified in the Capacities chart. If you don't have an oil can spout, you will need a funnel. Be certain you do not overfill the engine, which can cause serious damage. Replace the cap.

12. Check the oil level on the dipstick. It is normal for the level to be a bit above the full mark. Start the engine and allow it to idle for a few minutes.

CAUTION: *Do not run the engine above idle speed until it has built up oil pressure, indicated when the oil light goes out.*

Check around the filter and and drain plug for any leaks.

13. Shut off the engine, allow the oil to drain for a minute, and check the oil level.

After completing this job, you will have several quarts of oil to dispose of. The best thing to do with it is to funnel it into old plastic mile containers or bleach bottles. Then, you can either pour it into the recycling barrel at the gas station (if you're on good terms with the attendant), or put the containers into the trash.

## Manual Transaxle Lubricant

### RECOMMENDATIONS

Under normal conditions, the lubricant used in the manual transaxle does not require periodic changing. The fluid level in the transaxle should be checked every 12 months or 7500 miles, whichever comes first. The manual transaxle is designed for use with Dexron®II automatic transmission. Don't use standard manual transmission lubricant in the A-Body transaxle.

### CHECKING THE FLUID LEVEL

1. Park the car on a level surface. Before proceeding, the transaxle case must be cool to the touch. Due to the expansion characteristics of the Dexron®II fluid, it will be above the level of the filler plug when the transmission is hot.

2. Slowly remove the filler plug from the driver's side of the transaxle (see the illustration). The lubricant level should be right at the bottom of the filler plug hole. If the fluid trick-

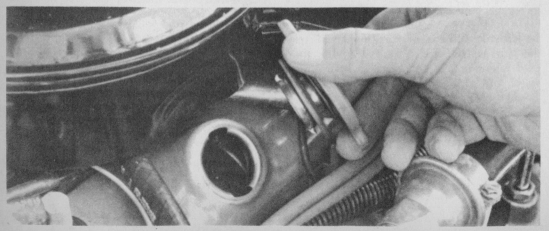

Add oil through the capped filler hole in the valve cover

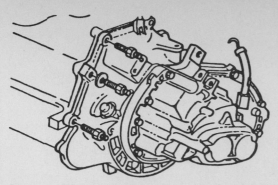

Some models use a dipstick to check the level of the manual transaxle lubricant

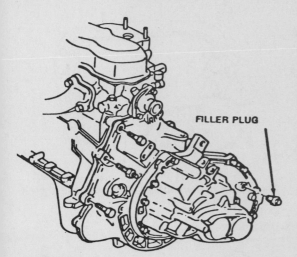

FILLER PLUG

Some models use a filler plug to check the level of the manual transaxle lubricant

les out as the plug is removed, or if you can just touch the fluid through the filler plug hole, the level is correct.

3. If you cannot feel the fluid level with your finger through the filler plug hole, add Dexron®II automatic transmission through the hole until the fluid begins to trickle out of the hole.

4. When the level is correct, install the filler plug and tighten it snugly.

### DRAIN AND REFILL

1. Park the car on a level surface, turn off engine and apply the parking brake.

2. Place a container of adequate capacity beneath the drain plug which is located underneath the car, on the bottom of the transaxle housing.

3. Use the proper size wrench to loosen the drain plug slowly, while maintaining a slight upward pressure, to keep the oil from leaking out around the plug.

4. Allow all of the lubricant to drain from the

transaxle, then install the drain plug and gasket (if so equipped).

5. Remove the transaxle dipstick and fill the transaxle to the capacity shown in the Capacities chart. Do not overfill.

6. Check the oil level as outlined above.

## Automatic Transaxle Fluid

### RECOMMENDATIONS

Under normal operating conditions, the automatic transmission fluid only needs to be changed every 100,000 miles, according to G.M. If one or more of the following driving conditions is encountered, the fluid and filter should be changed every 15,000 miles: a) driving in heavy city traffic when the outside temperature regularly reached 90°F, b) driving regularly in hilly or mountainous areas, c)towing a trailer, or d) using the vehicle as a taxi or police car, or for delivery purposes. Remember, these are the factory recommendations, and in this case are considered to be the minimum. You must determine a change interval which fits your driving habits. If your vehicle is never subjected to these conditions, a 100,000 mile change interval is adequate. If you are a normal driver, a two-year/30,000 mile interval will be more than sufficient to maintain the long life for which your automatic transaxle was designed.

When replacing or adding fluid, use only fluid labeled Dexron®II. Use of other fluids could cause erratic shifting and transmission damage.

### CHECKING THE FLUID LEVEL

The fluid level may be checked with the transaxle code, warm, or hot, as this is accounted for on the dipstick graduations.

NOTE: *If the vehicle has just been driven in extreme conditions, allow the fluid to cool for about 30 minutes.*

1. Park the car on a level surface and set the parking brake.

2. Start the engine, apply the regular brakes, and move the shift lever through all of the gear ranges, ending up in Park.

3. Let the engine idle for at least 5 minutes with the transaxle in Park.

4. The dipstick is located on the driver's side of the engine compartment, ahead of the engine.

5. Raise the hood, pull the dipstick out and wipe it off with a clean cloth.

6. Reinsert the dipstick, being sure that it is fully seated.

7. Again, remove the dipstick. Hold it horizontally and read the fluid level. Touch the fluid — if it feels cold or warm, the level should be between the dimples above the **FULL HOT**

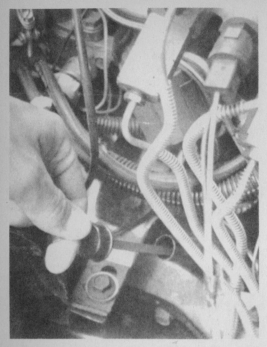

Automatic transaxle fluid dipstick and filler tube location

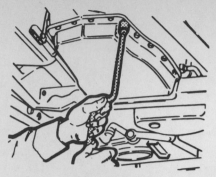

Loosen the pan bolts and allow one corner of the pan to tilt slightly to drain the fluid

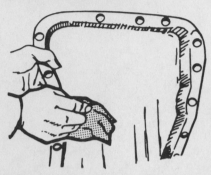

Clean the pan thoroughly with solvent and allow it to air dry completely

mark. If the fluid feels hot, the level should be in the hatched area, between the **ADD 1 PT** and **FULL HOT** marks.

8. If required, add just enough Dexron®II automatic transmission fluid to bring the level to where it should be. One pint of fluid will raise the level from **ADD** to **FULL** when the transaxle is hot. Recheck the level.

9. Reinsert the dipstick, again making sure that it is fully seated. Lower the hood.

WARNING: *NEVER overfill the transaxle, as fluid foaming and subsequent transaxle damage will occur!*

## CHANGING THE FLUID AND FILTER

NOTE: *Some transaxle use RTV sealer in place of a gasket. Do not attempt to replace the sealer with a gasket.*

1. Jack up the front of your vehicle and support it with jackstands.

2. Remove the front and side pan bolts.

3. Loosen the rear bolts about 4 turns.

4. Carefully pry the oil pan loose, allowing the fluid to drain.

5. Remove the remaining bolts, the pan, and the gasket or RTV. Discard the gasket.

6. Clean the pan with solvent and dry thoroughly, with compressed air.

7. Remove the strainer and O-ring seal.

8. Install new strainer and new O-ring seal locating the strainer against the dipstick stop.

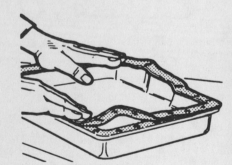

Install a new gasket on the pan

9. Install a new gasket or RTV. Tighten the pan bolts to 12 ft.lb.

10. Lower the car. Add about 4 quarts of Dexron®II transmission fluid.

11. Start the engine; let it idle. Block the wheels and apply the parking brake.

12. Move the shift lever through the ranges.

13. With the lever in park check the fluid level. Add fluid if necessary.

NOTE: *Always replace the filter with a new one, don't attempt to clean the old filter. The transmission fluid currently being used may appear to be darker and have a strong odor. This is normal and not a sign of required maintenance or transmission failure.*

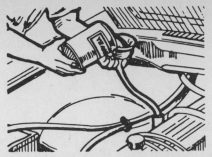

Fill the transaxle with the required amount of fluid. Do not overfill. Check the fluid level and add fluid if necessary

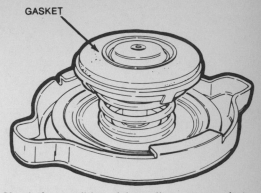

GASKET

Check the condition of the radiator cap gasket

## Cooling System

Every 12 months or 15,000 miles, the following services should be performed:
1. Wash and inspect the radiator cap and the filler neck.
2. Check the coolant level and the degree of freezing protection.
3. If a pressure tester is available, pressure test the system and the radiator cap.
4. Inpsect the hoses of the cooling system (expect to replace the hoses at 24 months/30,000 miles).
5. Check the fins of the radiator (or air conditioning condenser, if equipped as such) for blockage.

### RADIATOR CAP

Before removing the cap. squeeze the upper radiator hose. If it compresses easily (indicating little or no pressure in the system), the cap may be removed by turning it counterclockwise until it reaches the stop. If any hissing is noted at this point (indicating the release of pressure), wait until the hissing stops before you remove the cap. To completely remove the cap, press downward and turn it counterclockwise.

CAUTION: *To avoid personal injury, DO NOT ATTEMPT to remove the radiator cap while the engine is hot.*

If the upper radiator hose is hard, pressure is indicated within the system. In this case, a greater degree of caution should be used in removing the cap. Cover the radiator cap with a thick cloth, and while wearing a heavy glove, carefully turn the cap to the stop. This will allow the pressure to be relieved from the system. After the hissing stops, completely remove the cap (press and turn counterclockwise).

Check the condition of the radiator cap gasket and the seal inside of the cap. The radiator cap is designed to seal the cooling system under normal operating conditions which allows the system to build-up a certain amount of pressure (this pressure rating is stamped or printed on the cap). The pressure in the system raises the boiling point of the coolant to help prevent overheating. If the radiator cap does not seal, the boiling point of the coolant is lowered and overheating will occur. If the cap must be replaced, purchase the new cap according to the pressure rating which is specified for your vehicle.

Prior to installing the cap, inspect and clean the radiator filler neck. If you are reusing the old cap, clean it thoroughly with clear water. After turning the cap on, make sure that the arrows on the cap align with the overflow hose.

### CHECKING THE COOLANT

Any time the hood is raised, check the level of the coolant in the see-through plastic coolant recovery tank. With the engine cold, the coolant level should be near the **ADD** mark on the tank. At normal engine operating temperature, the level should be at the **FULL** mark on the bottle. If coolant must be added to the tank, use a 50/50 mix of coolant/water to adjust the fluid level on models with gasoline engines. On models with diesel engines, use straight, undiluted coolant to adjust the level in the tank. See Coolant Requirements for additional information.

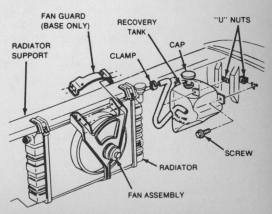

The coolant recovery tank is at the right front of the engine compartment

**You can use an inexpensive tester to check antifreeze protection**

An inexpensive tester may be purchased to test the freezing protection of the coolant. Follow the instructions provided with the tester. The coolant used in models with gasoline engines should protect to –37°F; diesels must have protection to –75°F.

## COOLANT REQUIREMENTS

The coolant used in any General Motors engine must:

a. Be a high quality ehtylene glycol-based solution. Do not use alcohol or methanol-based solutions at any time.

b. Have built-in rust inhibitors.

c. Be designed for year-round use.

d. Offer complete protection for a minimum of 1 years/30,000 miles, without replacement, as long as the proper concentration is maintained.

e. Meet G.M. Specification 1825-M (as specified on the container). This point is critical for diesel engines; coolant meeting other specifications could result in cooling system damage and engine damage due to overheating.

f. Be mixed in the proper proportions: 50% coolant/50% water for gasoline engines; 64% Coolant/36% water for diesel engines.

NOTE: *On diesels, this proportion can be accurately attained only when refilling the system entirely. See Draining and Refilling.*

The use of self-sealing coolants is not recommended. Also, the use of a coolant meeting the above requirements negates the need for supplemental additives. Use of such supplemental products is an unnecessary expense and may cause less than optimum cooling system performance.

## DRAINING AND REFILLING

At least every 2 years or 30,000 miles (whichever comes first), the cooling system should be completely drained and refilled with the proper mixture of coolant and water. Many mechanics recommend that this be done once a year for extra protection against corrosion and subsequent overheating.

Though most coolants are labeled permanent, this only means that the coolant will retain its anti-freezing characteristics. The required rust inhibitors and other chemicals which were added to the coolant during its manufacture will become less effective over a period of time. The following procedure covers the factory recommended procedure for draining and refilling the system.

NOTE: *If you are only replacing the hoses, perform steps 1-3, and 11-16 as required.*

1. Remove the radiator cap.

2. Raise the front of the vehicle and support it safely with jackstands.

3. Open the radiator fitting (located at the bottom of the radiator) by turning it counterclockwise. It may be wise to coat the fitting with penetrating lubricant before you attempt to turn it. Allow the coolant to drain from the radiator.

CAUTION: *When draining the coolant, keep in mind that cats and dogs are attracted by the ethylene glycol antifreeze, and are quite likely to drink any that is left in an uncovered container or in puddles on the ground. This will prove fatal in sufficient quantity. Always drain the coolant into a sealable container. Coolant should be reused unless it is contaminated or several years old.*

4. Remove the drain plug(s) from the engine block (located on the engine block, above the engine oil pan) and allow the coolant to drain.

5. Close the radiator drain fitting and reinstall the engine block plugs.

6. Add clear water to the system until it is filled.

7. Start the engine and repeat steps 3-6 until the drained water is almost colorless. Turn the engine OFF.

8. Allow the system to drain completely and repeat step 5. Remove the cap from the coolant recovery tank, leaving the hoses connected to the cap.

9. Unbolt and remove the coolant recovery tank, drain it, and flush it with clear water. Reinstall the tank.

10. Fill the radiator to the base of the radiator filler neck with a 50/50 mixture of coolant/water. Remember, on diesel equipped models, add a gallon of undiluted coolant first, then add the 50/50 solution.

NOTE: *If only the radiator was drained, use a 50/50 solution to refill it, then check the freezing protection after the level stabilizes.*

11. Fill the coolant recovery tank to the **FULL** mark with the 50/50 solution.

12. With the radiator cap still removed, start the engine and allow it to idle until the upper radiator hose becomes hot, indicating that the thermostat has opened.

13. With the engine still idling, fill the radiator to the base of the filler neck with the 50/50 solution.

14. Install the radiator cap, being sure to align the arrows on the cap with the overflow tube.

15. Turn the engine Off, check for leakage, and double check that the radiator drain is closed and the drain plug(s) is tighten.

### CLEAN RADIATOR OF DEBRIS

Periodically clean any debris — leaves, paper, insects, etc. — from the radiator fins. Pick the large pieces off by hand. The smaller pieces can be washed away with water pressure from a hose.

Carefully straighten any bent radiator fins with a pair of needle nose pliers. Be careful — the fins are very soft. Don't wiggle the fins back and forth too much. Straighten them once and try not to move them again.

### FLUSHING AND CLEANING THE SYSTEM

Several aftermarket radiator flushing and cleaning kits can be purchased at your local auto parts store. It is recommended that the radiator be cleaned and flushed of sludge and any rust build-up once a year. Manufacturers directions for proper use, and safety precautions, come in each kit.

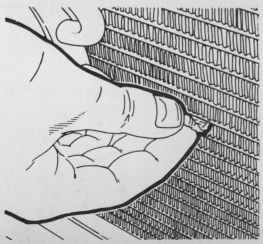

**Clean the front of the radiator as part of the yearly cooling system service**

## Brake Master Cylinder
### RECOMMENDATIONS

Only extra-heavy duty fluid meeting DOT 3 specifications must be used. Using an inferior fluid will result in component damage and reduced braking capabilities.

### CHECKING

About once a month, the fluid level in the master cylinder should be checked.

1. Park the car on a level surface, turn it off and raise the hood.

2. Wipe off the master cylinder cover before you remove it, to prevent contaminating the fluid with dirt.

NOTE: *On most models, a see-through reservoir is used, eliminating the need of removing the cylinder cover.*

3. The cover is snapped into place on the master cylinder. To remove the cover, just press up on the two tabs on the side of the cover, tilt it, then remove it. Be careful not to damage the rubber seal under the cover.

CAUTION: *If you value the paint on your car, don't spill brake fluid on the finish. Brake fluid destroys paint.*

NOTE: *Don't leave the cover off of the master cylinder or the cap off of the brake fluid container any longer than necessary.*

4. The fluid level in each master cylinder reservoir should be ¼" below the lowest edge of the filler opening. Use fresh brake fluid to adjust the level if necessary.

It is normal for the master cylinder fluid level to drop as the brake linings wear (⅛" drop about every 10,000 miles). If the fluid level is constantly low, the system should be checked for leaks.

5. Carefully seat the cover seal into the cover, then snap the cover into place on the master cylinder. Be sure that all four snaps latch completely.

## Power Steering Pump
### FLUID RECOMMENDATIONS

When adding power steering fluid use G.M. part #1050017 or its equal. Dexron®II automatic transmission fluid is an acceptable substitute.

### LEVEL CHECK

The power steering fluid level should be checked at every oil change. On models with gasoline engines, the power steering pump and reservoir are integrated into one unit bolted to the front of the engine. On diesel engined models, the pump is mounted on the engine, and a separate, translucent reservoir is attached to the firewall in the engine compartment.

To check the fluid level, run the engine until it reaches normal operating temperature, then turn the engine off. Remove the reservoir filler cap and check the oil level on the dipstick. The fluid level must be between the HOT and COLD marks on the filler cap indicator. Add power steering fluid as required then reinstall the cap.

## Steering Gear

### FLUID RECOMMENDATIONS AND LEVEL CHECK

All models use integral rack and pinion power steering. The power steering pump delivers hydraulic pressure through two hoses to the steering gear itself. Refer to the power steering pump fluid recommendation and level check procedures above to check the steering gear fluid level.

## Chassis Greasing

### Front Suspension and Steering Linkage

These parts should be greased every 12 months or 7,500 miles (12,000 Km.) with an EP grease meeting G.M. specification 6031M.

If you choose to do this job yourself, you will need to purchase a hand operated grease gun, if you do not own one already, and a long flexible extension hose to reach the various grease fittings. You will also need a cartridge of the appropriate grease.

Press the fitting of the grease gun hose onto the grease fitting of the suspension or steering linkage component. Pump a few shots of grease into the fitting, until the rubber boot on the joint begins to expand, indicating that the joint is full. Remove the gun from the fitting. Be careful not to overfill the joints, which will rupture the rubber boots, allowing the entry of dirt. You can keep the grease fittings clean by covering them with a small square of tin foil.

### Transaxle Shift Linkage

Lubricate the manual transaxle shift linkage contact points with the EP grease used for chassis greasing, which should meet G.M. specification 6031M. The automatic transaxle linkage should be lubricated with clean engine oil.

## Body Lubrication

Clean the latch surfaces and apply clean engine oil to the latch pilot bolts and the spring anchor. Use the engine oil to lubricate the hood hinges as well. Use a chassis grease to lubricate all the pivot points in the latch release mechanism.

### DOOR HINGES

The gas tank filler door, car door, and rear hatch or trunk lid hinges should be wiped clean and lubricated with clean engine oil. Silicone spray also works well on these parts, but must be applied more often. Use engine oil to lubricate the trunk or hatch lock mechanism and the lock bolt and striker. The door lock cylinders can be lubricated easily with a shot of silicone spray or one of the many dry penetrating lubricants commercially available.

### PARKING BRAKE LINKAGE

Use chassis grease on the parking brake cable where is contacts the guides, links, levers, and pulleys. The grease should be a water resistant one for durability under the car.

### ACCELERATOR LINKAGE

Lubricate the carburetor stud, carburetor lever, and the accelerator pedal lever at the support inside the car with clean engine oil.

## Rear Wheel Bearings

### REMOVAL AND INSTALLATION

1. Raise and support the car on a hoist.
2. Remove the wheel and brake drum.
CAUTION: *Do not hammer on the brake drum as damage to the bearing could result.*
3. Remove the hub and bearing assembly to rear axle attaching bolts and remove the rear axle.
NOTE: *The bolts which attach the hub and bearing assembly also support the brake assembly. When removing these bolts, support the brake assembly with a wire or other means. Do not let the brake line support the brake assembly.*
4. Install the hub and bearing assembly to the rear axle and torque the hub and bearing bolts to 45 ft.lb.
5. Install the brake drum, tire and wheel assembly and lower the car.

### ADJUSTMENT

There is no necessary adjustment to the rear wheel bearing and hub assembly.

## Trailer Towing

Your A body car is designed and intended to be used mainly to carry people. Towing a trailer will affect handling, durability and economy.

Your safety and satisfaction depend upon proper use and correct equipment. You should also avoid overloads and other abusive use.

Information on trailer towing ability, special

# JUMP STARTING A DEAD BATTERY

The chemical reaction in a battery produces explosive hydrogen gas. This is the safe way to jump start a dead battery, reducing the chances of an accidental spark that could cause an explosion.

## Jump Starting Precautions

1. Be sure both batteries are of the same voltage.
2. Be sure both batteries are of the same polarity (have the same grounded terminal).
3. Be sure the vehicles are not touching.
4. Be sure the vent cap holes are not obstructed.
5. Do not smoke or allow sparks around the battery.
6. In cold weather, check for frozen electrolyte in the battery. Do not jump start a frozen battery.
7. Do not allow electrolyte on your skin or clothing.
8. Be sure the electrolyte is not frozen.

CAUTION: *Make certain that the ignition key, in the vehicle with the dead battery, is in the OFF position. Connecting cables to vehicles with on-board computers will result in computer destruction if the key is not in the OFF position.*

## Jump Starting Procedure

1. Determine voltages of the two batteries; they must be the same.
2. Bring the starting vehicle close (they must not touch) so that the batteries can be reached easily.
3. Turn off all accessories and both engines. Put both cars in Neutral or Park and set the handbrake.
4. Cover the cell caps with a rag—do not cover terminals.
5. If the terminals on the run-down battery are heavily corroded, clean them.
6. Identify the positive and negative posts on both batteries and connect the cables in the order shown.
7. Start the engine of the starting vehicle and run it at fast idle. Try to start the car with the dead battery. Crank it for no more than 10 seconds at a time and let it cool off for 20 seconds in between tries.
8. If it doesn't start in 3 tries, there is something else wrong.
9. Disconnect the cables in the reverse order.
10. Replace the cell covers and dispose of the rags.

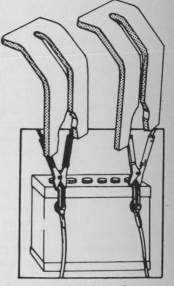

Side terminal batteries occasionally pose a problem when connecting jumper cables. There frequently isn't enough room to clamp the cables without touching sheet metal. Side terminal adaptors are available to alleviate this problem and should be removed after use.

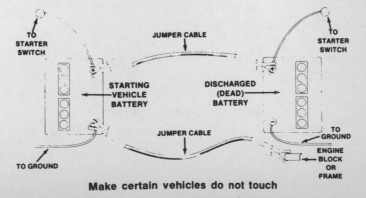

TO STARTER SWITCH

JUMPER CABLE

TO STARTER SWITCH

STARTING VEHICLE BATTERY

DISCHARGED (DEAD) BATTERY

JUMPER CABLE

TO GROUND

ENGINE BLOCK OR FRAME

TO GROUND

**Make certain vehicles do not touch**

**This hook-up for negative ground cars only**

equipment required and optional equipment available should be obtained from your dealer.

### PUSHING AND TOWING

DO NOT attempt to start your A-Body by pushing or towing as damage to the catalytic convertor or other components may result. If the battery is weak, the vehicle may be jump started, using the procedure found after this section.

As long as the driveline and steering are normally operable, your A-Body may be towed on all four wheels. If this is done, don't exceed 35 mph or travel further than 50 miles. The steering wheel must be unlocked, the transaxle in Neutral, and the parking brake released. Never attach towing equipment to the bumpers or bumper brackets—the equipment must be attached to the main structural members of the car.

NOTE: *Remember that there will be no power assist for brakes and steering with the engine Off. Also, be sure to check into state and local towing laws before flat-towing your vehicle.*

If the car is to be towed by a wrecker, instructions supplied by the wrecker manufacturer should be followed. Because of the front wheel drive, towing on the rear wheels is preferred. If absolutely necessary, the A-Body may be towed on the front wheels as long as the speed does not exceed 25 mph and the towing distance does not exceed 10 miles.

CAUTION: *Don't exceed the speed or dis-* *tance limits which are outlined here. Severe transaxle damage could result.*

## JACKING

### Precautions

•. NEVER use the jack supplied with the vehicle for anything but changing tire and wheel assemblies.

•. NEVER crawl underneath the vehicle while it is supported by the factory supplied jack.

•. NEVER start or run the engine while the car is supported by only a jack.

•. ALWAYS secure the spare tire, jack, etc., to prevent loose parts from causing personal injury during hard braking.

### Instructions (Factory supplied Jack Only)

Please refer to the accompanying illustrations for detailed jacking instructions and spare tire/jack stowage instructions.

CAUTION: *Be especially careful not to damage the catalytic convertor when jacking from the floor side rails.*

The accompanying illustrations depict the preferred jacking and jack stand support points underneath the vehicle. When using a floor jack, either the center of the engine cradle crossmember or the center of the rear axle bar can be used as jacking points in addition to the previous hoisting points.

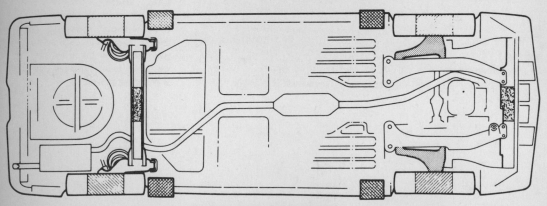

**Jacking and hoisting locations**

## Maintenance Intervals

| Perform | Check | Change | Service | Gasoline-fueled | Diesel-fueled |
|---|---|---|---|---|---|
| X | | | Chassis lubrication | 12 mo./7500 mi. | 12 mo./5000 mi. |
| | X | | Fluid levels | 12 mo./7500 mi. | 12 mo./5000 mi. |
| | | X | Engine oil | 12 mo./7500 mi.② ⑥ | 5000 mi.② |
| | | X | Engine oil filter | ① | every oil change |
| X | X | | Clutch adjustment | ③ | ③ |
| | X | | Engine drive belts | 12 mo./15,000 mi. | 5000 mi. |
| | X | | Front suspension | 12 mo./7500 mi. | 12 mo./10,000 mi. |
| | X | | Exhaust system | 12 mo./7500 mi. | ④ |
| X | X | | Rotate tires and wheels | ⑤ | ④ |
| | X | | Disc Brakes | ⑤ | 12 mo./10,000 mi. |
| | X | | Brake lines | 12 mo./7500 mi. | 12 mo./10,000 mi. |
| | X | | Drum and parking brakes | 12 mo./15,000 mi. | 12 mo./15,000 mi. |
| | X | | Throttle linkage | 12 mo./15,000 mi. | 12 mo./15,000 mi. |
| | X | | Cooling system | 12 mo./15,000 mi. | 12 mo./15,000 mi. |
| X | | | Cooling system drain & refill | 24 mo./30,000 mi. | 24 mo./30,000 mi. |
| | X | | Manual transaxle fluid level | 12 mo./7500 mi. | 12 mo./7500 mi. |
| | X | | Auto. transaxle fluid/filter | see text | see text |
| | | X | Auto. transaxle fluid/filter | see text | see text |

① See the text for recommendations
② Under normal conditions. See the text for additional information.
③ Adjust every 5000 miles or less. See chapter 6 for information.
④ 1st 5000 miles, then every 15,000 thereafter.
⑤ 1st 7500 miles, then every 15,000 thereafter.
⑥ 1987 and later models, every 3 months or 3,000 miles.

## Capacities

| Year | Engine Displacement Cu. In. (Liters) | Crankcase Quarts (Liters) w/filter | Crankcase Quarts (Liters) wo/filter | Transaxle Pints (Liters) 4-Speed | Transaxle Pints (Liters) 5-Speed | Transaxle Pints (Liters) Auto. | Gas Tank Gal. (Liters) | Cooling Systems Quarts (Liters) wo/A.C. | Cooling Systems Quarts (Liters) w/A.C. | Cooling Systems Quarts (Liters) w/H.D. |
|---|---|---|---|---|---|---|---|---|---|---|
| '82–'88 | 151 (2.5) | 3 (2.8) | 3 (2.8) | 5.9 (2.8) | — | 18① (4.6) | 15.7 (59.4) | 9.4 (9.9) | 9.7 (10.25) | 12.1 (12.8) |
| | 173 (2.8) | 4 (3.8) | 4 (3.8) | 5.9 (2.8) | 4.5 (1.5) | 18① (4.6) | 16.4 (62.1) | 11.3 (11.9) | 11.7 (12.4) | 12.1 (12.7) |
| | 183 (3.0) | 4 (3.8) | 4 (3.8) | 5.9 (2.8) | — | 18 (4.6) | 16 (60) | 14.4 (15.2) | 13.6 (14.3) | 14.0 (14.8) |
| | 263 (4.3) | 6 (5.7) | 6 (5.7) | 5.9 (2.8) | — | 18 (4.6) | 16.6 (62.8) | 13.2 (13.9) | 13.9 (14.7) | 13.9 (14.7) |
| | 231 (3.8) | 4 (3.8) | 4 (3.8) | 5.9 (2.8) | 4.5 (2.5) | 18① (4.6) | 16 (60) | 11.4 (10.8) | 12 (11.4) | 12 (11.4) |

① 12.0 pts w/125c transaxle

# Engine Performance and Tune-Up

## 2

## Tune-Up Specifications

When analyzing compression test results, look for uniformity among cylinders rather than specific pressures.

| Year | Engine No. Cyl. Displacement (cu. in.) | hp | Spark Plugs Orig Type | Gap (in.) | Distributor Point Dwell (deg) | Point Gap (in.) | Ignition Timing (deg)▲● Man Trans | Auto Trans | Valves Intake Opens (deg.)■ | Fuel Pump Pressure (psi) | Idle Speed (rpm)▲● Man Trans | Auto Trans |
|---|---|---|---|---|---|---|---|---|---|---|---|---|
| '82–'85 | 4-151 | 90 | R-44TSX | .060 | Electronic | | 8B | 8B | 33 | 6–8 | 950 ① | 750 ② |
| | 6-173 | 112 | R-43TS | .045 | Electronic | | 10B | 10B | 25 | 6–7.5 | 800 | 600 |
| | 6-183 | 110 | R-44TS8 | .080 | Electronic | | ③ | 15B | 16 | 6–8 | ③ | ③ |
| | 6-263 | 85 | — | — | — | | — | 6A | NA | 5.8–8.7 | — | 650 |
| '84–'88 | 6-231 ④ | 125 | R44TS8 | .080 | Electronic | | — | ③ | NA | 30–40 | — | ③ |
| '85–'88 | 6-173 ④ | 94 | R42CTS | .045 | Electronic | | — | ③ | NA | 30–46 | — | ③ |
| '86–'88 | 4-151 | 90 | R-43TSX | .060 | Electronic | | ③ | ③ | NA | 6–7 | ③ | ③ |

NOTE: *The underhood specifications sticker often reflects tune-up specification changes made in production. Sticker figures must be used if they disagree with those in this chart.*
▲ See text for procedure
● Figure in parenthesis indicates California and High Altitude engine
■ All figures Before Top Dead Center
B Before Top Dead Center
Part numbers in this chart are not recommendations by Chilton for any product by brand name.
① Without air conditioning: 850
② Without air conditioning: 680
③ See underhood sticker
④ Multi Port Fuel Injection
NA: not available

## TUNE-UP PROCEDURES

In order to extract the full measure of performance and economy from your car's engine it is essential that it be properly tuned at regular intervals. Although the tune-up intervals for the A-Body have been stretched to limits which would have been thought impossible a few years ago, periodic maintenance is still required. A regularly scheduled tune-up will keep your car's engine running smoothly and will prevent the annoying minor breakdowns and poor performance associated with an untuned engine.

A complete tune-up should be performed at the interval specified in the Maintenance Intervals chart in Chapter 1. This interval should be halved if the car is operated under severe conditions, such as trailer towing, prolonged idling, continual stop-and-start driving, or if starting and running problems are noticed. It is assumed that the routine maintenance described

## Troubleshooting Engine Performance

| Problem | Cause | Solution |
|---|---|---|
| Hard starting (engine cranks normally) | · Binding linkage, choke valve or choke piston | · Repair as necessary |
| | · Restricted choke vacuum diaphragm | · Clean passages |
| | · Improper fuel level | · Adjust float level |
| | · Dirty, worn or faulty needle valve and seat | · Repair as necessary |
| | · Float sticking | · Repair as necessary |
| | · Faulty fuel pump | · Replace fuel pump |
| | · Incorrect choke cover adjustment | · Adjust choke cover |
| | · Inadequate choke unloader adjustment | · Adjust choke unloader |
| | · Faulty ignition coil | · Test and replace as necessary |
| | · Improper spark plug gap | · Adjust gap |
| | · Incorrect ignition timing | · Adjust timing |
| | · Incorrect valve timing | · Check valve timing; repair as necessary |
| Rough idle or stalling | · Incorrect curb or fast idle speed | · Adjust curb or fast idle speed |
| | · Incorrect ignition timing | · Adjust timing to specification |
| | · Improper feedback system operation | · Refer to Chapter 4 |
| | · Improper fast idle cam adjustment | · Adjust fast idle cam |
| | · Faulty EGR valve operation | · Test EGR system and replace as necessary |
| | · Faulty PCV valve air flow | · Test PCV valve and replace as necessary |
| | · Choke binding | · Locate and eliminate binding condition |
| | · Faulty TAC vacuum motor or valve | · Repair as necessary |
| | · Air leak into manifold vacuum | · Inspect manifold vacuum connections and repair as necessary |
| | · Improper fuel level | · Adjust fuel level |
| | · Faulty distributor rotor or cap | · Replace rotor or cap |
| | · Improperly seated valves | · Test cylinder compression, repair as necessary |
| | · Incorrect ignition wiring | · Inspect wiring and correct as necessary |
| | · Faulty ignition coil | · Test coil and replace as necessary |
| | · Restricted air vent or idle passages | · Clean passages |
| | · Restricted air cleaner | · Clean or replace air cleaner filler element |
| | · Faulty choke vacuum diaphragm | · Repair as necessary |
| Faulty low-speed operation | · Restricted idle transfer slots | · Clean transfer slots |
| | · Restricted idle air vents and passages | · Clean air vents and passages |
| | · Restricted air cleaner | · Clean or replace air cleaner filter element |
| | · Improper fuel level | · Adjust fuel level |
| | · Faulty spark plugs | · Clean or replace spark plugs |
| | · Dirty, corroded, or loose ignition secondary circuit wire connections | · Clean or tighten secondary circuit wire connections |
| | · Improper feedback system operation | · Refer to Chapter 4 |
| | · Faulty ignition coil high voltage wire | · Replace ignition coil high voltage wire |
| | · Faulty distributor cap | · Replace cap |
| Faulty acceleration | · Improper accelerator pump stroke | · Adjust accelerator pump stroke |
| | · Incorrect ignition timing | · Adjust timing |
| | · Inoperative pump discharge check ball or needle | · Clean or replace as necessary |
| | · Worn or damaged pump diaphragm or piston | · Replace diaphragm or piston |

## Troubleshooting Engine Performance (cont.)

| Problem | Cause | Solution |
|---|---|---|
| Faulty acceleration (cont.) | • Leaking carburetor main body cover gasket | • Replace gasket |
| | • Engine cold and choke set too lean | • Adjust choke cover |
| | • Improper metering rod adjustment (BBD Model carburetor) | • Adjust metering rod |
| | • Faulty spark plug(s) | • Clean or replace spark plug(s) |
| | • Improperly seated valves | • Test cylinder compression, repair as necessary |
| | • Faulty ignition coil | • Test coil and replace as necessary |
| | • Improper feedback system operation | • Refer to Chapter 4 |
| Faulty high speed operation | • Incorrect ignition timing | • Adjust timing |
| | • Faulty distributor centrifugal advance mechanism | • Check centrifugal advance mechanism and repair as necessary |
| | • Faulty distributor vacuum advance mechanism | • Check vacuum advance mechanism and repair as necessary |
| | • Low fuel pump volume | • Replace fuel pump |
| | • Wrong spark plug air gap or wrong plug | • Adjust air gap or install correct plug |
| | • Faulty choke operation | • Adjust choke cover |
| | • Partially restricted exhaust manifold, exhaust pipe, catalytic converter, muffler, or tailpipe | • Eliminate restriction |
| | • Restricted vacuum passages | • Clean passages |
| | • Improper size or restricted main jet | • Clean or replace as necessary |
| | • Restricted air cleaner | • Clean or replace filter element as necessary |
| | • Faulty distributor rotor or cap | • Replace rotor or cap |
| | • Faulty ignition coil | • Test coil and replace as necessary |
| | • Improperly seated valve(s) | • Test cylinder compression, repair as necessary |
| | • Faulty valve spring(s) | • Inspect and test valve spring tension, replace as necessary |
| | • Incorrect valve timing | • Check valve timing and repair as necessary |
| | • Intake manifold restricted | • Remove restriction or replace manifold |
| | • Worn distributor shaft | • Replace shaft |
| | • Improper feedback system operation | • Refer to Chapter 4 |
| Misfire at all speeds | • Faulty spark plug(s) | • Clean or replace spark plug(s) |
| | • Faulty spark plug wire(s) | • Replace as necessary |
| | • Faulty distributor cap or rotor | • Replace cap or rotor |
| | • Faulty ignition coil | • Test coil and replace as necessary |
| | • Primary ignition circuit shorted or open intermittently | • Troubleshoot primary circuit and repair as necessary |
| | • Improperly seated valve(s) | • Test cylinder compression, repair as necessary |
| | • Faulty hydraulic tappet(s) | • Clean or replace tappet(s) |
| | • Improper feedback system operation | • Refer to Chapter 4 |
| | • Faulty valve spring(s) | • Inspect and test valve spring tension, repair as necessary |
| | • Worn camshaft lobes | • Replace camshaft |
| | • Air leak into manifold | • Check manifold vacuum and repair as necessary |
| | • Improper carburetor adjustment | • Adjust carburetor |
| | • Fuel pump volume or pressure low | • Replace fuel pump |
| | • Blown cylinder head gasket | • Replace gasket |
| | • Intake or exhaust manifold passage(s) restricted | • Pass chain through passage(s) and repair as necessary |
| | • Incorrect trigger wheel installed in distributor | • Install correct trigger wheel |

## Troubleshooting Engine Performance (cont.)

| Problem | Cause | Solution |
|---|---|---|
| Power not up to normal | · Incorrect ignition timing | · Adjust timing |
| | · Faulty distributor rotor | · Replace rotor |
| | · Trigger wheel loose on shaft | · Reposition or replace trigger wheel |
| | · Incorrect spark plug gap | · Adjust gap |
| | · Faulty fuel pump | · Replace fuel pump |
| | · Incorrect valve timing | · Check valve timing and repair as necessary |
| | · Faulty ignition coil | · Test coil and replace as necessary |
| | · Faulty ignition wires | · Test wires and replace as necessary |
| | · Improperly seated valves | · Test cylinder compression and repair as necessary |
| | · Blown cylinder head gasket | · Replace gasket |
| | · Leaking piston rings | · Test compression and repair as necessary |
| | · Worn distributor shaft | · Replace shaft |
| | · Improper feedback system operation | · Refer to Chapter 4 |
| Intake backfire | · Improper ignition timing | · Adjust timing |
| | · Faulty accelerator pump discharge | · Repair as necessary |
| | · Defective EGR CTO valve | · Replace EGR CTO valve |
| | · Defective TAC vacuum motor or valve | · Repair as necessary |
| | · Lean air/fuel mixture | · Check float level or manifold vacuum for air leak. Remove sediment from bowl |
| Exhaust backfire | · Air leak into manifold vacuum | · Check manifold vacuum and repair as necessary |
| | · Faulty air injection diverter valve | · Test diverter valve and replace as necessary |
| | · Exhaust leak | · Locate and eliminate leak |
| Ping or spark knock | · Incorrect ignition timing | · Adjust timing |
| | · Distributor centrifugal or vacuum advance malfunction | · Inspect advance mechanism and repair as necessary |
| | · Excessive combustion chamber deposits | · Remove with combustion chamber cleaner |
| | · Air leak into manifold vacuum | · Check manifold vacuum and repair as necessary |
| | · Excessively high compression | · Test compression and repair as necessary |
| | · Fuel octane rating excessively low | · Try alternate fuel source |
| | · Sharp edges in combustion chamber | · Grind smooth |
| | · EGR valve not functioning properly | · Test EGR system and replace as necessary |
| Surging (at cruising to top speeds) | · Low carburetor fuel level | · Adjust fuel level |
| | · Low fuel pump pressure or volume | · Replace fuel pump |
| | · Metering rod(s) not adjusted properly (BBD Model Carburetor) | · Adjust metering rod |
| | · Improper PCV valve air flow | · Test PCV valve and replace as necessary |
| | · Air leak into manifold vacuum | · Check manifold vacuum and repair as necessary |
| | · Incorrect spark advance | · Test and replace as necessary |
| | · Restricted main jet(s) | · Clean main jet(s) |
| | · Undersize main jet(s) | · Replace main jet(s) |
| | · Restricted air vents | · Clean air vents |
| | · Restricted fuel filter | · Replace fuel filter |
| | · Restricted air cleaner | · Clean or replace air cleaner filter element |
| | · EGR valve not functioning properly | · Test EGR system and replace as necessary |
| | · Improper feedback system operation | · Refer to Chapter 4 |

in the first chapter has been kept up, as this will have a decided effect on the results of a tune-up. All of the applicable steps should be followed in order, as the result is a cumulative one.

If the specifications on the tune-up label in the engine compartment of your A-Body disagree with the Tune-Up Specifications chart in this chapter, the figures on the sticker must be used. The label often reflects changes made during the production run.

## Spark Plugs

Spark plugs ignite the air and fuel mixture in the cylinder as the piston reaches the top of the compression stroke. The controlled explosion

### TROUBLESHOOTING BASIC POINT-TYPE IGNITION SYSTEM PROBLEMS

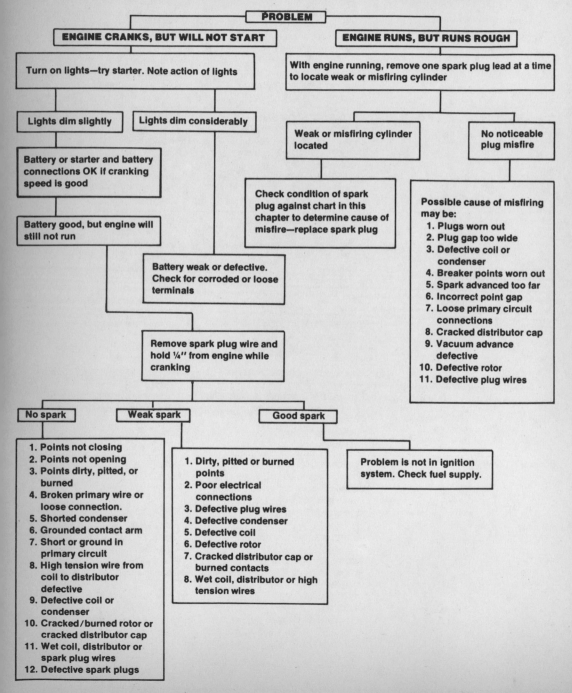

that results forces the piston down, turning the crankshaft and the rest of the drive train.

The average life of a spark plug in an A-Body is 30,000 miles. Part of the reason for this extraordinarily long life is the exclusive use of unleaded fuel, which reduces the amount of deposits within the combustion chamber and on the spark plug electrodes themselves, compared with the deposits left by the leaded gasoline used in the past. An additional contribution to long life is made by the HEI (High Energy Ignition) System, which fires the spark plugs with over 35,000 volts of electricity. The high voltage serves to keep the electrodes clear, and because it is a cleaner blast of electricity than that produced by conventional breaker points ignitions, the electrodes suffer less pitting and wear.

Nevertheless, the life of a spark plug is dependent on a number of factors, including the mechanical condition of the engine, driving conditions, and the driver's habits.

When you remove the plugs, check the condition of the electrodes, they are a good indicator of the internal state of the engine. Since the spark plug wires must be checked every 15,000 miles, the spark plugs can be removed and examined at the same time. This will allow you to keep an eye on the mechanical status of the engine.

A small deposit of light tan or rust/red material on a spark plug that has been used for any period of time is to be considered normal. Any other color, or abnormal amounts of wear or deposits, indicates that there is something amiss in the engine.

The gap between the center electrode and the side or ground electrode can be expected to increase not more than 0.001″ every 1,000 miles under normal conditions.

When a spark plug is functioning normally or, more accurately, when the plug is installed in an engine that is functioning properly, the plugs can be taken out, cleaned, regapped, and reinstalled in the engine without doing the engine any harm.

When, and if, a plug fouls and begins to misfire, you will have to investigate, correct the cause of the fouling, and either clean or replace the plug.

There are several reasons why a spark plug will foul and you can learn which is at fault by just looking at the plug. A few of the most common reasons for plug fouling, and a description of the fouled plug's appearance, are listed in the color insert section.

Spark plugs suitable for use in your car's engine are offered in a number of different heat ranges. The amount of heat which the plug absorbs is determined by the length of the lower insulator. The longer the insulator, the hotter the plug will operate; the shorter the insulator, the cooler it will operate. A spark plug that absorbs (or retains) little heat and remains too cool will accumulate deposits of oil and carbon, because it is not hot enough to burn them off. This leads to fouling and consequent misfiring. A spark plug that absorbs too much heat will have no deposits, but the electrodes will burn away quickly and, in some cases, pre-ignition may result. Pre-ignition occurs when the spark plug tips get so hot that they ignite the fuel/mixture before the actual spark fires. This premature ignition will usually cause a pinging sound under conditions of low speed and heavy load. In severe cases, the heat may become high enough to start the fuel/air mixture burning throughout the combustion chamber rather than just to the front of the plug. In this case, the resultant explosion (detonation) will be strong enough to damage pistons, rings, and valves.

In most cases, the factory recommended heat range is correct; it is chosen to perform well under a wide range of operating conditions. However, if most of your driving is long distance, high speed travel, you may want to install a spark plug one range colder than standard. If most of your driving is of the short trip variety, when the engine may not always reach operating temperature, a hotter plug may help burn off the deposits normally accumulated under those conditions.

### REMOVAL

1. Number the wires with pieces of adhesive tape so that you won't cross them when you replace them.

2. The spark plug boots have large grips to aid in removal. Grasp the wire by the rubber boot and twist the boot ½ turn in either direction to break the tight seal between the boot and the plug. Then twist and pull on the boot to remove the wire from the spark plug. Do not

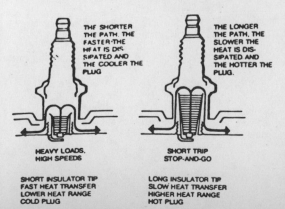

THE SHORTER THE PATH. THE FASTER THE HEAT IS DISSIPATED AND THE COOLER THE PLUG.

THE LONGER THE PATH. THE SLOWER THE HEAT IS DISSIPATED AND THE HOTTER THE PLUG.

HEAVY LOADS, HIGH SPEEDS

SHORT TRIP STOP-AND-GO

SHORT INSULATOR TIP
FAST HEAT TRANSFER
LOWER HEAT RANGE
COLD PLUG

LONG INSULATOR TIP
SLOW HEAT TRANSFER
HIGHER HEAT RANGE
HOT PLUG

**Spark plug heat range**

Twist and pull on the rubber boot to remove the spark plug wires; never pull on the wire itself

Plugs that are in good condition can be filed and reused

pull on the wire itself or you will damage the carbon cord conductor.

3. Use a ⅝" spark plug socket to loosen all of the plugs about two turns. A universal joint installed at the socket end of the extension will ease the process.

If removal of the plugs is difficult, apply a few drops of penetrating oil or silicone spray to the area around the base of the plug, and allow it a few minutes to work.

4. If compressed air is available, apply it to the area around the spark plug holes. Otherwise, use a rag or a brush to clean the area. Be careful not to allow any foreign material to drop into the spark plug holes.

5. Remove the plugs by unscrewing them the rest of the way.

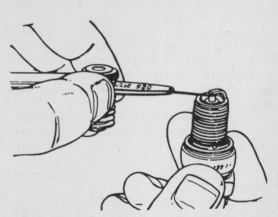

Always use a wire gauge to check the electrode gap

## INSPECTION

Check the plugs for deposits and wear. If they are not going to be replaced, clean the plugs thoroughly. Remember that any kind of deposit will decrease the efficiency of the plug. Plugs can be cleaned on a spark plug cleaning machine, which can sometimes be found in service stations, or you can do an acceptable job of cleaning with a stiff brush. If the plugs are cleaned, the electrodes must be filed flat. Use an ignition points file, not an emery board or the like, which will leave deposits. The electrodes must be filed perfectly flat with sharp edges; rounded edges reduce the spark plug voltage by as much as 50%.

Check the spark plug gap before installation. The ground electrode must be parallel to the center electrode and the specified size wire

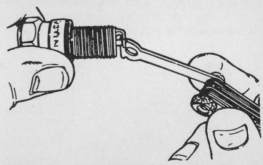

Adjust the electrode gap by bending the side electrode

gauge should pass through the gap with a slight drag. Always check the gap on new plugs, too; they are not always correctly set at the factory. Do not use a flat feeler gauge when measuring the gap, because the reading will be inaccurate. Wire gapping tools usually have a bending tool attached. Use that to adjust the side electrode until the proper distance is obtained. Also, be careful not to bend the side electrode too far or too often; it may weaken and break off within the engine, requiring removal of the cylinder head to retrieve it.

### INSTALLATION

1. Lubricate the threads of the spark plugs with a drop of oil or a shot of silicone spray. Install the plugs and tighten them handtight. Take care not to crossthread them.

2. Tighten the spark plugs with the socket. Do not apply the same amount of force you would use for a bolt; just snug them in. These spark plugs do not use gaskets, and over-tightening will make future removal difficult. If a torque wrench is available, tighten to 7-15 ft.lb.
   NOTE: *While over-tightening the spark plug is to be avoided,*
   *under-tightening is just as bad. If combustion gases leak past the*
   *threads, the spark plug will overheat and rapid electrode wear will*
   *result.*

3. Install the wires on their respective plugs. Make sure the wires are firmly connected. You will be able to feel them click into place. Spark plug wiring diagrams are in this chapter if you get into trouble.

## Spark Plug Wires

Every 15,000 miles, inspect the spark plug wires for burns, cuts, or breaks in the insulation. Check the boots and the nipples on the distributor cap. Replace any damaged wiring.

Every 45,000 miles or so, the resistance of the wires should be checked with an ohmmeter. Wires with excessive resistance will cause misfiring, and may make the engine difficult to start in damp weather. Generally, the useful life of the cables is 45,000-60,000 miles.

To check resistance, remove the distributor cap, leaving the wires in place. Connect one lead of an ohmmeter to an electrode within the cap; connect the other lead to the corresponding spark plug terminal (remove it from the spark plug for this test). Replace any wire which shows a resistance over 30,000Ω. The following chart gives resistance values as a function of length. Generally speaking, however, resistance should not be considered the outer limit of acceptability.
- 0-15": 3,000-10,000 ;
- 15-25": 4,000-15,000 ;

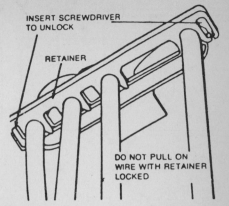

**Unlock the plastic retainers to replace the spark plug wires**

- 25-35": 6,000-20,000 ;
- Over 35": 25,000.

It should be remembered that resistance is also a function of length; the longer the wire, the greater the resistance. Thus, if the wires on your car are longer than the factory originals, resistance will be higher, quite possibly outside these limits.

When installing new wires, replace them one at a time to avoid mixups. Start by replacing the longest one first. Install the boot firmly over the spark plug. Route the wire over the the same path as the original. Insert the nipple firmly onto the tower on the distributor cap, then install the cap cover and latches to secure the wires.

## Firing Orders

NOTE: *To avoid confusion, remove and tag the wires one at a time, for replacement*

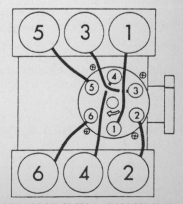

**GM (Buick) 183 V6 (3.0L) and 231 V6 (3.8L) engines firing order: 1-6-5-4-3-2; distributor rotation: clockwise**

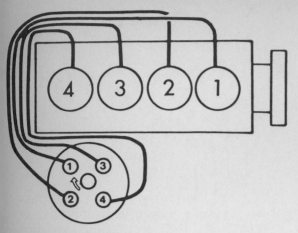

GM (Pontiac) 151-4
Engine firing order: 1-3-4-2
Distributor rotation: clockwise

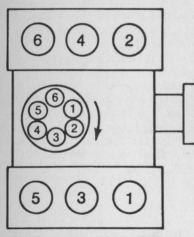

GM (Chevrolet) 173 V6 (2.8 L)
Engine firing order: 1-2-3-4-5-6
Distributor rotation: clockwise

## Ignition System

The General Motors High Energy Ignition (H.E.I.) system is virtually maintenance free, since it is electronic and, therefore, uses no breaker points. The only required service for the H.E.I. distributor is to check the distributor cap and rotor for cracks, carbon tracking, and corrosion every 30,000 miles.

## High Energy Ignition (HEI) System

NOTE: *This book contains simple testing procedures for your vehicle's electronic ignition. More comprehensive testing in this system and other electronic control systems on your vehicle can be found in CHILTON'S GUIDE TO ELECTRONIC ENGINE CONTROLS, book part number 7535, available at most book stores and auto parts stores or available directly from Chilton Co.*

The General Motors HEI system is a pulse-triggered, transistor-controlled, inductive discharge ignition system. The entire HEI system is contained within the distributor cap.

The distributor, in addition to housing the mechanical and vacuum advance mechanisms, contains the ignition coil, the electronic control module, and the magnetic pick-up assembly contains a permanent magnet, a pole piece with internal teeth, and a pick-up coil (not to be confused with the ignition coil).

For 1982 and later an HEI distributor with Electronic Spark Timing is used (for more information on EST, refer to Chapter 4).

All spark timing changes in the 1982 and later distributors are done electronically by the Electronic Control Module (ECM) which monitors information from various engine sensors, computes the desired spark timing and then signals the distributor to change the timing accordingly. No vacuum or mechanical advance systems are used whatsoever.

In the HEI system, as in other electronic ignition systems, the breaker points have been replaced with an electronic switch, a transistor, which is located within the control module. This switching transistor performs the same function the points did in a conventional ignition system; it simply turns coil primary current on and off at the correct time. Essentially then, electronic and conventional ignition systems operate on the same principle.

The module which houses the switching transistor is controlled (turned on and off) by a magnetically generated impulse induced in the pick-up coil. When the teeth of the rotating timer align with the teeth of the pole piece, the induced voltage in the pick-up coil signals the electronic module to open the coil primary circuit. The primary current then decreases, and a high voltage is induced in the ignition coil secondary windings which is then directed through the rotor and high voltage leads. (spark plug wires) to fire the spark plugs.

In essence then, the pick-up coil module system simply replaces the conventional breaker points and condenser. The condenser found within the distributor is for radio suppression purposes only and has nothing to do with the ignition process. The module automatically controls the dwell period, increasing it with increasing engine speed. Since dwell is automatically controlled, it cannot be adjusted. The module itself is non-adjustable and non-repairable and must be replaced if found defective.

## HEI SYSTEM PRECAUTIONS

Before going on to troubleshooting, it might be a good idea to take note of the following precautions:

### Timing Light Use

Inductive pick-up timing lights are the best kind of use with HEI. Timing light which connect between the spark plug and the spark plug wire occasionally (not always) give false readings.

### Spark Plug Wires

The plug wires used with HEI systems are of a different construction than conventional wires. When replacing them, make sure you get the correct wires, since conventional wires won't carry the voltage. Also, handle them carefully to avoid cracking or splitting them and never pierce them.

### Tachometer Use

Not all tachometers will operate or indicate correctly when used on a HEI system. While some tachometers may give a reading, this does not necessarily mean the reading is correct. In addition, some tachometers hook up differently from others. If you can't figure out whether or not your tachometer will work on your car, check with the tachometer manufacturer. Dwell readings, or course, have no significance at all.

### HEI System Testers

Instruments designed specifically for testing HEI systems are available from several tool manufacturers. Some of these will even test the module itself. However, the tests given in the following section will require only ohmmeter and a voltmeter.

## TROUBLESHOOTING THE HEI SYSTEM

The symptoms of a defective component within the HEI system are exactly the same as those you would encounter in a conventional system. Some of these symptoms are:
- Hard or no Starting
- Rough Idle
- Poor Fuel Economy
- Engine misses under load or while accelerating

If you suspect a problem in your ignition system, there are certain preliminary checks which you should carry out before you begin to check the electronic portions of the system. First, it is extremely important to make sure the vehicle battery is in a good state of charge. A defective or poorly charged battery will cause the various components of the ignition system to read incorrectly when they are being tested. Second, Make sure all wiring connections are clean and tight, not only at the battery, but also at the distributor cap, ignition coil, and at the electronic control module.

Since the only change between electronic and conventional ignition systems is in the distributor component area, it is imperative to check the secondary ignition circuit first. If the secondary circuit checks out properly, then the engine condition is probably not the fault of the ignition system. To check the secondary ignition system, perform a simple spark test. Remove one of the plug wires and insert some sort of extension in the plug socket. An old spark plug with the ground electrode removed makes a good extension. Hold the wire and extension about ¼" away from the block and crank the engine. If a normal spark occurs, then the problem is most likely not in the ignition system. Check for fuel system problems, or fouled spark plugs.

If, however, there is no spark or a weak spark, then further ignition system testing will have to be done. Troubleshooting techniques fall into two categories, depending on the nature of the problem. The categories are (1) Engine cranks, but won't start or (2) Engine runs, but runs rough or cuts out. To begin with, let's consider the first case.

### Engine Fail to Start

If the engine won't start, perform a spark test as described earlier. This will narrow the problem area down considerably. If no spark occurs, check for the presence of normal battery voltage of the battery (BAT) terminal in the distributor cap. The ignition switch must be in the ON position for this test. Either a voltmeter or a test light may be used for this test. Connect the test light wire to ground and probe end to the BAT terminal at the distributor. If the light comes on, you have voltage on the distributor. If the light fails to come on, this indicates an open circuit in the ignition primary wiring leading to the distributor. In this case, you will have to check wiring continuity back to the ignition switch using a test light. If there is battery voltage at the BAT terminal, but no spark at the plugs, then the problem lies within the distributor assembly. Go on to the distributor components test section.

### Engine Runs, But Runs Rough or Cuts Out

1. Make sure the plug wires are in good shape first. There should be no obvious cracks or breaks. You can check the plug wires with an ohmmeter, but do not pierce the wires with a

probe. Check the chart for the correct plug wire resistance.

2. If the plug wires are OK, remove the cap assembly and check of moisture, cracks, ships, or carbon tracks, or any other high voltage leaks or failures. Replace the cap if any defects are found. Make sure the timer wheel rotates when the engine is cranked. If everything is all right so far, go on to the distributor components test section following.

### DISTRIBUTOR COMPONENTS TESTING

If the trouble has been narrowed down to the units within the distributor, the following tests can help pinpoint the defective component. An ohmmeter with both high and low ranges should be used. These tests are made with the cap assembly removed and the battery wire disconnected. If a tachometer is connected to the TACH terminal, disconnect it before making these tests.

1. Connect an ohmmeter between the TACH and BAT terminals in the distributor cap. The primary coil resistance should be less than $1\Omega$.

2. To check the coil secondary resistance, connect an ohmmeter between the rotor button and BAT terminal. Note the reading. Connect the ohmmeter between the rotor button and the TACH terminal. Note the reading. The resistance in both cases should be between 6,000 and $30,000\Omega$. Be sure to test between the rotor button and both the BAT and TACH terminals.

3. Replace the coil only if the readings in Step 1 and Step 2 are infinite.

NOTE: *These resistance checks will not disclose shorted could windings. This condition can only be detected with scope analysis or a suitably designed coil tester. If these instruments are unavailable, replace the coil with a known good coil as a final coil test.*

4. To test the pick-up coil, first disconnect the white and green module leads. Set the ohmmeter on the high scale and connect it between a ground and either the white or green lead. Any resistance measurement less than infinity requires replacement of the pick-up coil.

5. Pick-up coil continuity is tested by connecting the ohmmeter (on low range) between the white and green leads. Normal resistance is between $800\Omega$ and $1500\Omega$. Move the vacuum advance arm while performing this test. This will detect any break in coil continuity. Such a condition can cause intermittent misfiring. Replace the pick-up if the reading is outside the specified limits.

6. If no defects have been found at this time, you still have a problem, then the module will have to be checked. If you do not have access to a module tester, the only possible alternative is a substitution test. If the module fails the substitution test, replace it.

### HEI SYSTEM MAINTENANCE

Except for periodic checks of the spark plug wires, and an occasional check of the distributor cap for cracks (see Steps 1 and 2 under Engine Runs, But Runs Rough or Cuts Out for details), no maintenance is required on the HEI System. No periodic lubrication is necessary; engine oil lubricates the lower bushing, and an oil-filled reservoir lubricates the upper bushing.

### COMPONENT REPLACEMENT

#### Integral Ignition Coil

1. Disconnect the feed and module wire terminal connectors from the distributor cap.

2. Remove the ignition set retainer.

3. Remove the 4 coil cover-to-distributor cap screws.

5. Using a blunt drift, press the coil wire spade terminals up out of the distributor cap.

6. Lift the coil up out of the distributor cap.

7. Remove and clean the coil spring, rubber seal washer and coil cavity of the distributor cap.

8. Coat the rubber seal with a dielectric lubricant furnished in the replacement ignition coil package.

9. Reverse the above procedures to install.

#### Distributor Cap

1. Remove the feed and module wire terminal connectors from the distributor cap.

2. Remove the retainer and spark plug wires from the cap.

3. Depress and release the 4 distributor cap-to-housing retainers and lift off the cap assembly.

4. Remove the 4 coil cover screws and cover.

5. Using a finger or a blunt drift, push the spade terminals up out of the distributor cap.

6. Remove all 4 coil screws and lift the coil, coil spring and rubber seal washer out of the cap coil cavity.

7. Using a new distributor cap, reverse the above procedure to assemble being sure to clean and lubricate the rubber seal washer with dielectric lubricant.

#### Rotor

1. Disconnect the feed and module wire connector from the distributor.

2. Depress and release the 4 distributor cap-to-housing retainers and lift off the cap assembly.

3. Remove the two rotor attaching screws and rotor.

4. Reverse the above procedure to install.

### Module

1. Remove the distributor cap and rotor as previously described.

2. Disconnect the harness connector and pick-up coil spade connectors from the module. Be careful not to damage the wires when removing the connector.

3. Remove the two screws and module from the distributor housing.

4. Coat the bottom of the new module with dielectric lubricant supplied with the new module. Reverse the above procedure to install.

### HEI SYSTEM TACHOMETER HOOKUP

There is a terminal marked TACH on the distributor cap. Connect one tachometer lead to this terminal and the other lead to a ground. On some tachometer, the leads must be connected to the TACK terminal and to the battery positive terminal.

CAUTION: *Never ground the TACH terminal; serious module and ignition coil damage will result. If there is any doubt as to the correct tachometer hookup, check with the tachometer manufacturer.*

## Computer Controlled Coil Ignition (C3I) System

Starting in 1987, some models of the A body came with 4 and 6 cylinder engines equipped with Computer Controlled Coil Ignition (C3I), which eliminates the distributor. The C3I ignition system consists of a coil pack, ignition module, camshaft and crankshaft sensor. There are two types of C3I coils used. Type 1 coils have three plug wires on each side of the coil assembly; Type 2 coils have all six wires connected on one side of the coil. When troubleshooting or replacing components, it is important to determine which C3I system is installed on the engine.

The C3I system consists of the coil pack, ignition module, crankshaft sensor, interruptor rings and electronic control module (ECM). All components are serviced as complete assemblies, although individual coils are available for Type 2 coil packs. Since the ECM controls the ignition timing, no timing adjustments are necessary or possible.

## Crankshaft Sensor

### REMOVAL AND INSTALLATION

1. Disconnect the negative battery cable.
2. Remove the serpentine drive belt.
3. Raise the car and support it safely.

4. Remove the right front tire.

5. Remove the inner fender splash shield.

6. Remove the crankshaft balancer bolt and balancer.

7. Remove the mounting bolts and remove the crankshaft sensor from the front cover. Disconnect the electrical connector and remove the sensor from the vehicle.

8. Installation is the reverse of removal. Make sure the electrical T-latch connector is assembled properly or an intermittent loss of operation may occur. The sensor must be carefully aligned with the interruptor rings to avoid damage when the engine is cranked. Tighten the crankshaft sensor mounting bolts to 22 ft.lb. (30 Nm) and the crankshaft balancer bolt to 200 ft.lb. (270 Nm).

For all testing and diagnosis procedures on the C3I ignition system, please refer to *Chilton's Guide To Electronic Engine Controls.*

## Ignition Timing

Ignition timing is the point at which each spark plug fires in relation to its respective piston, during the compression stroke of the engine.

As far as ignition timing is concerned, the position of the piston can be related (in degrees) to the following reference terms: Top Dead Center (TDC), After Top Dead Center (ATDC), and Before Top Dead Center (BTDC). The movement of the piston is expressed in degrees due to the rotaton of the crankshaft. Even though the crankshaft turns 720° to complete one entire 4-stroke cycle, all we're concerned about here is the compression stroke, since this is when the ignition of the air/fuel mixture takes place (or more accurately, should take place).

Because it takes a fraction of a second for the spark (at the spark plug) to ignite the air/fuel mixture and for the mixture to burn completely, the spark should ideally occur just before the piston reaches TDC. If the spark didn't occur until exactly TDC or ATDC, the piston would already be on its way down before the mixture explosion would not exert as much downward force on the piston as it would if the ignition timing was properly set. The result of this would be reduced power and fuel economy.

Should ignition of the air/fuel mixture occur too far BTDC (advanced), the mixture explosion will try to force the piston downward before it can mechanically do so. This contest between the explosion forcing the piston downward and the crankshaft forcing the piston upward will result in a pinging sound if you're lucky; severe engine damage if you're not so lucky. If you experience pinging, check with a trusted mechanic to determine if the pinging is

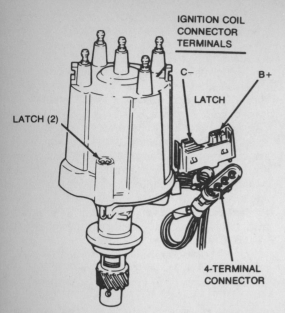

**HEI EST distributor**

mild or severe. Only a trained car mechanic can safely determine this.

NOTE: *Pinging can also be caused by inferior gasoline, since lower*
*octane gas burns at a faster, more uncontrolled rate than a higher octane fuel.*

In order to compensate for low quality gas, the ignition timing may be retarded a couple of degrees, though this is not recommended since performance and fuel economy will suffer.

On United States engines, after the initial (base) timing is set, the emission control computer and related components electronically determine and adjust the degree of spark advance under all conditions. On Canadian models, total ignition timing advance is determined by three things: initial timing setting, distributor vacuum control and distributor mechanical control.

### ADJUSTMENT

To check the timing before and after adjustment, a timing light is used. The timing light will visually show you a) when the spark is sent to the spark plug, and b) the position of the crankshaft when the spark occurs.

There are three basic types of timing light available. The first is a simple neon bulb with two wire connections (one for the spark plug and one for the plug wire, connecting the light in series). This type of light is quite dim, and must be held closely to the marks to be seen, but it is quite inexpensive. The second type of light operates form the car's battery. Two alligator clips connect to the battery terminals, while a third wire connects to the spark plug with an adapter. This type of light is more expensive, but the xenon bulb provides a nice bright flash which can even be seen in sunlight. The third type replaces the battery source with 110 volt house current. Some timing lights

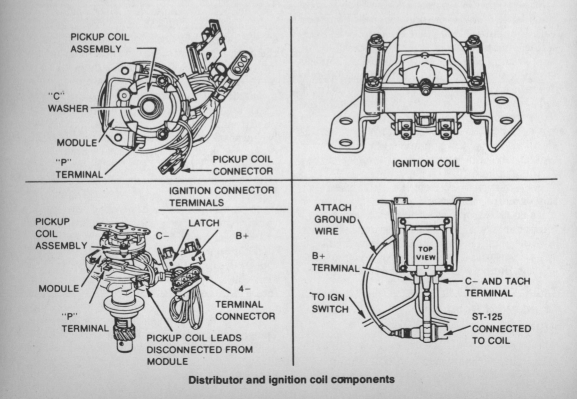

**Distributor and ignition coil components**

have other functions built into them, such as dwell meters, tachometers, or remote starting switches. These are convenient, in that they reduce the tangle of wires under the hood, but may duplicate the functions of tools you already have.

Because your car has electronic ignition, you should use a timing light which has an inductive pick-up. This type of pick-up merely clamps around the No. 1 spark plug wire, eliminating any kind of adapter. Other types of timing lights may cause false timing readings when used with H.E.I. systems.

CAUTION: *NEVER use a timing light which requires piercing of the spark plug wire.*

1. Refer to the instructions listed on the emission control label inside the engine compartment. Follow all instructions on the label.

2. Locate the timing marks on the front of the engine and on the crankshaft balances.

3. Clean off the marks so that they are readable. Chalk or white paint on the balancer mark (line) and at the correct point on the timing scale will make the marks much easier to accurately align.

4. If specified on the emissions label, attach a tachometer to the engine according to the tachometer manufacturer's instructions.

NOTE: *On 4-cylinder engines, the TACH terminal is at the brown wire connection at the ignition coil; on V6's, it is next to the BAT connector on the distributor cap.*

5. Attach a timing light according to the timing light manufacturer's instructions. Remember that the inductive pick-up is clamped around the No. 1 spark plug wire.

6. Check that all wiring is clear of the fan, then start the engine. Allow the engine to reach normal operating temperature.

7. Aim the timing light at the timing marks. The line on the crankshaft balancer will line up at a timing mark. If the line is within 1° of where it should be, no adjustment is necessary.

8. If adjustment is necessary, loosen the distributor holddown bolt slightly. Slowly rotate the distributor until the proper setting is attained.

9. Tighten the holddown bolt, recheck the timing and readjust if required.

10. Turn the engine off and disconnect the timing light (and tachometer, if in use).

NOTE: *Disregard the short tube which may be integral with the timing scale on some engines. This tube is used to connect magnetic timing equipment which is marketed to professional shops.*

## Valve Lash
### *ADJUSTMENT*
#### 4-151, 6-181, 6-231 and 6-263 Engines

All models utilize an hydraulic valve lifter system to obtain zero lash. No adjustment is necessary. An initial adjustment is required anytime that the lifters are removed or the

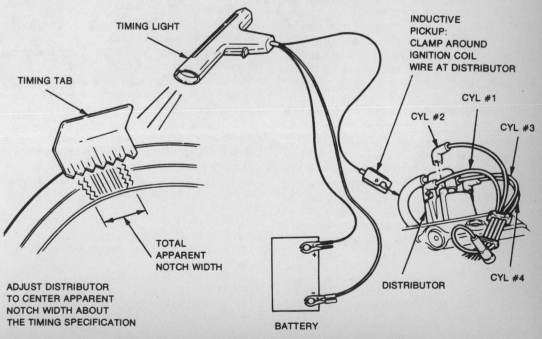

TIMING LIGHT

TIMING TAB

INDUCTIVE PICKUP: CLAMP AROUND IGNITION COIL WIRE AT DISTRIBUTOR

CYL #1

CYL #2

CYL #3

TOTAL APPARENT NOTCH WIDTH

ADJUST DISTRIBUTOR TO CENTER APPARENT NOTCH WIDTH ABOUT THE TIMING SPECIFICATION

DISTRIBUTOR

CYL #4

BATTERY

**Ignition timing is accomplished using the averaging method**

valve train is disturbed, this procedure is covered in Chapter 3.

### 6-173 Engine

Anytime the V6 valve train is disturbed, the valve lash must be adjusted. Crank the engine until the timing mark aligns with the **O** mark on the timing scale, and both valves in the No. 1 cylinder are closed. If the valves are moving as the timing marks align, the engine is in the No. 4 firing position. Turn the crankshaft one more revolution. With the engine in the No. 1 firing position, adjust the following valves:

- exhaust — 1,2,3
- intake — 1,5,6

Rotate the crankshaft one full revolution, until it is in the No. 4 firing position. Adjust the following valves:

- Exhaust — 4,5,6
- Intake — 2,3,4

Adjustment is made by backing off the rocker arm adjusting nut until there is play in the pushrod. Tighten the nut to remove the pushrod clearance (this can be determined by rotating the pushrod with your fingers while tightening the adjusting nut). When the pushrod cannot be freely turned, tighten the nut $1\frac{1}{2}$ additional turns to place the hydraulic lifter in the center of its travel. No further adjustment is required.

## Idle Speed And Mixture Adjustment Gasoline Engines

### U.S. Carbureted Models

Mixture adjustments are a function of the Computer Command Control (CCC) system. The idle speed on models equipped with an Idle Speed Control (ISC) motor is also automatically adjusted by the Computer Command Control System, making manual adjustment unnecessary. The underhood specifications sticker will indicate ISC motor use. We strongly recommend that mixture adjustments be referred to a qualified, professional technician.

On non-A/C models not equipped with ISC, the idle speed is adjusted at the idle speed screw on the carburetor. Before adjusting, check the underhood sticker for any preparations required. On A/C equipped models which do not have an ISC motor, an idle speed solenoid is used. This solenoid is adjusted at the solenoid screw. Consult the underhood specifications sticker for special instructions.

### Canadian Models

The idle speed may be adjusted on Canadian models, though this is not part of a normal tune-up. Be sure to follow the instructions on the underhood emissions label to the letter in order to properly perform this adjustment.

As on U.S. models, the idle mixture screws are concealed under hardened plugs and mixture adjustments are not normally required. Since carburetor removal is necessary in order to gain access to the screws, the plug removal and adjustment procedures are covered in Chapter 5. The mixture adjustment procedures for U.S. and Canadian models are different. Be sure to follow the proper procedure.

### U.S. Fuel Injected Models

No idle speed or mixture adjustments are possible on fuel injected engines.

## Idle Speed — Diesel Engine

### ADJUSTMENT

Adjustments to diesel fuel injection units are to be performed only in the case of parts replacement on the injection unit.

1. Apply the parking brake, place the transmission selector lever in Park and block the drive wheels.
2. Start engine and allow it to run until warm, usually 10-15 minutes.
3. Shut off the engine, remove the air cleaner assembly.
4. Clean the front cover rpm counter (probe holder) and the crankshaft balancer rim.
5. Install the magnetic pick-up probe of tool J-26925 fully into the rpm counter. Connect the battery leads; red to positive ( + ) and black to negative (–).
6. Disconnect the two-lead connector at the generator.
7. Turn off all electrical accessories.
8. Allow no one to touch either the steering wheel or service brake pedal.
9. Start the engine and place the transmission selector lever in Drive.
10. Check the slow idle speed reading against the one given on the underhood emission control sticker. Reset if required.
11. Unplug the connector from the fast idle cold advance (engine temp.) switch and install a jumper between the connector terminals. Do not allow the jumper to touch ground.
12. Check the fast idle solenoid speed against the one given on the underhood sticker and reset if required.
13. Remove the jumper and reconnect the connector to the temperature switch.
14. Recheck and reset the slow idle speed if necessary.
15. Shut off the engine.
16. Reconnect the lead at the generator.
17. Disconnect and remove the tachometer.
18. If equipped with cruise control adjust the servo throttle cable to minimum slack then install the clip on the servo stud.

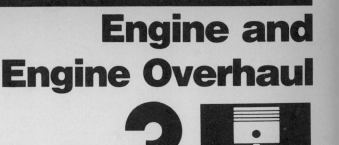

# Engine and Engine Overhaul

# 3

## UNDERSTANDING THE ENGINE ELECTRICAL SYSTEM

The engine electrical system can be broken down into three separate and distinct systems: (1) the starting system; (2) the charging system; (3) the ignition system.

### Battery and Starting System

The battery is the first link in the chain of mechanisms which work together to provide cranking of the automobile engine. In most modern cars, the battery is a lead-acid electrochemical device consisting of six two-volt (2V) subsections connected in series so the unit is capable of producing approximately 12 V of electrical pressure. Each subsection, or cell, consists of a series of positive and negative plates held a short distance apart in a solution of sulfuric acid and water. The two types of plates are of dissimilar metals. This causes a chemical reaction to set up, and it is this reaction which produces current flow from the battery when its positive and negative terminals are connected to an electrical appliance such as a lamp or motor. The continued transfer of electrons would eventually convert the sulfuric acid in the electrolyte to water, and make the two plates identical in chemical composition. As electrical energy is removed from the battery, its voltage output tends to drop. Thus, measuring battery voltage and battery electrolyte composition are two ways of checking the ability of the unit to supply power. During the starting of the engine, electrical energy is removed from the battery. However, if the charging circuit is in good condition and the operating conditions are normal, the power removed from the battery will be replaced by the generator (or alternator) which will force electrons back through the battery, reversing the normal flow, and re-

storing the battery to its original chemical state.

The battery and starting motor are linked by very heavy electrical cables designed to minimize resistance to the flow of current. The major power supply cable that leaves the battery goes directly to the starter, while other electrical system needs are supplied by a smaller cable. During the starter operation, power flows from the battery to the starter and is grounded through the car's frame and the battery's negative ground strap.

The starting motor is a specially designed, direct current electric motor capable of producing a very great amount of power for its size. One thing that allows the motor to produce a great deal of power is its tremendous rotating speed. It drives the engine through a tiny pinion gear (attached to the starter's armature), which drives the very large flywheel ring gear at a greatly reduced speed. Another factor allowing it to produce so much power is that only intermittent operation is required of it. Thus, little allowance for air circulation is required, and the windings can be built into a very small space.

The starter solenoid is a magnetic device which employs the small current supplied by the starting switch circuit of the ignition switch. This magnetic action moves a plunger which mechanically engages the starter and electrically closes the heavy switch which connects it to the battery. The starting switch circuit consists of the starting switch contained within the ignition switch, a transmission neutral safety switch or clutch pedal switch, and the wiring necessary to connect these with the starter solenoid or relay.

A pinion, which is a small gear, is mounted to a one-way drive clutch. This clutch is splined to the starter armature shaft. When the ignition switch is moved to the start position, the solenoid plunger slides the pinion toward the flywheel ring gear via a collar and spring. If the teeth on the pinion and flywheel match properly, the pinion will engage the flywheel immediately. If the gear teeth butt one another, the spring will be compressed and will force the gears to mesh as soon as the starter turns far enough to allow them to do so. As the solenoid plunger reaches the end of its travel, it closes the contacts that connect the battery and starter and then the engine is cranked.

As soon as the engine starts, the flywheel ring gear begins turning fast enough to drive the pinion at an extremely high rate of speed. At this point, the one-way clutch begins allowing the pinion to spin faster than the starter shaft so that the starter will not operate at excessive speed. When the ignition switch is released from the start position, the solenoid is de-energized, and a spring contained within the solenoid assembly pulls the gear out of mesh and interrupts the current flow to the starter.

## The Charging System

The automobile charging system provides electrical power for operation of the vehicle's ignition and starting systems and all the electrical accessories. The battery serves as an electrical surge or storage tank, storing (in chemical form) the energy originally produced by the engine driven A.C. (alternator). The system also provides a means of regulating alternator output to protect the battery from being overcharged and to avoid excessive voltage to the accessories.

The storage battery is a chemical device incorporating parallel lead plates in a tank containing a sulfuric acid/water solution. Adjacent plates are slightly dissimilar, and the chemical reaction of the two dissimilar plates produces electrical energy when the battery is connected to a load such as the starter motor. The chemical reaction is reversible, so that when the alternator is producing a voltage (electrical pressure) greater than that produced by the battery, electricity is forced into the battery, and the battery is returned to its fully charged state.

The vehicle's alternator is driven mechanically, through belts, by the engine crankshaft. It consists of two coils of fine wire, cone stationary (the stator), and one movable (the rotor). The rotor may also be known as the armature, and consists of fine wire wrapped around an iron core which is mounted on a shaft. The electricity which flows through the two coils of wire (provided initially by the battery in some cases) creates an intense magnetic field around both rotor and stator, and the interaction between the two fields creates voltage, allowing the generator to power the accessories and charges the battery.

Newer automobiles, including your A-Body, use alternating current alternators because they are efficient, can be rotated at high speeds, and have few brush problems. In an alternator, the field rotates while all the current produced passes only through the stator windings. The brushes bear against continuous slip rings rather than a commutator. This causes the current produced to periodically reverse the direction of its flow. Diodes (electrical one-way switches) block the flow of current from traveling in the wrong direction. A series of diodes is wired together to permit the alternating flow of the stator to be converted to a pulsating, but unidirectional flow at the alternator output. the alternator's field is wired in series with the voltage regulator. Alternators are self-limiting as far as maximum current is concerned.

### SAFETY PRECAUTIONS

Observing these precautions will ensure safe handling of the electrical system components, and will avoid damage to the vehicle's electrical system:

a. Be absolutely sure of the polarity of a booster battery before making connections. Connect the cables positive to positive, and negative to negative. Connect positive cables first and then make the last connection to a ground on the body of the booster vehicle so that arcing cannot ignite hydrogen gas that may have accumulated near the battery. Even momentary connection of a booster battery with the polarity reserved will damage alternator diodes.

b. Disconnect both vehicle battery cables before attempting to charge a battery.

c. Never ground the alternator output or battery terminal. Be cautious when using metal tools around a battery to avoid creating a short circuit between the terminals.

d. Never run an alternator or generator without load unless the field circuit is disconnected.

e. Never attempt to polarize an alternator.

## Ignition Coil

### TESTING

An ohmmeter with both high and low ranges should be used for these test. Tests are made with the cap assembly removed and the battery wire disconnected. If a tachometer is connected to the TACH terminal, disconnect it before making these test.

1. Connect an ohmmeter between the TACH and BAT terminals in the distributor cap. The primary coil resistance should be less than $1\Omega$.

2. To check the coil secondary resistance, connect an ohmmeter between the rotor button and the BAT terminal. Note the reading. Con-

nect an ohmmeter between the rotor button and the TACH terminal. Note the reading. The resistance in both cases should be between 6,000 and 30,000 ohms. Be sure to test between the rotor button and both the BAT and TACH terminals.

3. Replace the coil ONLY if the readings in Step 1 and Step 2 are infinite.

NOTE: *These resistance checks will not disclose shorted coil windings. This condition can only be detected with scope analysis or a suitably designed coil tester. If these instruments are not available, replace the coil with a known good coil as a final coil test.*

### REMOVAL AND INSTALLATION

1. Disconnect the feed and module wire terminal connectors from the distributor cap.

2. Remove the ignition wire set retainer.

3. Remove the 4 coil cover-to-distributor cap screws and the coil cover.

4. Remove the 4 coil-to-distributor cap screws.

5. Using a blunt drift, press the coil wire spade terminals up and out of the distributor cap.

6. Lift the coil up and out of the distributor cap.

7. Remove and clean the coil spring, rubber seal washer and coil cavity of the distributor cap.

8. Reverse the above process to install the new coil.

## Ignition Module
### REMOVAL AND INSTALLATION

1. Remove the distributor cap and rotor as previously described.

2. Disconnect the harness connector and pick-up coil spade connectors from the module (note their positions).

3. Remove the 2 screws and the module from the distributor housing.

4. Coat the bottom of the new module with silicone dielectric compound.

NOTE: *If a five terminal or seven terminal module is replaced, the ignition timing must be checked and reset as necessary.*

5. To install, reverse the above process.

## Distributor
### REMOVAL
#### 4-Cylinder Engines

1. Disconnect the negative battery cable.

2. Raise the front of the vehicle and support is safely with jackstands. DO NOT place the jackstands under the engine cradle.

3. Place a jack under the engine cradle then extend the jack so that it just touches the cra-

dle. The jack must not block any of the engine cradle bolts.

4. Remove the two rear engine cradle attaching bolts and lower the cradle just enough to gain access to the distributor.

5. Remove the five screws which attach the brake line support to the floorpan.

6. Remove the coil wire from the distributor.

7. Remove the distributor cap.

8. Mark the position of the rotor firing tip on the distributor body, then mark the relationship between the distributor body and some on the engine.

WARNING: *DO NOT attempt to crank the engine while the distributor is removed.*

9. Loosen the distributor holddown clamp bolt and slide the holddown clamp aside to clear the distributor body.

10. Lift the distributor out of the engine and mark the point at which the rotor stops turning while you're pulling upward. The rotor will have to be positioned at this same spot in order to install the distributor correctly.

#### V6 Engines

1. Disconnect the negative battery cable at the battery.

2. Release the distributor and ignition coil electrical connections at the distributor cap.

3. Follow steps 8 through 10 of the previous procedure to complete the removal of the distributor.

### INSTALLATION – ENGINE NOT DISTURBED

1. Align the ignition rotor with the mark made during the previous step 10.

2. Install the distributor into the engine, noting that the marks made during the previous step 8 must align. If they don't line up the first time, remove the distributor and try again.

3. Reposition the holddown clamp on the distributor body and tighten the bolt until the distributor is snug, but can be moved with a little effort.

4. Connect all wiring to the distributor, and on four cylinder models, jack the engine cradle back into place, install the engine cradle bolts and the brake line support bolts.

5. Connect the battery cable and lower the vehicle if necessary.

6. Adjust the ignition timing as previously outlined.

### INSTALLATION – ENGINE DISTURBED WITH DISTRIBUTOR REMOVED

1. Remove the spark plug from the No. 1 cylinder.

2. Place your thumb over the spark plug hole and turn the crankshaft by hand with a wrench until pressure is felt at the plug hole.

3. Look at the timing marks on the front of

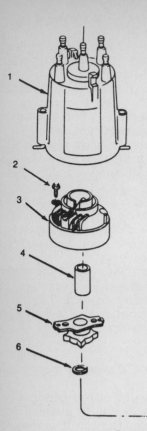
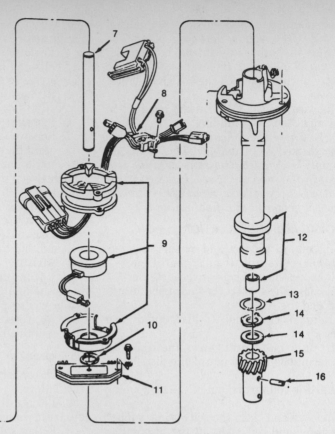

1. Distributor cap
2. Screw
3. Rotor
4. Bushing
5. Distributor shaft
6. Retainer
7. Distributor shaft
8. Wiring harness
9. Pole piece and plate assy. (pick-up coil)
10. Seal
11. Module
12. Housing assembly
13. O-ring
14. Washer
15. Distributor gear
16. Pin

**Exploded view of the distributor**

the engine and check to see if the balancer slash is aligned with the **0** on the timing scale. If necessary, turn the crankshaft until it does align.

4. On the four cylinder engine, turn the rotor until the rotor firing tip is positioned between the Nos. 1 and 3 spark plug towers of the distributor cap. On the V6, position the firing tip between the Nos.1 and 6 towers of the cap.

5. Install the distributor and follow steps 3 through 6 of the first (previous) installation procedure to complete the installation.

## Alternator

Two models of the SI series alternator are used on A-cars. The 10 SI, 12SI, 15 SI and 17 SI are of similar construction; the 15 SL and 17 SI are slightly larger, use different stator windings, and produce more current.

### PRECAUTIONS

1. When installing a battery, make sure that the positive and negative cables are not reversed.

2. When jump-starting the car, be sure that like terminals are connected. This also applies to using a battery charger. Reverse polarity will burn out the alternator and regulator in a matter of seconds.

3. Never operate the alternator with the battery disconnected or on an otherwise uncontrolled open circuit.

4. Do not short across or ground any alternator or regulator terminals.

5. Do not try to polarize the alternator.

6. Do not apply full battery voltage to the field (brown) connector.

7. Always disconnect the battery ground cable before disconnecting the alternator lead.

8. Always disconnect the battery (negative cable first) when charging it.

9. Never subject the alternator to excessive heat or dampness. If you are steam cleaning the engine, cover the alternator.

10. Never use arc-welding equipment on the car with the alternator connected.

### REMOVAL AND INSTALLATION

1. Disconnect the negative battery cable.

2. Remove the two-terminal plug and the battery leads from the rear of the alternator.

3. Remove the adjusting bolt from the alternator on gasoline engined models. The adjusting bolt is the one within the slotted hole.

4. On diesel equipped models, fit the end of a ratchet extension into the square hole of the belt tensioner bracket, then attach a ratchet to the extension. Lever the tensioner towards the firewall side of the engine compartment and remove the serpentine drive belt from the alternator.

5. On gasoline engined models, move the alternator to loosen the drive belt, then remove the belt.

6. On four cylinder models, remove the upper alternator bracket.

7. On diesel models, remove the alternator brace bolt from the rear of the alternator.

8. On gasoline engined models, remove the alternator pivot bolt and remove the alternator.

9. On diesel models, remove both alternator attaching bolts and remove the alternator.

10. Installation is the reverse of removal. Be sure to adjust the tension of the drive belt properly, then tighten the adjusting bolt(s) (on gasoline engined models).

## Regulator

A solid regulator is mounted within the alternator. All regulator components are enclosed in a solid mold. The regulator is non-adjustable and requires no maintenance.

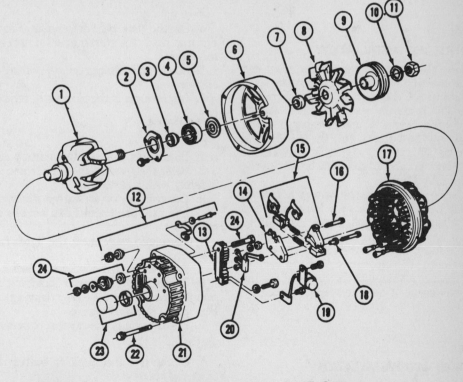

| | | |
|---|---|---|
| 1. Rotor | 9. Pulley | 17. Stator |
| 2. Front bearing retainer | 10. Lockwasher | 18. Insulating washer |
| 3. Inner collar | 11. Pulley nut | 19. Capacitor |
| 4. Bearing | 12. Terminal assembly | 20. Diode trio |
| 5. Washer | 13. Rectifier bridge | 21. Rear housing |
| 6. Front housing | 14. Regulator | 22. Through bolt |
| 7. Outer collar | 15. Brush assembly | 23. Bearing and seal assembly |
| 8. Fan | 16. Screw | 24. Terminal assembly |

Exploded view of the 10-SI alternator (others are similiar)

## Troubleshooting Basic Charging System Problems

| Problem | Cause | Solution |
|---|---|---|
| Noisy alternator | • Loose mountings<br>• Loose drive pulley<br>• Worn bearings<br>• Brush noise<br>• Internal circuits shorted (High pitched whine) | • Tighten mounting bolts<br>• Tighten pulley<br>• Replace alternator<br>• Replace alternator<br>• Replace alternator |
| Squeal when starting engine or accelerating | • Glazed or loose belt | • Replace or adjust belt |
| Indicator light remains on or ammeter indicates discharge (engine running) | • Broken fan belt<br>• Broken or disconnected wires<br>• Internal alternator problems<br>• Defective voltage regulator | • Install belt<br>• Repair or connect wiring<br>• Replace alternator<br>• Replace voltage regulator |
| Car light bulbs continually burn out— battery needs water continually | • Alternator/regulator overcharging | • Replace voltage regulator/alternator |
| Car lights flare on acceleration | • Battery low<br>• Internal alternator/regulator problems | • Charge or replace battery<br>• Replace alternator/regulator |
| Low voltage output (alternator light flickers continually or ammeter needle wanders) | • Loose or worn belt<br>• Dirty or corroded connections<br>• Internal alternator/regulator problems | • Replace or adjust belt<br>• Clean or replace connections<br>• Replace alternator or regulator |

## Battery

### REMOVAL AND INSTALLATION

1. Raise the hood and remove the front end diagonal brace(s) from above the battery(ies).

2. Disconnect the battery cables from the battery(ies). It may be necessary to use a small box end wrench or a ¼" drive ratchet to sneak in between the battery and the windshield washer (or coolant recovery) tank. Avoid using an open-end wrench for the cable bolts. See the previous CAUTION.

3. Loosen and remove the battery holddown bolt and block. The use of a long extension which places the ratchet above the battery makes it very easy to get to the holddown bolt.

4. Carefully lift the battery from the engine compartment. It may be necessary to remove the air cleaner intake duct (except 4-cyl.) or the intake resonator (4-cyl. only) for clearance.

## Starter

### REMOVAL AND INSTALLATION

#### Except Diesel Engines

1. Disconnect the negative battery cable.

2. Raise the front of the vehicle and support it safely with jackstands.

3. From underneath the vehicle, remove the two starter motor-to-engine bolts and carefully lower the starter. Note the location of shims (if so equipped).

4. On the four cylinder engine, remove the nut that holds the starter bracket to the rear of the starter.

5. Mark and disconnect all wiring at the starter.

6. Installation is the reverse of removal.

#### Diesel Engine

*1982*

1. Disconnect the negative battery cable(s).

2. Raise the front of the vehicle and support it safely with jackstands.

3. Remove the lower starter shield nut and flex the starter shield for access during removal.

4. Mark and disconnect the wires from the starter.

5. Remove the front starter attaching bolt.

6. Loosen the rear starter attaching bolt and remove the starter assembly, leaving the rear bolt in the starter housing.

7. Installation is the reverse of removal.

*1983-85*

1. Disconnect the negative battery cable(s) from the battery(s).

2. Install tool J-28467 to the engine, then raise the vehicle on a hoist.

3. Remove the left and the center engine mounting stud nuts.

4. Move the intermediate shaft seal upwards, then remove the intermediate shaft-to-stud shaft pinch bolt and disconnect the shaft from the gear.

CAUTION: *It is necessary to disconnect the intermediate shaft from the rack and pinion stud shaft; otherwise, damage to the steering gear and/or the intermediate shaft can occur, which may result in the loss of steering control.*

5. Remove the 2 front cradle mounting bolts, then lower the cradle at the front to gain access to the flywheel cover bolts.

6. Remove the flywheel cover bolts and the cover.

7. Remove the starter shield nut from the starter and the flex shield.

8. Mark and disconnect the wires from the starter. Remove the starter mounting bolts and the starter.

9. To install, reverse the removal procedures. Torque the stub shaft pinch bolt to 45 ft.lb. (62 Nm.) and the starter-to-engine bolts to 32 ft.lb. (43 Nm.).

*1986-88*

NOTE: *On some models it may be necessary to move the fuel lines out of the way. Remove the fuel lines from the retaining clamp and loosen at the regulator. If equipped with fuel injection, relieve the pressure from the fuel system before disconnecting fuel lines. See "Electric Fuel Pump Removal" for procedure.*

1. Disconnect battery ground cable.

2. Raise and support vehicle.

3. Disconnect all wires at solenoid terminals. Note color coding of wires for reinstallation.

4. Remove starter support bracket mount bolts (4 cylinder engines use two nuts; V6 engines use one nut). On engines with solenoid heat shield, remove front bracket upper bolt and detach bracket from starter motor.

5. Loosen the front bracket bolt or nut and rotate bracket clear. Lower and remove starter. Note the location of any shims so that they may be replaced in the same positions upon installation.

6. Reverse procedure to install.

7. Torque the starter-to-engine bolts to 32 ft.lb. (43 Nm.).

## STARTER SOLENOID REMOVAL AND INSTALLATION

### Except Diesel Aluminum Starter

1. Remove the starter and solenoid assembly as previously outlined.

2. Remove the screw and washer from the motor connector strap terminal.

3. Remove the two screws which retain the solenoid housing to the end frame assembly.

4. Twist the solenoid clockwise to remove the flange key from the keyway slot in the housing.

5. Remove the solenoid assembly.

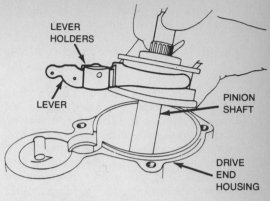

**Aluminum starter**

6. With the solenoid return spring installed on the plunger, position the solenoid body on the drive housing and turn it counterclockwise to engage the flange key in the key way slot.

7. Install the two screws which retain the solenoid housing to the end frame.

### Diesel Aluminum Starter (Type 2)

After the field coil connector nut and the two solenoid attaching screws are removed, pull the solenoid upward and forward to remove it. Installation is simply a matter of bolting the solenoid into place, fastening the field coil connector and reinstalling the starter. It is recommended by G.M., however, to check the pinion position as outline (Step 35a-35e of the Diesel Type 2 assembly procedure).

## STARTER OVERHAUL – GASOLINE ENGINES

### Drive Replacement

1. Disconnect the field coil straps from the solenoid.

2. Remove the through-bolts, and separate the commutator end frame, field frame assembly, drive housing, and armature assembly from each other.

3. Slide the thrust washer off the end of the armature shaft.

4. Slide a suitably metal cylinder, such as a standard half-inch pipe coupling, or an old pinion, on the shaft so that the end of the coupling or pinion butts up against the edge of the pinion retainer.

5. Support the lower end of the armature securely on a soft surface, such as a wood block, and tap the end of the coupling or pinion, driving the retainer towards the armature end of the snapring.

6. Remove the snapring from the groove in the armature shaft with a pair of pliers. Then, slide the retainer and starter drive from the shaft.

7. To reassemble, lubricate the drive end of the armature shaft with silicone lubricant, and then slide the starter drive onto the shaft with the pinion facing outward. Slide the retainer onto the shaft with the cupped surface facing outward.

8. Again, support the armature on a soft surface, with the pinion at the upper end. Center the snapring on the top of the shaft (use a new snap if the original was damaged during removal). Gently place a block of wood flat on top of the snapring so as not to move it from a centered position. Tap the wooden block with a hammer in order to force the snapring around the shaft. Then, slide the ring down into the snapring groove.

9. Lay the armature down flat on the surface you're working on. Slide the retainer up on to the shaft and position it and the thrust collar next to the snapring. Using two pairs of pliers on opposite sides of the shaft, squeeze the thrust collar and the retainer together until the snapring is forced into the retainer.

10. Lube the drive housing bushing with a silicone lubricant. Then, install the armature and clutch assembly into the drive housing, engaging the solenoid shift lever with the clutch, and positioning the front end of armature shaft into the bushing.

11. Apply a sealing compound approved for this application onto the drive housing; then position the field frame around the armature shaft and against the drive housing. Work slowly and carefully to prevent damaging the starter brushes.

12. Lubricate the bushing in the commutator end frame with a silicone lubricant, place the leather brake washer onto the armature shaft, and then slide the commutator end frame over the shaft and into position against the field frame. Line up the bolt holes, and then install and tighten the through-bolts.

13. Reconnect the field coil straps to the **motor** terminal of the solenoid.

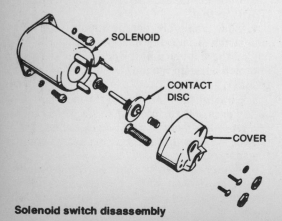

**Solenoid switch disassembly**

NOTE: *If replacement of the starter drive fails to cure the improper engagement of the starter pinion to the flywheel, there are probably defective parts in the solenoid and/or shift lever. The best procedure would probably be to take the assembly to a shop where a pinion clearance check can be made by energizing the solenoid on a test bench. If the pinion clearance is incorrect, disassemble the solenoid and the shift lever, inspect, and replace worn parts.*

**Brush Replacement**

1. After removing the starter from the engine, disconnect the field coil from the motor solenoid terminal.

2. Remove the starter through-bolts and remove the commutator end frame and washer.

3. Remove the field frame and the armature assembly from the drive housing.

4. Remove the brush holder pivot pin which positions one insulated and one grounded brush.

5. Remove the brush springs.

6. Remove the brushes.

7. Installation is in the reverse order of removal.

## STARTER OVERHAUL – DIESEL TYPE ONE

NOTE: *The Type One diesel starter is identified by having a cast iron housing, whereas the Type Two unit covered later, has an aluminum housing.*

**Drive Replacement**

1. Remove the starter from the vehicle as previously outlined.

2. Remove the screw from the field coil connector strap at the solenoid.

3. Separate the field frame assembly from the drive gear assembly.

4. Remove the solenoid mounting screws, turn the solenoid 90 degrees and remove the solenoid.

5. Remove the shift lever shaft retaining ring, lever shaft, and the housing through-bolts in order to separate the drive assembly, drive housing and gear housing.

6. Remove the thrust washer or collar from the drive shaft, in front of the drive assembly.

7. Slide a ⅝" deep socket (or a piece of suitably sized pipe) over the shaft and against the retainer.

8. Tap the socket (or pipe) to move the retainer off the snapring.

9. Remove the snapring from the groove in the shaft. If the ring becomes distorted during removal, it must be replaced with a new ring during assembly.

10. Remove the starter drive assembly from the shaft.

11. Slide the new drive assembly onto the drive shaft, then place the snapring retainer over the shaft with the cupped side of the retainer facing away from the gear of the drive unit.

12. Position the armature upright (drive unit facing upward), resting the lower end on a block of wood.

13. Center the snapring on the top of the shaft. Remember that a new ring should be used if the old one was damaged during removal.

14. Carefully place a block of wood on the ring then tap on the block of wood (using a light hammer) to force the ring onto the shaft. Slide the ring down into the snapring groove.

15. Place the thrust collar onto the drive shaft, then squeeze the thrust collar and retainer together, which will force the retainer over the snapring.

16. Assemble the plunger and shift lever into the drive housing with the lever shaft and the retaining ring.

17. Place the drive shaft washer over the drive shaft on the side of the gear opposite the drive assembly. Lubricate the gear teeth with G.M. #1960954 lubricant or its equivalent.

18. Assemble the gear housing with the attaching screws.

19. Assemble the solenoid to the drive housing.

20. Lubricate the bushing in the commutator end frame with the same lubricant mentioned previously.

21. Assemble the armature, field frame and the commutator end frame to the gear housing with the through-bolts.

22. Attach the field coil connector to the solenoid terminal. Install the starter assembly as previously outlined.

### Brush Replacement

1. Please follow steps 1-5 of the last Drive Replacement procedure in order to separate the field coil and frame assembly from the armature.

2. Remove the commutator end frame in order to gain access to the brushes.

3. Remove the brush holder pivot pin which positions one insulated and one grounded brush.

4. Remove the brush spring.

5. Replace the brushes as required, then reinstall the brush spring and the pivot pin.

6. Repeat steps 3, 4, and 5 for the remaining pair of brushes.

7. Re-assemble the remaining starter components in the reverse of removal.

### STARTER OVERHAUL – DIESEL TYPE TWO

NOTE: *The Type Two diesel starter is identified by having an aluminum housing.*

### Drive and Brush Replacement

NOTE: *G.M. special tool #J-22888 and a dial indicator will be needed to properly assemble the starter.*

1. Remove the starter assembly from the vehicle as previously outlined.

2. Remove the nut from the field coil connector at the solenoid.

3. Remove the two solenoid mounting screws then remove the solenoid by pulling it upward and forward.

NOTE: *In some cases, shims will be present between the solenoid and the drive end housing. These shims are used to set the drive pinion position.*

4. Remove the two through bolts and the two brush holder retaining screws. Remove the commutator end frame from the armature and bearing assembly.

5. Remove the field frame assembly and the armature from the center housing.

6. Carefully pry each brush spring back so that each brush can be backed away from the armature about ¼". Release the spring to hold the brushes in the backed out position, then remove the armature from the field frame and brush holder.

7. Remove the cover retaining screws, cover, C-washer and plate from the armature side of the center housing.

8. Remove the two center housing bolts, the center housing and the shim thrust washers.

9. Remove the reduction gear, spring holder and two lever springs.

10. Slide a ⅝" socket or suitably sized piece of pipe over the nose of the pinion shaft, against the drive pinion stopper.

11. Tap on the socket (or pipe) to drive the stopper off of the snapring. Using a pair of snapring pliers, remove the drive pinion snapring from the groove in the pinion shaft.

NOTE: *If the ring becomes distorted during removal, it must be replaced with a new ring during assembly.*

12. Remove the stopper, drive pinion gear and spring.

13. Remove the pinion shaft/overrunning clutch from the drive end housing.

### To replace the brushes:

14. Remove the brush holder and the negative brush assembly from the field frame by removing the positive brushes from the brush holder.

15. Cut the old positive brush leads from the field coil bar as close to the brush connection

point as possible; cut the negative brush leads from the brush holder plate.

16. Connection tangs are provided for installation of new brushes. Clean the connection tangs then solder the new brush leads on the tangs. Use only high temperature solder to connect the new brushes, and make sure that the positive brush connections are made properly in order to prevent grounding of the brush connection.

17. Reinstall the positive and the negative brushes in the brush holder assembly. Position the brushes in the backed-out position as described earlier.

### To assemble the starter:

NOTE: *The lubricant mentioned during assembly should be G.M. #1960954 or its equivalent.*

18. Lubricate the splines and bearing surfaces of the pinion shaft/overrunning clutch, the nylon lever holders and both ends of the lever.

19. Install the lever assembly on the overrunning clutch (see the accompanying illustration). The lever MUST be installed as shown; if not, the clutch mechanism could lock during operation.

20. Install the pinion shaft/overrunning clutch and lever assembly into the drive end housing.

21. Slide the spring, drive pinion and stopper (in that order) over the pinion shaft, making sure that the cupped side of the stopper faces the end of the shaft.

22. Press the drive pinion and stopper towards the drive end housing and install the snapring into the groove of the pinion shaft.

23. Using tool J-22888, force the drive pinion towards the end of the pinion shaft, which will force the stopper over the snapring. It may be necessary to tap the ring with a drift pin to seat the ring in the groove of the stopper.

24. Install the two lever springs and the spring holder into the drive end housing.

25. Lubricate the reduction gear teeth, then install the gear and shim thrust washer(s) onto the pinion shaft assembly.

26. Position the center housing to the drive end housing and install the two attaching bolts.

27. Check the end-play of the pinion shaft as follows:

a. Install the plate and the C-shaped washer onto the pinion shaft.

b. With the drive end housing suitably supported, insert an appropriately sized feeler gauge between the C-washer and the cover plate. Using a screwdriver, move the pinion shaft axially to determine the total end play. Try different sized feeler gauges until the thickest gauge fits the clearance. Total end-

play should be 0.004-0.020". Replace or remove the shim thrust washers as required to bring the clearance within specification.

c. Remove the cover plate (if it is not already removed) and fill the cover ½ full with lubricant.

d. Reinstall the cover and install and tighten the two cover bolts.

28. Install the armature by carefully engaging the splines of the shaft with the reduction gear.

29. Position the field frame and brush holder assembly on the center housing, noting that the rubber grommet for the field coil lead must align with the locating ribs of the center housing.

30. Pry the brush spring back, which will allow the brushes to seat against the commutator bars of the armature.

31. Position the commutator end frame onto the field frame, aligning the marks made during disassembly.

32. Install and tighten the two brush holder screws, then the through bolts.

33. Install the solenoid switch and shims onto the drive end housing. Make sure that the slot of the solenoid plunger engages with the top of the lever. Install and tighten the solenoid retaining bolts.

34. Connect the field coil connector to the solenoid switch terminal.

35. Because the starter has been disassembled, it is necessary to check the pinion position as follows:

a. Connect one 12V lead of a battery to the terminal marked **S** on the solenoid. Momentarily touch the other 12V lead to the starter frame. This action will shift the drive pinion into its cranking position until one of the battery leads is disconnected. DO NOT leave the pinion in the cranking position for more than 30 seconds at a time.

b. With the pinion in the cranking position, set up a dial indicator as shown, then zero the indicator needle.

c. Push the pinion shaft back by hand and record the amount of movement indicated by the indicator needle. Detach one of the battery leads to bring the drive pinion back to its off position.

d. The indicator reading should have been between 0.020 and 0.080". The clearance is adjusted by adding or removing shims between the solenoid and the front bracket. Shims are available in 0.010" and 0.020" thicknesses.

e. If a shim thickness adjustment was required, reinstall the solenoid with the new shims and repeat the clearance check.

## Troubleshooting Basic Starting System Problems

| Problem | Cause | Solution |
| --- | --- | --- |
| Starter motor rotates engine slowly | • Battery charge low or battery defective | • Charge or replace battery |
| | • Defective circuit between battery and starter motor | • Clean and tighten, or replace cables |
| | • Low load current | • Bench-test starter motor. Inspect for worn brushes and weak brush springs. |
| | • High load current | • Bench-test starter motor. Check engine for friction, drag or coolant in cylinders. Check ring gear-to-pinion gear clearance. |
| Starter motor will not rotate engine | • Battery charge low or battery defective | • Charge or replace battery |
| | • Faulty solenoid | • Check solenoid ground. Repair or replace as necessary. |
| | • Damage drive pinion gear or ring gear | • Replace damaged gear(s) |
| | • Starter motor engagement weak | • Bench-test starter motor |
| | • Starter motor rotates slowly with high load current | • Inspect drive yoke pull-down and point gap, check for worn end bushings, check ring gear clearance |
| | • Engine seized | • Repair engine |
| Starter motor drive will not engage (solenoid known to be good) | • Defective contact point assembly | • Repair or replace contact point assembly |
| | • Inadequate contact point assembly ground | • Repair connection at ground screw |
| | • Defective hold-in coil | • Replace field winding assembly |
| Starter motor drive will not disengage | • Starter motor loose on flywheel housing | • Tighten mounting bolts |
| | • Worn drive end busing | • Replace bushing |
| | • Damaged ring gear teeth | • Replace ring gear or driveplate |
| | • Drive yoke return spring broken or missing | • Replace spring |
| Starter motor drive disengages prematurely | • Weak drive assembly thrust spring | • Replace drive mechanism |
| | • Hold-in coil defective | • Replace field winding assembly |
| Low load current | • Worn brushes | • Replace brushes |
| | • Weak brush springs | • Replace springs |

# ENGINE MECHANICAL

## Engine Overhaul Tips

Most engine overhaul procedures are fairly standard. In addition to specific parts replacement procedures and complete specifications for your individual engine, this chapter also is a guide to accept rebuilding procedures. Examples of standard rebuilding practice are shown and should be used along with specific details concerning your particular engine.

Competent and accurate machine shop services will ensure maximum performance, reliability and engine life.

In most instances it is more profitable for the do-it-yourself mechanic to remove, clean and inspect the component, buy the necessary parts

and deliver these to a shop for actual machine work.

On the other hand, much of the rebuilding work (crankshaft, block, bearings, piston rods, and other components) is well within the scope of the do-it-yourself mechanic.

## TOOLS

The tools required for an engine overhaul or parts replacement will depend on the depth of your involvement. With a few exceptions, they will be the tools found in a mechanic's tool kit (see Chapter 1). More in-depth work will require any or all of the following:
- a dial indicator (reading in thousandths) mounted on a universal base
- micrometers and telescope gauges
- jaw and screw-type pullers
- scraper
- valve spring compressor
- ring groove cleaner
- piston ring expander and compressor
- ridge reamer
- cylinder hone or glaze breaker
- Plastigage®
- engine stand

Use of most of these tools is illustrated in this chapter. Many can be rented for a one-time use from a local parts jobber or tool supply house specializing in automotive work.

Occasionally, the use of special tools is called for. See the information on Special Tools and Safety Notice in the front of this book before substituting another tool.

## INSPECTION TECHNIQUES

Procedures and specifications are given in this chapter for inspecting, cleaning and assessing the wear limits of most major components. Other procedures such as Magnaflux® and Zyglo® can be used to locate material flaws and stress cracks. Magnaflux® is a magnetic process applicable only to ferrous materials. The Zyglo® process coats the material with a fluorescent dye penetrant and can be used on any material Check for suspected surface cracks can be more readily made using spot check dye. The dye is sprayed onto the suspected area, wiped off and the area sprayed with a developer. Cracks will show up brightly.

## OVERHAUL TIPS

Aluminum has become extremely popular for use in engines, due to its low weight. Observe the following precautions when handling aluminum parts:
- Never hot tank aluminum parts (the caustic hot tank solution will eat the aluminum.
- Remove all aluminum parts (identification tag, etc.) from engine parts prior to the tanking.
- Always coat threads lightly with engine oil or antiseize compounds before installation, to prevent siezure.
- Never over-torque bolts or spark plugs especially in aluminum threads.

Stripped threads in any component can be re-paired using any of several commercial repair kits (Heli-Coil®, Microdot®, Keenserts®, etc.).

When assembling the engine, any parts that will be frictional contact must be prelubed to provide lubrication at initial start-up. Any product specifically formulated for this purpose can be used, but engine oil is not recommended as a prelube.

When semi-permanent (locked, but removable) installation of bolts or nuts is desired, threads should be cleaned and coated with Loctite® or other similar, commercial non-hardening sealant.

## REPAIRING DAMAGED THREADS

Several methods of repairing damaged threads are available. Heli-Coil® (shown here), Keenserts® and Microdot® are among the most widely used. All involve basically the same principle – drilling out stripped threads, tapping the hole and installing a prewound insert – making welding, plugging and oversize fasteners unnecessary.

Two types of thread repair inserts are usually supplied – a standard type for most Inch Coarse, Inch Fine, Metric Course and Metric Fine thread sizes and a spark lug type to fit most spark plug port sizes. Consult the individual manufacturer's catalog to determine exact applications. Typical thread repair kits will contain a selection of prewound threaded inserts, a tap (corresponding to the outside diameter threads of the insert) and an installation tool. Spark plug inserts usually differ because they require a tap equipped with pilot threads and a combined reamer/tap section. Most manufacturers also supply blister-packed thread repair inserts separately in addition to a master kit containing a variety of taps and inserts plus installation tools.

Before effecting a repair to a threaded hole, remove any snapped, broken or damaged bolts

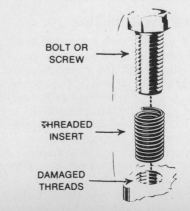

BOLT OR SCREW

THREADED INSERT

DAMAGED THREADS

**Damaged bolt holes can be repaired with thread repair inserts**

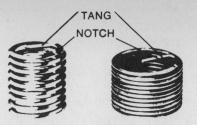

Standard thread repair insert (left) and spark plug thread insert (right)

Drill out the damaged threads with specified drill. Drill completely through the hole or to the bottom of a blind hole

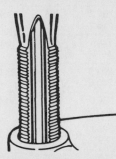

With the tap supplied, tap the hole to receive the thread insert. Keep the tap well oiled and back it out frequently to avoid clogging the threads

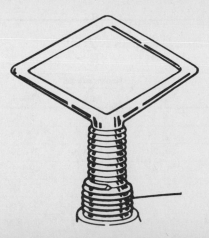

Screw the threaded insert onto the installation tool until the tang engages the slot. Screw the insert into the tapped hole until it is ¼–½ turn below the top surface, After installation break off the tang with a hammer and punch

or studs. Penetrating oil can be used to free frozen threads; the offending item can be removed with locking pliers or with a screw or stud extractor. After the hole is clear, the thread can be repaired, as follows:

## Checking Engine Compression

A noticeable lack of engine power, excessive oil consumption and/or poor fuel mileage measured over an extended period are all indicators of internal engine war. Worn piston rings, scored or worn cylinder bores, blown head gaskets, sticking or burnt valves and worn valve seats are all possible culprits here. A check of each cylinder's compression will help you locate the problems.

As mentioned in the Tools and Equipment section of Chapter 1, a screw-in type compression gauge is more accurate that the type you simply hold against the spark plug hole, although it takes slightly longer to use. It's worth it to obtain a more accurate reading. Follow the procedures below for gasoline and diesel engined trucks.

### GASOLINE ENGINES

1. Warm up the engine to normal operating temperature.
2. Remove all spark plugs.
3. Disconnect the high tension lead from the ignition coil.
4. On fully open the throttle either by operating the carburetor throttle linkage by hand or by having an assistant floor the accelerator pedal.
5. Screw the compression gauge into the no.1 spark plug hole until the fitting is snug.

NOTE: *Be careful not to crossthread the plug hole. On aluminum cylinder heads use extra care, as the threads in these heads are easily ruined.*

6. Ask an assistant to depress the accelerator pedal fully on both carbureted and fuel injected trucks. Then, while you read the compression gauge, ask the assistant to crank the engine two or three times in short bursts using the ignition switch.
7. Read the compression gauge at the end of each series of cranks, and record the highest of these readings. Repeat this procedure for each of the engine's cylinders. Compare the highest reading of each cylinder to the compression pressure specification in the Tune-Up Specifications chart in Chapter 2. The specs in this chart are maximum values.

A cylinder's compression pressure is usually acceptable if it is not less than 80% of maximum. The difference between each cylinder should be no more than 12-14 pounds.

## Standard Torque Specifications and Fastener Markings

In the absence of specific torques, the following chart can be used as a guide to the maximum safe torque of a particular size/grade of fastener.

- There is no torque difference for fine or coarse threads.
- Torque values are based on clean, dry threads. Reduce the value by 10% if threads are oiled prior to assembly.
- The torque required for aluminum components or fasteners is considerably less.

### U.S. Bolts

| SAE Grade Number | 1 or 2 | | | 5 | | | 6 or 7 | | |
|---|---|---|---|---|---|---|---|---|---|
| Number of lines always 2 less than the grade number. | | | | | | | | | |
| Bolt Size (Inches)—(Thread) | Maximum Torque | | | Maximum Torque | | | Maximum Torque | | |
| | Ft./Lbs. | Kgm | Nm | Ft./Lbs. | Kgm | Nm | Ft./Lbs. | Kgm | Nm |
| ¼ — 20 | 5 | 0.7 | 6.8 | 8 | 1.1 | 10.8 | 10 | 1.4 | 13.5 |
| — 28 | 6 | 0.8 | 8.1 | 10 | 1.4 | 13.6 | | | |
| 5/16 — 18 | 11 | 1.5 | 14.9 | 17 | 2.3 | 23.0 | 19 | 2.6 | 25.8 |
| — 24 | 13 | 1.8 | 17.6 | 19 | 2.6 | 25.7 | | | |
| 3/8 — 16 | 18 | 2.5 | 24.4 | 31 | 4.3 | 42.0 | 34 | 4.7 | 46.0 |
| — 24 | 20 | 2.75 | 27.1 | 35 | 4.8 | 47.5 | | | |
| 7/16 — 14 | 28 | 3.8 | 37.0 | 49 | 6.8 | 66.4 | 55 | 7.6 | 74.5 |
| — 20 | 30 | 4.2 | 40.7 | 55 | 7.6 | 74.5 | | | |
| ½ — 13 | 39 | 5.4 | 52.8 | 75 | 10.4 | 101.7 | 85 | 11.75 | 115.2 |
| — 20 | 41 | 5.7 | 55.6 | 85 | 11.7 | 115.2 | | | |
| 9/16 — 12 | 51 | 7.0 | 69.2 | 110 | 15.2 | 149.1 | 120 | 16.6 | 162.7 |
| — 18 | 55 | 7.6 | 74.5 | 120 | 16.6 | 162.7 | | | |
| 5/8 — 11 | 83 | 11.5 | 112.5 | 150 | 20.7 | 203.3 | 167 | 23.0 | 226.5 |
| — 18 | 95 | 13.1 | 128.8 | 170 | 23.5 | 230.5 | | | |
| ¾ — 10 | 105 | 14.5 | 142.3 | 270 | 37.3 | 366.0 | 280 | 38.7 | 379.6 |
| — 16 | 115 | 15.9 | 155.9 | 295 | 40.8 | 400.0 | | | |
| 7/8 — 9 | 160 | 22.1 | 216.9 | 395 | 54.6 | 535.5 | 440 | 60.9 | 596.5 |
| — 14 | 175 | 24.2 | 237.2 | 435 | 60.1 | 589.7 | | | |
| 1 — 8 | 236 | 32.5 | 318.6 | 590 | 81.6 | 799.9 | 660 | 91.3 | 894.8 |
| — 14 | 250 | 34.6 | 338.9 | 660 | 91.3 | 849.8 | | | |

### Metric Bolts

| Relative Strength Marking | 4.6, 4.8 | | | 8.8 | | |
|---|---|---|---|---|---|---|
| Bolt Markings | | | | | | |
| Bolt Size Thread Size x Pitch (mm) | Maximum Torque | | | Maximum Torque | | |
| | Ft./Lbs. | Kgm | Nm | Ft./Lbs. | Kgm | Nm |
| 6 x 1.0 | 2–3 | .2–.4 | 3–4 | 3–6 | .4–.8 | 5–8 |
| 8 x 1.25 | 6–8 | .8–1 | 8–12 | 9–14 | 1.2–1.9 | 13–19 |
| 10 x 1.25 | 12–17 | 1.5–2.3 | 16–23 | 20–29 | 2.7–4.0 | 27–39 |
| 12 x 1.25 | 21–32 | 2.9–4.4 | 29–43 | 35–53 | 4.8–7.3 | 47–72 |
| 14 x 1.5 | 35–52 | 4.8–7.1 | 48–70 | 57–85 | 7.8–11.7 | 77–110 |
| 16 x 1.5 | 51–77 | 7.0–10.6 | 67–100 | 90–120 | 12.4–16.5 | 130–160 |
| 18 x 1.5 | 74–110 | 10.2–15.1 | 100–150 | 130–170 | 17.9–23.4 | 180–230 |
| 20 x 1.5 | 110–140 | 15.1–19.3 | 150–190 | 190–240 | 26.2–46.9 | 160–320 |
| 22 x 1.5 | 150–190 | 22.0–26.2 | 200–260 | 250–320 | 34.5–44.1 | 340–430 |
| 24 x 1.5 | 190–240 | 26.2–46.9 | 260–320 | 310–410 | 42.7–56.5 | 420–550 |

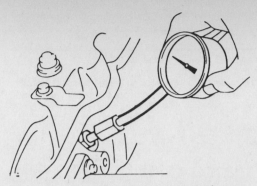

The screw-in type compression gauge is more accurate

8. If a cylinder is unusually low, pour a tablespoon of clean engine oil into the cylinder through the spark plug hole and repeat the compression test. If the compression comes up after adding the oil, it appears that the cylinder's piston rings or bore are damaged or worn. If the pressure remains low, the valves may not be seating properly (a valve job is needed), or the head gasket may be blown near that cylinder. If compression in any two adjacent cylinders is low, and if the addition of oil doesn't help the compression, there is leakage past the head gasket. Oil and coolant water in the combustion chamber can result from this problem. There may be evidence of water droplets on the engine dipstick when a head gasket has blown.

**Diesel Engines**

Checking cylinder compression on diesel engines is basically the same procedure as on gasoline engines except for the following:

1. A special compression gauge adaptor suitable for diesel engines (because these engines have much greater compression pressures) must be used.

2. Remove the injector tubes and remove the injectors from each cylinder.

NOTE: *Don't forget to remove the washer underneath each injector; otherwise, it may get lost when the engine is cranked.*

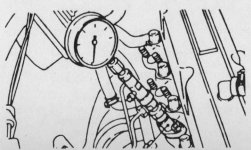

Diesel engines require a special compression gauge adaptor

3. When fitting the compression gauge adaptor to the cylinder head, make sure the bleeder of the gauge (if equipped) is closed.

4. When reinstalling the injector assemblies, install new washers underneath each injector.

## Engine
### REMOVAL AND INSTALLATION
#### 4-151 with Manual Transaxle

NOTE: *Relieve the pressure in the fuel system as described under Fuel Pump.*

1. Disconnect battery cables at battery.
2. Hoist car.
3. Remove front mount-to-cradle nuts.
4. Remove forward exhaust pipe.
5. Remove starter assembly (wires attached and swing to side).
6. Remove flywheel inspection cover.
7. Lower car.
8. Remove air cleaner.
9. Remove all bell housing bolts.
10. Remove forward torque reaction rod from engine and core support.
11. If equipped with air conditioning, remove air conditioning belt and compressor and swing to side.
12. Remove emission hoses at canister.
13. Remove power steering hose (if so equipped).
14. Remove vacuum hoses and electrical connectors at solenoid.
15. Remove heater blower motor.
16. Disconnect throttle cable.
17. Drain heater hose.

CAUTION: *When draining the coolant, keep in mind that cats and dogs are attracted by the ethylene glycol antifreeze, and are quite likely to drink any that is left in an uncovered container or in puddles on the ground. This will prove fatal in sufficient quantity. Always drain the coolant into a sealable container. Coolant should be reused unless it is contaminated or several years old.*

18. Disconnect heater hose.
19. Disconnect radiator hose.
20. Disconnect engine harness at bulkhead connector.
21. With engine lifting tool, hoist engine (remove heater hose at intake manifold and disconnect fuel line).

**To install:**

22. Lower the engine into the engine compartment.
23. Connect engine harness at bulkhead connector.
24. Connect radiator hose.
25. Connect heater hose.

## Troubleshooting Engine Mechanical Problems

| Problem | Cause | Solution |
|---|---|---|
| External oil leaks | • Fuel pump gasket broken or improperly seated | • Replace gasket |
| | • Cylinder head cover RTV sealant broken or improperly seated | • Replace sealant; inspect cylinder head cover sealant flange and cylinder head sealant surface for distortion and cracks |
| | • Oil filler cap leaking or missing | • Replace cap |
| | • Oil filter gasket broken or improperly seated | • Replace oil filter |
| | • Oil pan side gasket broken, improperly seated or opening in RTV sealant | • Replace gasket or repair opening in sealant; inspect oil pan gasket flange for distortion |
| | • Oil pan front oil seal broken or improperly seated | • Replace seal; inspect timing case cover and oil pan seal flange for distortion |
| | • Oil pan rear oil seal broken or improperly seated | • Replace seal; inspect oil pan rear oil seal flange; inspect rear main bearing cap for cracks, plugged oil return channels, or distortion in seal groove |
| | • Timing case cover oil seal broken or improperly seated | • Replace seal |
| | • Excess oil pressure because of restricted PCV valve | • Replace PCV valve |
| | • Oil pan drain plug loose or has stripped threads | • Repair as necessary and tighten |
| | • Rear oil gallery plug loose | • Use appropriate sealant on gallery plug and tighten |
| | • Rear camshaft plug loose or improperly seated | • Seat camshaft plug or replace and seal, as necessary |
| | • Distributor base gasket damaged | • Replace gasket |
| Excessive oil consumption | • Oil level too high | • Drain oil to specified level |
| | • Oil with wrong viscosity being used | • Replace with specified oil |
| | • PCV valve stuck closed | • Replace PCV valve |
| | • Valve stem oil deflectors (or seals) are damaged, missing, or incorrect type | • Replace valve stem oil deflectors |
| | • Valve stems or valve guides worn | • Measure stem-to-guide clearance and repair as necessary |
| | • Poorly fitted or missing valve cover baffles | • Replace valve cover |
| | • Piston rings broken or missing | • Replace broken or missing rings |
| | • Scuffed piston | • Replace piston |
| | • Incorrect piston ring gap | • Measure ring gap, repair as necessary |
| | • Piston rings sticking or excessively loose in grooves | • Measure ring side clearance, repair as necessary |
| | • Compression rings installed upside down | • Repair as necessary |
| | • Cylinder walls worn, scored, or glazed | • Repair as necessary |
| | • Piston ring gaps not properly staggered | • Repair as necessary |
| | • Excessive main or connecting rod bearing clearance | • Measure bearing clearance, repair as necessary |
| No oil pressure | • Low oil level | • Add oil to correct level |
| | • Oil pressure gauge, warning lamp or sending unit inaccurate | • Replace oil pressure gauge or warning lamp |
| | • Oil pump malfunction | • Replace oil pump |
| | • Oil pressure relief valve sticking | • Remove and inspect oil pressure relief valve assembly |
| | • Oil passages on pressure side of pump obstructed | • Inspect oil passages for obstruction |

## Troubleshooting Engine Mechanical Problems (cont.)

| Problem | Cause | Solution |
|---|---|---|
| No oil pressure (cont.) | • Oil pickup screen or tube obstructed<br>• Loose oil inlet tube | • Inspect oil pickup for obstruction<br>• Tighten or seal inlet tube |
| Low oil pressure | • Low oil level<br>• Inaccurate gauge, warning lamp or sending unit<br>• Oil excessively thin because of dilution, poor quality, or improper grade<br>• Excessive oil temperature<br>• Oil pressure relief spring weak or sticking<br>• Oil inlet tube and screen assembly has restriction or air leak<br><br><br>• Excessive oil pump clearance<br>• Excessive main, rod, or camshaft bearing clearance | • Add oil to correct level<br>• Replace oil pressure gauge or warning lamp<br>• Drain and refill crankcase with recommended oil<br>• Correct cause of overheating engine<br>• Remove and inspect oil pressure relief valve assembly<br>• Remove and inspect oil inlet tube and screen assembly. (Fill inlet tube with lacquer thinner to locate leaks.)<br>• Measure clearances<br>• Measure bearing clearances, repair as necessary |
| High oil pressure | • Improper oil viscosity<br><br>• Oil pressure gauge or sending unit inaccurate<br>• Oil pressure relief valve sticking closed | • Drain and refill crankcase with correct viscosity oil<br>• Replace oil pressure gauge<br><br>• Remove and inspect oil pressure relief valve assembly |
| Main bearing noise | • Insufficient oil supply<br><br>• Main bearing clearance excessive<br><br>• Bearing insert missing<br>• Crankshaft end play excessive<br><br>• Improperly tightened main bearing cap bolts<br>• Loose flywheel or drive plate<br><br>• Loose or damaged vibration damper | • Inspect for low oil level and low oil pressure<br>• Measure main bearing clearance, repair as necessary<br>• Replace missing insert<br>• Measure end play, repair as necessary<br>• Tighten bolts with specified torque<br><br>• Tighten flywheel or drive plate attaching bolts<br>• Repair as necessary |
| Connecting rod bearing noise | • Insufficient oil supply<br><br>• Carbon build-up on piston<br>• Bearing clearance excessive or bearing missing<br>• Crankshaft connecting rod journal out-of-round<br>• Misaligned connecting rod or cap<br>• Connecting rod bolts tightened improperly | • Inspect for low oil level and low oil pressure<br>• Remove carbon from piston crown<br>• Measure clearance, repair as necessary<br>• Measure journal dimensions, repair or replace as necessary<br>• Repair as necessary<br>• Tighten bolts with specified torque |
| Piston noise | • Piston-to-cylinder wall clearance excessive (scuffed piston)<br>• Cylinder walls excessively tapered or out-of-round<br>• Piston ring broken<br>• Loose or seized piston pin<br><br>• Connecting rods misaligned<br><br>• Piston ring side clearance excessively loose or tight<br>• Carbon build-up on piston is excessive | • Measure clearance and examine piston<br>• Measure cylinder wall dimensions, rebore cylinder<br>• Replace all rings on piston<br>• Measure piston-to-pin clearance, repair as necessary<br>• Measure rod alignment, straighten or replace<br>• Measure ring side clearance, repair as necessary<br>• Remove carbon from piston |

## Troubleshooting Engine Mechanical Problems (cont.)

| Problem | Cause | Solution |
|---|---|---|
| Valve actuating component noise | • Insufficient oil supply | • Check for:<br>(a) Low oil level<br>(b) Low oil pressure<br>(c) Plugged push rods<br>(d) Wrong hydraulic tappets<br>(e) Restricted oil gallery<br>(f) Excessive tappet to bore clearance |
| | • Push rods worn or bent | • Replace worn or bent push rods |
| | • Rocker arms or pivots worn | • Replace worn rocker arms or pivots |
| | • Foreign objects or chips in hydraulic tappets | • Clean tappets |
| | • Excessive tappet leak-down | • Replace valve tappet |
| | • Tappet face worn | • Replace tappet; inspect corresponding cam lobe for wear |
| | • Broken or cocked valve springs | • Properly seat cocked springs; replace broken springs |
| | • Stem-to-guide clearance excessive | • Measure stem-to-guide clearance, repair as required |
| | • Valve bent | • Replace valve |
| | • Loose rocker arms | • Tighten bolts with specified torque |
| | • Valve seat runout excessive | • Regrind valve seat/valves |
| | • Missing valve lock | • Install valve lock |
| | • Push rod rubbing or contacting cylinder head | • Remove cylinder head and remove obstruction in head |
| | • Excessive engine oil (four-cylinder engine) | • Correct oil level |

## Troubleshooting the Cooling System

| Problem | Cause | Solution |
|---|---|---|
| High temperature gauge indication—overheating | • Coolant level low | • Replenish coolant |
| | • Fan belt loose | • Adjust fan belt tension |
| | • Radiator hose(s) collapsed | • Replace hose(s) |
| | • Radiator airflow blocked | • Remove restriction (bug screen, fog lamps, etc.) |
| | • Faulty radiator cap | • Replace radiator cap |
| | • Ignition timing incorrect | • Adjust ignition timing |
| | • Idle speed low | • Adjust idle speed |
| | • Air trapped in cooling system | • Purge air |
| | • Heavy traffic driving | • Operate at fast idle in neutral intermittently to cool engine |
| | • Incorrect cooling system component(s) installed | • Install proper component(s) |
| | • Faulty thermostat | • Replace thermostat |
| | • Water pump shaft broken or impeller loose | • Replace water pump |
| | • Radiator tubes clogged | • Flush radiator |
| | • Cooling system clogged | • Flush system |
| | • Casting flash in cooling passages | • Repair or replace as necessary. Flash may be visible by removing cooling system components or removing core plugs. |
| | • Brakes dragging | • Repair brakes |
| | • Excessive engine friction | • Repair engine |
| | • Antifreeze concentration over 68% | • Lower antifreeze concentration percentage |
| | • Missing air seals | • Replace air seals |
| | • Faulty gauge or sending unit | • Repair or replace faulty component |
| | • Loss of coolant flow caused by leakage or foaming | • Repair or replace leaking component, replace coolant |
| | • Viscous fan drive failed | • Replace unit |

## Troubleshooting the Cooling System (cont.)

| Problem | Cause | Solution |
|---|---|---|
| Low temperature indication— undercooling | • Thermostat stuck open<br>• Faulty gauge or sending unit | • Replace thermostat<br>• Repair or replace faulty component |
| Coolant loss—boilover | • Overfilled cooling system<br><br>• Quick shutdown after hard (hot) run<br>• Air in system resulting in occasional "burping" of coolant<br>• Insufficient antifreeze allowing coolant boiling point to be too low<br>• Antifreeze deteriorated because of age or contamination<br>• Leaks due to loose hose clamps, loose nuts, bolts, drain plugs, faulty hoses, or defective radiator<br>• Faulty head gasket<br>• Cracked head, manifold, or block<br>• Faulty radiator cap | • Reduce coolant level to proper specification<br>• Allow engine to run at fast idle prior to shutdown<br>• Purge system<br><br>• Add antifreeze to raise boiling point<br><br>• Replace coolant<br><br>• Pressure test system to locate source of leak(s) then repair as necessary<br><br>• Replace head gasket<br>• Replace as necessary<br>• Replace cap |
| Coolant entry into crankcase or cylinder(s) | • Faulty head gasket<br>• Crack in head, manifold or block | • Replace head gasket<br>• Replace as necessary |
| Coolant recovery system inoperative | • Coolant level low<br>• Leak in system<br><br>• Pressure cap not tight or seal missing, or leaking<br>• Pressure cap defective<br>• Overflow tube clogged or leaking<br>• Recovery bottle vent restricted | • Replenish coolant to FULL mark<br>• Pressure test to isolate leak and repair as necessary<br>• Repair as necessary<br><br>• Replace cap<br>• Repair as necessary<br>• Remove restriction |
| Noise | • Fan contacting shroud<br><br>• Loose water pump impeller<br>• Glazed fan belt<br>• Loose fan belt<br>• Rough surface on drive pulley<br>• Water pump bearing worn<br><br>• Belt alignment | • Reposition shroud and inspect engine mounts<br>• Replace pump<br>• Apply silicone or replace belt<br>• Adjust fan belt tension<br>• Replace pulley<br>• Remove belt to isolate. Replace pump.<br>• Check pulley alignment. Repair as necessary. |
| No coolant flow through heater core | • Restricted return inlet in water pump<br>• Heater hose collapsed or restricted<br>• Restricted heater core<br>• Restricted outlet in thermostat housing<br>• Intake manifold bypass hole in cylinder head restricted<br>• Faulty heater control valve<br>• Intake manifold coolant passage restricted | • Remove restriction<br><br>• Remove restriction or replace hose<br>• Remove restriction or replace core<br>• Remove flash or restriction<br><br>• Remove restriction<br><br>• Replace valve<br>• Remove restriction or replace intake manifold |

**NOTE:** *Immediately after shutdown, the engine enters a condition known as heat soak. This is caused by the cooling system being inoperative while engine temperature is still high. If coolant temperature rises above boiling point, expansion and pressure may push some coolant out of the radiator overflow tube. If this does not occur frequently it is considered normal.*

## Troubleshooting the Serpentine Drive Belt

| Problem | Cause | Solution |
|---|---|---|
| Tension sheeting fabric failure (woven fabric on outside circumference of belt has cracked or separated from body of belt) | • Grooved or backside idler pulley diameters are less than minimum recommended<br>• Tension sheeting contacting (rubbing) stationary object<br>• Excessive heat causing woven fabric to age<br>• Tension sheeting splice has fractured | • Replace pulley(s) not conforming to specification<br><br>• Correct rubbing condition<br><br>• Replace belt<br><br>• Replace belt |
| Noise (objectional squeal, squeak, or rumble is heard or felt while drive belt is in operation) | • Belt slippage<br>• Bearing noise<br>• Belt misalignment<br>• Belt-to-pulley mismatch<br>• Driven component inducing vibration<br>• System resonant frequency inducing vibration | • Adjust belt<br>• Locate and repair<br>• Align belt/pulley(s)<br>• Install correct belt<br>• Locate defective driven component and repair<br>• Vary belt tension within specifications. Replace belt. |
| Rib chunking (one or more ribs has separated from belt body) | • Foreign objects imbedded in pulley grooves<br>• Installation damage<br>• Drive loads in excess of design specifications<br>• Insufficient internal belt adhesion | • Remove foreign objects from pulley grooves<br>• Replace belt<br>• Adjust belt tension<br><br>• Replace belt |
| Rib or belt wear (belt ribs contact bottom of pulley grooves) | • Pulley(s) misaligned<br>• Mismatch of belt and pulley groove widths<br>• Abrasive environment<br>• Rusted pulley(s)<br>• Sharp or jagged pulley groove tips<br>• Rubber deteriorated | • Align pulley(s)<br>• Replace belt<br><br>• Replace belt<br>• Clean rust from pulley(s)<br>• Replace pulley<br>• Replace belt |
| Longitudinal belt cracking (cracks between two ribs) | • Belt has mistracked from pulley groove<br>• Pulley groove tip has worn away rubber-to-tensile member | • Replace belt<br><br>• Replace belt |
| Belt slips | • Belt slipping because of insufficient tension<br>• Belt or pulley subjected to substance (belt dressing, oil, ethylene glycol) that has reduced friction<br>• Driven component bearing failure<br>• Belt glazed and hardened from heat and excessive slippage | • Adjust tension<br><br>• Replace belt and clean pulleys<br><br><br>• Replace faulty component bearing<br>• Replace belt |
| "Groove jumping" (belt does not maintain correct position on pulley, or turns over and/or runs off pulleys) | • Insufficient belt tension<br>• Pulley(s) not within design tolerance<br>• Foreign object(s) in grooves<br><br>• Excessive belt speed<br><br>• Pulley misalignment<br>• Belt-to-pulley profile mismatched<br>• Belt cordline is distorted | • Adjust belt tension<br>• Replace pulley(s)<br><br>• Remove foreign objects from grooves<br>• Avoid excessive engine acceleration<br>• Align pulley(s)<br>• Install correct belt<br>• Replace belt |
| Belt broken (Note: identify and correct problem before replacement belt is installed) | • Excessive tension<br><br>• Tensile members damaged during belt installation<br>• Belt turnover<br>• Severe pulley misalignment<br>• Bracket, pulley, or bearing failure | • Replace belt and adjust tension to specification<br>• Replace belt<br><br>• Replace belt<br>• Align pulley(s)<br>• Replace defective component and belt |

## Troubleshooting the Serpentine Drive Belt (cont.)

| Problem | Cause | Solution |
|---|---|---|
| Cord edge failure (tensile member exposed at edges of belt or separated from belt body) | • Excessive tension<br>• Drive pulley misalignment<br>• Belt contacting stationary object<br>• Pulley irregularities<br>• Improper pulley construction<br>• Insufficient adhesion between tensile member and rubber matrix | • Adjust belt tension<br>• Align pulley<br>• Correct as necessary<br>• Replace pulley<br>• Replace pulley<br>• Replace belt and adjust tension to specifications |
| Sporadic rib cracking (multiple cracks in belt ribs at random intervals) | • Ribbed pulley(s) diameter less than minimum specification<br>• Backside bend flat pulley(s) diameter less than minimum<br>• Excessive heat condition causing rubber to harden<br>• Excessive belt thickness<br>• Belt overcured<br>• Excessive tension | • Replace pulley(s)<br><br>• Replace pulley(s)<br><br>• Correct heat condition as necessary<br>• Replace belt<br>• Replace belt<br>• Adjust belt tension |

## General Engine Specifications

| Year | Engine No. Cyl Displacement (cu. in.) | Carburetor Type | Horsepower @ rpm | Torque @ rpm (ft. lbs.) | Bore x Stroke (in.) | Compression Ratio | Oil Pressure @ rpm |
|---|---|---|---|---|---|---|---|
| 1982–88 | 4-151 | T.B.I.① | 90 @ 4000 | 132 @ 2800 | 4.000 x 3.000 | 8.2:1 | 36–41 |
| | 6-173 | 2 bbl | 112 @ 4800 | 145 @ 2400 | 3.500 x 3.000 | 8.5:1 | 36–41 |
| | 6-183 | 2 bbl | 110 @ 4800 | 145 @ 2600 | 3.800 x 2.660 | 8.45:1 | 35–42 |
| | 6-263 | Diesel | 85 @ 3600 | 165 @ 1600 | 4.057 x 3.385 | 21.6:1 | 40–45 |
| 1984–88 | 6-231 | M.F.I.②④ | 125 @ 4400 ⑤ | 195 @ 2000 ⑥ | 3.800 x 3.400 | 8.0:1 | 36–41 |
| 1985 | 6-173 | M.F.I.② | 130 @ 4800 | 155 @ 3600 | 3.500 x 3.000 | 8.9:1 | 50–65 |
| 1984 | 6-173③ | 2 bbl | 130 @ 5400 | 145 @ 2400 | 3.500 x 3.000 | 8.9:1 | 50–65 |

① Throttle Body Injection
② Multi Port Fuel Injection
③ High Output
④ S.F.I.—Single Port Fuel Injection 1986–88
⑤ S.F.I.—150 @ 4400
⑥ S.F.I.—200 @ 2000
NOTE: *Some models equipped with the 4-151 engine use a 2 bbl. carburetor rather than T.B.I.*

## Valve Specifications

| Year | Engine No. Cyl Displacement (cu. in.) | Seat Angle (deg) | Face Angle (deg) | Spring Test Pressure (lbs. @ in.) | Spring Installed Height (in.) | Stem to Guide Clearance (in.) | | Stem Diameter (in.) | |
|---|---|---|---|---|---|---|---|---|---|
| | | | | | | Intake | Exhaust | Intake | Exhaust |
| '82–'88 | 4-151 | 46 | 45 | 176 @ 1.25 | 1.66 | .0010–.0027 | .0010–.0027 | .3418–.3425 | .3418–.3425 |
| | 6-173 | 46 | 45 | 195 @ 1.18 | 1.57 | .0010–.0027 | .0010–.0027 | .3418–.3425 | .3418–.3425 |
| | 6-183 | 46 | 45 | 184 @ 1.34 | 1.727 | .0015–.0032 | .0015–.0035 | .3401–.3412 | .3405–.3412 |
| | 6-263 | ① | ② | 210 @ 1.22 | 1.67 | .0010–.0027 | .0015–.0032 | .3425–.3432 | .3420–.3427 |
| '84–'88 | 6-231 | 46 | 45 | 184 @ 1.34 | 1.73 | .0015–.0035 | .0015–.0032 | .3401–.3412 | .3405–.3412 |

① Intake: 45
  Exhaust: 31
② Intake: 44
  Exhaust: 30

## Crankshaft and Connecting Rod Specifications
All measurements are given in inches

| Year | Engine No. Cyl Displacement (cu in.) | Crankshaft | | | | Connecting Rod | | |
| | | Main Brg Journal Dia | Main Brg Oil Clearance | Shaft End-Play | Thrust on No. | Journal Diameter | Oil Clearance | Side Clearance |
|---|---|---|---|---|---|---|---|---|
| '82–'88 | 4-151 | 2.2995–3.3005 | .0005–.0022 | .0035–.0085 | 5 | 1.995–2.0005 | .0005–.0026 | .006–.022 |
| | 6-173 | 2.4937–2.4946 ② | .0017–.0030 | .0020–.0067 | 3 | 1.9984–1.9994 | .0014–.0036 | .006–.017 |
| | 6-183 | 2.4990–2.5000 | .0003–.0018 | .0030–.0090 | 2 | 2.2487–2.2495 | .0005–.0026 | .006–.023 |
| | 6-263 | 2.9993–3.0003 | ① | .0035–.0135 | 3 | 2.2498–2.2500 | .0003–.0025 | .008–.021 |
| '84–'88 | 6-231 | 2.4990–2.5000 | .0003–.0018 | .0030–.0090 | 2 | 2.2487–2.2495 | .0005–.0026 | .006–.023 |

① #1, 2, 3: .0005–.0021
   #4: .0020–.0034
② 2.6473–2.6483: 1987–88

## Camshaft Specifications
All measurements in inches

| Year | Engine | Journal Diameter | | | | | Bearing Clearance | Lobe Lift | | Camshaft End Play |
| | | 1 | 2 | 3 | 4 | 5 | | Intake | Exhaust | |
|---|---|---|---|---|---|---|---|---|---|---|
| '82–'88 | 4-151 | 1.869 | 1.869 | 1.869 | 1.869 | 1.869 | .0007–.0027 | .398 ③ | .398 ③ | .0015–.0050 |
| | 6-173 | 1.869 | 1.869 | 1.869 | 1.869 | — | .0010–.0040 | .231 | .263 | — |
| | 6-183 | 1.786 | 1.786 | 1.786 | 1.786 | — | ① | .406 | .406 | — |
| | 6-263 | ② | 2.205 | 2.185 | 2.165 | — | .0020–.0059 | N/A | N/A | .0008–.0228 |
| '84–'88 | 6-231 | 1.786 | 1.786 | 1.786 | 1.786 | — | ① | .406 | .406 | — |

① #1: .0005–.0025        ③ .232: 1985–88
   #2–5: .0005–.0035
② #1 bearing is not borable, but must be replaced separately
N/A—not available

## Torque Specifications
(All readings in ft. lbs.)

| Year | Engine No. Cyl Displacement (cu. in.) | Cylinder Head Bolts | Rod Bearing Bolts | Main Bearing Bolts | Crankshaft Bolt | Flywheel to Crankshaft Bolts | Manifold | |
| | | | | | | | Intake | Exhaust |
|---|---|---|---|---|---|---|---|---|
| '82–'88 | 4-151 | 85 | 32 | 70 | 200 | 44 | 29 | 44 |
| | 6-173 | 70 | 37 | 68 | 75 | 50 | 23 | 25 |
| | 6-183 | 80 | 40 | 100 | 225 | 60 | 45 | 25 |
| | 6-263 | ① | 42 | 107 | 255 ② | 76 | 41 | 29 |
| '84–'88 | 6-231 | 80 | 40 | 100 | 225 | 60 | 45 | 25 |

① All exc. #5, 6, 11, 12, 13, 14: 142
   #5, 6, 11, 12, 13, 14: 59
② Range: 160–350 ft. lb.

## Piston and Ring Specifications
All measurements are given in inches.

| Year | Engine Type/ Disp. cu. in. | Piston-to-Bore Clearance | Ring Gap | | | Ring Side Clearance | | |
|---|---|---|---|---|---|---|---|---|
| | | | Top Compression | Bottom Compression | Oil Control | Top Compression | Bottom Compression | Oil Control |
| '82–'85 | 4-151 | 0.0025–0.0033 ① | 0.010–0.022 | 0.010 0.027 | 0.020–0.060 | 0.0020–0.0030 | 0.0010–0.0030 | 0.0150–0.0550 |
| | 6-173 | 0.0012–0.0022 ② | 0.0098–0.0197 | 0.0098–0.0197 | 0.020–0.055 | 0.0012–0.0028 | 0.0016–0.0037 | 0.008 max |
| | 6-183 | 0.0015–0.0035 | 0.013–0.023 | 0.013–0.023 | 0.015–0.035 | 0.0030–0.0050 | 0.0030–0.0050 | 0.0035 max |
| | 6-263 | 0.0030–0.0040 | 0.015–0.025 | 0.015–0.025 | 0.015–0.055 | 0.0050–0.0070 | 0.0030–0.0050 | 0.001–0.005 |
| '84–'85 | 6-231 | 0.0015–0.0035 | 0.013–0.023 | 0.013–0.023 | 0.015–0.035 | 0.0030–0.0050 | 0.0030–0.0050 | 0.0035 max. |

① 0.0014–0.0022—1986–88
② 0.0020–0.0028—1986–88

26. Connect the throttle cable
27. Install the heater blower motor.
28. Install the vacuum hoses and electrical connectors at the solenoid.
29. Install the power steering hose.
30. Install the emission hoses at the canister.
31. Install the air conditioning compressor and belt.
32. Install the forward torque reaction rod to the engine and core support.
33. Install all bell housing bolts.
34. Install the air cleaner.
35. Raise the vehicle.
36. Install the flywheel inspection cover.
37. Install the starter assembly.
38. Connect the forward exhaust pipe.
39. Install the front mount-to-cradle nuts.
40. Lower the vehicle and install the battery.

**4-151 with Automatic Transaxle**

NOTE: *Relieve the pressure in the fuel system as described under Fuel Pump.*
1. Disconnect battery cables at battery.
2. Drain cooling system.
CAUTION: *When draining the coolant, keep in mind that cats and dogs are attracted by the ethylene glycol antifreeze, and are quite likely to drink any that is left in an uncovered container or in puddles on the ground. This will prove fatal in sufficient quantity. Always drain the coolant into a sealable container. Coolant should be reused unless it is contaminated or several years old.*
3. Remove air cleaner and pre-heat tube.
4. Disconnect engine harness connector.
5. Disconnect all external vacuum hose connections.
6. Remove throttle and transaxle linkage at E.F.I. assembly and intake manifold.

7. Remove upper radiator hose.
8. If equipped with air conditioning, remove air conditioning compressor from mounting brackets and set aside. Do not disconnect hoses.
9. Remove the front engine strut assembly.
10. Disconnect heater hose at intake manifold.
11. Remove transaxle to engine bolts leaving upper two bolts in place.
12. Remove front mount-to-cradle nuts.
13. Remove forward exhaust pipe.
14. Remove flywheel inspection cover and remove starter motor.
15. Remove torque converter to flywheel bolts.
16. Remove power steering pump and bracket and move to one side.
17. Remove heater hose and lower radiator hose.
18. Remove two rear transaxle support bracket bolts.
19. Remove fuel supply line at fuel filter.
20. Using a floor jack and a block of wood placed under the transaxle, raise engine and transaxle until engine front mount studs clear cradle.
21. Connect engine lift equipment and put tension on engine.
22. Remove two remaining transaxle bolts.
23. Slide engine forward and lift from car.
**To Install:**
24. Lower the engine into the vehicle. Do not completely lower the engine with a jack supporting the transaxle.
25. Install two transaxle bolts.
26. Remove the floor jack and lower the engine completely into the vehicle.
27. Connect the fuel supply line and install the filter.

28. Install the two transaxle rear support bracket bolts.
29. Install the heater and lower radiator hoses.
30. Connect the power steering bracket and pump.
31. Install the torque converter-to-flywheel bolts.
32. Install the starter motor and the flywheel inspection cover.
33. Connect the forward exhaust pipe.
34. Install the front mount-to-cradle nuts.
35. Install the transaxle to engine bolts.
36. Connect the heater hose at intake manifold.
37. Install the front engine strut assembly.
38. Install the air conditioning compressor mounting brackets and the compressor.
39. Install the upper radiator hose.
40. Connect the throttle and transaxle linkage at the E.F.I. assembly and intake manifold.
41. Connect all external vacuum hose connections.
42. Connect the engine harness connector.
43. Install the air cleaner and pre-heat tube.
44. Fill the cooling system.
45. Connect battery cables at battery.

### 6-173 with Manual Transaxle

1. Disconnect cables from battery.
2. Remove air cleaner.
3. Drain cooling system.
CAUTION: *When draining the coolant, keep in mind that cats and dogs are attracted by the ethylene glycol antifreeze, and are quite likely to drink any that is left in an uncovered container or in puddles on the ground. This will prove fatal in sufficient quantity. Always drain the coolant into a sealable container. Coolant should be reused unless it is contaminated or several years old.*
4. Disconnect vacuum hosing to all non-engine mounted components.
5. Disconnect accelerator linkage from carburetor.
6. Disconnect engine harness connector from the ECM and pull the connector through the front of the dash.
7. Disconnect radiator hoses from raidator.
8. Disconnect heater hoses from engine.
9. If equipped, remove power steering pump and bracket assembly from engine.
10. Disconnect clutch cable from transaxle.
11. Disconnect shift linkage from transaxle shift levers. Remove cables from transaxle bosses.
12. Disconnect speedometer cable from transaxle.
13. Raise and support the vehicle on jack stands.

14. Remove exhaust crossover.
15. Remove all but one of the transaxle to engine retaining bolts.
16. Remove side and crossmember assembly.
17. Disconnect exhaust pipe.
18. Remove all power train mount to cradle attachments.
19. Disconnect the engine harness from the junction block at the left side of the dash.
20. Lower vehicle. If equipped with MFI, disconnect the throttle, the T.V. and the cruise control cables at the throttle body.
21. Install engine support fixture. Raise engine until weight is relieved from mount assemblied.
22. Lower left side of engine/transaxle assembly by loosening tool J-22825.
23. Place jack under transaxle.
24. Remove the final transaxle to engine attaching bolt and separate transaxle from engine and lower.
25. Lower vehicle.
26. Install engine lifting fixture.
27. If air conditioning equipped, remove compressor from mounting bracket and swing aside.
28. Disconnect forward strut bracket from radiator support. Swing aside.
29. Lift engine out of vehicle.
**To Install:**
30. Lower the engine into the vehicle.
31. Connect forward strut bracket to radiator support.
32. Install the air conditioning compressor and mounting bracket.
33. Raise the vehicle and place the transaxle jack under the transaxle.
34. Raise the transaxle flush with the engine and install the engine-to-transaxle attaching bolts.
35. Remove the transaxle jack and lower the vehicle just enough to install the engine support fixture.
36. Raise engine until weight is relieved from mount assemblies.
37. Connect all power train mount to cradle attachments.
38. Connect exhaust pipe.
39. Install the side and crossmember assembly. Connect the engine harness to the junction block at the left side of the dash.
40. Install all remaining transaxle to engine retaining bolts.
41. Install the exhaust crossover.
42. Remove the engine support fixture.
43. Lower the vehicle.
44. Connect the speedometer cable to the transaxle.
45. Install the cables to the transaxle bosses.
46. Connect the transaxle shift linkage.
47. Connect the clutch cable.

48. Install the power steering bracket and pump assembly.

49. Connect the heater hoses to the engine.

50. Install the radiator hoses to the radiator.

51. Feed the engine harness connector through the front of the dash and connect it to the ECM.

52. Connect the throttle, the T.V. and the cruise control cables at the throttle body.

53. Connect the accelerator linkage to the carburetor.

54. Connect vacuum hosing to all non-engine mounted components.

55. Fill the cooling system.

56. Install the air cleaner.

58. Connect the battery cables.

### 6-173 with Automatic Transaxle

1. Disconnect battery cables from battery.

2. Remove air cleaner.

3. Drain cooling system.

CAUTION: *When draining the coolant, keep in mind that cats and dogs are attracted by the ethylene glycol antifreeze, and are quite likely to drink any that is left in an uncovered container or in puddles on the ground. This will prove fatal in sufficient quantity. Always drain the coolant into a sealable container. Coolant should be reused unless it is contaminated or several years old.*

4. Disconnect vacuum hosing to all non-engine mounted components.

5. Disconnect detent cable from carburetor lever.

6. Disconnect accelerator linkage. If equipped with MFI, disconnect the throttle at the T.V. and the cruise control cables at the throttle body.

7. Disconnect engine harness connector from the ECM and pull the connector through the front of the dash, then disconnect it from the junction block at the left side of the dash.

8. Disconnect ground strap from engine at engine forward strut.

9. Disconnect radiator hoses from radiator.

10. Disconnect heater hoses from engine.

11. Remove power steering pump and bracket assembly from engine, if equipped.

12. Raise vehicle.

13. Disconnect exhaust pipe.

14. Disconnect fuel lines at rubber hose connections at right side of engine.

15. Remove engine front mount to cradle retaining nuts (right side of vehicle).

16. Disconnect battery cables from engine (Starter and transaxle housing bolt).

17. Remove flex plate cover and disconnect torque convertor from flex plate.

18. Remove transaxle case to cylinder case support bracket bolts.

19. Lower vehicle. Place a support under the transaxle rear extension.

20. Remove engine strut bracket from radiator support and swing rearward.

21. Remove exhaust crossover pipe.

22. Remove transaxle to cylinder case retaining bolts. Make note of ground stud location.

23. If air conditioning equipped, remove compressor from mounting bracket and lay aside.

24. Install lift fixture to engine and remove engine from vehicle.

**To Install:**

25. Lower the engine into the vehicle.

26. Install the compressor mounting bracket and the compressor.

27. Install the transaxle to cylinder case retaining bolts and the ground stud.

28. Install the exhaust crossover pipe.

29. Install the engine stud bracket to the radiator support.

30. Raise the vehicle and remove the support from the transaxle rear extension.

31. Install the transaxle case to cylinder case support bracket bolts.

32. Connect the torque converter to the flex plate and install the flex plate cover.

33. Connect the battery cables to the engine (Starter and transaxle housing bolt).

34. Install the engine front mount to cradle retaining nuts (right side of vehicle).

35. Connect fuel lines at rubber hose connections at right side of engine.

36. Connect exhaust pipe.

37. Lower the vehicle.

38. Install the power steering pump and bracket assembly to the engine.

39. Connect the heater hoses to the engine.

40. Connect the radiator hoses to the radiator.

41. Connect the ground strap to the engine at the engine forward strut.

42. Connect the engine harness connector to the junction block at the left side of the dash then push the connector through the front of the dash and connect it to the ECM.

43. Connect accelerator linkage. If equipped with MFI, connect the throttle at the T.V. and the cruise control cables at the throttle body.

44. Connect detent cable from carburetor lever.

45. Connect vacuum hosing to all non-engine mounted components.

46. Fill the cooling system.

47. Install the air cleaner.

48. Connect battery cables.

### 6-181

1. Disconnect battery cables from battery.

2. Remove air cleaner.

3. Drain cooling system.

CAUTION: *When draining the coolant, keep*

*in mind that cats and dogs are attracted by the ethylene glycol antifreeze, and are quite likely to drink any that is left in an uncovered container or in puddles on the ground. This will prove fatal in sufficient quantity. Always drain the coolant into a sealable container. Coolant should be reused unless it is contaminated or several years old.*

4. Disconnect vacuum hosing to all non-engine mounted components.

5. Disconnect detent cable from carburetor lever.

6. Disconnect accelerator linkage.

7. Disconnect engine harness connector.

8. Disconnect ground strap from engine at engine forward strut.

9. Disconnect radiator hoses from radiator.

10. Disconnect heater hoses from engine.

11. Remove power steering pump and bracket assembly from engine.

12. Raise vehicle.

13. Disconnect exhaust pipe at manifold.

14. Disconnect fuel lines at rubber hose connections.

15. Remove engine front mount to cradle retaining nuts (right side of vehicle).

16. Disconnect battery cables from engine (Starter and transaxle housing bolt).

17. Remove flex plate cover and disconnect torque converter from flex plate.

18. Remove transaxle case to cylinder case support bracket bolts.

19. Lower vehicle. Place a support under the transaxle rear extension.

20. Remove engine strut bracket from radiator support and swing rearward.

21. Remove transaxle to cylinder case retaining bolts. Make note of ground stud location.

22. If air conditioning equipped, remove compressor from mounting bracket and lay aside.

23. Install a lift fixture to the engine.

24. Remove the engine from the vehicle.

**To Install:**

25. Lower the engine into the vehicle.

26. Install the compressor mounting bracket and the compressor.

27. Install the transaxle to cylinder case retaining bolts and the ground stud.

28. Install the exhaust crossover pipe.

29. Install the engine stud bracket to the radiator support.

30. Raise the vehicle and remove the support from the transaxle rear extension.

31. Install the transaxle case to cylinder case support bracket bolts.

32. Connect the torque converter to the flex plate and install the flex plate cover.

33. Connect the battery cables to the engine (Starter and transaxle housing bolt).

34. Install the engine front mount to cradle retaining nuts (right side of vehicle).

35. Connect fuel lines at rubber hose connections at right side of engine.

36. Connect exhaust pipe.

37. Lower the vehicle.

38. Install the power steering pump and bracket assembly to the engine.

39. Connect the heater hoses to the engine.

40. Connect the radiator hoses to the radiator.

41. Connect the ground strap to the engine at the engine forward strut.

42. Connect the engine harness connector to the junction block at the left side of the dash then push the connector through the front of the dash and connect it to the ECM.

43. Connect the accelerator linkage.

44. Connect detent cable from carburetor lever.

45. Connect vacuum hosing to all non-engine mounted components.

46. Fill the cooling system.

47. Install the air cleaner.

48. Connect battery cables.

**6-231**

1. Disconnect the negative battery cable and place fender covers on the fenders.

2. Using a sharp tool, scribe marks around the hood hinges and remove the hood.

3. Raise the vehicle and support on jackstands.

4. Remove the electrical connections from the starter and the starter.

5. Remove the flex cover and disconnect the torque converter-to-flex plate bolts.

NOTE: *When removing the torque converter bolts, be sure to mark the position of the converter to the flex plate.*

6. If equipped with air conditioning, disconnect the electrical connector, then remove the compressor and move it aside.

7. Drain the cooling system, then remove the radiator hoses and the radiator.

CAUTION: *When draining the coolant, keep in mind that cats and dogs are attracted by the ethylene glycol antifreeze, and are quite likely to drink any that is left in an uncovered container or in puddles on the ground. This will prove fatal in sufficient quantity. Always drain the coolant into a sealable container. Coolant should be reused unless it is contaminated or several years old.*

8. Remove the right front engine mount bolts and the inner fender splash shield.

9. Remove the lower engine-to-transaxle mounting bolts, then the right rear engine mount bolts.

10. Remove the exhaust pipe-to-manifold bolts, then the heater hoses. Lower the vehicle.

11. Remove the serpentine drive belt, then the alternator wiring and the alternator.

12. Remove the power steering pump and move it aside, it may be necessary to disconnect the pressure hoses.

13. Remove the Mass Air Flow sensor and the air intake duct.

14. Connect a vertical engine lift to the engine and apply tension to the lift.

15. Remove the upper left transaxle mounting bolts, the master cylinder (DO NOT disconnect the fluid lines) and the fuel lines at the fuel rail (MFI equipped engines).

16. Disconnect the throttle, the T.V. and the cruise control cables from the throttle body.

17. Remove the remaining engine-to-transaxle bolts and the engine from the vehicle.

**To install:**

18. Lower the engine into the vehicle and install the engine to transaxle bolts.

19. Connect the throttle, T.V. and cruise control cables to the throttle body.

20. Install the upper left transaxle mounting bolts (if not done previously), the master cylinder and the fuel lines.

21. Remove the lifting device from the engine.

22. Connect the Mass air flow sensor and the air intake duct.

23. Connect the power steering pump and pressure hoses.

24. Install the alternator, connect the electrical wiring and install the serpentine drive belt.

25. Raise the vehicle and connect the heater hoses and the exhaust system.

26. Install the the right rear engine mount bolts, then the 6 lower engine-to-transaxle mounting bolts.

27. Install inner fender splash shield and the right front engine mount bolts.

28. Install the radiator and radiator hoses, the fill the system with engine coolant.

29. Install the air conditioning compressor and connect the electrical connector.

NOTE: *Be sure to properly position the converter to the flex plate.*

30. Install the torque converter to flex plate bolts and the flex cover.

31. Install the starter and connect the starter electrical connectors.

32. Lower the vehicle.

33. Install and adjust the hood.

34. Connect the battery cables.

### 6-263 Diesel

1. Drain the cooling system. Remove the serpentine drive belt (and vacuum pump drive belt, if air conditioning equipped).

CAUTION: *When draining the coolant, keep in mind that cats and dogs are attracted by the ethylene glycol antifreeze, and are quite likely to drink any that is left in an uncovered container or in puddles on the ground. This will prove fatal in sufficient quantity. Always drain the coolant into a sealable container. Coolant should be reused unless it is contaminated or several years old.*

2. Remove air cleaner and install cover J-26996.

3. Disconnect battery negative cable(s) at batteries and ground wires at inner fender panel. Disconnect engine ground strap, rear (right) head to cowl.

4. Hoist car.

5. Remove the flywheel cover.

6. Remove the flywheel to torque converter bolts.

7. Disconnect the exhaust pipe from the rear exhaust manifold.

8. Remove the engine to transaxle brace.

9. Remove the engine mount to cradle retaining nuts and washers.

10. Disconnect the leads to the starter motor, #2 cylinder glow plug and battery ground cable at transaxle to engine bolt.

11. Disconnect the lower oil cooler hose and cap the openings.

12. Remove the accessible power steering pump bracket fasteners.

13. Lower the car.

14. Remove the remaining power steering pump bracket/brace fasteners and lower the power steering pump with hoses out of the way.

15. Remove heater water return pipe.

16. Disconnect all remaining glow plug leads at the glow plugs.

17. Disconnect all other leads at the engine, disconnect the engine harness at the cowl connector and body mounted relays and position the engine harness aside.

18. If air conditioning equipped, disconnect the compressor with brackets and lines attached and position aside.

19. Disconnect the fuel and vacuum hoses, cap all fuel line openings.

20. Disconnect the throttle and T.V. cables at the injection pump and cable bracket. Position cables aside.

21. Disconnect the upper oil cooler hose and cap the openings.

22. Remove the exhaust crossover pipe heat shield.

23. Disconnect and move aside the transaxle filler tube.

24. Remove the exhaust crossover pipe.

25. Remove the engine mounting strut and strut brackets.

26. Install a suitable engine lifting device. Make certain that when installing chains to the cylinder heads that washers are used under the chains and bolt heads and that the bolts are torqued to 20 ft.lb.

CAUTION: *Failure to properly secure the engine lift to the aluminum cylinder heads can result in personal injury.*

27. Position a support under the transaxle rear extension. It may be necessary to raise the support as the engine is being removed.

28. Remove the engine to transaxle bolts and remove the engine.

29. To install, reverse the removal process noting the following:

a. Before installing the flex plate-to-converter bolts, make sure that the weld nuts on the converter are flush with the flex plate, and the converter rotates freely by hand.

b. Use only new O-rings at all connections.

c. Adjust the throttle valve cable as outlined in the Chapter 7.

## Valve Cover(s)
### REMOVAL AND INSTALLATION
#### 4-151 Engine

1. Remove the air cleaner assembly, being sure to tag all disconnected hoses for reassembly purposes.

2. Remove the P.C.V. valve and hose from the valve cover grommet.

3. Remove the valve cover retaining bolts.

4. Remove the spark plug wires from the spark plugs and the locating clips. Be sure to tag the wires so that they may be attached properly.

5. Remove the cover retaining bolts, then the valve cover by tapping it with a rubber mallet. This must be done to break the R.T.V. seal. DON'T attempt to pry the cover off, as it is easily damaged.

6. Remove the valve cover retaining bolts then remove the valve cover. If the cover sticks, tap it loose with a rubber mallet. DON'T attempt to pry it off of the head, as the cover may be easily damaged.

7. Refer to steps 6-8 of the previous 4-151 procedure to prepare and seal the valve cover during installation.

8. The remainder of the installation is performed in the reverse of removal. Torque the front engine strut bracket bolts to 35 ft.lb.

#### 6-173 Engine-Rear

1. Disconnect the negative battery cable at the battery.

2. Remove the air cleaner assembly, being sure to tag all disconnected hoses for reassembly purposes.

NOTE: *If equipped with an MFI system, remove any component which will interfere with the valve cover removal.*

3. Remove the spark plug wires from the spark plugs and the locating clips. Be sure to tag the wires so that they may be attached properly.

4. Disconnect the accelerator linkage and springs from the carburetor.

5. If your vehicle has an automatic transaxle, disconnect the T.V. (throttle valve) linkage at the carburetor.

6. If your vehicle has cruise control remove the diaphragm actuator mounting bracket.

7. Remove the air management valve and the necessary hoses (see Chapter 4).

8. Remove the valve cover retaining bolts, then remove the valve cover. If the cover sticks, tap it loose with a rubber mallet. DON'T attempt to pry it off of the head, as the cover may be easily damaged.

9. Refer to steps 6-8 of the previous 4-151 procedure to prepare and seal the valve cover during installation. The valve cover retaining bolts must be torqued to 11 ft.lb.

10. The remainder of the installation is performed in the reverse order of removal.

#### 6-183 and 6-231 Engine Front

1. Disconnect the negative battery cable.

2. Remove the crankcase breather tube.

3. Remove the spark plug wire harness cover and disconnect the spark plug wires at the spark plugs.

4. Remove the valve cover nuts, washers, seals and valve cover.

5. Using a putty knife, clean the gasket mounting surfaces.

6. To install, use a new gasket and reverse the removal procedures. Torque the valve cover nuts to 7 ft.lb. (10 Nm.).

#### 6-183 and 6-231 Engine Rear

1. Disconnect the negative battery cable.

2. Remove the C3 ignition coil module, the spark plug cables, the wiring connectors, the EGR solenoid wiring and vacuum hoses.

NOTE: *If equipped with an MFI system, remove any component which will interfere with the valve cover removal.*

3. Remove the serpentine drive belt.

4. Remove the alternator's wiring connectors, then the mounting bolt and swing the alternator toward the front of the vehicle.

5. Remove the power steering pump from the belt tensioner (move it aside) and the belt tensioner assembly.

6. Remove the engine lift bracket and the rear alternator brace.

7. Drain the cooling system below the level of the heater hose, then disconnect the throttle body heater hoses.

CAUTION: *When draining the coolant, keep in mind that cats and dogs are attracted by the ethylene glycol antifreeze, and are quite likely to drink any that is left in an uncovered container or in puddles on the ground. This will prove fatal in sufficient quantity. Always drain the coolant into a sealable container. Coolant should be reused unless it is contaminated or several years old.*

8. Remove the valve cover nuts, the washers, the seals, the valve cover and the gasket.

9. Using a putty knife, clean the gasket mounting surfaces.

10. To install, use a new gasket and reverse the removal procedures. Torque the valve cover nuts to 7 ft.lb. (10 Nm.).

### 6-263 Diesel Engine Front

1. Disconnect the negative battery cable.
2. Remove the fuel injection lines.
3. Remove the forward engine support strut, which is bolted to the radiator support strut and an engine bracket.
4. Unbolt and remove the strut bracket from the engine.
5. If necessary, remove any additional piece(s) which may interfere with removal of the cover.
6. Unbolt and remove the cover. If the cover sticks, tap it loose with a rubber mallet. DON'T attempt to pry it off of the head, as the cover may be easily damaged.
7. Raise the jack until it just starts to lift the vehicle.
8. Remove the two front body mount bolts from the cradle, along with the cushions and the retainers. Remove the cushions from the bolts.
9. Thread the body mount bolts (with the retainers) back into place, making sure to turn them at least three full turns each.
10. Carefully and slowly lower the jack until the cradle contacts the retainers. While you are lowering the jack, be sure to watch for any component interference and correct as required.

CAUTION: *DO NOT attempt to lower the cradle without the bolts and retainers in place, as this could cause damage of various underhood components.*

11. Unbolt and remove the cover. If the cover sticks, tap it loose with a rubber mallet. DON'T attempt to pry it off of the head, as the cover may be easily damaged.

12. Refer to steps 6-8 of the previous 4-151 procedure to prepare and seal the valve cover during installation.

13. To install reverse steps 1 through 12.

## Rocker Arm and Pushrod
### REMOVAL AND INSTALLATION
#### 4-151 Engine

1. Remove the valve cover.
2. On fuel injected engines, see the fuel pump section to relieve pressure, in the fuel system before disconnecting any fuel lines.
3. If only the pushrod is being removed, loosen the rocker arm bolt and swing the rocker arm aside.
4. Remove the rocker arm nut and ball.
5. Lift the rocker arm off the stud, keeping rocker arms in order for installation.
6. To install reverse steps 1 through 5. Tighten the rocker arm bolt to 20 ft.lb.; the rocker cover to 5 ft.lb.

#### 6-173 Engine

Rocker arms are removed by removing the adjusting nut. Be sure to adjust valve lash after replacing rocker arms.

NOTE: *When replacing an exhaust rocker, move an old intake rocker arm to the exhaust rocker arm stud and install the new rocker arm on the intake stud.*

Cylinder heads use threaded rocker arm studs. If the threads in the head are damaged or stripped, the head can be retapped and a helical type insert installed.

NOTE: *If engine is equipped with the A.I.R. exhaust emission control system, the interfering components of the system must be removed. Disconnect the lines at the air injection nozzles in the exhaust manifolds.*

#### 6-181 and 6-231 Engine

1. Remove the rocker arm cover(s).
2. Remove the rocker arm shaft(s).
3. Place the shaft on a clean surface.
4. Remove the nylon rocker arm retainers. A pair of slip joint pliers is good for this.
5. Slide the rocker arms off the shaft and inspect them for wear or damage. Keep them in order!
6. To install reverse steps 1 through 5. If new rocker arms are being installed, note that they are stamped R (right) or L (left), meaning that they be used on the right or left of each cylinder, NOT right and left cylinder banks. Each rocker arm must be centered over its oil hole. New nylon retainers must be used.

#### 6-263 Diesel Engine

NOTE: *This procedure requires that the valve lifters be bled!*

1. Remove the valve cover(s). See the Valve Cover procedure.
2. Remove the rocker arm nuts, pivot and rocker arms.
3. If rocker arms are being replaced, they must be replaced in cylinder sets. Never replace just one rocker arm per cylinder! If a stud was replaced, coat the threads with locking compound and torque it to 11 ft. lb.
4. To installation reverse the above process.

NOTE: AT TIME OF INSTALLATION, FLANGES MUST BE FREE OF OIL. A ⅛ BEAD OF SEALANT MUST BE APPLIED TO FLANGES AND SEALANT MUST BE WET TO TOUCH WHEN BOLTS ARE TORQUED.

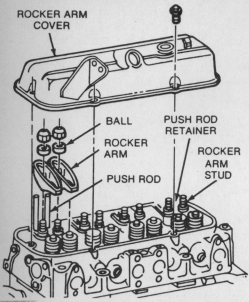

Exploded view of the rocker arm assembly—2.5L

See the section on Valve lifter bleed-down. This is absolutely necessary! If lifters are not bled, engine damage will be unavoidable! Torque the rocker arm nuts to 28 ft.lb.; the cover to 5 ft.lb.

## Thermostat
### REMOVAL AND INSTALLATION
#### All Models

1. Disconnect the negative battery cable.
2. Drain the cooling system.
CAUTION: *When draining the coolant, keep in mind that cats and dogs are attracted by the ethylene glycol antifreeze, and are quite likely to drink any that is left in an uncovered container or in puddles on the ground. This will prove fatal in sufficient quantity. Always drain the coolant into a sealable container. Coolant should be reused unless it is contaminated or several years old.*
3. Some models with cruise control have a vacuum modulator attached to the thermostat housing with a bracket. It your vehicle is equipped as such, remove the bracket from the housing.
4. On the 4-cyl. engines, unbolt the water outlet from the thermostat housing, remove the outlet from the housing and lift the thermostat out of the housing. On all other models, unbolt the water outlet from the intake manifold, remove the outlet and lift the thermostat out of the manifold.

Thermostat installation

### To install the new thermostat:

5. Clean both of the mating surfaces and run a ⅛″ bead of R.T.V.(room temperature vulcanizing) sealer in the groove of the water outlet.
6. Install the thermostat (spring towards engine) and bolt the water outlet into place while the R.T.V. sealer is still wet. Torque the bolts to 21 ft.lb. The remainder of the installation is the reverse of removal. Check for leaks after the car is started and correct as required.

## Intake Manifold
### REMOVAL AND INSTALLATION
#### 4-151 Engine

CAUTION: *Bleed pressure from the fuel system, if equipped with fuel injection, before servicing.*
1. Remove the air cleaner and the PCV valve.
2. Drain the cooling system into a clean container.
CAUTION: *When draining the coolant, keep in mind that cats and dogs are attracted by the ethylene glycol antifreeze, and are quite likely to drink any that is left in an uncovered container or in puddles on the ground. This will prove fatal in sufficient quantity. Always drain the coolant into a sealable container. Coolant should be reused unless it is contaminated or several years old.*
3. Disconnect the fuel and vacuum lines and the electrical connections at the carburetor and manifold.
4. Disconnect the throttle linkage at the EFI unit and disconnect the transaxle downshift linkage and cruise control linkage.

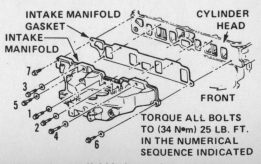

4-151 intake manifold bolt torquing sequence

5. Remove the carburetor and the spacer.

6. Remove the bell crank and the throttle linkage. Position to the side for clearance.

7. Remove the heater hose at the intake manifold.

8. Remove the pulse air check valve bracket from the manifold.

9. Remove the manifold attaching bolt and remove the manifold.

### 6-173 Engine

1. Remove the rocker covers.

2. Drain the cooling system.

CAUTION: *When draining the coolant, keep in mind that cats and dogs are attracted by the ethylene glycol antifreeze, and are quite likely to drink any that is left in an uncovered container or in puddles on the ground. This will prove fatal in sufficient quantity. Always drain the coolant into a sealable container. Coolant should be reused unless it is contaminated or several years old.*

3. If equipped, remove the AIR pump and bracket.

4. Remove the distributor cap. Mark the position of the ignition rotor in relation to the distributor body, and remove the distributor. Do not crank the engine with the distributor removed.

5. Remove the heater and radiator hoses from the intake manifold.

6. Remove the power brake vacuum hose.

7. Disconnect and label the vacuum hoses. Remove the EFE pipe from the rear of the manifold.

8. Remove the carburetor linkage. Disconnect and plug the fuel line.

NOTE: *If equipped with an MFI system, remove any component which will interfere with the intake manifold removal.*

9. Remove the manifold retaining bolts and nuts.

10. Remove the intake manifold. Remove and discard the gaskets, and scrape off the old silicone seal from the front and rear ridges.

**To install:**

1. The gaskets are marked for right and left side installation; do not interchange them. Clean the sealing surface of the engine block, and apply a $3/16''$ bead of silicone sealer to each ridge.

2. Install the new gaskets onto the heads. The gaskets will have to be cut slightly to fit past the center pushrods. Do not cut any more material than necessary. Hold the gaskets in place by extending the ridge bead of sealer $1/4''$ onto the gasket ends.

3. Install the intake manifold. The area between the ridges and the manifold should be completely sealed.

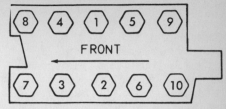

**173 V6 intake manifold torque sequence**

4. Install the retaining bolts and nuts, and tighten in sequence to 23 ft.lb. Do not overtighten; the manifold is made from aluminum, and can be warped or cracked with excessive force.

5. The rest of installation is the reverse of removal. Adjust the ignition timing after installation, and check the coolant level after the engine has warmed up.

### 6-183 and 6-231 Engine

1. Disconnect the battery ground.

2. Drain the cooling system.

CAUTION: *When draining the coolant, keep in mind that cats and dogs are attracted by the ethylene glycol antifreeze, and are quite likely to drink any that is left in an uncovered container or in puddles on the ground. This will prove fatal in sufficient quantity. Always drain the coolant into a sealable container. Coolant should be reused unless it is contaminated or several years old.*

3. Remove the air cleaner.

4. Disconnect all hoses and wiring from the manifold.

5. Disconnect the accelerator linkage and cruise control chain.

NOTE: *If equipped with an MFI system, remove any component which will interfere with the intake manifold removal.*

6. Disconnect the fuel line.

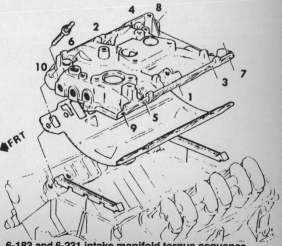

**6-183 and 6-231 intake manifold torque sequence**

7. Remove the distributor cap and rotor and remove the Torx® head bolt from the left side of the manifold.

8. Unbolt and remove the manifold.

9. To install reverse steps 1 through 8. When installing the front and rear seals, make sure that the ends of the seals fit snugly against the block and head. Install nos. 1 & 2 bolts first and tighten them until snug, then install the other bolts in order.

### 6-263 Diesel Engine

NOTE: *This procedure requires the removal, disassembly draining and reassembly of the valve lifters. Read that procedure, below, before continuing.*

1. Remove the air cleaner assembly.

2. Drain the radiator, then disconnect the upper radiator hose from the water outlet.

CAUTION: *When draining the coolant, keep in mind that cats and dogs are attracted by the ethylene glycol antifreeze, and are quite likely to drink any that is left in an uncovered container or in puddles on the ground. This will prove fatal in sufficient quantity. Always drain the coolant into a sealable container. Coolant should be reused unless it is contaminated or several years old.*

3. Disconnect the heater inlet hose from the outlet on intake manifold and disconnect the heater outlet pipe from the intake manifold attachments and move it aside.

4. Remove air crossover and the fuel injection pump.

5. Disconnect wiring as necessary at the generator (and air conditioning compressor) and switches (if so equipped).

6. Remove the cruise control servo if so equipped.

7. Remove the air conditioning compressor bracket and brace bolts and position the compressor (if so equipped) with lines attached out of the way.

8. Remove the generator assembly.

9. Disconnect the engine mounting strut.

10. Remove the fuel lines, filter and brackets. Cap all openings.

11. Disconnect the electrical leads to the glow plug controller and sending units.

12. Disconnect the exhaust crossover pipe heat shield.

13. Remove the left (forward) injection lines and cap all openings. Use backup wrench on the nozzles.

14. Disconnect the throttle and T.V. cables from the bracket.

15. Remove the drain tube.

16. Remove the intermediate pump adapter.

17. Remove pump adapter and seal.

18. Remove the intake manifold.

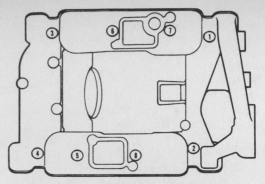

**6-263 intake manifold torque sequence**

19. Clean the machined surfaces of cylinder head and intake manifold with a putty knife. Use care not to gouge or scratch the machined surfaces. Clean all bolts and bolt holes.

20. Coat both sides of gasket sealing surface that seal the intake manifold to the head with 1050026 sealer or equivalent and position intake manifold gasket. Install end seals, making sure that ends are positioned under the cylinder heads. The seals and mating surfaces must be dry. Any liquid, including sealer will act as a lubricant and cause the seal to move during assembly. Use RTV sealer only on each end of the seal.

21. Position intake manifold on engine. Lubricate the entire intake manifold bolt (all) with lubricant 1052080 or equivalent.

22. Torque the bolts in sequence shown to 20 ft.lb. Then retorque to 41 ft.lb.

23. Install the drain tube.

24. Install the pump adapter.

25. Apply chassis lube to seal area of intake manifold and pump adapter.

26. Apply chassis lube to inside and outside diameter of seal and seal area of tool J-28425.

27. Install seal on tool and install the seal.

28. Install intermediate pump adapter.

29. Reverse the order of removal and install all other removed parts except the air crossover.

30. Fill the cooling system.

31. Install manifold covers, J-29657.

32. Start engine and check for leaks.

33. Check and if necessary, reset the injection pump timing.

34. Remove screen covers from manifold.

35. Install air crossover.

36. Install the air cleaner.

37. Road test car and inspect for leaks.

## Diesel Engine Valve Lifter Bleed-Down

If the intake manifold and valve rocker arms have been removed, it will be necessary to remove, disassemble, drain and reassemble the lifters on that side. If the rocker arms have been loosened or removed, but the intake manifold was not removed, skip down to the Bleed-Down procedure.

### REMOVAL

Keep lifters and pushrods in order! This is absolutely necessary for installation, since these parts have differences which could result in engine damage if not installed in their original positions!

1. Remove intake manifold. Refer to Intake Manifold.
2. Remove valve covers, rocker arm assemblies and pushrods.
3. Remove the valve lifter guide retainer bolts.
4. Remove the retainer guides and valve lifters.

### DISASSEMBLY

1. Remove the retainer ring with a small screwdriver.
2. Remove pushrod seat and oil metering valve.
3. Remove plunger and plunger spring.
4. Remove check valve retainer from plunger, then remove valve and spring.

### CLEANING AND INSPECTION

After lifters are disassembled, all parts should be cleaned in clean solvent. A small particle of foreign material under the check valve will cause malfunctioning of the lifter. Close inspection should be made for nicks, burrs or scoring of parts. If either the roller body or plunger is defective, replace with a new lifter assembly. Whenever lifters are removed, check as follows:

1. Roller should rotate freely, but without excessive play.
2. Check for missing or broken needle bearings.
3. Roller should be free of pits or roughness. If present, check camshaft for similar condition. If pits or roughness are evident replace lifter and camshaft.

### ASSEMBLY

1. Coat all lifter parts with a coating of clean kerosene or diesel fuel.
2. Assemble the ball check, spring and retainer into the plunger.
3. Install plunger spring over check retainer.
4. Hold plunger with spring up and insert into lifter body. Hold plunger vertically to prevent cocking spring.
5. Submerge the lifter in clean kerosene or diesel fuel.

6. Install oil metering valve and pushrod seat into lifter and install retaining ring.

### INSTALLATION

Prime new lifters by working lifter plunger while submerged in clean kerosene or diesel fuel. Lifter could be damaged when starting engine if dry.

1. When a rocker arm is loosened or removed, valve lifter bleed down is required. Lifters must be bled down as possible valve to piston interference due to the close tolerances could exist. Before installing a new or used lifter in the engine, lubricate the roller and bearings of the lifter with No. 1052365 lubricant or equivalent.
2. Install lifters and pushrods into original position in cylinder block. See note under Removal.
3. Install manifold gaskets and manifold.
4. Position rocker arms, pivots and bolts on cylinder head.
5. Install valve covers.
6. Install intake manifold assembly.

### BLEED-DOWN

1. Before installing any removed rocker arms, rotate the engine crankshaft to a position of number 1 cylinder being 32 degrees before top dead center. This is a 50 mm (2") counterclockwise from the 0 pointer. If only the right valve cover was removed, remove No. 1 cylinder's glow plug to determine if the position of the piston is the correct one. The compression pressure will tell you that you are in the right position. If the left valve cover was removed, rotate the crankshaft until the number 5 cylinder intake valve pushrod ball is 7.0 mm (0.28") above the number 5 cylinder exhaust valve pushrod ball.

NOTE: *Use only hand wrenches to torque the rocker arm pivot nuts to avoid engine damage.*

2. If removed, install the No. 5 cylinder pivot and rocker arms. Torque the nuts alternately between the intake and exhaust valves until the intake valve begins to open, then stop.
3. Install remaining rocker arms except No. 3 exhaust valve. (If this rocker arm was removed).
4. If removed, install but do not torque No. 3 valve pivots beyond the point that the valve would be fully open. This is indicated by strong resistance while still turning the pivot retaining bolts. Going beyond this would bend the pushrod. Torque the nuts SLOWLY allowing the lifter to bleed down.
5. Finish torquing No. 5 cylinder rocker arm pivot nut SLOWLY. Do not go beyond the point

that the valve would be fully open. This is indicated by strong resistance while still turning the pivot retaining bolts. Going beyond this would bend the pushrod.

6. DO NOT turn the engine crankshaft for at least 45 minutes.

7. Finish reassembling the engine as the lifters are being bled.

NOTE: *Do not rotate the engine until the valve lifters have been bleed down, or damage to the engine will occur.*

## Exhaust Manifold
### REMOVAL AND INSTALLATION

#### 4-151 Engine

1. Remove the air cleaner and the EFI preheat tube.

2. Remove the manifold strut bolts from the radiator support panel and the cylinder head.

3. Remove the air conditioning compressor bracket bolts and position the compressor to one side. Do not disconnect any of the refrigerant lines.

4. If necessary, remove the dipstick tube attaching bolt, and the engine mount bracket from the cylinder head. Remove the oxygen sensor connector.

5. Raise the car and disconnect the exhaust pipe from the manifold.

6. Remove the manifold attaching bolts and remove the manifold.

7. Reverse steps 1 through 6 to install.

#### 6-173 Engine Left Side

1. Remove the air cleaner. Remove the exhaust crossover pipe.

2. Remove the air supply plumbing from the exhaust manifold, if equipped.

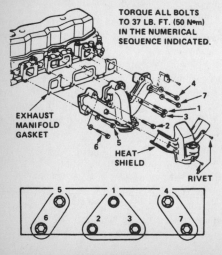

TORQUE ALL BOLTS TO 37 LB. FT. (50 N•m) IN THE NUMERICAL SEQUENCE INDICATED.

EXHAUST MANIFOLD GASKET

HEAT SHIELD

RIVET

BOLT LOCATIONS

**4-151 exhaust manifold torque sequence**

3. Raise and support the car. Unbolt and remove the exhaust pipe at the manifold.

4. Unbolt and remove the manifold.

**To install:**

1. Clean the mating surfaces of the cylinder head and manifold. Install the manifold onto the head, and install the retaining bolts finger tight.

2. Tighten the manifold bolts in a circular pattern, working from the center to the ends, to 25 ft.lb. in two stages.

3. Connect the exhaust pipe to the manifold.

4. The remainder of installation is the reverse of removal.

#### 6-183 and 6-231 Engine Left Side

1. Disconnect the battery ground.

2. Unbolt and remove the crossover pipe.

3. Remove the upper engine support strut.

4. Unbolt and remove the manifold.

5. To install reverse steps 1 through 4.

#### 6-263 Diesel Engine Left Side

1. Remove the crossover pipe from the manifolds.

2. Raise and support the car on jackstands.

3. Unbolt and remove the manifold.

4. Installation is the reverse of removal. Lubricate the entire length of each manifold bolt with lubricant 1052080 or its equivalent.

#### 6-263 Diesel Engine Right Side

1. Remove the engine support strut.

2. Place a floor jack under the front crossmember and take up the weight of the car.

3. Remove the two front body mount bolts. Remove the cushions from the bolts.

4. Thread the body mount bolts with their retainers into the cage nuts so that the bolts restrict movement of the engine cradle.

5. Lower the jack until the crossmember contacts the body mount bolt retainers. Check for any hose or wire interference.

6. Remove the crossover pipe.

7. Raise and support the car on jackstands.

8. Disconnect the exhaust pipe from the manifold.

9. Lower the car.

10. Unbolt and remove the manifold.

11. Installation is the reverse of removal. Lubricate the entire length of each manifold bolt with lubricant 1052080 or its equivalent.

#### 6-173 Engine Right Side

1. Disconnect the negative battery cable.

2. Remove the air cleaner and the A.I.R. bracket at the exhaust flange.

3. Raise and support the vehicle on jackstands.

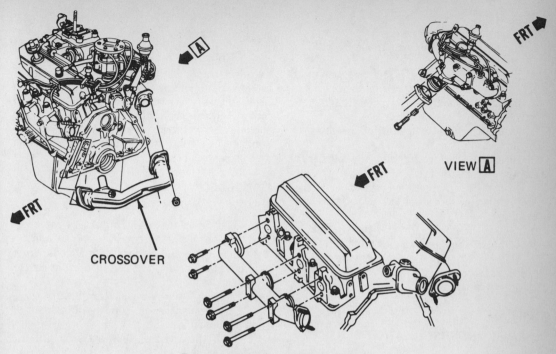

**Exhaust manifold installation—typical**

4. Remove the exhaust pipe from the manifold, then lower the vehicle.

5. Disconnect the oxygen sensor connector and the A.I.R. management hose from the valve.

6. Remove the exhaust crossover pipe, the manifold bolts and the exhaust manifold.

7. To install, use a new gasket and reverse the removal procedures. Torque the manifold bolts to 25 ft.lb. (34 Nm.).

### 6-183 and 6-231 Engine Right Side

1. Disconnect the negative battery cable.

2. Remove the intermediate shaft pinch bolt and separate the intermediate shaft from the stub shaft.

CAUTION: *Failure to disconnect the intermediate shaft from the rack and pinion stub shaft can result in damage to the steering gear and/or the intermediate shaft. This damage can cause loss of steering control.*

3. Raise the support the vehicle on jackstands.

4. Remove the exhaust pipe-to-manifold bolts, then lower the vehicle.

5. Place a jack under the front crossmember of the cradle, then raise the jack until it starts to raise the vehicle and remove the two front body mount bolts.

6. With the cushions removed, thread the body mount bolts and retainers at least three turns into the cage nuts, then slowly release the jack.

7. Remove the power steering pump and bracket, then move it aside.

8. Disconnect the oxygen sensor connector.

9. Remove the crossover pipe-to-manifold nuts, the exhaust manifold bolts and the manifold.

10. To install, reverse the removal procedures.

## Air Conditioning Compressor

### REMOVAL AND INSTALLATION

1. Disconnect the negative battery cable.

2. Disconnect the compressor clutch coil wire.

3. Remove the engine fan and fan shroud.

4. Remove the drive belt from the compressor.

5. Remove the compressor bracket.

6. Refer to Chapter 1 and discharge the air conditioning system.

7. Remove the screw attaching the muffler to the compressor support.

8. Remove the hose and muffler assembly from the compressor.

9. Remove the vacuum pump hose from the metal vacuum line.

10. Remove the four nuts and one bolt and spacer from the compressor support.

11. Remove the compressor support by pulling forward.

12. Pull the compressor forward to remove it from the vehicle.

**To install**

1. Position the compressor.
2. Install the compressor support by pulling forward.
3. Install the four nuts and one bolt and spacer from the compressor support.
4. Install the vacuum pump hose to the metal vacuum line.
5. Install the hose and muffler assembly to the compressor.
6. Install the screw attaching the muffler to the compressor support.
7. Install the compressor bracket.
8. Install the drive belt to the compressor and adjust.
9. Install the engine fan and fan shroud.
10. Connect the compressor clutch coil wire.
11. Refer to Chapter 1 and charge the air conditioning system.
12. Connect the negative battery cable.

## Radiator

### REMOVAL AND INSTALLATION

#### All Models

1. Disconnect the negative battery cable.
2. Drain the cooling system.
CAUTION: *When draining the coolant, keep in mind that cats and dogs are attracted by the ethylene glycol antifreeze, and are quite likely to drink any that is left in an uncovered container or in puddles on the ground. This will prove fatal in sufficient quantity. Always drain the coolant into a sealable container. Coolant should be reused unless it is contaminated or several years old.*
3. Remove the forward strut brace for the engine at the radiator. Loosen the bolt to prevent shearing the rubber bushing, then swing the strut rearward.
4. Disconnect the headlamp wiring harness from the fan frame. Unplug the fan electrical connector.
5. Remove the attaching bolts for the fan.
6. Scribe the hood latch location on the radiator support, then remove the latch.
7. Disconnect the coolant hoses from the radiator. Remove the coolant recovery tank hose from the radiator neck. Disconnect and plug the automatic transmission fluid cooler lines from the radiator, if so equipped. On the diesel engine, disconnect the engine oil cooler hoses.
8. Remove the radiator attaching bolts and remove the radiator. If the car has air conditioning, if first may be necessary to raise the left side of the radiator so that the radiator neck will clear the compressor.
**To install:**
1. Install the radiator in the car, tightening the mounting bolts to 7 in.lb. Connect the

transmission cooler lines and hoses. Install the coolant recovery hose.
2. Install the hood latch. Tighten to 6 ft.lb.
3. Install the fan, making sure the bottom leg of the frame fits into the rubber grommet at the lower support. Install the fan wires and the headlamp wiring harness. Swing the strut and brace forward, tightening to 11 ft.lb. Connect the engine ground strap to the strut brace. Install the negative battery cable, fill the cooling system, and check for leaks.

## Condenser

### REMOVAL AND INSTALLATION

1. Disconnect the negative battery cable.
2. Discharge the air conditioning system.
NOTE: *Refer to Chapter 1 for Discharging, Evacuating and Charging of the air conditioning System.*
3. Remove the upper radiator shroud.
4. Disconnect the air conditioning lines at the condenser.
5. Push the radiator forward and pull the condensor out from the top.
6. Reverse steps 1 through 5 to install.

## Water Pump

### REMOVAL AND INSTALLATION

#### 4-151 Engine

1. Disconnect battery negative cable and drain the cooling system.
CAUTION: *When draining the coolant, keep in mind that cats and dogs are attracted by the ethylene glycol antifreeze, and are quite likely to drink any that is left in an uncovered container or in puddles on the ground. This will prove fatal in sufficient quantity. Always drain the coolant into a sealable container. Coolant should be reused unless it is contaminated or several years old.*
2. Remove accessory drive belts.
3. Remove water pump attaching bolts and remove pump.
4. If installing a new water pump, transfer pulley from old unit. With sealing surfaces cleaned, place a 3mm (⅛") bead of sealant #1052289 or equivalent on the water pump sealing surface. While sealer is still wet, install pump and torque bolts to 20 ft.lb.
5. Install accessory drive belts.
6. Connect battery negative cable and refill the cooling system.

#### 6-173 Engine

1. Disconnect battery negative cable.
2. Drain cooling system and remove heater hose.
CAUTION: *When draining the coolant, keep*

in mind that cats and dogs are attracted by the ethylene glycol antifreeze, and are quite likely to drink any that is left in an uncovered container or in puddles on the ground. This will prove fatal in sufficient quantity. Always drain the coolant into a sealable container. Coolant should be reused unless it is contaminated or several years old.

3. Remove water pump attaching bolts and nut and remove pump.

4. With the sealant surfaces cleaned, place a 2mm ($^3/_{32}$") bead of sealant #1052357 or equivalent on the water pump sealing surface.

5. Clean old sealant from pump.

6. Coat bolt threads with pipe sealant #1052080 or equivalent.

7. Install pump and torque bolts to 10 ft.lb.

8. Connect battery negative battery cable.

NOTE: *When replacing the water pump on a car equipped with the V6 engine, the timing cover must be clamped to the cylinder block PRIOR TO removing the water pump bolts. Certain bolts holding the water pump pass through the front cover and when removed, may allow the front cover to pull away from the cylinder block, breaking the seal. This may or may not be readily apparent and if left undetected, could allow coolant to enter the crankcase. To prevent this possible separation during water pump removal, Special Tool #J29176 will have to be installed.*

### 6-183 and 6-231 Engine

1. Disconnect the negative battery cable and drain the coolant.

CAUTION: *When draining the coolant, keep in mind that cats and dogs are attracted by the ethylene glycol antifreeze, and are quite likely to drink any that is left in an uncovered container or in puddles on the ground. This will prove fatal in sufficient quantity. Always drain the coolant into a sealable container. Coolant should be reused unless it is contaminated or several years old.*

2. Remove accessory drive belts. Removed the radiator and the heater hoses from the water pump.

3. Remove water pump attaching bolts.

4. Remove the engine support strut.

5. Place a floor jack under the front crossmember of the cradle and raise the jack until the jack just starts to raise the car.

6. Remove the front two body mount bolts with the lower cushions and retainers.

7. Remove the cushions from the bolts.

8. Thread the body mount bolts with retainers a minimum of three (3) turns into the cage nuts so that the bolts restrain cradle movement.

9. Release the floor jack slowly until the

crossmember contacts the body mount bolts retainers. As the jack is being lowered watch and correct any interference with hoses, lines, pipes and cables.

NOTE: *Do not lower the cradle without its being restrained as possible damage can occur to the body and underhood items.*

10. Remove water pump from engine.

11. Reverse removal procedure.

12. Install pump and torque to 25 ft.lb.

13. Connect negative battery cable.

14. Fill with coolant and check for leaks.

### 6-263 Diesel Engine

1. Drain radiator. Remove the negative battery cable.

CAUTION: *When draining the coolant, keep in mind that cats and dogs are attracted by the ethylene glycol antifreeze, and are quite likely to drink any that is left in an uncovered container or in puddles on the ground. This will prove fatal in sufficient quantity. Always drain the coolant into a sealable container. Coolant should be reused unless it is contaminated or several years old.*

2. Disconnect lower radiator hose at water pump.

3. Disconnect the heater return hose at the water pump, remove the bolt retaining the heater water return pipe to the intake manifold and position the pipe out-of-the-way.

4. If equipped with AC, remove the vacuum pump drive belt.

5. Remove the serpentine drive belt.

6. Remove the generator, air conditioning compressor or vacuum pump brackets.

7. Remove the water pump attaching bolts and remove the water pump assembly.

8. Using tools J-29785 and J-29786, remove the water pump pulley.

9. Clean gasket material from engine block.

10. Apply a thin coat of 1050026 sealer or equivalent to the water pump housing to retain the gasket, then position new gasket on the housing. Also apply sealer to water pump mounting bolts. Torque bolts to 12-15 ft.lb.

## Cylinder Head
### REMOVAL AND INSTALLATION
#### 4-151 Engine

CAUTION: *On fuel injected engines, relieve the pressure in the fuel system before disconnecting any fuel line connections.*

NOTE: *The engine should be overnight cold.*

1. Drain the cooling system into a clean container.

CAUTION: *When draining the coolant, keep in mind that cats and dogs are attracted by the ethylene glycol antifreeze, and are quite*

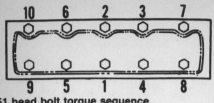

**4-151 head bolt torque sequence**

*likely to drink any that is left in an uncovered container or in puddles on the ground. This will prove fatal in sufficient quantity. Always drain the coolant into a sealable container. Coolant should be reused unless it is contaminated or several years old.*

2. Remove the air cleaner, the negative battery cable, the oil indicator tube, the ignition coil, the engine-to-upper strut rod bolt and the power steering pump bracket.

3. Remove the intake and exhaust manifolds as previously outlined.

4. Remove the alternator bracket bolts.

5. Remove the air conditioning compressor bracket bolts and position the compressor to one side. Do not disconnect any of the refrigerant lines.

6. Disconnect all vacuum and electrical connections from the cylinder head.

7. Disconnect the upper radiator hose.

8. Disconnect the spark plug wires and remove the plugs.

9. Remove the rocker arm cover, rocker arms, and pushrods.

10. Unbolt and remove the cylinder head.

11. Clean the gasket surfaces thoroughly.

12. Install a new gasket over the dowels and position the cylinder head.

13. Coat the head bolt threads with sealer and install finger tight.

14. Tighten the bolts in sequence, in three equal steps to the specified torque.

15. Install all parts in the reverse of removal.

### 6-173 Engine Left Side

1. Raise and support the car.

2. Drain the coolant from the block and lower the car.

CAUTION: *When draining the coolant, keep in mind that cats and dogs are attracted by the ethylene glycol antifreeze, and are quite likely to drink any that is left in an uncovered container or in puddles on the ground. This will prove fatal in sufficient quantity. Always drain the coolant into a sealable container. Coolant should be reused unless it is contaminated or several years old.*

3. Remove the intake manifold.

4. Remove the crossover.

5. Remove the alternator and AIR pump brackets.

6. Remove the dipstick tube.

7. Loosen the rocker arm bolts and remove the pushrods. Keep the pushrods in the same order as removed.

8. Remove the cylinder head bolts in stages and in the reverse order of the tightening sequence.

9. Remove the cylinder head. Do not pry on the head to loosen it.

10. Installation is the reverse of removal.

NOTE: *The words This Side Up on the new cylinder head gasket should face upward. Coat the cylinder head bolts with sealer and torque to specifications in the sequence shown. Make sure the pushrods seat in the lifter seats and adjust the valves.*

### 6-173 Engine Right Side

1. Raise the car and drain the coolant from the block.

CAUTION: *When draining the coolant, keep in mind that cats and dogs are attracted by the ethylene glycol antifreeze, and are quite likely to drink any that is left in an uncovered container or in puddles on the ground. This will prove fatal in sufficient quantity. Always drain the coolant into a sealable container. Coolant should be reused unless it is contaminated or several years old.*

2. Disconnect the exhaust pipe and lower the car.

3. If equipped, remove the cruise control servo bracket.

4. Remove the air management valve and hose.

5. Remove the intake manifold.

6. Remove the exhaust crossover.

7. Loosen the rocker arm nuts and remove the pushrods. Keep the pushrods in the order in which they were removed.

8. Remove the cylinder head bolts in stages and in the reverse order of the tightening sequence.

9. Remove the cylinder head. Do not pry on the cylinder head to loosen it.

NOTE: *The words This Side Up on the new cylinder head gasket should face upwards. Coat the cylinder head bolts with sealer and tighten them to specifications in the sequence shown. Make sure the lower ends of the push-*

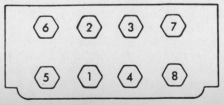

**6-173 head bolt torque sequence**

*rods seat in the lifter seats and adjust the valves.*

### 6-183 and 6-231 Engine

1. Disconnect negative battery cable.
2. Remove intake manifold.
3. Loosen the remove belt(s).
4. When removing LEFT cylinder head;
   a. Remove oil dipstick.
   b. Remove air and vacuum pumps with mounting bracket if present, and move out of the way with hoses attached.
5. When removing RIGHT cylinder head:
   a. Remove alternator.
   b. Disconnect power steering gear pump and brackets attached to cylinder head.
6. Disconnect wires from spark plugs, and remove the spark plug wire clips from the rocker arm cover studs.
7. Remove exhaust manifold bolts from head being removed.
8. With air hose and cloths, clean dirt off cylinder head and adjacent area to avoid getting dirt into engine. It is extremely important to avoid getting dirt into the hydraulic valve lifters.
9. Remove rocker arm cover and rocker arm and shaft assembly from cylinder head. Lift out pushrods.

NOTE: *If lifters are to be serviced, remove them at this time and place them in a container with numbered holes or a similar device, to keep them identified as to engine position. If they are not to be removed, protect lifters and camshaft from dirt by covering area with a clean cloth.*

10. Loosen all cylinder head bolts, then remove bolts and lift off the cylinder head.
11. With cylinder head on bench, remove all spark plugs for cleaning and to avoid damaging them during work on the head.
12. Installation is the reverse of removal. Clean all gasket surfaces thoroughly. Always use a new head gasket. The head gasket is installed with the bead downward. Coat the head bolt threads with heavy-bodied thread sealer. Torque the head bolts in three equal stages. Recheck head bolt torque after the engine has been warmed to operating temperature.

### 6-263 Diesel Engine

NOTE: *This procedure requires the complete disassembly of the valve lifters as explained under Diesel Engine Valve Lifter Bleed-Down.*

1. Remove intake manifold.
2. Remove valve cover. Loosen or remove any accessory brackets or pipe clamps which interfere.

NOTE: *If removing the left cylinder head, remove the oil level indicator guide.*

3. Disconnect glow plug wiring (and block heater lead if so equipped on rear bank).
4. Remove the ground strap from the rear cylinder head. Remove the fuel lines at the injector nozzles.
5. Remove rocker arm nuts, pivots, rocker arms and pushrods. Scribe pivots and keep rocker arms separated so they can be installed in their original locations.
6. Disconnect the exhaust crossover pipe from the exhaust manifold on the side being worked on and loosen it on the other.
7. Remove engine block drain plug, from side of the block where head is being removed.
8. Remove the pipe plugs covering the upper cylinder head bolts.
9. Remove all the cylinder head bolts and remove the cylinder head.
10. If necessary to remove the prechamber, remove the glow plug and injection nozzle, then tap out with a small blunt 1/8" drift. Do NOT use a tapered drift.
11. Installation is the reverse of removal. Do not use sealer on the head gasket. If a prechamber was replaced, measure the chamber height and grind the new one to within 0.001" of the old chamber's height, using #80 grit wet sandpaper to polish it. Coat the head bolts with sealer, preventing coolant leakage.
12. Torque the cylinder head bolts, except No. 5, 6, 11, 12, 13 and 14, to 100 ft.lb. (135 Nm.);

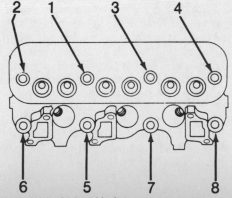

6-183 and 6-231 head bolt torque sequence

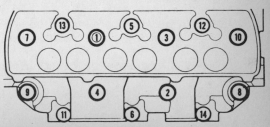

6-263 head bolt torque sequence

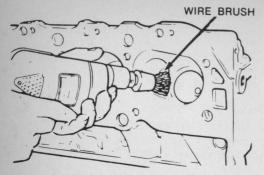

WIRE BRUSH

**Remove the carbon from the cylinder head with a wire brush and electric drill**

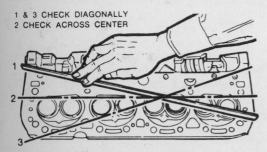

1 & 3 CHECK DIAGONALLY
2 CHECK ACROSS CENTER

**Check the cylinder head for warpage**

No. 5, 6, 11, 12, 13 and 14 bolts to 41 ft.lb. (55 Nm.). Retorque the cylinder head bolts, except No. 5, 6, 11, 12, 13 and 14, to 142 ft.lb. (193 Nm.); No. 5, 6, 11, 12, 13 and 14 bolts to 59 ft.lb. (80 Nm.).

### CLEANING AND INSPECTION

Chip carbon away from the valve heads, combustion chambers, and ports, using a chisel made of hardwood. Remove the remaining deposits with a stiff wire brush.

WARNING: *DO NOT use a steel wire brush to clean an aluminum cylinder head. Special brushes are sold just for use on aluminum.*

Be sure that the deposits are actually removed, rather than burnished. Have cylinder head hot-tanked to remove grease, corrosion, and scale from the water passages. Clean the remaining cylinder head parts in an engine cleaning solvent. Do not remove the protective coating from the springs.

### RESURFACING

NOTE: *All machine work should be performed by a competent, professional machine shop.*

Place a straightedge across the gasket surface of the cylinder head. Using feeler gauges, determine the clearance at the center of the straightedge. If warpage exceeds 0.003" in a 6" span, or 0.006" over the total length, the cylinder head must be resurfaced.

NOTE: *If warpage exceeds the manufacturer's maximum tolerance for material removal, the cylinder head must be replaced.*

When milling the cylinder heads of V-type engines, the intake manifold mounting position is latered, and must be corrected by milling the manifold flange a proportionate amount.

## Valves and Springs

### ADJUSTMENT

NOTE: *This procedure must be performed with the engine COLD.*

1. Remove the valve cover and the No. 1 spark plug.
2. Rotate the engine until the 0 degree mark on the crankshaft pulley aligns with the timing tab and the No. 1 cylinder is on the TDC of the compression stroke.
3. With the engine in this position, adjust the exhaust valves of No. 1, 2 and 3 and the intake valves of N. 1, 5 and 6. Back out the adjusting nut until lash is felt at the push rod, then turn the nut to remove the lash. With the lash removed, turn the nut an additional 1½ turns.
4. Rotate the engine 1 complete revolution until the 0 degree mark on the crankshaft pulley aligns with the timing tab and the No. 4 piston is on the TDC of the compression stroke.
5. With the engine in this position, adjust the exhaust valves of No. 2, 3 and 4; adjust the valves the same way as in Step No. 3.
6. Install the valve covers and the spark plug(s).

### REMOVAL AND INSPECTION

1. Remove the cylinder head(s) from the vehicle as previously outlined.
2. Using a suitable valve spring compressor, compress the valve spring and remove the valve keys using a magnetic retrieval tool.
3. Slowly release the compressor and remove the valve spring caps (or rotators) and the valve springs.
4. Fabricate a valve arrangement board to use when you remove the valves, which will indicate the port in which each valve was originally installed (and which cylinder head on V6 models). Also note that the valve keys, rotators, caps, etc. should be arranged in a manner which will allow you to reinstall them on the valve on which they were originally used.
5. Remove and discard the valve seals. On models using the umbrella type seals, note the location of the large and small seals for assembly purposes.
6. Thoroughly clean the valves on the wire wheel of a bench grinder, then clean the cylinder head mating surface with a) a soft wire

wheel, b) a soft wire brush, or c) a wooden scraper. Avoid using a metallic scraper, since this can cause damage to the cylinder head mating surface, especially on models with aluminum heads.

7. Using a valve guide cleaner chucked into a drill, clean all of the valve guides.

8. Reinstall each valve into its respective port (guide) of the cylinder head.

9. Mount a dial indicator so that the stem is at 90 degrees to the valve stem, as close to the valve guide as possible.

10. Move the valve off its seat, and measure the valve guide-to-stem clearance by rocking the stem back and forth to actuate the dial indicator.

11. Measure the valve stems using a micrometer, and compare to specifications, to determine whether stem or guide wear is responsible for excessive clearance.

NOTE: *Consult the Specifications tables earlier in this chapter.*

### REFACING

Using a valve grinder, resurface the valves according to specifications in this chapter. All machine work should be performed by a competent, professional machine shop.

NOTE: *Valve face angle is not always identical to valve seat angle.*

A minimum margin of $\frac{1}{32}''$ should remain after grinding the valve. The valve stem top should also be squared and resurfaced, by placing the stem in the V-block of the grinder, and turning it while pressing lightly against the grinding wheel. Be sure to chamfer the edge of the tip so that the squared edges don't dig into the rocker arm.

### LAPPING

This procedure should be performed after the valves and seats have been machined, to insure that each valve mates to each seat precisely.

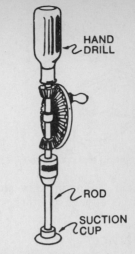

Home-made valve lapping tool

1. Invert the cylinder head, lightly lubricate the valve stems, and install the valves in the head as numbered.

2. Coat valve seats with fine grinding compound, and attach the lapping tool suction cup to a valve head.

NOTE: *Moisten the suction cup.*

3. Rotate the tool between the palms, changing position and lifting the tool often to prevent grooving.

4. Lap the valve until a smooth, polished seat is evident.

5. Remove the valve and tool, and rinse away all traces of grinding compound.

## Valve Spring Testing

Place the spring on a flat surface next to a square. Measure the height of the spring and rotate it against the edge of the square to measure distortion. If spring height varies (by comparison) by more than $\frac{1}{16}''$ or if distortion exceeds $\frac{1}{16}''$, replace the spring. In addition to evaluating the spring as above, test the spring pressure at the installed and compressed (installed height minus valve lift) height using a

Lapping the valves by hand

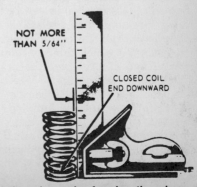

Check the valve spring free length and squareness

**Check the valve spring test pressure**

valve spring tester. Spring pressure should be ± 1 lb. of all other springs in either position.

## Valve Seat Service

The valve seats are integral with the cylinder head on all engines except the V6 diesel with aluminum cylinder heads. On all engines except that particular diesel, the seats are machined into the cylinder head casting itself. On the aluminum head diesel, the valve seats are separate inserts, which may be replaced by a competent machine shop if required. The reason for using inserts on this engine is basically because the aluminum could not withstand the constant pounding of the valves opening and closing as well as the hardened steel insert which is used.

Machining of the valve seats, or replacement of the seats in the case of the diesel, should be referred to a professional machine shop.

## Valve Guide Service

The valve guides used in any of the A-Body engines are integral with the cylinder head, that is, they cannot be replaced.

NOTE: *Refer to the previous Valves Removal and Installation to check the valve guides for wear.*

Valve guides are most accurately repaired using the bronze wall rebuilding method. In this operation, threads are cut into the bores of the valve guide and bronze wire is turned into the threads. The bronze wall is then reamed to the proper diameter. This method is well received for a number of reasons: a) it is relatively inexpensive, b) offers better valve lubrication (the wire forms channels which retain oil), c) less valve friction, and d) preserves the original valve guide-to-seat relationship.

Another popular method of repairing valve guides is to have the guides knurled. The knurling entails cutting action raises metal off of the guide bore which actually narrows the inner diameter of the bore, thereby reducing the clearance between the valve guide bore and the valve stem. This method offers the same advan-

tages as the bronze wall method, but will generally wear faster.

Another method of repairing the guides is to ream the bores and install oversize valves.

Either of the above services must be performed by a professional machine shop which has the specialized knowledge and tools necessary to perform the service.

## Valve and Spring Installation

NOTE: *Be sure that all traces of lapping compound have been cleaned off before the valves are installed.*

1. Lubricate all of the valve stems with a light coating of engine oil, then install the valves into the proper ports/guides.

2. If umbrella-type valve seals are used, install them at this time. Be sure to use a seal protector to prevent damage to the seals as they are pushed over the valve keeper grooves.

NOTE: *If O-ring seals are used, don't install them yet.*

3. Install the valve springs and the spring retainers (or rotators), and using the valve compressing tool, compress the springs.

4. If umbrella-type seals are used, just install the valve keepers (white grease may be used to hold them in place) and release the pressure on the compressing tool. If O-ring type seals are used, carefully work the seals into the second groove of the valve (closest to the head), install the valve keepers and release the pressure on the tool.

NOTE: *If the O-ring seals are installed BEFORE the springs and retainers are compressed, the seal will be destroyed.*

5. After all of the valves are installed and retained, tap each valve spring retainer with a rubber mallet to seat the keepers in the retainer.

## Oil Pan

### REMOVAL AND INSTALLATION

#### 4-151 Engine

1. Raise and support the car. Drain the oil.

2. Remove the engine cradle-to-front engine mounts.

3. Disconnect the exhaust pipe at both the exhaust manifold and at the front of the converter.

4. Disconnect and remove the starter. Remove the flywheel housing or torque converter cover.

5. Remove the alternator upper bracket. Remove the splash shield.

6. Install an engine lifting chain and raise the engine. If equipped, remove the power steering pump and bracket and move it aside.

7. Remove the lower alternator bracket. Remove the engine support bracket.

8. Remove the oil pan retaining bolts and remove the pan.

9. Reverse the procedure to install. Clean all gasket surfaces thoroughly. Install the rear oil pan gasket into the rear main bearing cap, then apply a thin bead of silicone sealer to the pan gasket depressions. Install the front pan gasket into the timing cover. Install the side gaskets onto the pan, not the block. They can be retained in place with grease. Apply a thin bead of silicone seal to the mating joints of the gaskets. Install the oil pan; install the timing gear bolts last, after the other bolts have been snugged down.

### 6-173 Engine

1. Disconnect the battery ground.
2. Raise and support the car on jackstands.
3. Drain the oil.
4. Remove the bellhousing cover.
5. Remove the starter.
6. Support the engine.
7. Unbolt the engine from its mounts.
8. Remove the oil pan bolts.

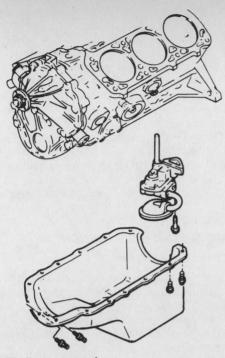

**6-173 oil pan removal**

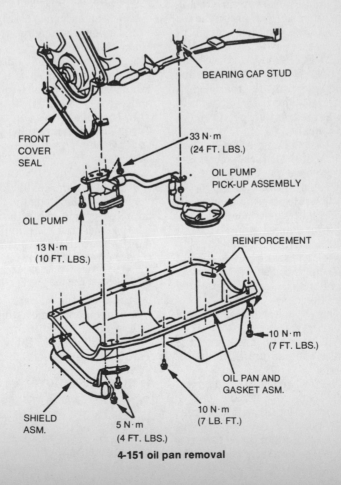

BEARING CAP STUD

FRONT COVER SEAL

33 N·m (24 FT. LBS.)

OIL PUMP PICK-UP ASSEMBLY

OIL PUMP

13 N·m (10 FT. LBS.)

REINFORCEMENT

10 N·m (7 FT. LBS.)

OIL PAN AND GASKET ASM.

SHIELD ASM.

5 N·m (4 FT. LBS.)

10 N·m (7 LB. FT.)

**4-151 oil pan removal**

9. Raise the engine with a jack, just enough to remove the oil pan.

10. Installation is the reverse of removal. The pan is installed using RTV gasket material in place of a gasket. Make sure that the sealing surfaces are free of old RTV material. Use a ⅛" bead of RTV material on the pan sealing flange. Torque the pan bolts to 8-10 ft.lb.

### 6-183 and 6-231 Engine

1. Disconnect the battery ground.
2. Raise and support the car on jackstands.
3. Drain the oil.
4. Remove the bellhousing cover.
5. Unbolt and remove the oil pan.
6. Installation is the reverse of removal.

RTV gasket material is used in place of a gasket. Make sure that the sealing surfaces are free of all old RTV material. Use a ⅛" bead of RTV material on the oil pan sealing flange. Torque the pan bolts to 10 ft.lb.

### 6-263 Diesel Engine

CAUTION: *The following procedure will be personally hazardous unless the procedures are followed exactly.*

1. Install the engine support fixture tool J-28467. Be certain to arrange washers on the fixture so that the bolt securing the chain to the cylinder head can be torqued to 20 ft.lb. THIS IS ABSOLUTELY NECESSARY!

2. Raise the front and rear of the car and support it on jackstands with the rear slightly lower than the front. The front jackstands should be located at the front lift points shown in your owner's manual.

3. Turn the intermediate steering shaft so that the steering gear stub shaft clamp bolt is in the UP position. Remove the clamp bolt and disconnect the two shafts. Drain the oil.

4. Remove the left side steering gear cradle bolt and loosen the right side cradle bolt.

5. Remove the front stabilizer bar.

6. Using a ½" drill bit, drill through the spot weld located between the rear holes at the left front stabilizer bar mounting.

7. Remove the nuts securing the engine and transaxle to its cradle.

8. Disconnect the left lower ball joint from the knuckle.

9. Place a wood block on a floor jack and raise the transaxle under the pan until the mount studs clear the cradle.

10. Remove the bolts securing the front crossmember to the right side of the cradle.

11. Remove the bolts from the left side front body mounts.

12. Remove the left side and front crossmember assemblies. It will be necessary to lower the rear crossmember below the left side of the

body through the careful use of a large pry bar.

13. Remove the bellhousing cover.
14. Remove the starter.
15. Remove the engine from mount bracket.
16. Unbolt and remove the oil pan.

17. Installation is the reverse of removal. Apply sealer to both sides of the oil pan gasket and make sure that the tabs on the gaskets are installed in the seal notches. Apply RTV sealer to the front cover oil pan seal retainer, and to each seal where it contacts the block. Wipe the seal area of the pan with clean engine oil before installing the pan. Torque the pan bolts to 10 ft.lb. and the steering clamp bolt to 40 ft.lb.

## Oil Pump
### REMOVAL AND INSTALLATION
#### 4-151 and 6-173 Engines

1. Remove the oil pan as described earlier.
2. Unbolt and remove the oil pump and pickup.

3. Installation is the reverse of removal. Torque the 4-151 pump to 22 ft.lb. and the 6-173 pump bolts to 26-35 ft.lb.

#### 6-183 and 6-231 Engines

1. Remove the oil filter.
2. Unbolt the oil pump cover from the timing chain cover.

3. Slide out the oil pump gears. Clean all parts thoroughly in solvent and check for wear. Remove the oil pressure relief valve cap, spring and valve.

4. Installation is the reverse of removal. Torque the pressure relief valve cap to 35 ft.lb. Install the pump gears and check their clearances:
- End clearance: 0.002-0.006"
- Side clearance: 0.002-0.005"

Place a straightedge across the face of the pump cover and check that it is flat to within 0.001". Pack the oil pump cavity with petroleum jelly so that there is no air space. Install the cover and torque the bolts to 10 ft.lb.

#### 6-263 Diesel Engine

1. Remove the oil pan.
2. Unbolt and remove the oil pump and drive extension.

3. Installation is the reverse of removal. Torque the pump bolts to 18 ft.lb.

## Timing Gear Cover
### REMOVAL AND INSTALLATION
#### 4-151 Engine

1. Remove the crankshaft hub. It is necessary to remove the inner fender splash shield.

2. Remove the alternator lower bracket.

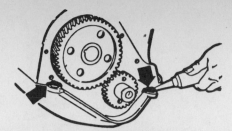

**Apply sealant where shown on the 4-151**

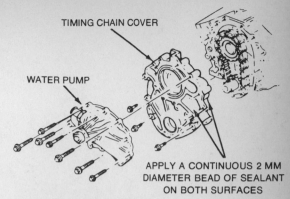

TIMING CHAIN COVER

WATER PUMP

APPLY A CONTINUOUS 2 MM
DIAMETER BEAD OF SEALANT
ON BOTH SURFACES

**6-173 timing cover removal**

3. Remove the front engine mounts.

4. Using a floor jack, raise the engine.

5. Remove the engine mount mounting bracket-to-cylinder block bolts. Remove the bracket and mount as an assembly.

6. Remove the oil pan-to-front cover screws.

7. Remove the front cover-to-block screws.

8. Pull the cover slightly forward, just enough to allow cutting of the oil pan front seal flush with the block on both sides.

9. Remove the front cover and attached portion of the pan seal.

10. Clean the gasket surfaces thoroughly.

11. Cut the tabs from the new oil pan front seal.

12. Install the seal on the front cover, pressing the tips into the holes provided. Install the centering tool J-23042 into the seal.

13. Coat the new gasket with sealer and position it on the front cover.

14. Apply a 1/8" bead of silicone sealer to the joint formed at the oil pan and block.

15. Align the front cover seal with a centering tool and install the front cover. Tighten the screws. Install the hub.

### 6-173 Engine

CAUTION: *The engines use a harmonic balancer. Breakage may occur as the balancer is hammered back onto the crankshaft. A press or special installation tool is necessary.*

1. Remove the negative battery cable, the drive belts, the inner splash shield, the damper retaining bolt and the water pump.

2. Remove the compressor without disconnecting any air conditioning lines and lay it aside. If equipped, remove the A.I.R. pump.

3. Remove harmonic balancer, using a puller tool J-23523.

NOTE: *The outer ring (weight) of the harmonic balancer is bonded to the hub with rubber. The balancer must be removed with a puller which acts on the inner hub only. Pulling on the outer portion of the balancer will break the rubber bond or destroy the tuning of the torsional damper.*

4. Disconnect the lower radiator hose and heater hose.

5. Remove timing gear cover attaching screws, cover and gasket.

6. Clean all the gasket mounting surfaces on the front cover and block. Apply a continuous 3/32" bead of sealer (1052357 or equivalent) to front cover sealing surface and around coolant passage ports and central bolt holes.

7. Apply a bead of silicone sealer to the oil pan-to-cylinder block joint.

8. Install a centering tool J-23042 in the crankshaft snout hole in the front cover and install the cover.

9. Install the front cover bolts finger tight, remove the centering tool and tighten and cover bolts. Install the harmonic balancer, pulley, water pump, belts, radiator, and all other parts.

### 6-183 and 6-231 Engine

1. Drain the cooling system.

CAUTION: *When draining the coolant, keep in mind that cats and dogs are attracted by the ethylene glycol antifreeze, and are quite likely to drink any that is left in an uncovered container or in puddles on the ground. This will prove fatal in sufficient quantity. Always drain the coolant into a sealable container. Coolant should be reused unless it is contaminated or several years old.*

2. Disconnect the radiator hoses and the heater hose at the water pump.

3. Remove the water pump pulley and all drive belts. Remove the front engine mount-to-cradle bolts and raise the engine.

4. Remove the alternator and brackets.

5. Remove the distributor. Remove the front and using a puller, remove the balancer.

6. Remove the balancer bolt and washer, and using a puller, remove the balancer.

7. Remove the cover-to-block bolts. Remove the two oil pan-to-cover bolts.

8. Remove the cover and gasket.

9. Installation is the reverse of removal. Always use a new gasket coated with sealer. Remove the oil pump cover and pack the area

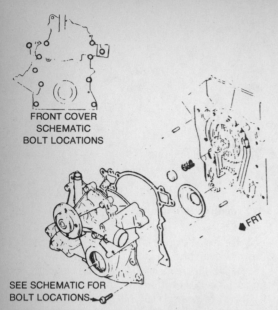

FRONT COVER
SCHEMATIC
BOLT LOCATIONS

SEE SCHEMATIC FOR
BOLT LOCATIONS

**6-183 and 6-231 timing cover removal**

**Installing an oil seal with the front cover removed—typical**

around the gears with petroleum jelly so that no air space is left within the pump. Apply sealer to the cover bolt threads.

### 6-263 Diesel Engine

1. Drain the cooling system.

CAUTION: *When draining the coolant, keep in mind that cats and dogs are attracted by the ethylene glycol antifreeze, and are quite likely to drink any that is left in an uncovered container or in puddles on the ground. This will prove fatal in sufficient quantity. Always drain the coolant into a sealable container. Coolant should be reused unless it is contaminated or several years old.*

2. Disconnect the radiator hoses and the heater hoses at the water pump. Disconnect the heater outlet pipe at the manifold.

3. Disconnect the power steering pump, vacuum pump, belt tensioner, air conditioning compressor and alternator brackets.

CAUTION: *Do not disconnect any refrigerant lines.*

4. Remove the crankshaft balancer using a puller.

5. Unbolt and remove the front cover and gasket.

6. Installation is the reverse of removal. Grind a chamfer on the end of each dowel pin to aid in cover installation. Trim ⅛″ from the ends of the new front pan seal. Apply RTV sealer to the oil pan seal retainer. After the cover gasket is in place, apply sealer to the junction of the pan, gasket and block. When installing the cover, rotate it right and left while guiding the pan seal into place with a small screwdriver.

## Oil Seal

### REMOVAL AND INSTALLATION

#### Cover Removed

*ALL ENGINES EXCEPT 6-183 AND 6-231*

1. After removing the timing cover, pry oil seal out of front of cover.

2. Install new lip seal with lip (open side of seal) inside and drive or press seal carefully into place.

#### 6-183 AND 6-231 ENGINE

1. Using a drift punch, drive the oil seal and the shedder from the front toward the rear of the timing cover.

2. To install the new oil seal, coil it around the opening with the ends toward the top. Using a punch, drive in the oil seal and stake it at three places. Rotate a hammer handle inside the seal until the crankshaft balancer can be inserted through the opening.

3. To complete the installation, reverse the removal procedures. Torque the balancer bolt to 225 ft.lb.

#### Cover Installed

*4-151 ENGINE*

The oil seal may be removed from the timing cover without removing the cover. To do this, remove the damper pulley and pry the oil seal from the timing cover, using a small pry bar.

Place a Seal Installation Tool J-34995 on the crankshaft (to prevent damaging the seal) when installing the new oil seal or the front cover. To install the new oil seal, place the seal's open end toward the inside of the cover and drive it into the cover. Torque the damper pulley bolt to 160 ft.lb.

*6-173 ENGINE*

The oil seal may be removed from the timing cover without removing the cover. To do this, remove the damper pulley and pry the oil seal from the timing cover, using a small pry bar.

To install the new oil seal, place the seal's open end toward the inside of the cover and drive it into the cover using tool J-23042. To install the damper pulley, lubricate the engine oil and use tool J-29113 to press it onto the crankshaft. Torque the damper pulley bolt to 67-85 ft.lb.

*6-263 ENGINE*

1. Refer to the Timing Cover, Removal and Installation procedures in the section and remove the crankshaft balancer from the crankshaft.

2. Using tools J-1859-03 and J-23129, press the oil seal from the timing cover.

3. Lubricate the seal lip with engine oil and the outer edge with sealant No. 1050026. Using tool J-29659, press the new oil seal into the timing cover until it seats.

4. To complete the installation, reverse the removal procedures. Torque the crankshaft balancer bolt to 203-350 ft.lb.

## Timing Gear and/or Chain
### REMOVAL AND INSTALLATION
#### 4-151 Engine

NOTE: *The timing gear is pressed onto the camshaft. To remove or install the timing gear an arbor must be used.*

1. Refer to the Camshaft, Removal and Installation procedures in this section and remove the camshaft from the engine.

2. Using an arbor press, a press plate and a gear removal tool J-971, press the timing from the camshaft.

NOTE: *When pressing the timing gear from the camshaft, be certain that the position of the press plate does not contact the woodruff key.*

3. To assemble, position the press plate to support the camshaft at the back of the front journal. Place the gear spacer ring and the thrust plate over the end of the camshaft, then install the woodruff key. Press the timing gear onto the camshaft, until it bottoms against the gear spacer ring.

NOTE: *The end clearance of the thrust plate should be 0.0015-0.005". If less than 0.0015", replace the spacer ring; if more than 0.005", replace the thrust plate.*

4. To complete the installation, align the marks on the timing gears and reverse the removal procedures.

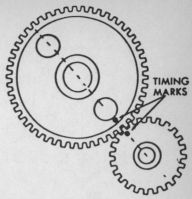

**4-151 timing gear alignment**

#### 6-173 Engine

1. Refer to the Timing Cover, Removal and Installation procedures in this section and remove the timing cover.

2. Turn the crankshaft to place the No. 1 cylinder on TDC and so that the camshaft sprocket the No. 4-cylinder TDC mark aligns with the crankshaft sprocket mark.

3. Remove the camshaft sprocket bolts, the sprocket and the timing chain.

NOTE: *If the camshaft sprocket does not come off easily, lightly strike the edge of it with a plastic hammer.*

4. To install, lubricate the timing chain, align the timing sprocket marks, the camshaft dowel pin with the sprocket and insert the bolts. Torque the camshaft sprocket bolts to 15-20 ft.lb.

5. To complete the installation, reverse the removal procedures.

#### 6-183 and 6-231 Engine

1. Remove the timing chain cover.

2. Turn the crankshaft so that the timing marks are aligned.

3. Remove the crankshaft oil slinger.

**6-173 timing chain and sprockets**

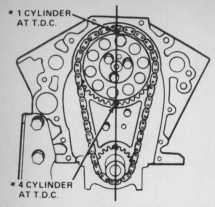

**6-173 timing gear alignment**

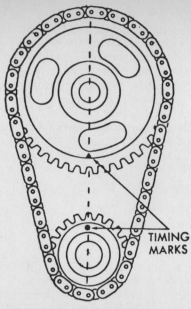

**6-183 and 6-231 timing gear alignment**

4. Remove the camshaft sprocket bolts.

5. Use two prybars to alternately pry the camshaft and crankshaft sprocket free along with the chain.

6. Installation is the reverse of removal. If the engine was turned, make sure that the #1 cylinder is at TDC.

### 6-263 Diesel Engine

NOTE: *The following procedure requires the bleed-down of the valve lifters. Read that procedure before proceeding.*

1. Remove the front cover.

2. Loosen all the rocker arms. See Rocker Arm Removal and Installation.

3. Remove the crankshaft oil slinger.

4. Remove the camshaft sprocket bolt.

5. Using two prybars, work the camshaft and crankshaft sprockets alternately off their shafts along with the chain. It may be necessary to remove the crankshaft sprocket with a puller.

6. Installation is the reverse of removal. If the engine was turned, make sure that the #1

piston is at TDC. Bleed the lifters following the procedure under Diesel Engine Valve Lifter Bleed-Down.

## Camshaft

### REMOVAL AND INSTALLATION

#### 4-151 Engine

CAUTION: *Relieve the pressure in the EFI system on fuel injected engines before disconnecting the fuel line connections.*

1. Remove the engine as previously outlined.

2. Remove the rocker cover, rocker arms, and pushrods.

3. Remove the distributor, spark plugs, and fuel pump.

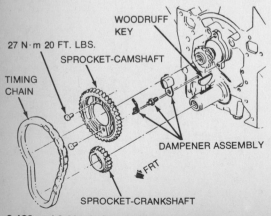

**6-183 and 6-231 timing chain and sprockets**

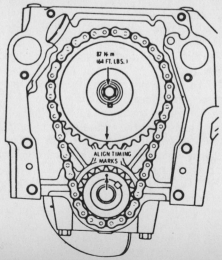

**6-263 timing gear alignment**

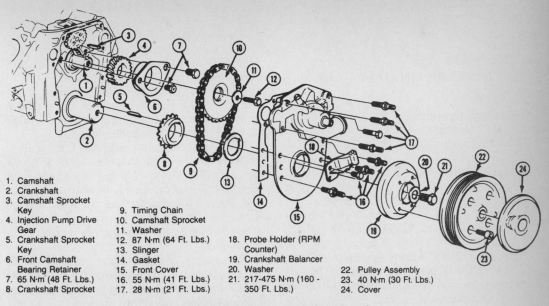

1. Camshaft
2. Crankshaft
3. Camshaft Sprocket
   Key
4. Injection Pump Drive
   Gear
5. Crankshaft Sprocket
   Key
6. Front Camshaft
   Bearing Retainer
7. 65 N·m (48 Ft. Lbs.)
8. Crankshaft Sprocket

9. Timing Chain
10. Camshaft Sprocket
11. Washer
12. 87 N·m (64 Ft. Lbs.)
13. Slinger
14. Gasket
15. Front Cover
16. 55 N·m (41 Ft. Lbs.)
17. 28 N·m (21 Ft. Lbs.)

18. Probe Holder (RPM
    Counter)
19. Crankshaft Balancer
20. Washer
21. 217-475 N·m (160 -
    350 Ft. Lbs.)

22. Pulley Assembly
23. 40 N·m (30 Ft. Lbs.)
24. Cover

**6-263 timing cover and chain removal**

4. Remove the pushrod cover and gasket. Remove the lifters.

5. Remove the alternator, the alternator lower bracket and the front engine mount bracket assembly.

6. Remove the oil pump driveshaft and gear assembly.

7. Remove the crankshaft hub and timing gear cover.

8. Remove the two camshaft thrust plate screws by working through the holes in the gear.

9. Remove the camshaft and gear assembly by pulling it through the front of the block. Take care not to damage the bearings.

10. Install in the reverse order. Torque the thrust plate screws to 75 in.lb.

### 6-173 Engine

Follow the 6-173 engine removal procedure then remove the camshaft as follows:

1. Remove intake manifold, valve lifters and timing chain cover as described in this section. If the car is equipped with air conditioning, unbolt the condenser and move it aside without disconnecting any lines.

2. Remove fuel pump and pump pushrod.

3. Remove camshaft sprocket bolts, sprocket and timing chain. A light blow to the lower edge of a tight sprocket should free it (use a plastic mallet.

4. Install two bolts in cam bolt holes and pull cam from block.

5. To install, reverse removal procedure aligning the sprocket timing marks.

### 6-183 Engine

1. Remove the engine as described earlier.

2. Remove the intake manifold.

3. Remove the rocker arm covers.

4. Remove the rocker arm assemblies, pushrods and lifters.

5. Remove the timing chain and camshaft sprocket as described earlier.

6. Installation is the reverse of removal.

### 6-263 and 6-231 Diesel Engine

NOTE: *This procedure requires the removal, disassembly, cleaning, reassembly and bleed-down of all the valve lifters. Read that procedure, described earlier, before proceeding.*

1. Remove the engine as described earlier.

2. Remove the intake manifold.

3. Remove the oil pump drive assembly.

4. Remove the timing chain cover.

5. Align the timing marks.

6. Remove the rocker arms, pushrods and lifters, keeping them in order for reassembly.

7. Remove the timing chain and camshaft lifters, keeping them in order for reassembly.

8. Remove the camshaft bearing retainer.

9. Remove the cam sprocket key.

10. Remove the injection pump drive gear.

11. Remove the injection pump driven gear, intermediate pump adapter and pump adapter. Remove the snapring and selective washer. Remove the driven gear and spring.

12. Carefully slide the camshaft out of the block.

13. If the camshaft bearings are being replaced, you'll have to remove the oil pan.

14. Installation is the reverse of removal. Perform the complete valve lifter bleed-down procedure mentioned earlier.

## Camshaft Bearings

### REMOVAL AND INSTALLATION

#### 4-151 Engine

1. Remove the engine from the vehicle as previously outlined.

2. Remove the camshaft from the engine as previously outlined.

3. Unbolt and remove the engine flywheel.

4. Drive the rear camshaft expansion plug out of the engine block from the inside.

5. Using a camshaft bearing service tool, J-21473-1 (1982-84) or J-33049 (1985-88 and later), drive the front camshaft bearing towards the rear and the rear bearing towards the front.

6. Install the appropriate extension tool J-21054-1 on the service tool and drive the center bearing out towards the rear.

7. Drive all of the new bearings into place in the opposite direction of which they were removed, making sure to align the oil holes of each bearing with each of the feed holes in the engine block bores.

NOTE: *The front camshaft bearing must be driven approximately 1/8" behind the front of the cylinder block to uncover the oil hole to the timing gear oiling nozzle.*

8. Install the camshaft into the engine then reinstall the engine as previously outlined.

#### 6-173 Engine

Camshaft bearings can be replaced with engine completely or partially disassembled. To replace bearings without complete disassembly remove the camshaft and crankshaft leaving cylinder heads attached and pistons in place. Before removing crankshaft, tape threads of connecting rod bolts to prevent damage to crankshaft. Fasten connecting rods against sides of engine so they will not be in the way while replacing camshaft bearings.

1. Remove the camshaft rear cover.

2. Using Tool J-6098 (1982-84) or J-33049 (1985-88 and later) or its equivalent, with nut and thrust washer installed to end of threads, index pilot in camshaft front bearing and install puller screw through pilot.

3. Install remover and installer tool with shoulder toward bearing, making sure a sufficient amount of threads are engaged.

4. Using two wrenches, hold puller screw while turning nut. When bearing has been pulled from bore, remove remover and installer tool and bearing from puller screws.

5. Remove remaining bearings (except front and rear) in the same manner. It will be necessary to index pilot in camshaft rear bearing to remove the rear intermediate bearing.

6. Assemble remover and installer tool on driver handle and remove camshaft front and rear bearings by driving towards center of cylinder block.

The camshaft front and rear bearings should be installed first. These bearings will act as guides for the pilot and center the remaining bearings being pulled into place.

1. Assemble remover and installer tool on driver handle and install camshaft front and rear bearings by driving towards center of cylinder block.

2. Using Tool Set J-6098 (1982-84) or J-33049 (1985-88), or its equivalent with nut then thrust washer installed to end of threads, index pilot in camshaft front bearing and install puller screw through pilot.

3. Index camshaft bearing in bore (with oil hole aligned as outlined below), then install remover and installer tool on puller screw with shoulder toward bearing.

• The rear and intermediate bearing oil holes must be aligned at 2:30 o'clock.

• The front bearing oil holes must be aligned at 1:00 and 2:30 o'clock (two holes).

4. Using two wrenches, hold puller screw while turning nut. After bearing has been pulled into bore, remove the remover and installer tool from puller screw and check alignment of oil hole in camshaft bearing.

5. Install remaining bearings in the same manner. It will be necessary to index pilot in the camshaft rear bearing to install the rear intermediate bearing. Clean the rear cover mating surfaces and bolt holes then apply a 1/8" bead of R.T.V. to the cover. Install the cover.

#### 6-183 and 6-231 Engine

Care must be exercised during bearing removal and installation, not to damage bearings that are not being replaced.

1. Remove camshaft as previously outlined.

2. Assemble puller screw to required length.

3. Select proper size expanding collet and back-up nut.

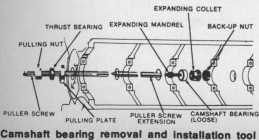

**Camshaft bearing removal and installation tool (OHV engines only)**

4. Install expanding collet on expanding mandrel. Install back-up nut.

5. Insert this assembly into camshaft bearing to be removed. Tighten back-up nut to expand collect to fit I.D. of bearing.

6. Thread end of puller screw assembly into end of expanding mandrel and collet assembly.

7. Install pulling plate, thrust bearing, and pulling nut on threaded end of puller screw.

8. Bearing can then be removed by turning pulling nut.

NOTE: *Make certain to grip the ⅝" hex end of the puller screw with a wrench to keep it from rotating when the pulling nut is turned. Failure to do this will result in the locking up of all threads in the pulling assembly and possible over expansion of the collet.*

9. Repeat the above procedure to remove any other bearings, except the front bearing, which may be pulled from the rear of the engine.

NOTE: *When removing rear cam bearing, it is necessary to remove welch plug at the back of cam bore. However, if only the front bearing is being replaced, it is not necessary to remove the engine or welch plug. The front bearing can be removed by using a spacer between the pulling plate and the cylinder block.*

## To install the bearings:

10. Assemble puller screw to required length.

11. Select proper size expanding collet and back-up nut.

12. Install expanding collet on expanding mandrel.

13. Install back-up nut.

14. Place new camshaft bearing on collet and GENTLY hand tighten back-up nut to expand collet to fit bearing. Do not over tighten back-up nut. A loose sliding fit between collet and bearing surface is adequate. This will provide just enough clearance to allow for the collapse which will occur when the new bearing is pulled into the engine block.

15. Slide mandrel assembly and bearing into bearing bore as far as it will go without force.

16. Thread end of puller screw onto the end of the mandrel. Make certain to align oil holes in bearing and block properly. One of the collet separation lines may be used as a reference point.

17. Install pulling plate, thrust bearing and pulling nut on threaded end of puller screw.

18. Install bearing in the same manner as described in Steps 8 and 9 under Bearing Removal.

NOTE: *When installing rear cam bearing, install new welch plug at back of cam bore. Coat O.D. of plug with non-hardening sealer before installation.*

## 6-263 Engine

The front camshaft bearing may be replaced separately but numbers 2, 3 and 4 must be replaced as a completed set. This is because it is necessary to remove the forward bearings to gain access to the rearward bearings.

Camshaft Bearing Remover and Installer Set BT-6409 and camshaft bearing pilot spacer BT-7817 are available tools. This set can be used to remove can bearings. To replace bearings with engine in car, proceed as follows:

NOTE: *The equivalents of special tools mentioned here may be used.*

1. Remove the camshaft as previously outlined.

2. Remove the rear camshaft plug:

    a. Drill a 12 mm or ½" hole in the center of the plug.

    b. Drive the plug inward carefully just enough to loosen it in the block.

    c. Place a punch or screwdriver in the drilled hole and remove the plug.

    d. Remove all the metal particles that entered the block and all traces of the old sealer.

NOTE: *Failure to remove the metal particles will result in engine damage.*

3. Front bearing removal and installation:

    a. To remove the front (No. 1) camshaft bearing, support the retainer in a vise and drive the bearing out using BT-6409-2 with driver BT-6409-7.

    b. To install the bearing use the same tools but make certain that the oil hole in the bearing is in alignment with the oil hole in the retainer.

4. #2, 3, & 4 bearing removal and installation:

    a. Install tool BT-6409-2 on handle BT-6409-7 and drive out No. 2 cam bearing.

    b. Remove the No. 3 bearing in the same manner using BT-6409-3 on handle BT-6409-7.

    c. Remove the No. 4 bearing using puller BT-6409-8.

To aid aligning the bearings with the oil passages, place each bearing in the front of the bore with tapered edge toward the block and align the oil hole in the bearing with the center of the oil slot in the bore. Mark bottom of bearing. When installing the bearings, the mark will act as a guide.

Using pilot BT-6409-1 will aid in installing the No. 4 and 3 bearings by preventing cocking of the bearings.

    d. Install No. 4 bearing using tool BT-6409-4.

NOTE: *Drive the bearing in carefully, stopping to make certain that the oil holes are in alignment otherwise it is possible to drive the bearing in beyond the oil passage opening.*

*Use a piece of $^3/_{32}$" brass rod with a 90 degree bend at the end to check the oil hole opening as shown in Figure 6A7-76.*

e. Install the No. 3 bearing using tool BT-6409-3 until the oil holes are in alignment.

f. Install the No. 2 bearing using tool BT-6409-2 carefully until the oil holes are in alignment.

g. Use a piece of $^3/_{32}$" brass rod with a 90 degree bend at the end to check all oil hole openings. Wire must enter hole or the bearing will not receive sufficient lubrication. (See Figure 6A7-76).

5. Install the rear plug:

a. Coat the block with R.T.V. sealer.

b. Drive the plug into the block until it is flush or no more than 0.5 mm (0.020") concave.

c. Install the camshaft and engine assembly. Road test the car and inspect for leaks.

### CHECKING CAMSHAFT

Degrease the camshaft, using solvent, and clean out all oil holes. Visually inspect cam lobes and bearing journals for excessive wear. If a lobe is questionable, check all lobes as indicated below. If a journal or lobe is worn, the camshaft must be reground or replaced.

NOTE: *If a journal is worn, there is a good chance that the bushings are worn. If lobes and journals appear intact, place the front and rear journals in V-blocks, and rest a dial indicator on the center journal. Rotate the camshaft to check straightness. If deviation exceeds 0.001", replace the camshaft.*

*Check the camshaft lobes with a micrometer, by measuring the lobes from the nose to base and again at 90 degrees (see illustration). The lift is determined by subtracting the second measurement from the first. If all exhaust lobes and all intake lobes are not identical, the camshaft must be reground or replaced.*

## Pistons and Connecting Rod Assemblies

### REMOVAL

1. Remove the engine assembly from the car, see Engine Removal and Installation.

2. Remove the intake manifold, cylinder head or heads.

3. Remove the oil pan.

4. Remove the oil pump assembly.

5. Stamp the cylinder number on the machined surfaces of the bolt bosses of the connecting rod and cap for identification when reinstalling. If the pistons are to be removed from the connecting rod, mark the cylinder number on the piston with a silver pencil or quick dry-ing paint for proper cylinder identification and cap to rod location. The 4-151 engine is numbered 1-4 from front to back; on the 183, 231 and diesel V6s, the right (rear) bank is numbered 2-4-6, left (front) bank 1-3-5; the V6-173 is numbered 1-3-5 on the right bank, 2-4-6 on the left bank.

6. Examine the cylinder bore above the ring travel. If a ridge exists, remove the ridge with a ridge reamer before attempting to remove the piston and rod assembly.

7. Remove the rod bearing cap and bearing.

8. Install a guide hose over threads of rod bolts. This is to prevent damage to bearing journal and rod bolt threads.

9. Remove the rod and piston assembly through the top of the cylinder bore.

10. Remove any other rod and piston assemblies in the same manner.

### CLEANING AND INSPECTION

#### Pistons

Clean varnish from piston skirts and pins with a cleaning solvent. DO NOT WIRE BRUSH ANY PART OF THE PISTON. Clean the ring grooves with a groove cleaner and make sure oil ring holes and slots are clean.

Inspect the piston for cracked ring lands, skirts or pin bosses, wavy or worn ring lands, scuffed or damaged skirts, eroded areas at top of the piston. Replace pistons that are damaged or show signs of excessive wear.

Inspect the grooves for nicks or burrs that might cause the rings to hang up.

Measure piston skirt (across center line of piston pin) and check piston clearance.

#### Connecting Rods

Wash connecting rods in cleaning solvent and dry with compressed air. Check for twisted or bent rods and inspect for nicks or cracks. Replace connecting rods that are damaged.

### PISTON PIN REPLACEMENT

#### Gasoline Engines

Use care at all times when handling and servicing connecting rods and pistons To prevent possible damage to these units, do not clamp rod or piston is vise since they may become distorted. Do not allow pistons to strike against one another, against hard objects or bench surfaces, since distortion of piston contour or nicks in the soft aluminum material may result.

1. Remove piston rings using suitable piston ring remover.

2. Install guide bushing of piston pin removing and installing tool.

3. Install piston and connecting rod assembly on support and place assembly in an arbor

press. Press pin out of connecting rod, using the appropriate piston pin tool.

### Diesel Engines

The piston pin is a free floating piston pin and the correct piston pin fit in the piston is 0.0076-0.0127mm (0.0003-0.0005″) and rod is 0.0076-0.033 mm (0.003-0.0013″) loose. If the pin to piston clearance is to the high limit 0.0127-0.033mm (0.005″ piston or 0.0013″ rod), the pin can be inserted in the piston or rod with very little hand pressure and will fall through the piston or rod by its own weight. If the clearance is 0.0076mm (0.0003″), the pin will not fall through. It is important that the piston and rod pin hole be clean and free of oil when checking pin fit.

The rod may be installed in the piston with either side facing up. Whenever the replacement of a piston pin is necessary, remove the snapring retaining the pin. Then remove pin.

It is very important that after installing the piston pin retaining snaprings that the rings be rotated to make sure they are fully seated in their grooves. The snapring must be installed with the flat side out.

### POSITIONING

NOTE: *Most pistons are notched or marked to indicate which way they should be installed. If your pistons are not marked, mark them before removal. Then reinstall them in the proper position.*

### MEASURING THE OLD PISTONS

Check used piston to cylinder bore clearance as follows:

1. Measure the cylinder bore diameter with a telescope gage.
2. Measure the piston diameter. When measuring piston for size or taper, measurement must be made with the piston pin removed.
3. Subtract piston diameter from cylinder bore diameter to determine piston-to-bore clearance.
4. Compare piston-to-bore clearance obtained with those clearances recommended. Determine is piston-to-bore clearance is in acceptable range.
5. When measuring taper, the largest reading must be at the bottom of the skirt.

### SELECTING NEW PISTONS

1. If the used piston is not acceptable, check service piston sizes and determine if a new piston can be selected. Service pistons are available in standard, high limit and standard 0.254mm (0.010″) oversize.
2. Occasionally during the honing operation, the cylinder bore should be thoroughly cleaned

and the selected piston checked for correct fit.

3. When finish honing a cylinder bore, the hone should be moved up and down at a sufficient speed to obtain very fine uniform surface finish marks in a cross hatch pattern of approximately 45 to 65 degrees included angle. The finish marks should be clean but not sharp, free from imbedded particles and torn or folded metal.

4. Permanently mark the piston for the cylinder to which it has been fitted and proceed to hone the remaining cylinders.

NOTE: *Handle pistons with care. Do not attempt to force pistons through cylinders through cylinders until the cylinders have been honed to correct size. Pistons can be distorted through careless handling.*

5. Thoroughly clean the bores with hot water and detergent. Scrub well with a stiff bristle brush and rinse thoroughly with hot water. It is extremely essential that a good cleaning operation be performed. If any of the abrasive material is allowed to remain in the cylinder bores, it will rapidly wear the new rings and cylinder bores. The bores should be swabbed several times with light engine oil and a clean cloth and then wiped with a clean dry cloth. CYLINDERS SHOULD NOT BE CLEANED WITH KEROSENE OR GASOLINE. Clean the remainder of the cylinder block to remove the excess material spread during the honing operation.

### CHECKING CYLINDER BORE

Cylinder bore size can be measured with inside micrometers or a cylinder gage. The most wear will occur at the top of the ring travel.

Reconditioned cylinder bores should be held to not more than 0.025mm (0.001″) out-of-round and 0.025mm (0.001″) taper.

If the cylinder bores are smooth, the cylinder walls should not be deglazed. If the cylinder walls are scored, the walls may have to be honed before installing new rings. It is important that reconditioned cylinder bores be thoroughly washed with a soap and water solution to remove all traces of abrasive material to eliminate premature wear.

### PISTON RING REPLACEMENT

Using a ring expander, remove the rings from the piston.

Clean the ring grooves using an appropriate tool, exercising care to avoid cutting too deeply. Thoroughly clean all carbon and varnish from the piston with solvent.

WARNING: *Do not use a wire brush or caustic solvent on pistons.*

Inspect the pistons for scuffing, scoring, cracks, pitting, or excessive ring groove wear. If wear is evident, the piston must be replaced.

**Fitting**

1. Slip the compression ring in the cylinder bore. Be sure the ring is square with the cylinder wall.

2. Measure the space between the ends of the ring with a feeler gauge.

3. If the gap between the ends of the ring is below specifications, remove the ring and try another for fit.

4. Fit each compression ring to the cylinder in which it is to be used.

5. If the pistons have not been cleaned, do so prior to installing them.

6. Slip the outer surface of the top and second compression ring into the respective ring groove and roll the ring around the groove. If binding is caused by a distorted ring, check another ring.

### INSTALLATION

1. Install oil ring spacer in the groove being sure the ends are butted and not overlapped.

2. Hold the spacer ends butted and install lower steel oil ring rail.

3. Install upper steel oil ring rail with the gap staggered.

4. Flex the oil ring to make sure it is free. If binding occurs, determine the cause.

5. Install the second compression ring. Stagger the gap.

6. Install the top compression ring. Stagger the gap.

NOTE: *In order to install the piston and rings, you will need a ring compressor. This tool squeezes the rings thereby allowing them to fit into the cylinder bore.*

## Connecting Rod Bearings

If you have already removed the connecting rod and piston assemblies from the engine, follow only steps 3-7 of the following procedure.

### REMOVAL, INSPECTION, INSTALLATION

The connecting rod bearings are designed to have a slight projection above the rod and cap faces to insure a positive contact. The bearings can be replaced without removing the rod and piston assembly from the engine.

1. Remove the oil pan, see Oil Pan. It may be necessary to remove the oil pump to provide access to rear connecting rod bearings.

2. With the connecting rod journal at the bottom, stamp the cylinder number on the machined surfaces of connecting rod and cap for identification when reinstalling, then remove caps.

3. Inspect journals for roughness and wear. Slight roughness may be removed with a fine grit polishing cloth saturated with engine oil.

Burrs may be removed with a fine oil stone by moving the stone on the journal circumference. Do not move the stone back and forth across the journal. If the journals are scored or ridged, the crankshaft must be replaced.

4. The connecting rod journals should be checked for out-of-round and correct size with a micrometer.

NOTE: *Cranshaft rod journals will normally be standard size. If any undersized crankshafts are used, all will be 0.254mm undersize and 0.254mm will be stamped the number 4 counterweight.*

If plastic gaging material is to be used:

5. Clean oil from the journal bearing cap, connecting rod and outer and inner surface of the bearing inserts. Position insert so that tang is properly aligned with notch in rod and cap.

6. Place a piece of plastic gaging material in the center of lower bearing shell.

7. Remove bearing cap and determine bearing clearances by comparing the width of the flattened plastic gaging material at its widest point with the graduation on the container. The number within the graduation on the envelopes indicates the clearance in thousandths of an inch or millimeters. If this clearance is excessive, replace the bearing and recheck clearance with plastic gaging material. Lubricate bearing with engine oil before installation. Repeat Steps 2 through 7 on remaining connecting rod bearings. All rods must be connected to their journals when rotating the crankshaft to prevent engine damage.

## Piston and Connecting Rod Assembly

### INSTALLATION

1. Install connecting rod bolt guide hose over rod bolt threads.

2. Apply engine oil to the rings and piston, then install piston ring compressing tool on the piston.

3. Install the assembly in its respective cylinder bore.

4. Lubricate the crankshaft journal with engine oil and install connecting rod bearing and cap, with bearing index tang in rod and cap on same side.

NOTE: *When more than one rod and piston assembly is being installed, the connecting rod cap attaching nuts should only be tightened enough to keep each rod in position until all have been installed. This will aid installation of remaining piston assemblies.*

5. Torque rod bolt nuts to specification.

6. Install all other removed parts.

7. Install the engine in the car, see Engine Removal and Installation.

# Rear Main Oil Seal

## REMOVAL AND INSTALLATION

### 4-151 Engine

1. Remove the transaxle and flywheel.
2. Being careful not to scratch the crankshaft, pry out the old seal with a screwdriver.
3. Coat the new seal with clean engine oil, and install it by hand onto the crankshaft. The seal backing must be flush with the block opening, use tool J-34924 to drive the new seal into the block.
4. Install all other parts in reverse of removal.

### 6-173 Engine

#### THIN SEAL

1. Remove the oil pan and pump.
2. Remove the rear main bearing cap.
3. Gently pack the upper seal into the groove approximately ¼″ on each side.
4. Measure the amount the seal was driven in on one side and add $\frac{1}{16}$″. Cut this length from the old lower cap seal. Be sure to get a sharp cut. Repeat for the other side.
5. Place the piece of cut seal into the groove and pack the seal into the block. Do this for each side.
NOTE: *G.M. makes a guide tool (J-29114-1) which bolts to the block via an oil pan bolt hole, and a packing tool (J-29114-2) which are machined to provide a built-in stop for the installation of the short cut pieces. Using the packing tool, work the short pieces of seal onto the guide tool, then pack them into the block with the packing tool.*
6. Install a new lower seal in the rear main cap.
7. Install a piece of Plastigage® or the equivalent on the bearing journal. Install the rear cap and tighten to 70 ft.lb. Remove the cap and check the gauge for bearing clearance. If out of specification, the ends of the seal may be frayed or not flush, preventing the cap from proper sealing. Correct as required.

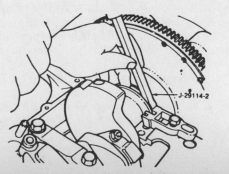

**Installing the upper rear main seal on 6-173 engines**

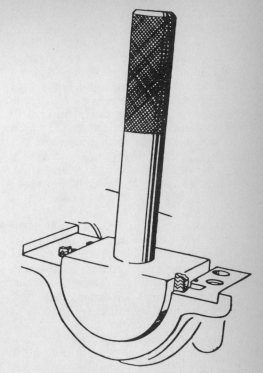

AFTER CORRECTLY POSITIONING SEAL, ROTATE TOOL SLIGHTLY AND CUT OFF EACH END OF SEAL FLUSH WITH BLOCK

**Installing the lower seal half**

8. Clean the journal, and apply a thin film of sealer to the mating surfaces of the cap and block. Do not allow any sealer to get onto the journal or bearing. Install the bearing cap and tighten to 70 ft.lb. Install the pan and pump.

#### THICK SEAL

1. Remove the transaxle and the flexplate.
2. Using a small pry bar, pry the seal from the block.
CAUTION: *Be careful not to damage the crankshaft surface when removing the oil seal.*
3. Clean and inspect the seal mounting surface for nicks and burrs.
4. Coat the new seal with engine oil. Using tool J-34686, press the seal into the block, until it seats.
5. To complete the installation, reverse the removal procedures. Start the engine and check for leaks.

### 6-183, 6-231 and 6-263 Engines

#### LOWER OIL SEAL REPAIR

Braided fabric seals are pressed into grooves formed in crankcase and rear bearing cap to rear of the oil collecting groove, to seal against leakage of oil around the crankshaft.

A new braided fabric seal can be installed in crankcase only when crankshaft is removed, but it can be repaired while crankshaft is installed, as outlined under Rear Main Bearing Upper Oil Seal Repair. The seal can be replaced in cap whenever the cap is removed. Remove old seal and place new seal in groove with both ends projecting surface of cap. Force seal into groove rubbing down with hammer handle or smooth stick until seal projects above the groove not more than $1/16$". Cut ends off flush with surface of cap, using sharp knife or razor blade.

The engine must be operated at slow speed when first started after a new braided seal is installed.

Neoprene composition seals are placed in grooves in the sides of bearing cap to seal against leakage in the joints between cap and crankcase. The neoprene composition swells in the presence of oil and heat. The seals are undersize when newly installed and may even leak for a short time until the seals have had time to swell and seal the opening.

The neoprene seals are slightly longer than the grooves in the bearing cap. The seals must not be cut to length. Before installation of seals, soak for 1 to 2 minutes in light oil or kerosene. After installation of bearing cap in crankcase, install seal in bearing cap.

To help eliminate oil leakage at the joint where the cap meets the crankcase, apply silastic sealer, or equivalent, to the rear main bearing cap split line. When applying sealer, use only a thin coat as an over abundance will not allow the cap to seat properly.

After seal is installed, force seals up into the cap with a blunt instrument to be sure of a seal at the upper parting line between the cap and case.

### REAR MAIN BEARING UPPER OIL SEAL REPAIR

1. Remove oil pan.
2. Insert packing tool (J-21526-2) against one end of the seal in the cylinder block. Drive the old seal gently into the groove until it is packed tight. This varies from ¼" to ¾" depending on the amount of pack required.
3. Repeat Step 2 on the other end of the seal in the cylinder block.
4. Measure the amount the seal was driven up on one side and add $1/16$". Using a single edge razor blade, cut that length from the old seal removed from the rear main bearing cap. Repeat the procedure for the other side. Use the rear main bearing cap as a holding fixture when cutting the seal.
5. Install Guide Tool (J-21526-1) onto cylinder block.
6. Using packing tool, work the short pieces

cut in Step 4 into the guide tool and then pack into cylinder block. The guide tool and packing tool have been machined to provide a built-in stop. Use this procedure for both sides. It may help to use oil on the short pieces of the rope seal when packing into the cylinder block.

7. Remove the guide tool.
8. Install a new fabric seal in the rear main bearing cap. Install cap and torque to specifications.
9. Install oil pan.

## Crankshaft

### REMOVAL

1. Remove the engine assembly as previously outlined.
2. Remove the engine front cover.
3. Remove the timing chain and sprockets or gears.
4. Remove the oil pan.
5. Remove the oil pump.
6. Stamp the cylinder number on the machined surfaces of the bolt bosses of the connecting rods and caps for identification when reinstalling. If the pistons are to be removed from the connecting rod, mark cylinder number on piston with a silver pencil or quick drying paint for proper cylinder identification and cap to rod location.
7. Remove the connecting rod caps and install thread protectors.
8. Mark the main bearing caps so that they can be reinstalled in their original positions.
9. Remove all the main bearing caps.
10. Note position of keyway in crankshaft so it can be installed in the same position.
11. Lift crankshaft out of block. Rods will pivot to the center of the engine when the crankshaft is removed.
12. Remove both halves of the rear main oil seal.

### INSTALLATION

1. Measure the crankshaft journals with a micrometer to determine the correct size rod and main bearings to be used. Whenever a new or reconditioned crankshaft is installed, new connect rod bearings and main bearings should be installed. See Main Bearings and Rod Bearings.
2. Clean all oil passages in the block (and crankshaft if it is being reused.

NOTE: *A new rear main seal should be installed anytime the crankshaft is removed or replaced.*

3. Install sufficient oil pan bolts in the block to align with the connecting rod bolts. Use rubber bands between the bolts to position the connecting rods as required. Connecting rod posi-

tion can be adjusted by increasing the tension on the rubber bands with additional turns around the pan bolts or thread protectors.

4. Position the upper half of main bearings in the block and lubricate with engine oil.

5. Position crankshaft keyway in the same position as removed and lower into block. The connecting rods will follow the crank pins into the correct position as the crankshaft is lowered.

6. Lubricate the thrust flanges with 1050169 Lubricant or equivalent. Install caps with lower half of bearings lubricated with engine oil. Lubricate cap bolts with engine oil and install, but do not tighten.

7. With a block of wood, bump shaft in each direction to align thrust flanges of main bearing. After bumping shaft in each direction, wedge the shaft to the front and hold it while torquing the thrust bearing cap bolts.

NOTE: *In order to prevent the possibility of cylinder block and/or main bearing cap damage, the main bearing caps are to be tapped into their cylinder block cavity using a brass or leather mallet before attaching bolts are installed. Do not use attaching bolts to pull main bearing caps into their seat. Failure to observe this information may damage the cylinder block or a bearing cap.*

8. Torque all main bearing caps to specification.

9. Remove the connecting rod bolt thread protectors and lubricate the connecting rod bearings with engine oil.

10. Install the connecting rod bearing caps in their original position. Torque the nuts to specification.

11. Complete the installation by reversing the removal steps.

## Main Bearings

### CHECKING BEARING CLEARANCE

1. Remove bearing cap and wipe oil from crankshaft journal and outer and inner surfaces of bearing shell.

2. Place a piece of plastic gaging material in the center of bearing.

3. Use a floor jack or other means to hold crankshaft against upper bearing shell. This is necessary to obtain accurate clearance readings when using plastic gaging material.

4. Reinstall bearing cap and bearing. Place engine oil on cap bolts and install Torque bolts to specification.

5. Remove bearing cap and determine bearing clearance by comparing the width of the flattened plastic gaging material at its widest point with graduations on the gaging material container. The number within the graduation

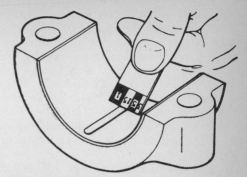

**Measure Plastigage® to determine main bearing clearance**

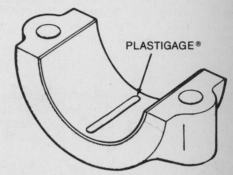

**Plastigage® installed on the lower bearing shell**

on the envelope indicates the clearance in millimeters or thousandths of an inch. If the clearance is greater than allowed, REPLACE BOTH BEARING SHELLS AS A SET. Recheck clearance after replacing shells. (Refer to Main Bearing Replacement).

### REPLACEMENT

Main bearing clearances must be corrected by the use of selective upper and lower shells. UNDER NO CIRCUMSTANCES should the use of shims behind the shells to compensate for wear be attempted. To install main bearing shells, proceed as follows:

1. Remove the oil pan as outlined elsewhere in this Chapter. On some models, the oil pump may also have to be removed.

2. Loosen all main bearing caps.

3. Remove bearing cap and remove lower shell.

4. Insert a flattened cotter pin or roll out pin in the oil passage hole in the crankshaft in the direction opposite to cranking rotation. The pin will contact the upper shell and roll it out.

5. The main bearing journals should be checked for roughness and wear. Slight roughness may be removed with a fine grit polishing cloth saturated with engine oil. Burrs may be removed with a fine oil stone. If the journals are scored or ridged, the crankshaft must be replaced.

NOTE: *The journals can be measured for out-of-round with the crankshaft installed by using a crankshaft caliper and inside micrometer or a main bearing micrometer. The upper bearing shell must be removed when measuring the crankshaft journals. Maximum out-of-round of the crankshaft journals must not exceed 0.037mm (0.0015").*

6. Clean crankshaft journals and bearing caps thoroughly before installing new main bearings.

7. Apply special lubricant, No. 1050169 to the thrust flanges of bearing shells.

8. Place new upper shell on crankshaft journal with locating tang incorrect position and rotate shaft to turn it into place using cotter pin or roll out pin as during removal.

9. Place new bearing shell in bearing cap.

10. Install a new oil seal in the rear main bearing cap and block.

11. Lubricate the removed or replaced main bearings with engine oil. Lubricate the thrust surface with lubricant 1050169 or equivalent.

12. Lubricate the main bearing cap bolts with engine oil.

NOTE: *In order to prevent the possibility of cylinder block and/or main bearing cap damage, the main bearing caps are to be tapped into their cylinder block cavity using a brass or leather mallet before attaching bolts are installed. Do not use attaching bolts to pull main bearing caps into their seats. Failure to observe this information may damage the cylinder block or a bearing cap.*

13. Torque the main bearing cap bolts.

## Flywheel and Ring Gear
### REMOVAL AND INSTALLATION

The ring gear is an integral part of the flywheel and is not replaceable.

1. Remove the transmission.

2. Remove the six bolts attaching the flywheel to the crankshaft flange. Remove the flywheel.

3. Inspect the flywheel for cracks, and inspect the ring gear for burrs or worn teeth. Replace the flywheel if any damage is apparent. Remove burrs with a mill file.

4. Install the flywheel. The flywheel will only attach to the crankshaft in one position, as the bolt holes are unevenly spaced. Install the bolts and torque to specification.

## EXHAUST SYSTEM

Whenever working on the exhaust system please observe the following:

1. Check the complete exhaust system for open seams, holes loose connections, or other deterioration which could permit exhaust fumes to seep into the passenger compartment.

2. The exhaust system is supported by free-hanging rubber mountings which permit some movement of the exhaust system, but do not permit transfer of noise and vibration into the passenger compartment.

3. Before removing any component of the exhaust system, ALWAYS squirt a liquid rust dissolving agent onto the fasteners for ease of removal.

4. Annoying rattles and noise vibrations in the exhaust system are usually caused by misalignment of the parts. When aligning the system, leave all bolts and nuts loose until all parts are properly aligned, then tighten, working from front to rear.

5. When replacing a muffler and/or resonator, the tailpipe(s) should also be replaced.

6. When installing exhaust system parts, make sure there is enough clearance between the hot exhaust parts, and pipes and hoses that would be adversely affected by excessive heat. Also make sure there is adequate clearance from the floor pan to avoid possible overheating of the floor.

7. Exhaust pipe sealers should be used at all slip joint connections except at the catalytic convertor. Do not use any sealers at the convertor as the sealer will not withstand convertor temperatures.

## Front Pipe
### REMOVAL AND INSTALLATION

1. Raise and support the front of the vehicle on jackstands.

2. Remove the exhaust pipe-to-manifold nuts.

3. Support the catalytic converter and disconnect the pipe from the converter. Remove the pipe.

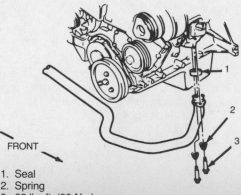

FRONT

1. Seal
2. Spring
3. 22 lbs.ft. (30 Nm)

**Exhaust manifold attachment 2.5L engine**

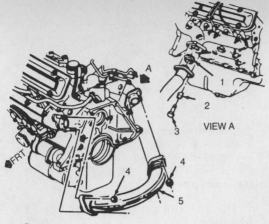

1. Seal
2. Spring
3. 22 lbs.ft. (30 Nm)
4. 18 lbs.ft. (24 Nm)
5. Cross over

**Exhaust manifold attachment 2.8L engine**

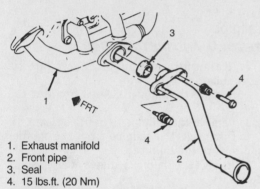

1. Exhaust manifold
2. Front pipe
3. Seal
4. 15 lbs.ft. (20 Nm)

**Exhaust manifold attachment 3.8L engine**

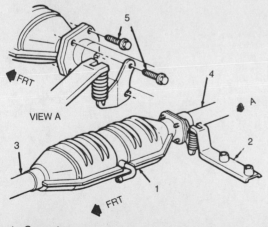

1. Converter
2. Hanger
3. Front exhaust pipe
4. Intermediate pipe
5. 35 lbs.ft. (48 Nm)

**Catalytic converter attachment all models**

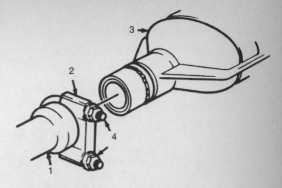

1. Replacement pipe
2. Guillotine clamp
3. Existing converter
4. 26 lbs.ft. (35 Nm)

**Intermediate pipe installation**

4. To install, use a new gasket, add sealer to the connecting surfaces, assembly the system, check the clearance and tighten the connectors.

## Intermediate Pipe

The intermediate pipe is the section between the catalytic converter and the muffler.

### REMOVAL AND INSTALLATION

1. Raise and support the front of the vehicle.
2. Disconnect the intermediate pipe from the catalytic converter.
3. At the muffler, remove the clamp and the intermediate pipe.
4. To install, use a new clamp and nuts/bolts, assembly the system, check the clearances and tighten the connectors.

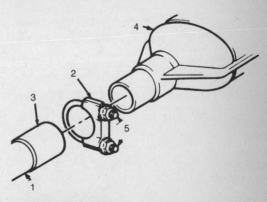

1. Replacement pipe
2. Guillotine type clamp
3. Sleeve
4. Replacement converter
5. 26 lbs.ft. (35 Nm)

**Replacement converter installation**

## Catalytic Converter

### REMOVAL AND INSTALLATION

1. Raise and support the front of the vehicle on jackstands and place a support under the catalytic converter.

2. Remove the clamp at the front of the converter, then cut the pipe at the front of the converter.

3. Remove the converter-to-intermediate pipe nuts/bolts.

4. Disconnect the converter-to-crossover pipe or front pipe.

6. To install, add sealer to the connecting surfaces, use new clamps and nuts/bolts, assemble the system, check the clearances and tighten all of the attachments.

## Muffler

The exhaust system pipes rearward of the mufflers, MUST BE replaced whenever a new muffler is installed.

### REMOVAL AND INSTALLATION

1. Raise and support the vehicle on jackstands.

2. On the single pipe system, cut the exhaust pipe near the front of the muffler. ON the dual pipe system, remove the U-bolt clamp at the front of the muffler and disengage the muffler from the exhaust pipe.

NOTE: *Before cutting the exhaust pipe, measure the service muffler exhaust pipe extension and make certain to allow 1½" for the exhaust pipe-to-muffler extension engagement.*

3. At the rear of the muffler, remove the U-bolt clamp and disengage the muffler from the tailpipe.

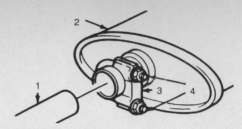

1. Existing intermediate pipe
2. Replacement muffler
3. Saddle/U bolt clamp
4. 22 lbs.ft. (30 Nm)

**Muffler installation**

4. Remove the tailpipe clamps and the tailpipe.

5. Inspect the muffler and the tailpipe hangers; replace if necessary.

6. To install, add sealer to the connecting surfaces, assemble the system, check the clearances and tighten all of the attachments.

## Tailpipe

### REMOVAL AND INSTALLATION

1. Raise and support the vehicle on jackstands.

2. Remove the hanger clamps from the tail pipe.

3. Remove the tailpipe-to-muffler clamp.

4. Disengage the tailpipe from the muffler and remove the tailpipe.

5. Inspect the tailpipe hangers and replace, if necessary.

6. To install, add sealer to the connecting surfaces, assemble the system, check the clearance and tighten the attachments.

# Emission Controls

## EMISSION CONTROLS

There are three sources of automotive pollutants: crankcase fumes, exhaust gases, and gasoline evaporation. The pollutants formed from these substances fall into three categories: unburnt hydrocarbons (HC), carbon monoxide (CO), and oxides of nitrogen (NOx). The equipment that is used to limit these pollutants is commonly called emission control equipment.

## Crankcase Ventilation System

### OPERATION

All A Body gasoline vehicles are equipped with a positive crankcase ventilation (PCV) system to control crankcase blow-by vapors. The system functions as follows:

When the engine is running, a small portion of the gases which are formed in the combustion chamber leak by the piston rings and enter the crankcase. Since these gases are under pressure, they tend to escape from the crankcase and enter the atmosphere. If these gases are allowed to remain in the crankcase for any period of time, they contaminate the engine oil and cause sludge to build up in the crankcase. If the gases are allowed to escape into the atmosphere, they pollute the air with unburned hydrocarbons.

The job of the crankcase emission control equipment is to recycle these gases back into the engine combustion chamber where they are reburned.

The crankcase (blow-by) gases are recycled in the following way: as the engine is running, clean, filtered air is drawn through the air filter and into the crankcase. As the air passes through the crankcase, it picks up the combustion gases and carries them out of the crankcase, through the oil separator, through the PCV valve, and into the induction system. As

they enter the intake manifold, they are drawn into the combustion chamber where they are reburned.

The most critical component in the system is the PCV valve. This valve controls the amount of gases which are recycled into the combustion chamber. At low engine speeds, the valve is partially closed, limiting the flow of gases into the intake manifold. As engine speed increases, the valve opens to admit greater quantities of gases into the intake manifold. If the valve should become blocked or plugged, the gases will be prevented from escaping from the crankcase by the normal route. Since these gases are under pressure, they will find their own way out of the crankcase. This alternate route is usually a weak oil seal or gasket in the engine. As the gas escapes by the gasket, it also creates an oil leak. Besides causing oil leaks, a clogged PCV valve also allows these gases to remain in the crankcase for an extended period of time, promoting the formation of sludge in the engine.

### SERVICE

Inspect the PCV system hose and connections at each tune-up and replace any deteriorated hoses. Check the PCV valve at every tune-up and replace it at 30,000 mile intervals.

### REMOVAL AND INSTALLATION

In replacing the PCV valve, make sure it is fully inserted in the hose, that the clamp is moved over the ridge on the valve so that the valve will not slip out of the hose, and that the valve is fully inserted into the grommet in the valve cover.

1. Slide the rubber coupling that joins the tube coming from the valve cover to the filter off the filter nipple. Then, remove the top of the air cleaner. Slide the spring clamp off the filter, and remove the filter.

2. Inspect the rubber grommet in the valve

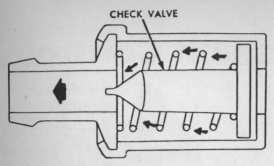

**Cross section of a PCV valve**

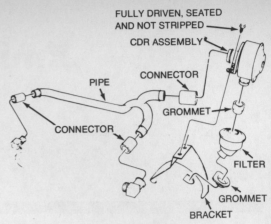

**V6 diesel crankcase ventilation**

cover and the rubber coupling for brittleness or cracking. Replace parts as necessary.

3. Insert the new PCV filter through the hole in the air cleaner with the open portion of the filter upward. Make sure that the square portion of filter behind the nipple fits into the (square) hole in the air cleaner.

4. Install a new spring clamp onto the nipple. Make sure the clamp goes under the ridge on the filter nipple all the way around. Then, reconnect the rubber coupling and install the air cleaner cover.

## Diesel Crankcase Ventilation

A crankcase depression regulator valve is used to regulate the flow of crankcase gases back into the engine. This valve is designed to limit vacuum in the crankcase. The gases are drawn from the valve cover through the CDRV and into the intake manifold.

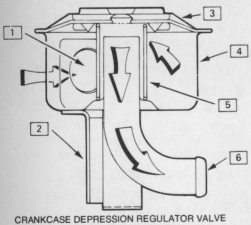

CRANKCASE DEPRESSION REGULATOR VALVE
V-TYPE DIESEL ENGINE

1. Inlet port (2) (Gases from crankcase
2. Mounting bracket
3. Cover diaphragm
4. Body
5. Spring
6. Outlet tube (Gases to intake manifold)

**Crankcase depression regulator valve (C.D.R.V.)**

Fresh air enters the engine through the combination filter, check valve, and oil fill cap. This air mixes with blow-by gases and enters the opposite valve cover. These gases pass through a filter on the valve cover and are drawn into the connected tubing.

Intake manifold vacuum acts against a spring loaded diaphragm to control the flow of crankcase gases. Higher vacuum levels pull the diaphragm closer to the top of the outlet tube. This reduces the amount of gases being drawn from the crankcase and decreases vacuum in the crankcase. As intake vacuum decreases, the spring pushes the diaphragm away from the top of the outlet tube allowing more gases into the manifold.

CAUTION: *Do not allow solvent to come in contact with the diaphragm of the CDRV, as it will cause diaphragm damage.*

## Evaporative Emission Control System

The basic Evaporative Emission Control System (EEC) used on all models is the carbon canister storage method. The system is used to reduce emissions of fuel vapors from the car's fuel system. Evaporated fuel vapors are stored for burning during combustion rather than being vented into the atmosphere when the engine is not running. To accomplish this, the fuel tank and the carburetor float bowl are vented through a vapor canister containing activated charcoal. The system utilizes a sealed fuel tank with a dome that collects fuel vapors and allows them to pass on into a line connected with the vapor canister. In addition, the vapors that form above the float chamber in the carburetor also pass into a line connected with the canister. The canister absorbs these vapors in a bed of activated charcoal and retains them until the

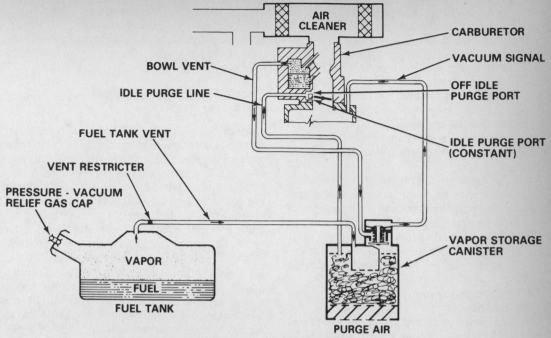

Evaporative emission control system (EECS)—open canister

canister is purged or cleared by air drawn through the filter at its bottom. The absorbing occurs when the car is not running, while the purging or cleaning occurs when the car is running. The amount of vapor being drawn into the engine at any given time is too small to have an effect on either fuel economy or engine performance.

The Electronic Control Module (ECM) controls the vacuum to the canister purge valve by using an electrically operated solenoid valve. When the system is in the 'Open Loop' mode,

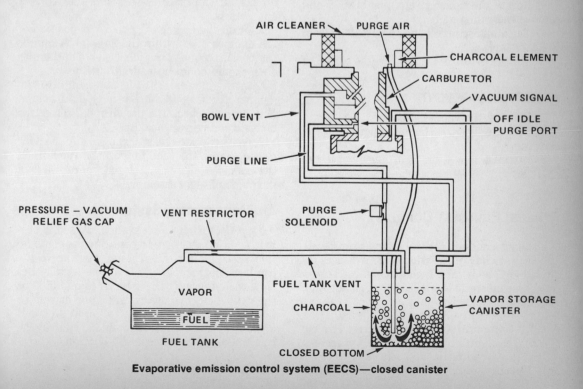

Evaporative emission control system (EECS)—closed canister

the solenoid valve is energized and blocks all vacuum to the canister purge valve. When the system is in the 'Closed Loop' mode, the solenoid valve is de-energized and vacuum is then supplied to operate the purge valve. This releases the fuel vapors, collected in the canister, into the induction system.

It is extremely important that only vapors be transferred to the engine. To avoid the possibility of liquid fuel being drawn into the system, the following features are included as part of the total system:

• A fuel tank overfill protector is provided to assure adequate room for expansion of liquid fuel volume with temperature changes.

• A one point fuel tank venting system is provided on all models to assure that the tank will be vented under any normal car attitude. This is accomplished by the use of a domed tank.

• A pressure-vacuum relief valve is located in the fuel cap.

NOTE: *Some canisters are of the closed design. They draw air from the air cleaner rather than the bottom of the canister.*

### VAPOR CANISTER REMOVAL AND INSTALLATION

1. Loosen the screw holding the canister retaining bracket.
2. If equipped with A/C, loosen the attachments holding the accumulator and pipe assembly.
3. Rotate the canister retaining bracket and remove the canister.
4. Tag and disconnect the hoses leading from the canister.
5. Installation is in the reverse order of removal.

### FILTER REPLACEMENT

1. Remove the vapor canister.
2. Pull the filter out from the bottom of the canister.
3. Install a new filter and then replace the canister.

## Exhaust Emission Controls

Exhaust emission control systems constitute the largest body of emission control devices installed on A body cars. Included in this category are: Thermostatic Air Cleaner (THERMAC); Air Management System; Early Fuel Evaporation System (EFE); Exhaust Gas Recirculation (EGR); Computer Command Control System (CCC); Deceleration Valve; Mixture Control Solenoid (M/C); Throttle Position Sensor (TPS); Idle Speed Control (ISC); Electronic Spark Timing (EST); Transmission Converter Clutch (TCC); Catalytic Converter and the Oxygen Sensor System. A brief description of each system and any applicable service procedures follows.

## Thermostatic Air Cleaner (THERMAC)

All engines use the THERMAC system. This system is designed to warm the air entering the carburetor when underhood temperatures are low, and to maintain a controlled air temperature into the carburetor at all times. By allowing preheated air to enter the carburetor, the amount of time the choke is on is reduced, resulting in better fuel economy and lower emissions. Engine warm-up time is a also reduced.

The THERMAC system is composed of the air cleaner body, a filter, sensor unit, vacuum diaphragm, damper door, and associated hoses and connections. Heat radiating from the exhaust manifold is trapped by a heat stove and is ducted to the air cleaner to supply heated air to the carburetor. A movable door in the air cleaner case snorkel allows air to be drawn in from the heat stove (cold operation). The door position is controlled by the vacuum motor, which receives intake manifold vacuum as modulated by the temperature sensor.

### SYSTEM CHECKS

1. Check the vacuum hoses for leaks, kinks, breaks, or improper connections and correct any defects.
2. With the engine off, check the position of the damper door within the snorkel. A mirror can be used to make this job easier. The damper door should be open to admit outside air.
3. Apply at least 7 in.Hg of vacuum to the damper diaphragm unit. The door should close. If it doesn't, check the diaphragm linkage for binding and correct hookup.
4. With the vacuum still applied and the door closed, clamp the tube to trap the vacuum. If the door doesn't remain closed, there is a leak in the diaphragm assembly.

## Air Management System

The AIR management system, is used to provide additional oxygen to continue the combustion process after the exhaust gases leave the combustion chamber. Air is injected into either the exhaust port(s), the exhaust manifold(s) or the catalytic converter by an engine driven air pump. The system is in operation at all times and will bypass air only momentarily during deceleration and at high speeds. The bypass function is performed by the AIR Management Valve, while the check valve protects the air

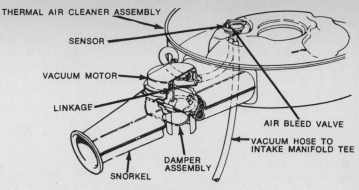

THERMAL AIR CLEANER ASSEMBLY

SENSOR

VACUUM MOTOR

LINKAGE

AIR BLEED VALVE

VACUUM HOSE TO
INTAKE MANIFOLD TEE

DAMPER
ASSEMBLY

SNORKEL

**Thermostatic air cleaner**

pump by preventing any backflow of exhaust gases.

The AIR management system helps reduce HC and CO content in the exhaust gases by injecting air into the exhaust ports during cold engine operation. This air injection also helps the catalytic converter to reach the proper temperature quicker during warmup. When the engine is warm (Closed Loop), the AIR system injects air into the beds of a three-way converter to lower the HC and the CO content in the exhaust.

The Air Management system utilizes the following components:

1. An engine driven AIR pump.
2. AIR management valves (Air Control, Air Switching).
3. Air flow and control hoses.
4. Check valves.
5. A dual-bed, three-way catalytic converter.
The belt driven, vane-type air pump is located at the front of the engine and supplies clean air to the AIR system for purposes already stated. When the engine is cold, the Electronic Control Module (ECM) energizes an AIR control solenoid. This allows air to flow to the AIR switching valve. The AIR switching valve is then energized to direct air to the exhaust ports.

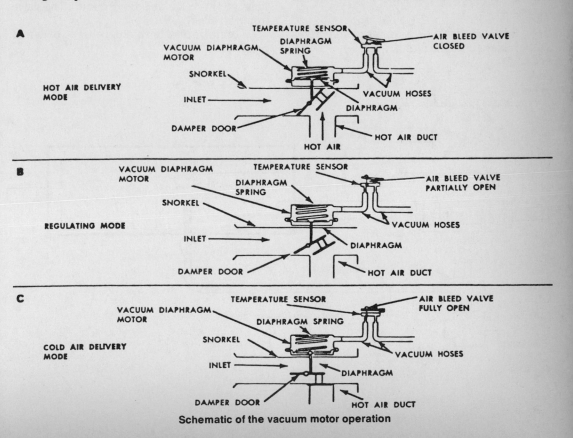

A

HOT AIR DELIVERY MODE

TEMPERATURE SENSOR
DIAPHRAGM SPRING
VACUUM DIAPHRAGM MOTOR
AIR BLEED VALVE CLOSED
SNORKEL
INLET
VACUUM HOSES
DIAPHRAGM
DAMPER DOOR
HOT AIR DUCT
HOT AIR

B

REGULATING MODE

VACUUM DIAPHRAGM MOTOR
TEMPERATURE SENSOR
DIAPHRAGM SPRING
AIR BLEED VALVE PARTIALLY OPEN
SNORKEL
VACUUM HOSES
INLET
DIAPHRAGM
DAMPER DOOR
HOT AIR DUCT

C

COLD AIR DELIVERY MODE

TEMPERATURE SENSOR
VACUUM DIAPHRAGM MOTOR
AIR BLEED VALVE FULLY OPEN
DIAPHRAGM SPRING
SNORKEL
VACUUM HOSES
INLET
DIAPHRAGM
DAMPER DOOR
HOT AIR DUCT

**Schematic of the vacuum motor operation**

When the engine is warm, the ECM de-energizes the AIR switching valve, thus directing the air between the beds of the catalytic converter. This provides additional oxygen for the oxidizing catalyst in the second bed to decrease HC and CO, while at the same time keeping oxygen levels low in the first bed, enabling the reducing catalyst to effectively decrease the levels of NOx.

If the AIR control valve detects a rapid increase in manifold vacuum (deceleration), certain operating modes (wide open throttle, etc.) or if the ECM self-diagnostic system detects any problem in the system, air is diverted to the air cleaner or directly into the atmosphere.

The primary purpose of the ECM's divert mode is to prevent backfiring. Throttle closure at the beginning of deceleration will temporarily create air/fuel mixtures which are too rich to burn completely. These mixtures become burnable when they reach the exhaust if combined with the injection air. The next firing of the engine will ignite this mixture causing an exhaust backfire. Momentary diverting of the injection air from the exhaust prevents this.

The AIR management system check valves and hoses should be checked periodically for any leaks, cracks or deterioration.

## REMOVAL AND INSTALLATION

### Air Pump

1. Remove the AIR management valves and/or adapter at the pump.

2. Loosen the air pump adjustment bolt and remove the drive belt.

3. Unscrew the pump mounting bolts and then remove the pump pulley.

4. Unscrew the pump mounting bolts and then remove the pump.

5. Installation is in the reverse order of removal. Be sure to adjust the drive belt tension after installing it.

### Check Valve

1. Release the clamp and disconnect the air hoses from the valve.

2. Unscrew the check valve from the air injection pipe.

3. Installation is in the reverse order of removal.

### Air Management Valve

1. Disconnect the negative battery cable.

2. Remove the air cleaner.

3. Tag and disconnect the vacuum hose from the valve.

4. Tag and disconnect the air outlet hoses from the valve.

5. Bend back the lock tabs and then remove the bolts holding the elbow to the valve.

6. Tag and disconnect any electrical connections at the valve and then remove the valve from the elbow.

7. Installation is in the reverse order of removal.

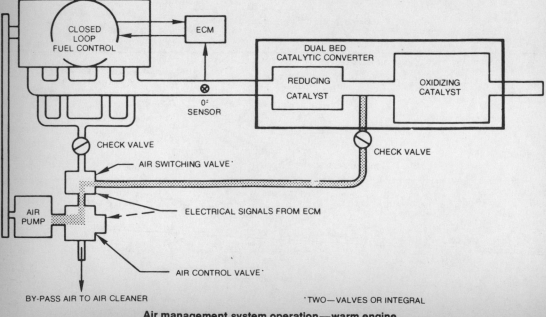

**Air management system operation—warm engine**

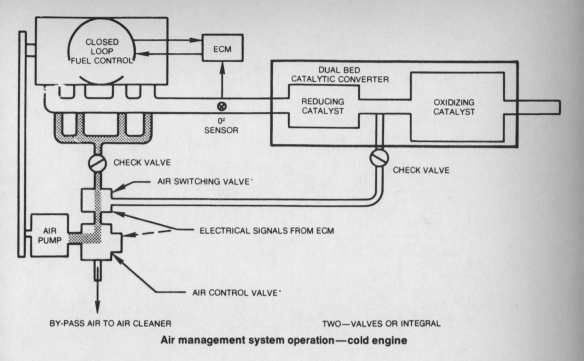

**Air management system operation—cold engine**

## Computer Command Control System (CCC)

### OPERATION

The Computer Command Control System (CCC) is an electronically controlled exhaust emission system that can monitor and control a large number of interrelated emission control systems. It can monitor up to 15 various engine/vehicle operating conditions and then use this information to control as many as 9 engine related systems. The System is thereby making constant adjustments to maintain good vehicle performance under all normal driving conditions while at the same time allowing the catalytic converter to effectively control the emissions of HC, CO and NOx.

In addition, the System has a built in diagnostic system that recognizes and identifies possible operational problems and alerts the driver through a Check Engine light in the instrument panel. The light will remain On until the problem is corrected. The System also has built in back-up systems that in most cases of an operational problem will allow for the continued operation of the vehicle in a near normal manner until the repairs can be made.

The CCC system has some components in common with the old G.M. C-4 system, although they are not interchangeable. These components include the Electronic Control Module (ECM), which controls many more functions than does its predecessor, an oxygen sensor system, an electronically controlled variable-mixture carburetor, a three-way catalytic converter, throttle position and coolant sensors, a Barometric Pressure Sensor (BARO), a Manifold Absolute Pressure Sensor (MAP) and a Check Engine light in the instrument panel.

Components unique to the CCC system include the Air Injection Reaction (AIR) management system, a charcoal canister purge solenoid, EGR valve controls, a vehicle speed sensor (in the instrument panel), a transmission converter clutch solenoid (only on models with automatic transmission), idle speed control and Electronic Spark Timing (EST).

The ECM, in addition to monitoring sensors and sending out a control signal to the carburetors, also controls the following components or sub-systems: charcoal canister purge control, the AIR system, idle speed, automatic transmission converter lockup, distributor ignition timing, the EGR valve, and the air conditioner converter clutch.

The EGR valve control solenoid is activated by the ECM in a fashion similar to that of the charcoal canister purge solenoid described earlier in this chapter. When the engine is cold, the ECM energizes the solenoid, which blocks the vacuum signal to the EGR valve. When the engine is warm, the ECM de-energizes the solenoid and the vacuum signal is allowed to reach and then activate the EGR valve.

The idle speed control adjusts the idle speed

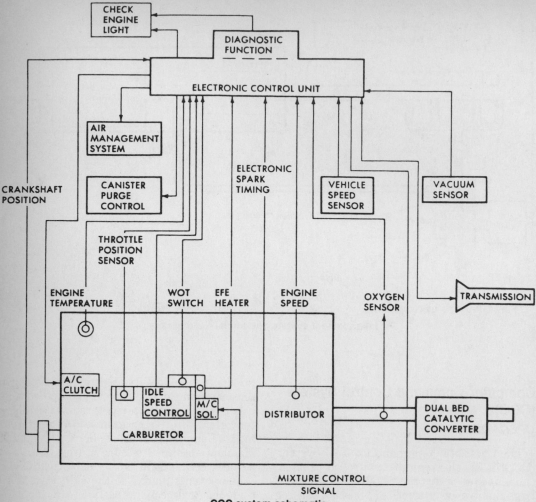

CCC system schematic

to all particular engine load conditions and will lower the idle under no-load or low-load conditions in order to conserve fuel.

## SERVICE

NOTE: *The following explains how to activate the Trouble Code signal light in the instrument cluster. This is not a full fledged CCC system troubleshooting and isolation procedure.*

Before suspecting the CCC system, or any of its components as being faulty, check the ignition system (distributor, timing, spark plugs and wires). Check the engine compression, the air cleaner and any of the emission control components that are not controlled by the ECM. Also check the intake manifold, the vacuum hoses and hose connectors for any leaks. Check the carburetor mounting bolts for tightness.

The following symptoms could indicate a possible problem area with the CCC system:

1. Detonation.

2. Stalling or rough idling when the engine is cold.

3. Stalling or rough idling when the engine is hot.

4. Missing.

5. Hesitation.

6. Surging.

7. Poor gasoline mileage.

8. Sluggish or spongy performance.

9. Hard starting when engine is cold

10. Hard starting when the engine is hot.

11. Objectionable exhaust odors.

12. Engine cuts out.

13. Improper idle speed

As a bulb and system check, the Check Engine light will come on when the ignition switch is turned to the ON position but the engine is not started.

The Check Engine light will also produce the trouble code/codes by a series of flashes which translate as follows: When the diagnostic test terminal under the instrument panel is grounded, with the ignition in the ON position and the engine not running, the Check Engine light will flash once, pause, and then flash twice in rapid succession. This is a Code 12, which indicates that the diagnostic system is working. After a long pause, the Code 12 will repeat itself two more times. This whole cycle will then repeat itself until the engine is started or the ignition switch is turned OFF.

When the engine is started, the Check Engine light will remain on for a few seconds and then turn off. If the Check Engine light remains on, the self-diagnostic system has detected a problem. If the test terminal is then grounded, the trouble code will flash (3) three times. If more than one problem is found to be in existence, each trouble code will flash (3) three times and then change to the next one. Trouble codes will flash in numerical order (lowest code number to highest). The trouble code series will repeat themselves for as long as the test terminal remains grounded.

A trouble code indicates a problem with a given circuit. For example, trouble code 14 indicates a problem in the coolant sensor circuit. This includes the coolant sensor, its electrical harness and the Electronic Control Module (ECM).

Since the self-diagnostic system cannot diagnose every possible fault in the system, the absence of a trouble code does not necessarily mean that the system is trouble-free. To determine whether or not a problem with the system exists that does not activate a trouble code, a system performance check must be made. This job should be left to a qualified service technician.

In the case of an intermittent fault in the system, the Check Engine light will go out when the fault goes away, but the trouble code will remain in the memory of the ECM. Therefore, if a trouble code can be obtained even though the Check Engine light is not on, it must still be evaluated. It must be determined if the fault is intermittent or if the engine must be operating

## Trouble Code Identification Chart

NOTE: *Always ground the test terminal AFTER the engine is running.*

| Trouble Code | Refers To: |
|---|---|
| 12 | No reference pulses to the ECM. This is not stored in the memory and will only flash when the fault is present (not to be confused with the Code 12 discussed earlier). |
| 13 | Oxygen sensor circuit. The engine must run for at least 5 min. before this code will set. |
| 14 | Shorted coolant circuit. The engine must run at least 2 min. before this code will set. |
| 15 | Open coolant sensor circuit. The engine must run at least 5 min. before this code will set. |
| 21 | Throttle position sensor circuit. The engine must run up to 25 sec., below 800 rpm, before this code will set. |
| 23 | Open or grounded carburetor solenoid circuit. |
| 24 | Vehicle Speed Sensor (VSS) circuit. The engine must run for at least 5 min. at road speed for this code to set. |
| 32 | Altitude Compensator circuit. |
| 34 | Vacuum sensor circuit. The engine must run up to 5 min., below 800 rpm, before this code will set. |
| 35 | Idle speed control switch circuit shorted. Over ½ throttle for at least 2 sec. |
| 41 | No distributor reference pulses to the ECM at specified engine vacuum. This code will store in memory. |
| 42 | Electronic Spark Timing (EST) bypass circuit grounded. |
| 44 | Lean oxygen sensor indication. The engine must run at least 5 min., in closed loop, at part throttle and road load for this code to set. |
| 45 | Rich system indication. The engine must run at least 5 min., in closed loop, at part throttle and road load for this code to set. |
| 44&45 | (at same time) Faulty oxygen sensor circuit. |
| 51 | Faulty calibration unit (PROM) or installation. It takes 30 sec. for this code to set. |
| 54 | Shorted M/C solenoid circuit and/or faulty ECM. |
| 55 | Gounded Vref (terminal 21), faulty oxygen sensor or ECM. |

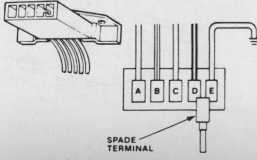

SPADE
TERMINAL

**Test terminal and ground location**

under certain conditions (acceleration, deceleration, etc.) before the Check Engine light will come on. In some cases, certain trouble codes will not be recorded in the ECM until the engine has been operated at part throttle for at least 5 to 18 minutes.

On the CCC system, a trouble code will be stored until the terminal **R** at the ECM has been disconnected from the battery for at least 10 seconds.

### ACTIVATING THE TROUBLE CODE

On the CCC system, locate the test terminal under the instrument panel (see illustration). Use a jumper wire and ground only the lead.

NOTE: *Ground the test terminal according to the instructions given previously in the Basic Troubleshooting section.*

## Pulse Air Injection (PULSAIR)

All engines use the Pulsair air injection system, which uses exhaust system air pulses to siphon fresh air into the exhaust manifold. The injected air supports continued combustion of the hot exhaust gases in the exhaust manifold, reducing exhaust emissions. A secondary purpose of the Pulsair system is to introduce more oxygen into the exhaust system upstream of the catalytic converter, to supply the converter with the oxygen required for the oxidation reaction.

Air is drawn into the Pulsair valve through a hose connected to the air cleaner. The air passes through a check valve (there is one check valve for each cylinder; all check valves are installed in the Pulsair valve), then through a manifold pipe to the exhaust manifold. All manifold pipes are the same length, to prevent uneven pulsation. The check valves open during pulses of negative exhaust back pressure, admitting air into the manifold pipe and the exhaust manifold. During pulses of positive exhaust back pressure, the check valves close, preventing backfiring into the Pulsair valve and air cleaner.

The Pulsair check valves, hoses and pipes should be checked occasionally for leaks, cracks, or breaks.

### REMOVAL AND INSTALLATION

1. Remove the air cleaner case. Disconnect the rubber hose(s) from the Pulsair valve(s).
2. Disconnect the support bracket, if present. Some V6 engines have a Pulsair solenoid and bracket, which must be removed.
3. Unscrew the attaching nuts and remove the Pulsair tubes from the exhaust manifold(s).
4. To install, first apply a light coat of clean oil to the ends of the Pulsair tubes.
5. Install the tubes to the exhaust manifold(s), tightening the nuts to 10-13 ft. lbs. (10Nm.). Connect the support bracket and sole-

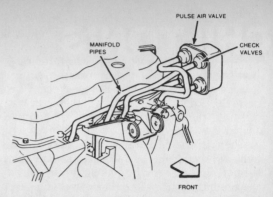

**Pulsair installed on the four cylinder engine; V6 similar**

noid and bracket, if used. Connect the rubber hose(s) and install the air cleaner.

## Deceleration Valve

The purpose of the deceleration valve is to prevent backfiring in the exhaust system during deceleration. The normal position of the valve is closed. When deceleration causes a sudden vacuum increase in the vacuum signal lines, the pressure differential on the diaphragm will overcome the closing force of the spring, opening the valve and bleeding air into the intake manifold.

Air trapped in the chamber above the vacuum diaphragm will bleed at a calibrated rate through the delay valve portion of the integral

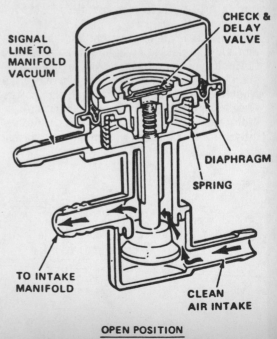

**OPEN POSITION**

**Cross section of the deceleration valve**

# CHILTON'S
# FUEL ECONOMY
# & TUNE-UP TIPS

**55 WAYS TO IMPROVE FUEL ECONOMY**

**Tune-up • Spark Plug Diagnosis • Emission Controls**

**Fuel System • Cooling System • Tires and Wheels**

**General Maintenance**

# CHILTON'S FUEL ECONOMY & TUNE-UP TIPS

Fuel economy is important to everyone, no matter what kind of vehicle you drive. The maintenance-minded motorist can save both money and fuel using these tips and the periodic maintenance and tune-up procedures in this Repair and Tune-Up Guide.

There are more than 130,000,000 cars and trucks registered for private use in the United States. Each travels an average of 10-12,000 miles per year, and, and in total they consume close to 70 billion gallons of fuel each year. This represents nearly ⅔ of the oil imported by the United States each year. The Federal government's goal is to reduce consumption 10% by 1985. A variety of methods are either already in use or under serious consideration, and they all affect you driving and the cars you will drive. In addition to "down-sizing", the auto industry is using or investigating the use of electronic fuel delivery, electronic engine controls and alternative engines for use in smaller and lighter vehicles, among other alternatives to meet the federally mandated Corporate Average Fuel Economy (CAFE) of 27.5 mpg by 1985. The government, for its part, is considering rationing, mandatory driving curtailments and tax increases on motor vehicle fuel in an effort to reduce consumption. The government's goal of a 10% reduction could be realized — and further government regulation avoided — if every private vehicle could use just 1 less gallon of fuel per week.

## How Much Can You Save?

Tests have proven that almost anyone can make at least a 10% reduction in fuel consumption through regular maintenance and tune-ups. When a major manufacturer of spark plugs sur-

## TUNE-UP

1. Check the cylinder compression to be sure the engine will really benefit from a tune-up and that it is capable of producing good fuel economy. A tune-up will be wasted on an engine in poor mechanical condition.

2. Replace spark plugs regularly. New spark plugs alone can increase fuel economy 3%.

3. Be sure the spark plugs are the correct type (heat range) for your vehicle. See the Tune-Up Specifications.

Heat range refers to the spark plug's ability to conduct heat away from the firing end. It must conduct the heat away in an even pattern to avoid becoming a source of pre-ignition, yet it must also operate hot enough to burn off conductive deposits that could cause misfiring.

The heat range is usually indicated by a number on the spark plug, part of the manufacturer's designation for each individual spark plug. The numbers in bold-face indicate the heat range in each manufacturer's identification system.

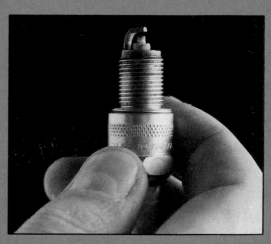

*Periodically, check the spark plugs to be sure they are firing efficiently. They are excellent indicators of the internal condition of your engine.*

| Manufacturer | Typical Designation |
|---|---|
| AC | R **45** TS |
| Bosch (old) | WA **145** T30 |
| Bosch (new) | HR **8** Y |
| Champion | RBL **15** Y |
| Fram/Autolite | 4**15** |
| Mopar | P-**62** PR |
| Motorcraft | BRF-**42** |
| NGK | BP **5** ES-15 |
| Nippondenso | W **16** EP |
| Prestolite | 14GR **5** 2A |

On AC, Bosch (new), Champion, Fram/Autolite, Mopar, Motorcraft and Prestolite, a higher number indicates a hotter plug. On Bosch (old), NGK and Nippondenso, a higher number indicates a colder plug.

4. Make sure the spark plugs are properly gapped. See the Tune-Up Specifications in this book.

5. Be sure the spark plugs are firing efficiently. The illustrations on the next 2 pages show you how to "read" the firing end of the spark plug.

6. Check the ignition timing and set it to specifications. Tests show that almost all cars have incorrect ignition timing by more than 2°.

veyed over 6,000 cars nationwide, they found that a tune-up, on cars that needed one, increased fuel economy over 11%. Replacing worn plugs alone, accounted for a 3% increase. The same test also revealed that 8 out of every 10 vehicles will have some maintenance deficiency that will directly affect fuel economy, emissions or performance. Most of this mileage-robbing neglect could be prevented with regular maintenance.

Modern engines require that all of the functioning systems operate properly for maximum efficiency. A malfunction anywhere wastes fuel. You can keep your vehicle running as efficiently and economically as possible, by being aware of your vehicle's operating and performance characteristics. If your vehicle suddenly develops performance or fuel economy problems it could be due to one or more of the following:

| PROBLEM | POSSIBLE CAUSE |
| --- | --- |
| Engine Idles Rough | Ignition timing, idle mixture, vacuum leak or something amiss in the emission control system. |
| Hesitates on Acceleration | Dirty carburetor or fuel filter, improper accelerator pump setting, ignition timing or fouled spark plugs. |
| Starts Hard or Fails to Start | Worn spark plugs, improperly set automatic choke, ice (or water) in fuel system. |
| Stalls Frequently | Automatic choke improperly adjusted and possible dirty air filter or fuel filter. |
| Performs Sluggishly | Worn spark plugs, dirty fuel or air filter, ignition timing or automatic choke out of adjustment. |

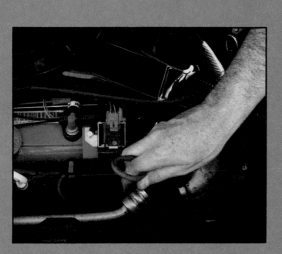

*Check spark plug wires on conventional point type ignition for cracks by bending them in a loop around your finger.*

*Be sure that spark plug wires leading to adjacent cylinders do not run too close together. (Photo courtesy Champion Spark Plug Co.)*

7. If your vehicle does not have electronic ignition, check the points, rotor and cap as specified.

8. Check the spark plug wires (used with conventional point-type ignitions) for cracks and burned or broken insulation by bending them in a loop around your finger. Cracked wires decrease fuel efficiency by failing to deliver full voltage to the spark plugs. One misfiring spark plug can cost you as much as 2 mpg.

9. Check the routing of the plug wires. Misfiring can be the result of spark plug leads to adjacent cylinders running parallel to each other and too close together. One wire tends to pick up voltage from the other causing it to fire "out of time".

10. Check all electrical and ignition circuits for voltage drop and resistance.

11. Check the distributor mechanical and/or vacuum advance mechanisms for proper functioning. The vacuum advance can be checked by twisting the distributor plate in the opposite direction of rotation. It should spring back when released.

12. Check and adjust the valve clearance on engines with mechanical lifters. The clearance should be slightly loose rather than too tight.

# SPARK PLUG DIAGNOSIS

## Normal

APPEARANCE: This plug is typical of one operating normally. The insulator nose varies from a light tan to grayish color with slight electrode wear. The presence of slight deposits is normal on used plugs and will have no adverse effect on engine performance. The spark plug heat range is correct for the engine and the engine is running normally.

CAUSE: Properly running engine.

RECOMMENDATION: Before reinstalling this plug, the electrodes should be cleaned and filed square. Set the gap to specifications. If the plug has been in service for more than 10-12,000 miles, the entire set should probably be replaced with a fresh set of the same heat range.

## Oil Deposits

APPEARANCE: The firing end of the plug is covered with a wet, oily coating.

CAUSE: The problem is poor oil control. On high mileage engines, oil is leaking past the rings or valve guides into the combustion chamber. A common cause is also a plugged PCV valve, and a ruptured fuel pump diaphragm can also cause this condition. Oil fouled plugs such as these are often found in new or recently overhauled engines, before normal oil control is achieved, and can be cleaned and reinstalled.

RECOMMENDATION: A hotter spark plug may temporarily relieve the problem, but the engine is probably in need of work.

## Incorrect Heat Range

APPEARANCE: The effects of high temperature on a spark plug are indicated by clean white, often blistered insulator. This can also be accompanied by excessive wear of the electrode, and the absence of deposits.

CAUSE: Check for the correct spark plug heat range. A plug which is too hot for the engine can result in overheating. A car operated mostly at high speeds can require a colder plug. Also check ignition timing, cooling system level, fuel mixture and leaking intake manifold.

RECOMMENDATION: If all ignition and engine adjustments are known to be correct, and no other malfunction exists, install spark plugs one heat range colder.

## Carbon Deposits

APPEARANCE: Carbon fouling is easily identified by the presence of dry, soft, black, sooty deposits.

CAUSE: Changing the heat range can often lead to carbon fouling, as can prolonged slow, stop-and-start driving. If the heat range is correct, carbon fouling can be attributed to a rich fuel mixture, sticking choke, clogged air cleaner, worn breaker points, retarded timing or low compression. If only one or two plugs are carbon fouled, check for corroded or cracked wires on the affected plugs. Also look for cracks in the distributor cap between the towers of affected cylinders.

RECOMMENDATION: After the problem is corrected, these plugs can be cleaned and reinstalled if not worn severely.

## MMT Fouled

APPEARANCE: Spark plugs fouled by MMT (Methycyclopentadienyl Maganese Tricarbonyl) have reddish, rusty appearance on the insulator and side electrode.

CAUSE: MMT is an anti-knock additive in gasoline used to replace lead. During the combustion process, the MMT leaves a reddish deposit on the insulator and side electrode.

RECOMMENDATION: No engine malfunction is indicated and the deposits will not affect plug performance any more than lead deposits (see Ash Deposits). MMT fouled plugs can be cleaned, regapped and reinstalled.

## High Speed Glazing

APPEARANCE: Glazing appears as shiny coating on the plug, either yellow or tan in color.

CAUSE: During hard, fast acceleration, plug temperatures rise suddenly. Deposits from normal combustion have no chance to fluff-off; instead, they melt on the insulator forming an electrically conductive coating which causes misfiring.

RECOMMENDATION: Glazed plugs are not easily cleaned. They should be replaced with a fresh set of plugs of the correct heat range. If the condition recurs, using plugs with a heat range one step colder may cure the problem.

## Ash (Lead) Deposits

APPEARANCE: Ash deposits are characterized by light brown or white colored deposits crusted on the side or center electrodes. In some cases it may give the plug a rusty appearance.

CAUSE: Ash deposits are normally derived from oil or fuel additives burned during normal combustion. Normally they are harmless, though excessive amounts can cause misfiring. If deposits are excessive in short mileage, the valve guides may be worn.

RECOMMENDATION: Ash-fouled plugs can be cleaned, gapped and reinstalled.

## Detonation

APPEARANCE: Detonation is usually characterized by a broken plug insulator.

CAUSE: A portion of the fuel charge will begin to burn spontaneously, from the increased heat following ignition. The explosion that results applies extreme pressure to engine components, frequently damaging spark plugs and pistons.

Detonation can result by over-advanced ignition timing, inferior gasoline (low octane) lean air/fuel mixture, poor carburetion, engine lugging or an increase in compression ratio due combustion chamber deposits or engine fication.

RECOMMENDATION: Replace the correcting the problem.

Photos Courtesy Champion Spark Plug Co.

ware of the general condition of the control system. It contributes to reduce pollution and should be serviced regularly to maintain efficient engine operation.

14. Check all vacuum lines for dried, cracked or brittle conditions. Something as simple as a leaking vacuum hose can cause poor performance and loss of economy.

15. Avoid tampering with the emission control system. Attempting to improve fuel econ-

# FUEL SYSTEM

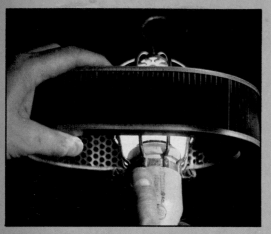

*Check the air filter with a light behind it. If you can see light through the filter it can be reused.*

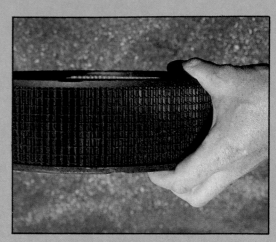

*Extremely clogged filters should be discarded and replaced with a new one.*

18. Replace the air filter regularly. A dirty air filter richens the air/fuel mixture and can increase fuel consumption as much as 10%. Tests show that ⅓ of all vehicles have air filters in need of replacement.

19. Replace the fuel filter at least as often as recommended.

20. Set the idle speed and carburetor mixture to specifications.

21. Check the automatic choke. A sticking or malfunctioning choke wastes gas.

22. During the summer months, adjust the automatic choke for a leaner mixture which will produce faster engine warm-ups.

# COOLING SYSTEM

29. Be sure all accessory drive belts are in good condition. Check for cracks or wear.

30. Adjust all accessory drive belts to proper tension.

31. Check all hoses for swollen areas, worn spots, or loose clamps.

32. Check coolant level in the radiator or expansion tank.

33. Be sure the thermostat is operating properly. A stuck thermostat delays engine warm-up and a cold engine uses nearly twice as much fuel as a warm engine.

34. Drain and replace the engine coolant at least as often as recommended. Rust and scale

# TIRES & WHEELS

38. Check the tire pressure often with a pencil type gauge. Tests by a major tire manufacturer show that 90% of all vehicles have at least 1 tire improperly inflated. Better mileage can be achieved by over-inflating tires, but never exceed the maximum inflation pressure on the side of the tire.

9. If possible, install radial tires. Radial tires deliver as much as ½ mpg more than bias belted tires.

40. Avoid installing super-wide tires. They only create extra rolling resistance and decrease fuel mileage. Stick to the manufacturer's recommendations.

41. Have the wheels properly balanced.

omy by tampering with emission controls is more likely to worsen fuel economy than improve it. Emission control changes on modern engines are not readily reversible.

16. Clean (or replace) the EGR valve and lines as recommended.

17. Be sure that all vacuum lines and hoses are reconnected properly after working under the hood. An unconnected or misrouted vacuum line can wreak havoc with engine performance.

23. Check for fuel leaks at the carburetor, fuel pump, fuel lines and fuel tank. Be sure all lines and connections are tight.

24. Periodically check the tightness of the carburetor and intake manifold attaching nuts and bolts. These are a common place for vacuum leaks to occur.

25. Clean the carburetor periodically and lubricate the linkage.

26. The condition of the tailpipe can be an excellent indicator of proper engine combustion. After a long drive at highway speeds, the inside of the tailpipe should be a light grey in color. Black or soot on the insides indicates an overly rich mixture.

27. Check the fuel pump pressure. The fuel pump may be supplying more fuel than the engine needs.

28. Use the proper grade of gasoline for your engine. Don't try to compensate for knocking or "pinging" by advancing the ignition timing. This practice will only increase plug temperature and the chances of detonation or pre-ignition with relatively little performance gain.

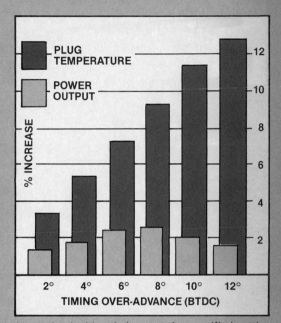

*Increasing ignition timing past the specified setting results in a drastic increase in spark plug temperature with increased chance of detonation or preignition. Performance increase is considerably less. (Photo courtesy Champion Spark Plug Co.)*

that form in the engine should be flushed out to allow the engine to operate at peak efficiency.

35. Clean the radiator of debris that can decrease cooling efficiency.

36. Install a flex-type or electric cooling fan, if you don't have a clutch type fan. Flex fans use curved plastic blades to push more air at low speeds when more cooling is needed; at high speeds the blades flatten out for less resistance. Electric fans only run when the engine temperature reaches a predetermined level.

37. Check the radiator cap for a worn or cracked gasket. If the cap does not seal properly, the cooling system will not function properly.

42. Be sure the front end is correctly aligned. A misaligned front end actually has wheels going in differed directions. The increased drag can reduce fuel economy by .3 mpg.

43. Correctly adjust the wheel bearings. Wheel bearings that are adjusted too tight increase rolling resistance.

*Check tire pressures regularly with a reliable pocket type gauge. Be sure to check the pressure on a cold tire.*

# GENERAL MAINTENANCE

Check the fluid levels (particularly engine oil) on a regular basis. Be sure to check the oil for grit, water or other contamination.

A vacuum gauge is another excellent indicator of internal engine condition and can also be installed in the dash as a mileage indicator.

44. Periodically check the fluid levels in the engine, power steering pump, master cylinder, automatic transmission and drive axle.

45. Change the oil at the recommended interval and change the filter at every oil change. Dirty oil is thick and causes extra friction between moving parts, cutting efficiency and increasing wear. A worn engine requires more frequent tune-ups and gets progressively worse fuel economy. In general, use the lightest viscosity oil for the driving conditions you will encounter.

46. Use the recommended viscosity fluids in the transmission and axle.

47. Be sure the battery is fully charged for fast starts. A slow starting engine wastes fuel.

48. Be sure battery terminals are clean and tight.

49. Check the battery electrolyte level and add distilled water if necessary.

50. Check the exhaust system for crushed pipes, blockages and leaks.

51. Adjust the brakes. Dragging brakes or brakes that are not releasing create increased drag on the engine.

52. Install a vacuum gauge or miles-per-gallon gauge. These gauges visually indicate engine vacuum in the intake manifold. High vacuum = good mileage and low vacuum = poorer mileage. The gauge can also be an excellent indicator of internal engine conditions.

53. Be sure the clutch is properly adjusted. A slipping clutch wastes fuel.

54. Check and periodically lubricate the heat control valve in the exhaust manifold. A sticking or inoperative valve prevents engine warm-up and wastes gas.

55. Keep accurate records to check fuel economy over a period of time. A sudden drop in fuel economy may signal a need for tune-up or other maintenance.

check and delay valve, reducing the vacuum acting on the diaphragm. When the vacuum load on the diaphragm and the spring load equalize, the valve assembly will close, shutting off the air flow into the intake manifold.

The check valve portion of the check and delay valve provides quick balancing of chamber pressure when a sudden decrease in vacuum is caused by acceleration rather than deceleration.

## Mixture Control Solenoid (M/C)

The fuel flow through the carburetor idle main metering circuits is controlled by a mixture control (M/C) solenoid located in the carburetor. The M/C solenoid changes the air/fuel mixture to the engine by controlling the fuel flow through the carburetor. The ECM controls the solenoid by providing a ground. When the solenoid is energized, the fuel flow through the carburetor is reduced, providing a leaner mixture. When the ECM removes the ground, the solenoid is de-energized, increasing the fuel flow and providing a richer mixture. The M/C solenoid is energized and de-energized at a rate of 10 times per second.

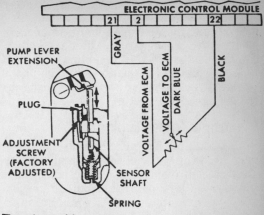

Throttle position sensor

## Throttle Position Sensor (TPS)

The throttle position sensor is mounted in the carburetor body and is used to supply throttle position information to the ECM. The ECM memory stores an average of operating conditions with the ideal air/fuel ratios for each of those conditions. When the ECM receives a signal that indicates throttle position change, it immediately shifts to the last remembered set of operating conditions that resulted in an ideal air/fuel ratio control. The memory is continually being updated during normal operations.

## Idle Speed Control (ISC)

The idle speed control does just what its name implies-it controls the idle. The ISC is used to maintain low engine speeds while at the same time preventing stalling due to engine load changes. The system consists of a motor assembly mounted on the carburetor which moves the throttle lever so as to open or close the throttle blades.

The whole operation is controlled by the

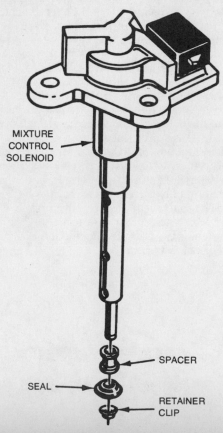

The mixture control (M/C) solenoid is located in the carburetor

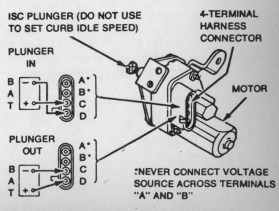

The idle speed control motor (ISC) is mounted on the carburetor

ECM. The ECM monitors engine load to determine the proper idle speed. To prevent stalling, it monitors the air conditioning compressor switch, the transmission, the park/neutral switch and the ISC throttle switch. The ECM processes all this information and then uses it to control the ISC motor which in turn will vary the idle speed as necessary.

## Electronic Spark Timing (EST)

All models use EST. The EST distributor, as described in an earlier chapter, contains no vacuum or centrifugal advance mechanism and uses a seven terminal HEI module. It has four wires going to a four terminal connector in addition to the connectors normally found on HEI distributors. A reference pulse, indicating engine rpm is sent to the ECM. The ECM determines the proper spark advance for the engine operating conditions and then sends an EST pulse back to the distributor.

Under most normal operating conditions, the ECM will control the spark advance. However, under certain operating conditions such as cranking or when setting base timing, the distributor is capable of operating without ECM control. This condition is called BYPASS and is determined by the BYPASS lead which runs from the ECM to the distributor. When the BYPASS lead is at the proper voltage (5), the ECM will control the spark. If the lead is grounded or open circuited, the HEI module itself will control the spark. Disconnecting the 4-terminal EST connector will also cause the engine to operate in the BYPASS mode.

## Transmission Converter Clutch (TCC)

All models with an automatic transmission use TCC. The ECM controls the converter by means of a solenoid mounted in the transmission. When the vehicle speed reaches a certain level, the ECM energizes the solenoid and allows the torque converter to mechanically couple the transmission to the engine. When the operating conditions indicate that the transmission should operate as a normal fluid coupled transmission, the ECM will de-energize the solenoid. Depressing the brake will also return the transmission to normal automatic operation.

## Catalytic Converter

The catalytic converter is a muffler-like container built into the exhaust system to aid in the reduction of exhaust emissions. The catalyst element consists of individual pellets or a honeycomb monolithic substrate coated with a noble metal such as platinum, palladium, rho-

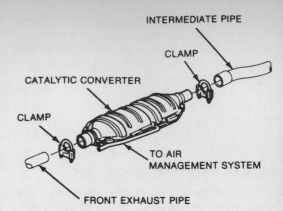

The catalytic converter is upstream of the muffler

dium or a combination. When the exhaust gases come into contact with the catalyst, a chemical reaction occurs which will reduce the pollutants into harmless substances like water and carbon dioxide.

There are essentially two types of catalytic converters: an oxidizing type and a three-way type. The oxidizing type requires the addition of oxygen to spur the catalyst into reducing the engine's HC and CO emissions into $H_2O$ and $CO_2$. The oxidizing catalytic converter, while effectively reducing HC and CO emissions, does little, if anything in the way of reducing NOx emissions. Thus, the three-way catalytic converter.

The three-way converter, unlike the oxidizing type, is capable of reducing HC, CO and NOx emmissions; all at the same time. In theory, it seems impossible to reduce all three pollutants in one system since the reduction of HC and CO requires the addition of oxygen, while the reduction of NOx calls for the removal of oxygen. In actuality, the three-way system really can reduce all three pollutants, but only if the amount of oxygen in the exhaust system is precisely controlled. Due to this precise oxygen control requirement, the three-way converter system is used only in conjunction with an oxygen sensor system.

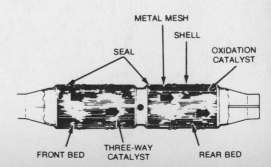

Cutaway view of the typical three-way catalytic converter

There are no service procedures required for the catalytic converter, although the converter body should be inspected occasionally for damage.

### PRECAUTIONS

1. Use only unleaded fuel.
2. Avoid prolonged idling; the engine should run no longer than 20 min. at curb idle and no longer than 10 min. at fast idle.
3. Do not disconnect any of the spark plug leads while the engine is running.
4. Make engine compression checks as quickly as possible.

### CATALYST TESTING

At the present time there is no known way to reliably test catalytic converter operation in the field. The only reliable test is a 12 hour and 40 min. soak test (CVS) which must be done in a laboratory.

An infrared HC/CO tester is not sensitive enough to measure the higher tailpipe emissions from a failing converter. Thus, a bad converter may allow enough emissions to escape so that the car is no longer in compliance with Federal or state standards, but will still not cause the needle on a tester to move off zero.

The chemical reactions which occur inside a catalytic converter generate a great deal of heat. Most converter problems can be traced to fuel or ignition system problems which cause unusually high emissions. As a result of the increased intensity of the chemical reactions, the converter literally burns itself up.

A completely failed converter might cause a tester to show a slight reading. As a result, it is occasionally possible to detect one of these.

As long as you avoid severe overheating and the use of leaded fuels it is reasonably safe to assume that the converter is working properly. If you are in doubt, take the car to a diagnostic center that has a tester.

## Early Fuel Evaporation (EFE)

All models are equipped with this system to reduce engine warm-up time, improve driveability and reduce emissions. The system is electric and uses a ceramic heater grid located underneath the primary bore of the carburetor as part of the carburetor insulator/gasket. When the ignition switch is turned on and the engine coolant temperature is low, voltage is applied to the EFE relay by the ECM. The EFE relay in turn energizes the heater grid. When the coolant temperature increases, the ECM de-energizes the relay which will then shut off the EFE heater.

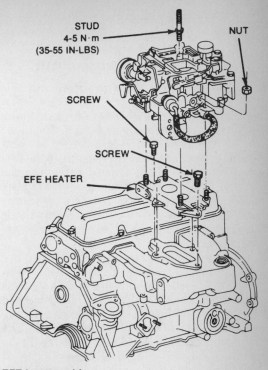

EFE heater grid

### REMOVAL AND INSTALLATION

1. Remove the air cleaner and disconnect the negative battery cable.
2. Disconnect all electrical, vacuum and fuel connections from the carburetor.
3. Disconnect the EFE heater electrical lead.
4. Remove the carburetor as detailed later in this chapter.
5. Lift off the EFE heater grid.
6. Installation is in the reverse order of removal.

### EFE HEATER RELAY REPLACEMENT

1. Disconnect the negative battery cable.
2. Remove the retaining bracket.
3. Tag and disconnect all electrical connections.
4. Unscrew the retaining bolts and remove the relay.

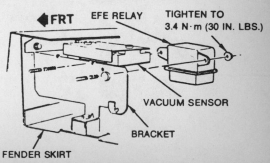

Heater relay installation details

5. Installation is in the reverse order of removal.

## Exhaust Gas Recirculation (EGR)

All gasoline models are equipped with this system, which consists of a metering valve, a vacuum line to the carburetor or intake manifold, and cast-in exhaust passages in the intake manifold. The EGR valve is controlled by vacuum, and opens and closes in response to the vacuum signals to admit exhaust gases into the air/fuel mixture. The exhaust gases lower peak combustion temperatures, reducing the formation of NOx. The valve is closed at idle and wide open throttle, but is open between the two extreme positions.

There are actually two types of EGR systems: Vacuum Modulated and Exhaust Back Pressure Modulated. The principle of both systems is the same; the only difference is in the method used to control how far the EGR valve opens.

In the Vacuum Modulated system, the amount of exhaust gas admitted into the intake manifold depends on a ported vacuum signal. A ported vacuum signal is one taken from the carburetor above the throttle plates; thus, the vacuum signal (amount of vacuum) is dependent on how far the throttle plates are opened. When the throttle is closed (idle or deceleration) there is no vacuum signal. Thus, the EGR valve is closed, and no exhaust gas enters the intake manifold. As the throttle is opened, a vacuum is produced, which opens the EGR valve, admitting exhaust gas into the intake manifold.

In the Exhaust Back Pressure Modulated system, a transducer is installed in the EGR valve body. The vacuum is still ported vacuum, but the transducer uses exhaust gas pressure to control an air bleed within the valve to modify this vacuum signal.

### SYSTEM CHECKS

1. Check to see if the EGR valve diaphragm moves freely. Use your finger to reach up under the valve and push on the diaphragm. If it doesn't move freely, the valve should be replaced. The use of a mirror will aid the inspection process.

CAUTION: *If the engine is hot, wear a glove to protect your hand.*

2. Install a vacuum gauge into the vacuum line between the EGR valve and the carburetor. Start the engine and allow it to reach operating temperature.

3. With the car in either Park or Neutral, increase the engine speed until at least 5 in.Hg is showing on the gauge.

4. Remove the vacuum hose from the EGR valve. The diaphragm should move downward (valve closed). The engine speed should increase.

5. Install the vacuum hose and watch for the EGR valve to open (diaphragm moving upward). The engine speed should decrease to its former level, indicating exhaust recirculation.

**If the diaphragm doesn't move:**

1. Check engine vacuum; it should be at least 5 in.Hg with the throttle open and engine running.

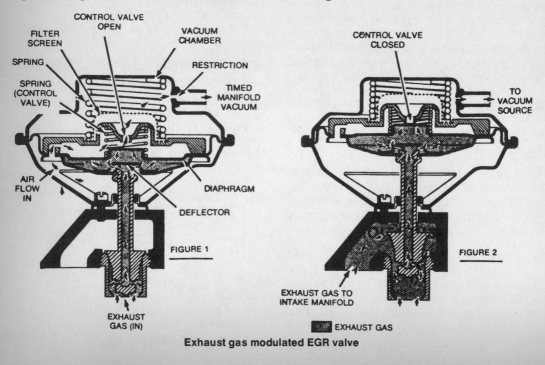

**Exhaust gas modulated EGR valve**

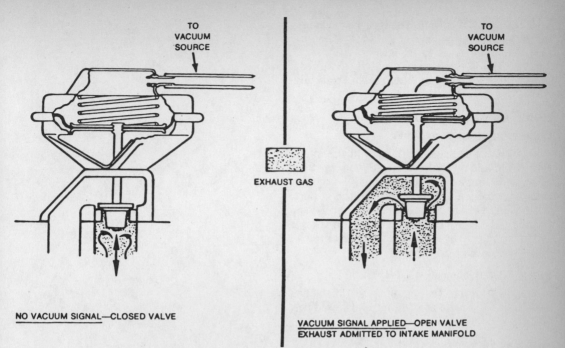

TO
VACUUM
SOURCE

TO
VACUUM
SOURCE

EXHAUST GAS

NO VACUUM SIGNAL—CLOSED VALVE

VACUUM SIGNAL APPLIED—OPEN VALVE
EXHAUST ADMITTED TO INTAKE MANIFOLD

**Vacuum modulated EGR valve**

2. Check to see that the engine is at normal operating temperature.

3. Check for vacuum at the EGR hose. If no vacuum is present, check the hose for leaks, breaks, kinks, improper connections, etc., and replace as necessary. If the diaphragm moves, but the engine speed doesn't change, check the EGR passages in the intake manifold for blockage.

### REMOVAL AND INSTALLATION

1. Disconnect the vacuum hose.

2. Remove the bolts or nuts holding the EGR valve to the engine.

3. Remove the valve.

4. Clean the mounting surfaces before replacing the valve. Install the valve onto the manifold, using a new gasket. Be sure to install the spacer, if used. Connect the vacuum hose and check the valve operation.

## Diesel EGR System

The diesel EGR systems work in the same basic manner as gasoline engine EGR systems: exhaust gases are introduced into the combustion chambers to reduce combustion temperatures, and thus lower the formation of nitrogen oxides (NOx).

Vacuum from the vacuum pump is modulated by the Vacuum Regulator Valve (VRV) mounted on the injection pump.

The amount of EGR valve opening is further modulated by a Vacuum Modulator Valve (VMV). The VMV allows for an increase in vac-

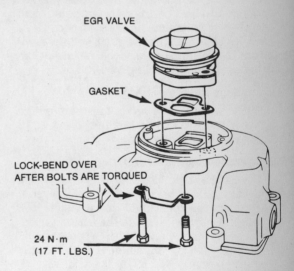

EGR VALVE

GASKET

LOCK-BEND OVER
AFTER BOLTS ARE TORQUED

24 N·m
(17 FT. LBS.)

**EGR valve—V6 diesel**

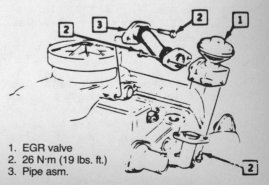

1. EGR valve
2. 26 N·m (19 lbs. ft.)
3. Pipe asm.

**View of the EGR valve—V6 diesel ('85)**

uum to the EGR valve as the throttle is closed, up to the switching point of the VMV. The system also employs an RVR valve.

In 1985, the EGR valve was moved to the rear of the engine and has become electronically controlled.

### BASIC COMPONENT TESTING

#### Vacuum Regulator Valve (VRV)

The VRV is attached to the side of the injection pump and regulates vacuum in proportion to throttle angle. Vacuum from the vacuum pump is supplied to port A and vacuum at port **B** (see illustration) is reduced as the throttle is opened. At closed throttle the vacuum is 15 in.Hg; at half throttle, 6"; at wide open throttle there should be zero vacuum.

#### Exhaust Gas Recirculation Valve

Apply vacuum to the vacuum port. The valve should be fully open at 12 in.Hg and closed below 6".

#### Response Vacuum Reducer (RVR)

Connect a vacuum gauge to the port marked To EGR valve or TCC solenoid. Connect a hand operated vacuum pump to the VRV port. Draw 15 in.Hg of vacuum on the pump and the reading on the vacuum gauge should be lower than the vacuum pump reading by 0.75".

#### Exhaust Pressure Regulator Valve

Apply vacuum to the vacuum port of the valve. The valve should be fully closed at 12 in.Hg and open below 6 in.

#### Vacuum Modulator Valve (VMV)

To test the VMV, block the drive wheels, and apply the parking brake. With the shift lever in Park, start the engine and run at a slow idle. Connect a vacuum gauge to the hose that connects to the port marked **MAN**. There should be at least 14 in.Hg of vacuum. If not, check the vacuum pump, VRV, RVR, solenoid, and all connecting hoses. Reconnect the hose to the **MAN** port. Connect a vacuum gauge to the **DIST** port on the VMV. The vacuum reading should be 12 in.Hg except on High Altitude cars, which should be 9 in.Hg.

## Service Lights

An emissions indicator flag may appear in the odometer window of the speedometer on some vehicles. The flag could say "Sensor", "Emissions" or "Catalyst" depending on the part or assembly that is scheduled for regular emissions maintenance replacement. The word "Sensor" indicates a need for oxygen sensor replacement and the words "Emissions" or "Cat-

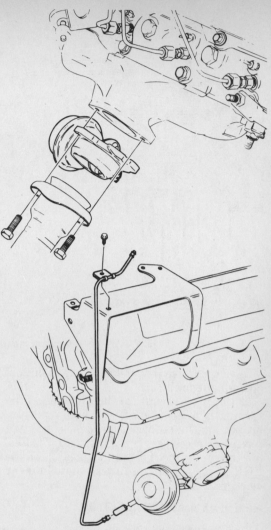

**Exhaust pressure regulator valve (EPR)**

alyst" indicate the need for catalytic converter catalyst replacement.

### Reset Procedure

1. Remove the instrument panel trim plate.
2. Remove the instrument cluster lens.
3. Locate the flag indicator reset notches at the drivers side of the odometer.
4. Use a pointed tool to apply light downward pressure on the notches, until the indicator is reset.
5. When the indicator is reset an alignment mark will appear in the left center of the odometer window.

## Oxygen Sensor

An oxygen sensor is used on all models. The sensor protrudes into the exhaust stream and monitors the oxygen content of the exhaust gases. The difference between the oxygen content of the exhaust gases and that of the outside air generates a voltage signal to the ECM. The ECM monitors this voltage and, depending upon the value of the signal received, issues a command to adjust for a rich or a lean condition.

No attempt should ever be made to measure the voltage output of the sensor. The current drain of any conventional voltmeter would be such that it would permanently damage the sensor. No jumpers, test leads or any other electrical connections should ever be made to the sensor. Use these tools ONLY on the ECM side of the wiring harness connector AFTER disconnecting it from the sensor.

### REMOVAL AND INSTALLATION

The oxygen sensor must be replaced every 30,000 miles (48,000 km.). The sensor may be difficult to remove when the engine temperature is below 120°F (48°C). Excessive removal force may damage the threads in the exhaust manifold or pipe; follow the removal procedure carefully.

1. Locate the oxygen sensor. It protrudes from the center of the exhaust manifold at the front of the engine compartment (it looks somewhat like a spark plug).

2. Disconnect the electrical connector from the oxygen sensor.

3. Spray a commercial heat riser solvent onto the sensor threads and allow it to soak in for at least five minutes.

4. Carefully unscrew and remove the sensor.

5. To install, first coat the new sensor's threads with G.M. anti-seize compound No. 5613695 or the equivalent. This is not a conventional anti-seize paste. The use of a regular compound may electrically insulate the sensor, rendering it inoperative. You must coat the

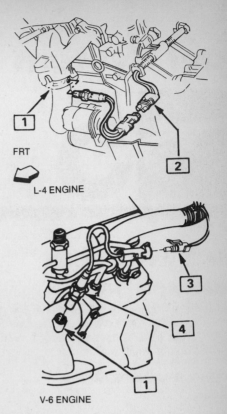

FRT

**L-4 ENGINE**

**V-6 ENGINE**

1. Exhaust manifold  3. Terminal (Wiring harness)
2. Engine harness    4. Oxygen sensor

**Oxygen sensor mounting**

threads with an electrically conductive anti-seize compound.

6. Installation torque is 30 ft. lbs. (42 Nm.). Do not overtighten.

7. Reconnect the electrical connector. Be careful not to damage the electrical pigtail. Check the sensor boot for proper fit and installation.

# Fuel System

## CARBURETED FUEL SYSTEM

### Mechanical Fuel Pump

Mechanical fuel pumps are used on 6-173 engines. The pump has a vapor return line for both emission control purposes and to reduce the likelihood of vapor lock.

#### *REMOVAL AND INSTALLATION*

#### All Models

The fuel pump is located at the left side of the engine.

1. Disconnect the negative cable at the battery. Raise and support the car.
2. Remove the pump shields and the oil filter, if so equipped.
3. Disconnect the inlet hose from the pump. Disconnect the vapor return hose, if equipped.
4. Loosen the fuel line at the carburetor, then disconnect the outlet pipe from the pump.
5. Remove the two mounting bolts and remove the pump from the engine.
6. To install, place a new gasket on the pump and install the pump on the engine. Tighten the two mounting bolts alternately and evenly.

## Troubleshooting Basic Fuel System Problems

| Problem | Cause | Solution |
|---|---|---|
| Engine cranks, but won't start (or is hard to start) when cold | • Empty fuel tank<br>• Incorrect starting procedure<br>• Defective fuel pump<br>• No fuel in carburetor<br>• Clogged fuel filter<br>• Engine flooded<br>• Defective choke | • Check for fuel in tank<br>• Follow correct procedure<br>• Check pump output<br>• Check for fuel in the carburetor<br>• Replace fuel filter<br>• Wait 15 minutes; try again<br>• Check choke plate |
| Engine cranks, but is hard to start (or does not start) when hot— (presence of fuel is assumed) | • Defective choke | • Check choke plate |
| Rough idle or engine runs rough | • Dirt or moisture in fuel<br>• Clogged air filter<br>• Faulty fuel pump | • Replace fuel filter<br>• Replace air filter<br>• Check fuel pump output |
| Engine stalls or hesitates on acceleration | • Dirt or moisture in the fuel<br>• Dirty carburetor<br>• Defective fuel pump<br>• Incorrect float level, defective accelerator pump | • Replace fuel filter<br>• Clean the carburetor<br>• Check fuel pump output<br>• Check carburetor |
| Poor gas mileage | • Clogged air filter<br>• Dirty carburetor<br>• Defective choke, faulty carburetor adjustment | • Replace air filter<br>• Clean carburetor<br>• Check carburetor |
| Engine is flooded (won't start accompanied by smell of raw fuel) | • Improperly adjusted choke or carburetor | • Wait 15 minutes and try again, without pumping gas pedal<br>• If it won't start, check carburetor |

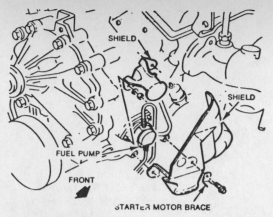

**V6 fuel pump installation**

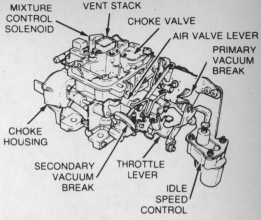

**Rochester E2SE carburetor**

7. Install the pump outlet pipe. This is easier if the pipe is disconnected from the carburetor. Tighten the fitting while backing up the pump nut with another wrench. Install the pipe at the carburetor.

8. Install the inlet and vapor hoses. Install the shields (if equipped) and oil filter. Lower the car, connect the negative battery cable, start the engine, and check for leaks.

### TESTING THE FUEL PUMP

To determine if the pump is in good condition, tests for both volume and pressure should be performed. The tests are made with the pump installed. Never replace a fuel pump without first performing these simple tests.

Be sure that the fuel filter has been changed at the specified interval. If in doubt, install a new filter first.

#### Pressure Test

1. Disconnect the fuel line at the carburetor and connect a fuel pump pressure gauge. Fill the carburetor float bowl with gasoline.

2. Start the engine and check the pressure with the engine at idle. If the pump has a vapor return hose, squeeze it off so that an accurate reading can be obtained. Pressure should measure 6.0-7.5 psi.

3. If the pressure is incorrect, replace the pump. If it is ok, go on to the volume test.

#### Volume Test

1. Disconnect the pressure gauge. Run the fuel line into a graduated container.

2. Run the engine at idle until one pint of gasoline has been pumped. One pint should be delivered in 30 seconds or less. There is normally enough fuel in the carburetor float bowl to perform this test, but refill it if necessary.

3. If the delivery rate is below the minimum, check the lines for restrictions or leaks, then replace the pump.

## Carburetor

The Rochester E2SE is used on all 1982 and later A-body cars. It is a two barrel, two stage carburetor of downdraft design used in conjunction with the Computer Command Control system of fuel control. The carburetor has special design features for optimum air/fuel mixture control during all ranges of engine operation.

### MODEL IDENTIFICATION

General Motors Rochester carburetors are identified by their model code. The first number indicates the number of barrels, while one of the last letters indicates the type of choke used. These are V for the manifold mounted choke coil, C for the choke coil mounted in the carburetor body, and E for electric choke, also mounted on the carburetor. Model codes ending in A indicate an altitude compensation carburetor.

### FLOAT ADJUSTMENT

1. Remove the air horn from the throttle body.

2. Use your fingers to hold the retainer in place, and to push the float down into light contact with the needle.

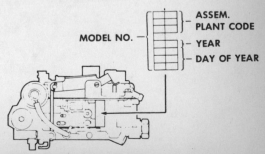

**The carburetor identification number is stamped on the float bowl**

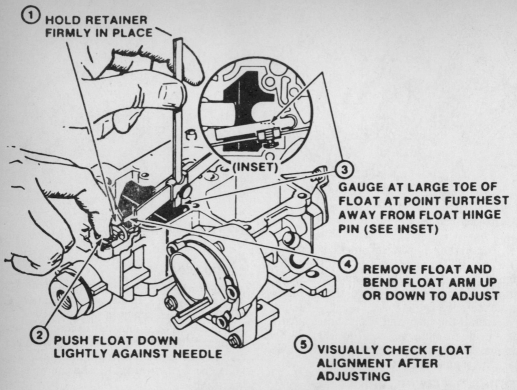

① HOLD RETAINER FIRMLY IN PLACE

(INSET)

③ GAUGE AT LARGE TOE OF FLOAT AT POINT FURTHEST AWAY FROM FLOAT HINGE PIN (SEE INSET)

④ REMOVE FLOAT AND BEND FLOAT ARM UP OR DOWN TO ADJUST

② PUSH FLOAT DOWN LIGHTLY AGAINST NEEDLE

⑤ VISUALLY CHECK FLOAT ALIGNMENT AFTER ADJUSTING

Float adjustment (1982–'84)

1. REMOVE AIR HORN, AIR HORN GASKET AND UPPER FLOAT BOWL INSERT.

2. ATTACH J-34817-1 OR BT-8227A-1 TO FLOAT BOWL.

3. PLACE J-34817-3 OR BT-8227A IN BASE, WITH CONTACT PIN RESTING ON OUTER EDGE OF FLOAT LEVER.

4. MEASURE DISTANCE FROM TOP OF CASTING TO TOP OF FLOAT, AT POINT FARTHEST FROM FLOAT HINGE. USE J-9789-90 OR BT-8037.

5. IF MORE THAN ±1.59mm (2/32") FROM SPECIFICATION, USE J-34817-20 OR BT-8045A TO BEND LEVER UP OR DOWN. REMOVE BENDING TOOL AND MEASURE, REPEATING UNTIL WITHIN SPECIFICATION.

6. VISUALLY CHECK FLOAT ALIGNMENT.

7. REASSEMBLE CARBURETOR.

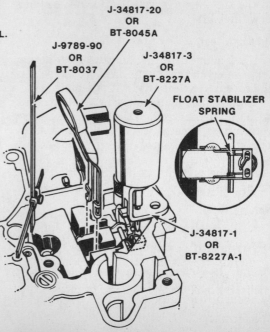

J-34817-20 OR BT-8045A

J-9789-90 OR BT-8037

J-34817-3 OR BT-8227A

FLOAT STABILIZER SPRING

J-34817-1 OR BT-8227A-1

Float adjustment—1985 and later

3. Measure the distance from the toe of the float (furthest from the hinge) to the top of the carburetor (gasket removed).

4. To adjust, remove the float and gently bend the arm to specification. After adjustment, check the float alignment in the chamber.

### PUMP ADJUSTMENT

E2SE carburetors have a non-adjustable pump lever. No adjustments are either necessary or possible.

### FAST IDLE ADJUSTMENT

1. Set the ignition timing and curb idle speed, and disconnect and plug hoses as directed on the emission control decal.

2. Place the fast idle screw on the highest step of the cam.

3. Start the engine and adjust the engine speed to specification with the fast idle screw.

### CHOKE COIL LEVER ADJUSTMENT

1. Remove the three retaining screws and remove the choke cover and coil. On models with a riveted choke cover, drill out the three rivets and remove the cover and choke coil.

NOTE: *A choke stat cover retainer kit is required for reassembly.*

2. Place the fast idle screw on the high step of the cam.

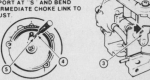

① IF RIVETED, DRILL OUT AND REMOVE RIVETS. REMOVE CHOKE COVER AND STAT ASSEMBLY.
② PLACE FAST IDLE SCREW ON HIGH STEP OF FAST IDLE CAM.
③ PUSH ON INTERMEDIATE CHOKE LEVER UNTIL CHOKE VALVE IS CLOSED.
④ INSERT .085" (2.18mm) PLUG GAGE IN HOLE.
⑤ EDGE OF LEVER SHOULD JUST CONTACT SIDE OF GAGE.
⑥ SUPPORT AT "S" AND BEND INTERMEDIATE CHOKE LINK TO ADJUST.

**Choke stat lever adjustment**

3. Close the choke by pushing in on the intermediate choke lever.

4. Insert a drill or gauge of the specified size into the hole in the choke housing. The choke lever in the housing should be up against the side of the gauge.

5. If the lever does not just touch the gauge, bend the intermediate choke rod to adjust.

### FAST IDLE CAM (CHOKE ROD) ADJUSTMENT

NOTE: *A special angle gauge should be used. If it is not available, an inch measurement can be made.*

1. Adjust the choke coil lever and fast idle first.

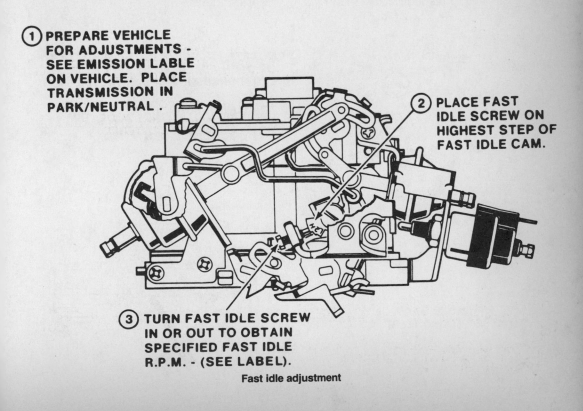

① **PREPARE VEHICLE FOR ADJUSTMENTS - SEE EMISSION LABLE ON VEHICLE. PLACE TRANSMISSION IN PARK/NEUTRAL .**

② **PLACE FAST IDLE SCREW ON HIGHEST STEP OF FAST IDLE CAM.**

③ **TURN FAST IDLE SCREW IN OR OUT TO OBTAIN SPECIFIED FAST IDLE R.P.M. - (SEE LABEL).**

**Fast idle adjustment**

① **ATTACH RUBBER BAND TO INTER-MEDIATE CHOKE LEVER.**

② **OPEN THROTTLE TO ALLOW CHOKE VALVE TO CLOSE.**

③ **SET UP ANGLE GAGE AND SET ANGLE TO SPECIFICATIONS.**

④ **PLACE FAST IDLE SCREW ON SECOND STEP OF CAM AGAINST RISE OF HIGH STEP.**

⑤ **PUSH ON CHOKE SHAFT LEVER TO OPEN CHOKE VALVE AND TO MAKE CONTACT WITH BLACK CLOSING TANG.**

⑥ **SUPPORT AT "S" AND ADJUST BY BENDING FAST IDLE CAM LINK UNTIL BUBBLE IS CENTERED.**

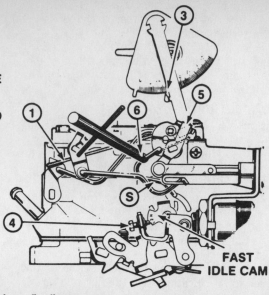

**Fast idle cam (choke rod) adjustment**

2. Rotate the degree scale until it is zeroed.

3. Close the choke and install the degree scale onto the choke plate. Center the leveling bubble.

4. Rotate the scale so that the specified degree is opposite the scale pointer.

5. Place the fast idle screw on the second step of the cam (against the high step). Close the choke by pushing in the intermediate lever.

6. Bend the fast idle cam rod at the U to adjust the angle to specifications.

### AIR VALVE ROD ADJUSTMENT

1. Seat the vacuum diaphragm with an outside vacuum source. Tape over the purge bleed hole if present.

2. Close the air valve.

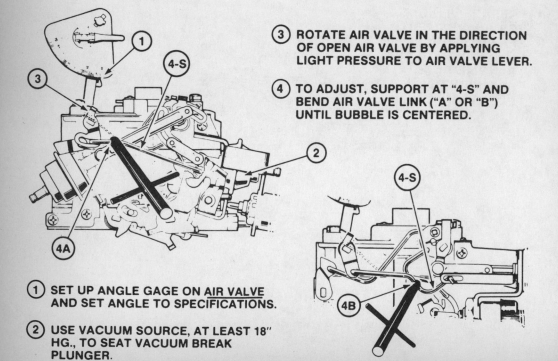

③ **ROTATE AIR VALVE IN THE DIRECTION OF OPEN AIR VALVE BY APPLYING LIGHT PRESSURE TO AIR VALVE LEVER.**

④ **TO ADJUST, SUPPORT AT "4-S" AND BEND AIR VALVE LINK ("A" OR "B") UNTIL BUBBLE IS CENTERED.**

① **SET UP ANGLE GAGE ON AIR VALVE AND SET ANGLE TO SPECIFICATIONS.**

② **USE VACUUM SOURCE, AT LEAST 18" HG., TO SEAT VACUUM BREAK PLUNGER.**

**Air valve rod adjustment**

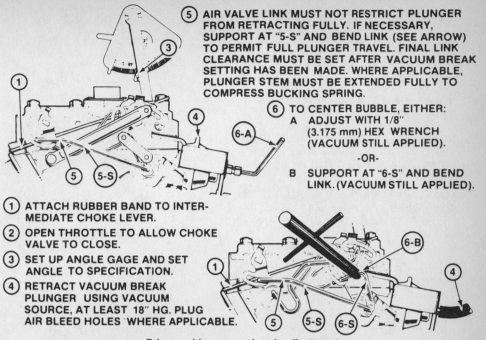

5. AIR VALVE LINK MUST NOT RESTRICT PLUNGER FROM RETRACTING FULLY. IF NECESSARY, SUPPORT AT "5-S" AND BEND LINK (SEE ARROW) TO PERMIT FULL PLUNGER TRAVEL. FINAL LINK CLEARANCE MUST BE SET AFTER VACUUM BREAK SETTING HAS BEEN MADE. WHERE APPLICABLE, PLUNGER STEM MUST BE EXTENDED FULLY TO COMPRESS BUCKING SPRING.

6. TO CENTER BUBBLE, EITHER:
A   ADJUST WITH 1/8" (3.175 mm) HEX WRENCH (VACUUM STILL APPLIED).
-OR-
B   SUPPORT AT "6-S" AND BEND LINK. (VACUUM STILL APPLIED).

1. ATTACH RUBBER BAND TO INTERMEDIATE CHOKE LEVER.
2. OPEN THROTTLE TO ALLOW CHOKE VALVE TO CLOSE.
3. SET UP ANGLE GAGE AND SET ANGLE TO SPECIFICATION.
4. RETRACT VACUUM BREAK PLUNGER USING VACUUM SOURCE, AT LEAST 18" HG. PLUG AIR BLEED HOLES WHERE APPLICABLE.

**Primary side vacuum break adjustment**

3. Insert the specified gauge between the rod and the end of the slot in the plunger.
4. Bend the rod to adjust the clearance.

### PRIMARY SIDE VACUUM BREAK ADJUSTMENT

1. Follow Steps 1-4 of the Fast Idle Cam Adjustment.
2. Seat the choke vacuum diaphragm with an outside vacuum source.
3. Push in on the intermediate choke lever to close the choke valve, and hold closed during adjustment.
4. Adjust by using a 1/8" hex wrench to turn the screw in the rear cover until the bubble is centered.
5. After adjusting, apply RTV silicone sealant over the screw to seal the setting.

### SECONDARY VACUUM BREAK ADJUSTMENT

1. Follow Steps 1-4 of the Fast Idle Cam Adjustment.
2. Seat the choke vacuum diaphragm with an outside vacuum source.
3. Push in on the intermediate choke lever to close the choke valve, and hold closed during adjustment. Make sure the plunger spring is compressed and seated, if present.
4. Adjust by using a 1/8" hex wrench to turn the screw in the rear cover until the bubble is centered.
5. After adjusting, apply RTV silicone sealant over the screw to seal the setting.

### CHOKE UNLOADER ADJUSTMENT

1. Follow Steps 1-4 of the Fast Idle Cam Adjustment.
2. Hold the primary throttle wide open.
3. If the engine is warm, close the choke valve by pushing in on the intermediate choke lever.
4. Bend the unloader tang until the bubble is centered.

### SECONDARY LOCKOUT ADJUSTMENT

1. Pull the choke wide open by pushing out on the intermediate choke lever.
2. Open the throttle until the end of the secondary actuating lever is opposite the toe of the lockout lever.
3. Gauge clearance between the lockout lever and secondary lever should be as specified.
4. To adjust, bend the lockout lever where it contacts the fast idle cam.

### AIR VALVE SPRING ADJUSTMENT

1. To gain access to the lock screw, remove the intermediate choke link.
2. Using a 3/32" hex wrench, loosen the lock screw.
3. Turn the adjusting screw clockwise until the air valve opens slightly, then turn the screw counterclockwise until the valve closes and continue the number of specified turns.
4. Tighten the lock screw and apply lithium grease to the pin and the spring contact area.

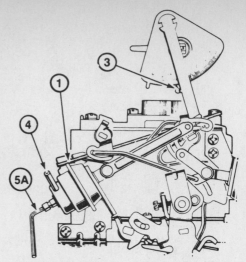

(1) ATTACH RUBBER BAND TO INTER-MEDIATE CHOKE LEVER.

(2) OPEN THROTTLE TO ALLOW CHOKE VALVE TO CLOSE.

(3) SET UP ANGLE GAGE AND SET ANGLE TO SPECIFICATION.

(4) RETRACT VACUUM BREAK PLUNGER USING VACUUM SOURCE, AT LEAST 18" HG. PLUG AIR BLEED HOLES WHERE APPLICABLE.

WHERE APPLICABLE, PLUNGER STEM MUST BE EXTENDED FULLY TO COMPRESS PLUNGER BUCKING SPRING.

(5) TO CENTER BUBBLE, EITHER:

   A.   ADJUST WITH 1/8" (3.175 mm) HEX WRENCH (VACUUM STILL APPLIED)

          -OR

   B.   SUPPORT AT "5-S", BEND LINK (VACUUM STILL APPLIED)

**Secondary vacuum break adjustment**

(1) ATTACH RUBBER BAND TO INTER-MEDIATE CHOKE LEVER.

(2) OPEN THROTTLE TO ALLOW CHOKE VALVE TO CLOSE.

(3) SET UP ANGLE GAGE AND SET ANGLE TO SPECIFICATIONS.

(4) HOLD THROTTLE LEVER IN WIDE OPEN POSITION.

(5) PUSH ON CHOKE SHAFT LEVER TO OPEN CHOKE VALVE AND TO MAKE CONTACT WITH BLACK CLOSING TANG.

(6) ADJUST BY BENDING TANG UNTIL BUBBLE IS CENTERED.

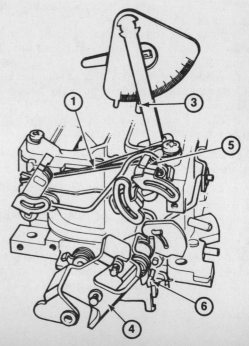

**Choke unloader adjustment**

① HOLD CHOKE VALVE WIDE OPEN BY PUSHING DOWN ON INTERMEDIATE CHOKE LEVER.

② OPEN THROTTLE LEVER UNTIL END OF SECONDARY ACTUATING LEVER IS OPPOSITE TOE OF LOCKOUT LEVER.

③ GAGE CLEARANCE - DIMENSION SHOULD BE .025".

④ IF NECESSARY TO ADJUST, BEND LOCKOUT LEVER TANG CONTACTING FAST IDLE CAM.

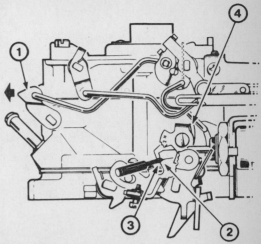

**Secondary lockout adjustment**

## CHOKE LINK/FAST IDLE CAM ADJUSTMENT

1. Connect a rubber band to the intermediate choke lever, then open the throttle valve to allow the choke valve to close.

2. Set up the angle gauge and the angle to specifications.

3. Position the fast idle screw on the second step of the fast idle cam (against the rise of the high step).

4. Turn the choke lever shaft to open the choke valve and make contact with the black closing tang.

5. Support at the **S** point and bend the fast idle cam link until the bubble is centered.

① IF NECESSARY, REMOVE INTERMEDIATE CHOKE LINK, TO GAIN ACCESS TO LOCK SCREW.

② LOOSEN LOCK SCREW USING 3/32" (2.381mm) HEX WRENCH.

③ TURN TENSION-ADJUSTING SCREW ↻ UNTIL AIR VALVE OPENS SLIGHTLY.

TURN ADJUSTING SCREW ↺ UNTIL AIR VALVE JUST CLOSES. CONTINUE ↺ SPECIFIED NUMBER OF TURNS.

④ TIGHTEN LOCK SCREW.

⑤ APPLY LITHIUM BASE GREASE TO LUBRICATE PIN AND SPRING CONTACT AREA.

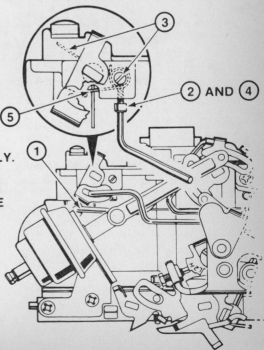

**Air valve spring adjustment**

## REMOVAL AND INSTALLATION

1. Remove the air cleaner and gasket.
2. Disconnect the fuel pipe and all vacuum lines.
3. Tag and disconnect all electrical connections.
4. If equipped with an Automatic Transaxle, disconnect the downshift cable.
5. If equipped with cruise control, disconnect the linkage.
6. Unscrew the carburetor mounting bolts and remove the carburetor.
7. Inspect the EFE heater for damage. Be sure that the throttle body and EFE mating surfaces are clean.
8. Install the carburetor and tighten the nuts alternately to the proper specifications.
9. Installation of the remaining components is in the reverse order of removal.

## OVERHAUL

Efficient carburetion depends greatly on careful cleaning and inspection during overhaul, since dirt, gum, water, or varnish in or on the carburetor parts are often responsible for poor performance.

Overhaul your carburetor in a clean, dust-free area. Carefully disassemble the carburetor, referring often to the exploded views and directions packaged with the rebuilding kit. Keep all similar and look-alike parts segregated during disassembly and cleaning to avoid accidental interchange during assembly. Make a note of all jet sizes.

When the carburetor is disassembled, wash all parts (except diaphragms, electric choke units, pump plunger, and any other plastic, leather, fiber, or rubber parts) in clean carburetor solvent. Do not leave parts in the solvent any longer than is necessary to sufficiently loosen the deposits. Excessive cleaning may remove the special finish from the float bowl and choke valve bodies, leaving these parts unfit for service. Rinse all parts in clean solvent and blow them dry with compressed air or allow them to air dry. Wipe clean all cork, plastic, leather, and fiber parts with a clean, lint-free cloth.

Blow out all passages and jets with compressed air and be sure that there are no restrictions or blockages. Never use wire or similar tools to clean jets, fuel passages, or air bleeds. Clean all jets and valves separately to avoid accidental interchange.

Check all parts for wear or damage. If wear or damage is found, replace the defective parts. Especially check the following:

1. Check the float needle and seat for wear. If wear is found, replace the complete assembly.
2. Check the float hinge pin for wear and the float(s) for dents or distortion. Replace the float if fuel has leaked into it.
3. Check the throttle and choke shaft bores for wear or an out-of-round condition. Damage or wear to the throttle arm, shaft, or shaft bore will often require replacement of the throttle body. These parts require a close tolerance of fit; wear may allow air leakage, which could affect starting and idling.

NOTE: *Throttle shafts and bushings are not included in overhaul kits. They can be purchases separately.*

4. Inspect the idle mixture adjusting needles for burrs or grooves. Any such condition requires replacement of the needle, since you will not be able to obtain a satisfactory idle.
5. Test the accelerator pump check valves. They should pass air one way but not the other. Test for proper seating by blowing and sucking on the valve. Replace the valve check ball and spring as necessary. If the valve is satisfactory, wash the valve parts again to remove breath moisture.
6. Check the bowl cover for warped surfaces with a straightedge.
7. Closely inspect the accelerator pump plunger for wear and damage, replacing as necessary.
8. After the carburetor is assembled, check the choke valve for freedom of operation.

Carburetor overhaul kits are recommended for each overhaul. These kits contain all gaskets and new parts to replace those which deteriorate most rapidly. Failure to replace all parts supplied with the kit (especially gaskets) can result in poor performance later.

Some carburetor manufacturers supply overhaul kits for three basic types: minor repair; major repair; and gasket kits. Basically, they contain the following:

**Minor Repair Kits:**
- All gaskets
- Float needle valve
- All diagrams
- Spring for the pump diaphragm

**Major Repair Kits:**
- All jets and gaskets
- All diaphragms
- Float needle valve
- Pump ball valve
- Float
- Complete intermediate rod
- Intermediate pump lever
- Some cover holddown screws and washers

**Gasket Kits:**
- All gaskets

After cleaning and checking all components, reassemble the carburetor, using new parts and referring to the exploded view. When reassembling, make sure that all screws and jets are tight in their seats, but do not overtighten as the tips will be distorted. Tighten all screws gradually, in rotation. Do not tighten needle valves into their seats; uneven jetting will result. Always use new gaskets. Be sure to adjust the float level when reassembling.

### PRELIMINARY CHECKS

The following should be observed before attempting any adjustments.

1. Thoroughly warm the engine. If the engine is cold, be sure that it reaches operating temperature.

2. Check the torque of all carburetor mounting nuts and assembly screws. Also check the intake manifold-to-cylinder head bolts. If air is leaking at any of these points, any attempts at adjustment will inevitably lead to frustration.

3. Check the manifold heat control valve (if used) to be sure that it is free.

4. Check and adjust the choke as necessary.

5. Adjust the idle speed and mixture. If the mixture screws are capped, don't adjust them unless all other causes of rough idle have been eliminated. If any adjustments are performed that might possible change the idle speed or mixture, adjust the idle and mixture again when you are finished.

Before you make any carburetor adjustments make sure that the engine is in tune. Many problems which are thought to be carburetor related can be traced to an engine which is simply out-of-tune. Any trouble in these areas will have symptoms like those of carburetor problems.

# GASOLINE FUEL INJECTION SYSTEM

NOTE: *This book contains testing and service procedures for your cars fuel injection system. More comprehensive testing and diagnosis procedures may be found in CHILTONS GUIDE TO FUEL INJECTION AND FEEDBACK CARBURETORS, book part number 7488, available at your local retailer.*

## Electric Fuel Pump

The electric fuel pumps are attached to the fuel sending unit, which is located in the fuel tank.

CAUTION: *Before opening any part of the fuel system, the pressure must be relieved. Follow the procedure below to relieve the pressure:*

### RELIEVING THE FUEL SYSTEM PRESSURE

1. Remove the fuel pump fuse from the fuse panel.

2. Start the engine and let it run until all fuel in the line is used.

3. Crank the starter an additional three seconds to relieve any residual pressure.

4. With the ignition OFF, replace the fuse.

### REMOVAL AND INSTALLATION

1. Relieve fuel system pressure.

2. Drain the fuel tank.

3. Disconnect wiring from the tank.

4. Remove the ground wire retaining screw from under the body.

5. Disconnect all hoses from the tank.

6. Support the tank on a jack and remove the retaining strap nuts.

7. Lower the tank and remove it.

8. Remove the fuel gauge/pump retaining ring using a spanner wrench such as tool J-24187.

9. Remove the gauge unit and the pump.

10. Installation is the reverse of removal. Always replace the O-ring under the gauge/pump retaining ring.

### TESTING THE FUEL PUMP

#### Pressure Test

1. Relive the fuel system pressure.

2. On TBI or MFI equipped engines, disconnect the fuel line from the EFI, then connect the fuel line to a pressure gauge.

NOTE: *If the system is equipped with a fuel return hose, squeeze it off so that an accurate reading can be obtained.*

3. On the TBI or MFI equipped engines, connect a jumper wire from the positive battery terminal to the G terminal of the ALCL unit or on the carbureted engines, start the engine, then check the fuel pressure.

4. The fuel pressure on the TBI unit, it is 9-13 psi and on the MFI system, it is 34-46 psi.

NOTE: *If the pressures do not indicate correctly, check the fuel line for restrictions or the pump for malfunctions.*

#### Volume Test

This test should be completed after the pressure test has been performed.

1. Disconnect the pressure gauge from the fuel line and connect a flexible tube from the fuel line to an unbreakable container.

NOTE: *If the engine is equipped with a fuel return line, squeeze off the line to obtain an accurate reading.*

2. Connect a jumper wire from the positive battery cable to the G terminal of the ALCL unit.

## E2SE Carburetor Specifications

| Year | Carburetor Identification | Float Level (in.) | Fast Idle Cam (deg.) | Choke Coil Lever (in.) | Air Valve Rod (deg.) | Primary Vacuum Break (deg.) | Secondary Vacuum Break (deg.) | Choke Unloader (deg.) |
|------|---------------------------|-------------------|----------------------|------------------------|----------------------|-----------------------------|-------------------------------|-----------------------|
| 1982 | 17082196 | 5/16 | 18° | .096 | — | 21° | 19° | 27° |
|      | 17082316 | 1/4 | 17° | .090 | 10 | 26° | 34° | 35° |
|      | 17082317 | 1/4 | 17° | .090 | 10 | 29° | 35° | 35° |
|      | 17082320 | 1/4 | 25° | .142 | 10 | 30° | 35° | 33° |
|      | 17082321 | 1/4 | 25° | .142 | 10 | 29° | 35° | 35° |
|      | 17082640 | 1/4 | 17° | .090 | 10 | 26° | 34° | 35° |
|      | 17082641 | 1/4 | 17° | .090 | 10 | 29° | 35° | 35° |
|      | 17082642 | 1/4 | 25° | .142 | 10 | 30° | 35° | 33° |
| 1983 | 17083356 | 13/32 | 22° | .085 | 1° | 25° | 35° | 30° |
|      | 17083357 | 13/32 | 22° | .085 | 1° | 25° | 35° | 30° |
|      | 17083358 | 13/32 | 22° | .085 | 1° | 25° | 35° | 30° |
|      | 17083359 | 13/32 | 22° | .085 | 1° | 25° | 35° | 30° |
|      | 17083368 | 1/8 | 22° | .085 | 1° | 25° | 35° | 30° |
|      | 17083370 | 1/8 | 22° | .085 | 1° | 25° | 35° | 30° |
|      | 17083450 | 1/8 | 28° | .085 | 1° | 27° | 35° | 45° |
|      | 17083451 | 1/8 | 28° | .085 | 1° | 27° | 35° | 45° |
|      | 17083452 | 1/8 | 28° | .085 | 1° | 27° | 35° | 45° |
|      | 17083453 | 1/8 | 28° | .085 | 1° | 27° | 35° | 45° |
|      | 17083454 | 1/8 | 28° | .085 | 1° | 27° | 35° | 45° |
|      | 17083455 | 1/8 | 28° | .085 | 1° | 27° | 35° | 45° |
|      | 17083456 | 1/8 | 28° | .085 | 1° | 27° | 35° | 45° |
|      | 17083630 | 1/4 | 28° | .085 | 1° | 27° | 35° | 45° |
|      | 17083631 | 1/4 | 28° | .085 | 1° | 27° | 35° | 45° |
|      | 17083632 | 1/4 | 28° | .085 | 1° | 27° | 35° | 45° |
|      | 17083633 | 1/4 | 28° | .085 | 1° | 27° | 35° | 45° |
|      | 17083634 | 1/4 | 28° | .085 | 1° | 27° | 35° | 45° |
|      | 17083635 | 1/4 | 28° | .085 | 1° | 27° | 35° | 45° |
|      | 17083636 | 1/4 | 28° | .085 | 1° | 27° | 35° | 45° |
|      | 17083650 | 1/8 | 28° | .085 | 1° | 27° | 35° | 45° |
| 1984 | 17072683 | 9/32 | 28° | .085 | 1° | 25° | 35° | 45° |
|      | 17074812 | 9/32 | 28° | .085 | 1° | 25° | 35° | 45° |
|      | 17084356 | 9/32 | 22° | .085 | 1° | 25° | 30° | 30° |
|      | 17084357 | 9/32 | 22° | .085 | 1° | 25° | 30° | 30° |
|      | 17084358 | 9/32 | 22° | .085 | 1° | 25° | 30° | 30° |
|      | 17084359 | 9/32 | 22° | .085 | 1° | 25° | 30° | 30° |
|      | 17084368 | 1/8 | 22° | .085 | 1° | 25° | 30° | 30° |
|      | 17084370 | 1/8 | 22° | .085 | 1° | 25° | 30° | 30° |
|      | 17084430 | 11/32 | 15° | .085 | 1° | 26° | 38° | 42° |

## E2SE Carburetor Specifications (cont.)

| Year | Carburetor Identification | Float Level (in.) | Fast Idle Cam (deg.) | Choke Coil Lever (in.) | Air Valve Rod (deg.) | Primary Vacuum Break (deg.) | Secondary Vacuum Break (deg.) | Choke Unloader (deg.) |
|------|---------------------------|-------------------|----------------------|------------------------|----------------------|-----------------------------|-------------------------------|-----------------------|
| 1984 (cont.) | 17084431 | $1\frac{1}{32}$ | 15° | .085 | 1° | 26° | 38° | 42° |
| | 17084434 | $1\frac{1}{32}$ | 15° | .085 | 1° | 26° | 38° | 42° |
| | 17084435 | $1\frac{1}{32}$ | 15° | .085 | 1° | 26° | 38° | 42° |
| | 17084452 | $\frac{5}{32}$ | 28° | .085 | 1° | 25° | 35° | 45° |
| | 17084453 | $\frac{5}{32}$ | 28° | .085 | 1° | 25° | 35° | 45° |
| | 17084455 | $\frac{5}{32}$ | 28° | .085 | 1° | 25° | 35° | 45° |
| | 17084456 | $\frac{5}{32}$ | 28° | .085 | 1° | 25° | 35° | 45° |
| | 17084458 | $\frac{5}{32}$ | 28° | .085 | 1° | 25° | 35° | 45° |
| | 17084532 | $\frac{5}{32}$ | 28° | .085 | 1° | 25° | 35° | 45° |
| | 17084534 | $\frac{5}{32}$ | 28° | .085 | 1° | 25° | 35° | 45° |
| | 17084535 | $\frac{5}{32}$ | 28° | .085 | 1° | 25° | 35° | 45° |
| | 17084537 | $\frac{5}{32}$ | 28° | .085 | 1° | 25° | 35° | 45° |
| | 17084538 | $\frac{5}{32}$ | 28° | .085 | 1° | 25° | 35° | 45° |
| | 17084540 | $\frac{5}{32}$ | 28° | .085 | 1° | 25° | 35° | 45° |
| | 17084542 | $\frac{1}{8}$ | 28° | .085 | 1° | 25° | 35° | 45° |
| | 17084632 | $\frac{9}{32}$ | 28° | .085 | 1° | 25° | 35° | 45° |
| | 17084633 | $\frac{9}{32}$ | 28° | .085 | 1° | 25° | 35° | 45° |
| | 17084635 | $\frac{9}{32}$ | 28° | .085 | 1° | 25° | 35° | 45° |
| | 17084636 | $\frac{9}{32}$ | 28° | .085 | 1° | 25° | 35° | 45° |
| 1985 | 17084534 | $\frac{5}{32}$ | 28° | .085 | 1° | 25° | 35° | 45° |
| | 17084535 | $\frac{5}{32}$ | 28° | .085 | 1° | 25° | 35° | 45° |
| | 17084540 | $\frac{5}{32}$ | 28° | .085 | 1° | 25° | 35° | 45° |
| | 17084542 | $\frac{1}{8}$ | 28° | .085 | 1° | 25° | 35° | 45° |
| | 17085356 | $\frac{1}{8}$ | 22° | .085 | 1° | 25° | 30° | 30° |
| | 17085357 | $\frac{9}{32}$ | 22° | .085 | 1° | 25° | 30° | 30° |
| | 17085358 | $\frac{1}{8}$ | 22° | .085 | 1° | 25° | 30° | 30° |
| | 17085359 | $\frac{9}{32}$ | 22° | .085 | 1° | 25° | 30° | 30° |
| | 17085368 | $\frac{1}{8}$ | 22° | .085 | 1° | 25° | 30° | 30° |
| | 17085369 | $\frac{9}{32}$ | 22° | .085 | 1° | 25° | 30° | 30° |
| | 17085370 | $\frac{1}{8}$ | 22° | .085 | 1° | 25° | 30° | 30° |
| | 17085371 | $\frac{9}{32}$ | 22° | .085 | 1° | 25° | 30° | 30° |
| | 17085452 | $\frac{5}{32}$ | 28° | .085 | 1° | 28° | 35° | 45° |
| | 17085453 | $\frac{5}{32}$ | 28° | .085 | 1° | 28° | 35° | 45° |
| | 17085458 | $\frac{5}{32}$ | 28° | .085 | 1° | 28° | 35° | 45° |
| 1986 | 17084534 | $\frac{5}{32}$ | 28° | .085 | 1° | 25° | 35° | 45° |
| | 17084535 | $\frac{5}{32}$ | 28° | .085 | 1° | 25° | 35° | 45° |
| | 17084540 | $\frac{5}{32}$ | 28° | .085 | 1° | 25° | 35° | 45° |
| | 17084542 | $\frac{5}{32}$ | 28° | .085 | 1° | 25° | 35° | 45° |

3. In 15 seconds, the fuel pump should supply ½ pint of fuel.

NOTE: *If the fuel volume is below minimum, check the fuel line for restrictions.*

4. After testing, reconnect the fuel line to the EFI unit.

## Throttle Body Injection (TBI)

Some 4-151 engines are equipped with electronic fuel injection. The computer (ECM) is in complete control of fuel metering under all driving conditions. The proper amount of fuel is injected directly into the intake manifold. An electric fuel pump located in the fuel tank maintains a constant fuel pressure between 9 and 13 psi. This electrical fuel pump is controlled by an electric fuel pump relay.

### THROTTLE BODY REMOVAL AND INSTALLATION

1. Relieve the fuel system pressure as described above.

2. Remove the air cleaner.

3. Disconnect all wiring from the unit.

4. Disconnect the linkage from the unit.

5. Mark and disconnect the vacuum lines from the unit.

6. Follow the CAUTION under the fuel Pressure Test above, then disconnect the fuel feed and return lines from the unit.

7. Unbolt and remove the unit.

8. Installation is the reverse of removal. Torque the TBI attaching bolts to 10-15 ft.lb.; the fuel lines to 19 ft.lb.

### INJECTOR REPLACEMENT

1. Relieve fuel system pressure as described above.

2. Remove the air cleaner.

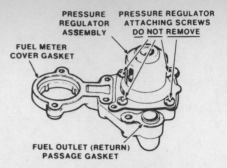

**Bottom view of the fuel meter cover**

3. Disconnect the injector by squeezing the two tabs together and pulling straight up.

4. Remove the fuel meter cover by removing the five attaching bolts; note the positions of the two short bolts.

CAUTION: *Do not remove the four screws securing the pressure regulator to the meter cover. The pressure regulator includes a large spring under heavy tension.*

5. Using a small pliers, grasp the center collar of the injector, between the terminals and remove it with a gentle, upward, twisting motion.

6. Installation is the reverse of removal. Always use new O-ring coated with clean automatic transmission fluid. Make sure all O-rings and steel washers are properly located. Make sure that the injector is fully seated with its locating lug mated with its notch and the electrical terminals parallel with the throttle shaft in the throttle body. Apply thread compound to the first three threads of the fuel meter cover bolts.

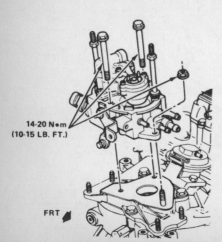

**Throttle Body Injection (TBI) unit mounting**

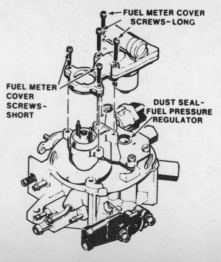

**Removing the fuel meter cover screws**

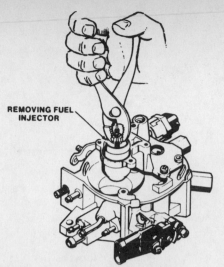

REMOVING FUEL
INJECTOR

Removing a fuel injector from the TBI

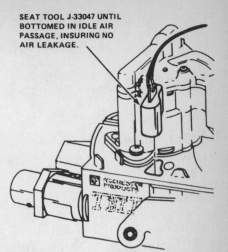

SEAT TOOL J-33047 UNTIL
BOTTOMED IN IDLE AIR
PASSAGE, INSURING NO
AIR LEAKAGE.

Installing tool J-33047 in the TBI for idle adjustment

## IDLE SPEED ADJUSTMENT

This procedure should be performed only when the throttle body parts have been replaced.

NOTE: *The following procedure requires the use of a special tool.*

1. Remove the air cleaner and gasket.
2. Plug the vacuum port on the TBI marked THERMAC.
3. If the car is equipped with a tamper resistant plug cover the throttle stop screw, the TBI unit must be removed as instructed above, to remove the plug.
4. Remove the throttle valve cable from the throttle control bracket to allow access to the throttle stop screw.
5. Connect a tachometer to the engine.
6. Start the engine and run it to normal operating temperature.
7. Install tool J-33047 into the idle air passage of the throttle body. Be sure that the tool is fully seated and that no air leaks exist.
8. Using a #20 Torx bit, turn the minimum air screw until the engine rpm is 675-725 with

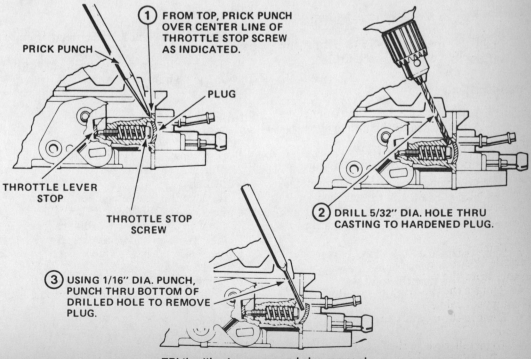

① FROM TOP, PRICK PUNCH OVER CENTER LINE OF THROTTLE STOP SCREW AS INDICATED.

PRICK PUNCH

PLUG

THROTTLE LEVER STOP

THROTTLE STOP SCREW

② DRILL 5/32" DIA. HOLE THRU CASTING TO HARDENED PLUG.

③ USING 1/16" DIA. PUNCH, PUNCH THRU BOTTOM OF DRILLED HOLE TO REMOVE PLUG.

TBI throttle stop screw and plug removal

auto. trans. or 725-825 with manual trans. The AT should be in Park; the MT in neutral.

9. Stop the engine and remove the special tool.

10. Install the cable on the throttle body.

11. Use RTV sealant to cover the throttle stop screw.

## Multi Port Fuel Injection

The system is controlled by the ECM which is in complete control of the fuel delivery during normal driving conditions.

The intake manifold functions like that of a diesel, to let air into the engine. The fuel is injected by separate injectors mounted over the intake valves; the injectors operate on every revolution of the crankshaft.

Of the various sensors which receive both temperature and barometric pressure information, the Mass Air Flow sensor (mounted between the air cleaner and the throttle body) measures the volume and temperature of the air moving through the intake manifold.

CAUTION: *Before opening any part of the fuel system, the pressure must be relieved. Follow the procedure below to relieve the pressure:*

The fuel pressure release fitting is located at the top rear of the fuel injection rail.

1. Remove the cap from the pressure release fitting, then connect a flexible tube to the fitting and place the other end in an unbreakable container.

NOTE: *Place a shop towel around the fitting to collect any excess fuel from spilling.*

2. Open the pressure release fitting and bleed off the fuel, then close the fitting.

## Throttle Body

The throttle body is located at the front of the engine and is attached to the intake plenum.

### REMOVAL AND INSTALLATION

1. Disconnect the negative battery cable.

2. Drain the coolant from the cooling system until the level is below the throttle body.

3. Remove the air inlet duct, the vacuum hoses and the coolant hoses from the throttle body.

4. Remove the Idle Air Control (IAC) and the Throttle Position Sensor (TPS) electrical connectors from the throttle body.

5. Remove the throttle and the cruise control (if equipped) cables.

6. Remove the mounting bolts and the throttle body.

7. To install, reverse the removal procedures and refill the cooling system.

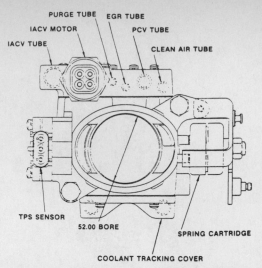

Location of the throttle body connections—MFI

## Plenum

The Plenum is the top portion of the intake manifold. This portion must be removed before servicing the injector system.

### REMOVAL AND INSTALLATION

1. Disconnect the negative battery cable.

2. Tag and disconnect the vacuum lines.

3. Remove the EGR to plenum nuts.

4. Remove the two throttle body bolts.

5. Remove the throttle cable bracket bolts.

6. Remove the ignition wire plastic shield bolts.

7. Remove the plenum bolts.

8. Remove the plenum and gaskets from the engine.

9. To install reverse steps 1 through 8. Torque the plenum bolts to 16 ft.lb.

## Fuel Rail

### REMOVAL AND INSTALLATION

1. Disconnect the negative battery cable.

2. Relieve the fuel system pressure as discribed above.

3. Remove the intake manifold plenum.

4. Remove the fuel line bracket bolt.

5. Remove the fuel lines at the rail.

NOTE: *Wrap a soft cloth around the fuel lines to collect fuel, then place the cloth in an approved container.*

6. Remove the fuel line O-rings.

7. Disconnect the vacuum line at the pressure regulator.

8. Remove the fuel rail retaining bolts.

9. Disconnect the injector electrical connectors.

10. Remove the fuel rail assembly.

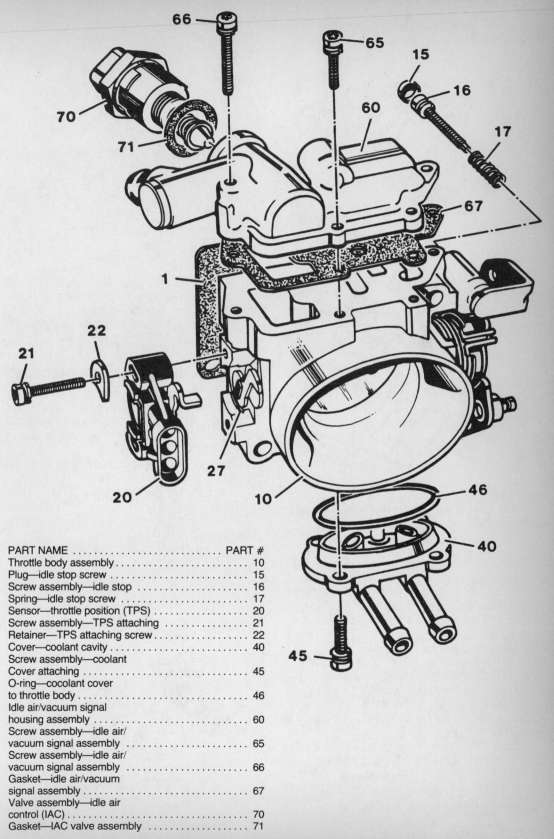

**Exploded view of the throttle body—MFI**

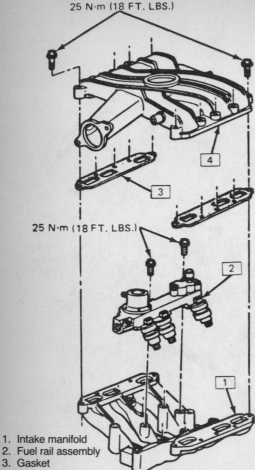

25 N·m (18 FT. LBS.)

25 N·m (18 FT. LBS.)

1. Intake manifold
2. Fuel rail assembly
3. Gasket
4. Plenum

**Exploded view of the plenum, fuel rail and intake manifold—MFI**

NOTE: *Use care in removing the fuel rail assembly, to prevent damage to the injector electrical connector terminals and injector spray tips. The fuel injector is an electrical component and should not be immersed in cleaner.*

11. If the injector seals were removed from the injectors, lubricate the new seals and install them on the spray tip end of each injector.

12. Tilt the fuel rail assembly so that the injectors fit into the intake manifold and install the fuel rail onto the manifold.

13. Install the fuel rail attaching bolts and torque to 19 ft.lb.

14. The ramainder of the installation process is the reverse of the removal procedure.

## Fuel Injectors

### REMOVAL AND INSTALLATION

1. Refer to the Fuel Rail, Removal and Installation procedures in this section and remove the fuel rail.

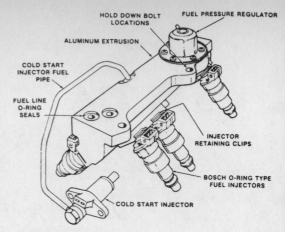

**View of the fuel rail—MFI**

2. At each injector, turn the retaining clip 90 degrees (to release the injector), then pull the injector from the fuel rail.

3. To install, use new O-rings and gaskets, then reverse the removal procedures.

## IDLE AIR CONTROL VALVE REPLACEMENT

The idle air control valve is mounted to the throttle body and controls the bypass air around the throttle plate; it is used to control the engine idle speed, to prevent stalls due to changes in the engine load.

1. Remove the electrical connector from the Idle Air Control (IAC) valve assembly.

2. Unscrew the IAC from the throttle body and discard the gasket.

NOTE: *Do not remove the thread locking compound from the threads.*

3. To install, use a new gasket and reverse the removal procedures.

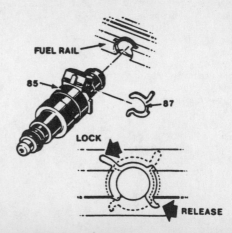

**85 INJECTOR - PORT**
**87 CLIP-INJECTOR RETAINER**
**Disconnect the fuel injector from the fuel rail—MFI**

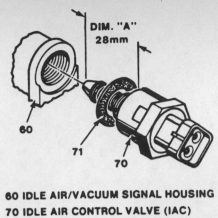

**60 IDLE AIR/VACUUM SIGNAL HOUSING**

**70 IDLE AIR CONTROL VALVE (IAC)**

**71 IAC GASKET**

View of the idle air control valve—MFI

## COLD START VALVE REPLACEMENT

The cold start valve (not controlled by the ECM) provides additional fuel during the starting mode to improve cold start ups.

1. Disconnect the negative battery cable.
2. Remove the IAC pipe and the engine mount strut brace.
3. Remove the fuel line from the fuel rail, the electrical connector from the valve and the valve retaining bolt.
4. Pull the cold start valve from the fuel rail.
5. To install, use new O-rings and reverse steps 1 through 4.

## ADJUSTMENTS

### Minimum Idle Speed

The engine should be at normal operating temperature before making this adjustment

1. Using an awl, pierce the idle stop screw plug (located on the side of the throttle body) and remove it by prying it from the housing.
2. Using a jumper wire, ground the diagnostic lead of the IAC motor.
3. Turn on the ignition, DO NOT start the

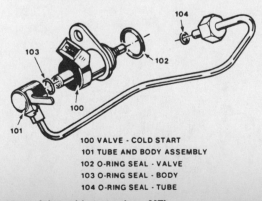

**100 VALVE - COLD START**

**101 TUBE AND BODY ASSEMBLY**

**102 O-RING SEAL - VALVE**

**103 O-RING SEAL - BODY**

**104 O-RING SEAL - TUBE**

View of the cold start valve—MFI

engine and wait for 30 seconds, then disconnect the IAC electrical connector. Remove the diagnostic lead ground lead and start the engine. Allow the system to go to closed loop.

4. Adjust the idle set screw to 550 rpm for the automatic transaxle (in Drive) or 650 rpm for the manual transaxle (in Neutral).
5. Turn the ignition Off and reconnect the IAC motor lead.
6. Using a voltmeter, adjust the TPS to 0.55 ± 0.1 volt and secure the TPS.
7. Recheck the setting, then start the engine and check for proper idle operation.
8. Seal the idle stop screw with silicone sealer.

### Cold Start Valve Assembly

This procedure is to be performed ONLY when installing the Cold Start Valve Assembly.

1. Turn the cold start valve completely into the body, until it seats.
2. Back out the valve one complete turn, until the electrical connector is at the top.
3. Bend the body tang forward to limit the rotation to less than a full turn.
4. Coat the new O-ring with engine oil and install it into the fuel rail.

## DIESEL FUEL SYSTEM

The diesel injection pump is mounted on top of the engine. It is gear driven by the camshaft and turns at camshaft speed. A light pressure rotary pump injects a metered amount of fuel into each cylinder at the precise time. Fuel delivery lines are the same length to prevent any difference in timing, from cylinder to cylinder. The timing advance is also controlled by the fuel pump. Engine rpm is controlled by the rotary fuel metering valve.

The fuel filter is located between the fuel pump and the injection pump at the left rear of the engine.

An electric fuel pump is used which is located at the front of the engine next to the fuel heater. Excess fuel returns to the tank via the fuel return line.

NOTE: *Because of the exacting nature of the diesel injection system all major repairs should be referred to your local GM dealer*

### Fuel Supply Pump

#### REMOVAL AND INSTALLATION

1. Disconnect the negative battery terminal.
2. Remove the air cleaner.
3. Unplug the electrical connection.
4. Using a ¾" wrench to support the inlet fitting, use a ⅝" wrench to unscrew the inlet tube.

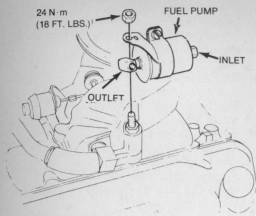

**Fuel pump—diesel**

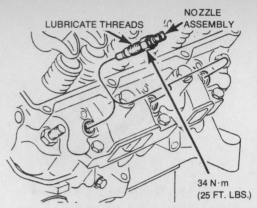

**V6 nozzle installation**

5. Remove the outlet tube.

6. Installation is the reverse of removal. After the pump has been replaced disconnect the fuel line at the filter. Turn the ignition on and bleed the lines. If the pump runs with a clicking sound, or air bubbles show up in the fuel, check the line for leaks. Check all connections to be sure they are dry. When the clicking noise disappears, tighten the line.

## Injection Pump
### REMOVAL AND INSTALLATION

1. Remove the air cleaner.

2. Remove the crankcase ventilation filter and pipes from the valve cover and air crossover.

3. Remove the air crossover and install special cover J-29657 or its equal. Remove the fuel lines, filter and fuel pump as an assembly. Cap all line openings.

4. Disconnect the throttle cable. Remove the return spring.

5. Remove the throttle and TV detent cables from the intake manifold brackets.

6. Disconnect the fuel return line from the injection pump.

7. Disconnect the injection line clamps, closest to the pump.

8. Disconnect the injection lines from the pump. Cap all openings. Carefully reposition the fuel lines.

9. Remove the two bolts retaining the injection pump.

10. Remove the pump. Discard the pump to adapter O-ring.

11. Installation is the reverse of removal, with the following recommendations. Position the number one cylinder to the firing position. Install a new O-ring, then install the pump fully, seating it by hand. If a new or intermediate adapter plate is used, set the pump at the center slots on the mounting flange. If the origi-

nal adapter is used align the pump timing mark and the adapter mark. Torque the pump bolts to 35 ft.lb.

## Injector
### REMOVAL AND INSTALLATION

NOTE: *When the lines are disconnected use a back-up wrench on the upper injection nozzle hex. It may also be necessary to jack up the engine to gain access to the back bank of injectors.*

1. Remove the fuel injection lines as described below.

2. Remove the injector nozzles.

NOTE: *When replacing the injectors, be sure to use new copper gaskets.*

3. Installation is the reverse of removal.

When reinstalling the injectors special lubricant (GM part 9985462 or its equal) must be applied to the nozzle threads. Torque the injectors to 25 ft.lb. Make sure the copper gasket is installed on the nozzle.

## Fuel Pump Lines
### REMOVAL AND INSTALLATION

All lines may be removed without moving the injection pump. It is not necessary to use a back-up wrench.

1. Remove the air cleaner.

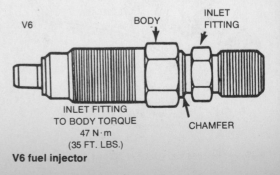

**V6 fuel injector**

2. Remove the filters and pipes from the valve covers and air crossover.

3. Remove the air crossover. Cap the intake manifold with special cover J-29657 or its equal.

4. Remove the injection pump line clamps. Remove the injection pump lines. Cap open lines, nozzles and pump fittings. Use a back-up wrench on the nozzle hex to prevent a fuel leak.

5. Installation is the reverse of removal.

### DIESEL IDLE SPEED ADJUSTMENT

1. Apply the parking brake, then place the transaxle in Park and block the drive wheels.

2. Start the engine and allow it to reach operating temperature, then turn it Off.

3. Remove the air cleaner cover and the MAP sensor retainer, then move the MAP sensor (with the leads and the hoses attached) aside.

4. Remove the air cleaner assembly and install tool J-26996-1 on the intake manifold.

5. Clean the rpm counter on the front cover and the crankshaft balancer rim. Install the magnetic pick-up probe tool J-26925 into the rpm counter, then connect the power leads to the battery.

6. If equipped with A/C, disconnect the compressor clutch lead from the compressor. If equipped with cruise control, remove the servo cable retainer and disconnect the servo throttle cable from the servo blade.

7. Make sure all of the electrical accessories are turned Off.

8. Start the engine and place the transaxle in Drive, then check the slow idle speed reading.

9. Turn Off the engine and unplug the engine coolant temperature sensor connector.

10. Start the engine and place the transaxle in Drive, then check the fast idle speed (allow the plunger to extend by opening the throttle slightly.

11. Connect the engine coolant temperature sensor connector and recheck and/or reset the slow idle speed.

12. Turn Off the engine and reconnect the A/C compressor lead, if equipped.

13. To complete the installation, reverse the removal procedures.

### INJECTION TIMING CHECKING

NOTE: *A special diesel timing meter is needed to check injection timing. There are a few variations of this meter, but the type desirable here uses a signal through a glow plug probe to determine combustion timing. The meter picks up the engine speed in RPM and the crankshaft position from the crankshaft balancer. This tool is available at automotive supply houses and from tool jobbers, and is the counterpart to a gasoline engine timing light, coupled with a tachometer. An intake manifold cover is also needed.*

*The marks on the pump and adapter flange will normally be aligned within 0.050".*

1. Place the transmission shift lever in Park, apply the parking brake and block the rear wheels.

2. Start the engine and let it run at idle until fully warm. Shut off the engine.

NOTE: *If the engine is not allowed to completely warm up, the probe may soot up, causing incorrect timing readings.*

3. Remove the air cleaner assembly and carefully install cover J-26996-1. This cover over the intake is important. Disconnect the EGR valve hose.

4. Clean away all dirt from the engine probe holder (RPM counter) and the crankshaft balancer rim.

5. Clean the lens on both ends of the glow plug probe and clean the lens in the photoelectric pick-up. Use a tooth pick to scrape the carbon from the combustion chamber side of the glow plug probe, then look through the probe to make sure it's clean. Cleanliness is crucial for accurate readings.

6. Install the probe into the crankshaft RPM counter (probe holder) on the engine front cover.

7. Remove the glow plug from No. 1 cylinder. Install the glow plug probe in the glow plug opening, and torque to 8 ft.lb.

8. Set the timing meter offset selector to **A** (20).

9. Connect the battery leads, red to positive, black to negative.

10. Disconnect the two-lead connector at the generator.

11. Start the engine. Adjust the engine RPM to the speed specified on the emissions control decal.

12. Observe the timing reading, then observe it again in 2 minutes. When the readings stabilize over the 2 minutes intervals, compare that final stabilized reading to the one specified on the emissions control decal. The timing reading will be an ATDC (After Top Dead Center) reading when set to specifications.

13. Disconnect the timing meter and install the removed glow plug, torquing it to 15 ft.lb.

14. Connect the generator two-lead connection.

15. Install the air cleaner assembly and connect the EGR valve hose.

### INJECTION TIMING ADJUSTING

1. Shut off the engine.

2. Note the relative position of the marks on

the pump flange and either the pump intermediate adapter.

3. Loosen the nuts or bolts holding the pump to a point where the pump can just be rotated. You may need a wrench with a slight offset to clear the fuel return line.

4. Rotate the pump to the left to advance the timing and to the right to retard the timing. The width of the mark on the intermediate adaptor is about ⅔ of a degree. Move the pump the amount that is needed and tighten the pump retaining nuts to 35 ft.lb.

5. Start the engine and recheck the timing as described earlier. Reset the timing if necessary.

6. Reset the fast and curb idle speeds.

NOTE: *Wild needle fluctuations on the timing meter indicate a cylinder not firing properly. Correction of this condition must be made prior to adjusting the timing.*

7. If after resetting the timing, the timing marks are far apart and the engine still runs poorly, the dynamic timing could still be off. It is possible that a malfunctioning cylinder will cause incorrect timing. If this occurs, it is essential that timing be checked in cylinder 1 or 4. If different timing exists between cylinders, try both positions to determine which timing works best.

### VACUUM REGULATOR VALVE ADJUSTMENT

1. Disconnect the EGR valve pipe assembly from the air crossover, then remove the air crossover.

2. Disconnect the throttle cable and the TV cable from the pump throttle lever.

3. Loosen the vacuum regulator valve-to-injection pump bolts.

4. Install tool BT-7944 or J-26701-15 to the injection pump throttle lever, then place angle gauge tool BT-7704 or J-26701 on the adapter.

NOTE: *It may be necessary to file the tool so that it can fit on the pump's thicker throttle lever.*

5. Move the throttle lever to the wide open position and set the angle gauge to zero degrees.

6. Center the bubble in the level, then set the gauge to 49 degrees. Rotate the throttle lever so that the bubble is centered.

7. Attach a vacuum source to port **A** and the vacuum gauge to port **B**, then apply 22 in.Hg vacuum to port **A**.

8. Rotate the vacuum valve clockwise until 10.3-10.9 in.Hg vacuum is obtained.

9. Tighten the vacuum bolts, then remove the vacuum source and the gauge.

10. Connect the throttle cable and the TV cables to the pump throttle lever, then remove the intake manifold screens.

11. Install the air crossover and the EGR valve pipe assembly to the crossover. Torque the bolts to 19 ft.lb.

### Glow Plugs

NOTE: *A burned out Fast Glow glow plug may bulge then break off and drop into the pre-chamber when the glow plug is removed. When this occurs the cylinder head must be removed and the pre-chamber removed from the head to remove the broken tip. When installing a glow plug, apply lubricant 1052771 or equivalent to the threads only when the engine is equipped with aluminum cylinder heads.*

*It is important that the pre-chamber be fully installed flush to the surface of the cylinder head. If this is not done, cylinder head gasket or piston damage can occur.*

*When servicing the right rear glow plugs, it may be necessary to follow the procedures below.*

#### REMOVAL AND INSTALLATION

1. Remove the engine support strut (see above figure).

2. Rotate the intermediate steering shaft so that the steering gear stub shaft clamp bolt is in the up position and remove the clamp bolt. Then disconnect the intermediate shaft from the stub shaft.

CAUTION: *Failure to disconnect the intermediate shaft from the rack and pinion stub shaft can result in damage to the steering gear and/or intermediate shaft. This damage can cause loss of steering control which could result in a vehicle crash with possible bodily injury.*

3. Place a floor jack under the front crossmember of the cradle and raise the jack until the jack just starts to raise the car.

4. Remove the front two body mount bolts with the lower cushions and retainers. Then remove the cushions from the bolts.

The removal of any one body mount requires the loosening of the adjacent body mounts to permit the cradle to seperate from the body. Take care to prevent breaking the plastic fan shroud, or damaging frame attachments such as steering hoses and brake pipes, during replacement of body mounts.

When installing a body mount, take care to ensure that the body is seated properly in the frame mounting hole; otherwise, direct metal to metal contact will result between the frame and the body. The tube spacer should be in all bolt-in-body mounts. The insulator and metal washer should be positioned to prevent contact with the frame rail. Do not overtighten the body mount; a collasped tube spacer or stripped bolt may result.

Proper clamping by the mount depends on clean dry surfaces. If the body mount bolt doesn't screw in smoothly, it may be necessary to run a tap through the cage nut in the body to remove foreign material. Take care to ensure that the tap does not punch through the underbody.

Whenever the body is going to be moved in relation to the cradle, the intermediate shaft should be disconnected from the rack and pinion steering gear stub shaft.

CAUTION: *Failure to disconnect the intermediate shaft from the rack and pinion steering gear stub shaft can result in damage to the steering gear and/or intermediate shaft. This damage can cause loss of steering control which could result in a vehicle crash with possible bodily injury.*

5. Thread the body mount bolts with retainers a minimum of three turns into the cage nuts so that the bolts retain cradle movement.

6. Release the floor jack slowly until the crossmember contacts the body mount bolt retainers. As the jack is being lowered, watch and correct any interference with hoses, lines, pipes and cables.

CAUTION: *Do not place your hands between the crossmember and body mount to remove objects or correct interference while the jack is lowering.*

*Do not lower the cradle without it being restrained as possible damage can occur to the body and underhood items.*

7. Reverse the procedure for installation. Torque the intermediate steering shaft clamp bolt to 46 ft.lb. and the body mount bolts to 77 ft.lb.

## Fuel Tank

### REMOVAL AND INSTALLATION

1. Disconnect the negative cable at the battery. Raise and support the car.

2. Drain the tank. There is no drain plug; remaining fuel in the tank must be siphoned through the fuel feed line (the line to the fuel pump), because of the restrictor in the filler neck.

3. Disconnect the hose and the vapor return hose from the level sending unit fittings.

4. Remove the ground wire screw.

5. Unplug the level sending unit electrical connector.

6. Disconnect the vent hose.

7. Unbolt the support straps, and lower and remove the tank.

8. To install reverse steps 1 through 7.

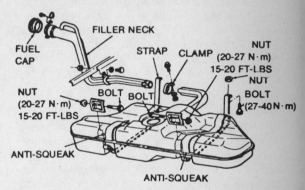

**Fuel tank removal and installation details**

# Chassis Electrical

**6**

## UNDERSTANDING BASIC ELECTRICTY

At the rate which both import and domestic manufacturers are incorporating electronic control systems into their production lines, it won't be long before every new vehicle is equipped with one or more on-board computer. These electronic components (with no moving parts) should theoretically last the life of the vehicle, provided nothing external happens to damage the circuits or memory chips.

While it is true that electronic components should never wear out, in the real world malfunctions do occur. It is also true that any computer-based system is extremely sensitive to electrical voltages and cannot tolerate careless or haphazard testing or service procedures. An inexperienced individual can literally do major damage looking for a minor problem by using the wrong kind of test equipment or connecting test leads or connectors with the ignition switch ON. When selecting test equipment, make sure the manufacturers instructions state that the tester is compatible with whatever type of electronic control system is being serviced. Read all instructions carefully and double check all test points before installing probes or making any test connections.

The following section outlines basic diagnosis techniques for dealing with computerized automotive control systems. Along with a general explanation of the various types of test equipment available to aid in servicing modern electronic automotive systems, basic repair techniques for wiring harnesses and connectors is given. Read the basic information before attempting any repairs or testing on any computerized system, to provide the background of information necessary to avoid the most common and obvious mistakes that can cost both time and money. Although the replacement and testing procedures are simple in themselves, the systems are not, and unless one has a thorough understanding of all components and their function within a particular computerized control system, the logical test sequence these systems demand cannot be followed. Minor malfunctions can make a big difference, so it is important to know how each component affects the operation of the overall electronic system to find the ultimate cause of a problem without replacing good components unnecessarily. It is not enough to use the correct test equipment; the test equipment must be used correctly.

### Safety Precautions

CAUTION: *Whenever working on or around any computer based microprocessor control system, always observe these general precautions to prevent the possibility of personal injury or damage to electronic components.*

• Never install or remove battery cables with the key ON or the engine running. Jumper cables should be connected with the key OFF to avoid power surges that can damage electronic control units. Engines equipped with computer controlled systems should avoid both giving and getting jump starts due to the possibility of serious damage to components from arcing in the engine compartment when connections are made with the ignition ON.

• Always remove the battery cables before charging the battery. Never use a high output charger on an installed battery or attempt to use any type of "hot shot" (24 volt) starting aid.

• Exercise care when inserting test probes into connectors to insure good connections without damaging the connector or spreading the pins. Always probe connectors from the rear (wire) side, NOT the pin side, to avoid accidental shorting of terminals during test procedures.

• Never remove or attach wiring harness connectors with the ignition switch ON, especially to an electronic control unit.

• Do not drop any components during service procedures and never apply 12 volts directly to any component (like a solenoid or relay) unless instructed specifically to do so. Some component electrical windings are designed to safely handle only 4 or 5 volts and can be destroyed in seconds if 12 volts are applied directly to the connector.

• Remove the electronic control unit if the vehicle is to be placed in an environment where temperatures exceed approximately 176°F (80°C), such as a paint spray booth or when arc or gas welding near the control unit location in the car.

## ORGANIZED TROUBLESHOOTING

When diagnosing a specific problem, organized troubleshooting is a must. The complexity of a modern automobile demands that you approach any problem in a logical, organized manner. There are certain troubleshooting techniques that are standard:

1. Establish when the problem occurs. Does the problem appear only under certain conditions? Were there any noises, odors, or other unusual symptoms?

2. Isolate the problem area. To do this, make some simple tests and observations; then eliminate the systems that are working properly. Check for obvious problems such as broken wires, dirty connections or split or disconnected vacuum hoses. Always check the obvious before assuming something complicated is the cause.

3. Test for problems systematically to determine the cause once the problem area is isolated. Are all the components functioning properly? Is there power going to electrical switches and motors? Is there vacuum at vacuum switches and/or actuators? Is there a mechanical problem such as bent linkage or loose mounting screws? Doing careful, systematic checks will often turn up most causes on the first inspection without wasting time checking components that have little or no relationship to the problem.

4. Test all repairs after the work is done to make sure that the problem is fixed. Some causes can be traced to more than one component, so a careful verification of repair work is important to pick up additional malfunctions that may cause a problem to reappear or a different problem to arise. A blown fuse, for example, is a simple problem that may require more than another fuse to repair. If you don't look for a problem that caused a fuse to blow, for example, a shorted wire may go undetected.

Experience has shown that most problems tend to be the result of a fairly simple and obvious cause, such as loose or corroded connectors or air leaks in the intake system; making careful inspection of components during testing essential to quick and accurate troubleshooting. Special, hand held computerized testers designed specifically for diagnosing the EEC-IV system are available from a variety of aftermarket sources, as well as from the vehicle manufacturer, but care should be taken that any test equipment being used is designed to diagnose that particular computer controlled system accurately without damaging the control unit (ECU) or components being tested.

NOTE: *Pinpointing the exact cause of trouble in an electrical system can sometimes only be accomplished by the use of special test equipment. The following describes commonly used test equipment and explains how to put it to best use in diagnosis. In addition to the information covered below, the manufacturer's instructions booklet provided with the tester should be read and clearly understood before attempting any test procedures.*

## TEST EQUIPMENT

### Jumper Wires

Jumper wires are simple, yet extremely valuable, pieces of test equipment. Jumper wires are merely wires that are used to bypass sections of a circuit. The simplest type of jumper wire is merely a length of multistrand wire with an alligator clip at each end. Jumper wires are usually fabricated from lengths of standard automotive wire and whatever type of connector (alligator clip, spade connector or pin connector) that is required for the particular vehicle being tested. The well equipped tool box will have several different styles of jumper wires in several different lengths. Some jumper wires are made with three or more terminals coming from a common splice for special purpose testing. In cramped, hard-to-reach areas it is advisable to have insulated boots over the jumper wire terminals in order to prevent accidental grounding, sparks, and possible fire, especially when testing fuel system components.

Jumper wires are used primarily to locate open electrical circuits, on either the ground (−) side of the circuit or on the hot (+) side. If an electrical component fails to operate, connect the jumper wire between the component and a good ground. If the component operates only with the jumper installed, the ground circuit is open. If the ground circuit is good, but the component does not operate, the circuit between the power feed and component is open. You can sometimes connect the jumper wire directly from the battery to the hot terminal of the component, but first make sure the component uses 12 volts in operation. Some electrical components, such as fuel injectors, are designed to operate on about 4 volts and running 12 volts directly to the injector terminals can burn out the wiring. By inserting an inline fuseholder between a set of test leads, a fused jumper wire can be used for bypassing open circuits. Use a 5 amp fuse to provide protection against voltage spikes. When in doubt, use a voltmeter to check the voltage input to the component and measure how much voltage is being applied normally. By moving the jumper wire successively back from the lamp toward the power source, you can isolate the area of the circuit where the open is located. When the component stops functioning, or the power is cut off, the open is in the segment of wire between the jumper and the point previously tested.

CAUTION: *Never use jumpers made from wire that is of lighter gauge than used in the circuit under test. If the jumper wire is of too small gauge, it may overheat and possibly melt. Never use jumpers to bypass high resistance loads (such as motors) in a circuit. Bypassing resistances, in effect, creates a short circuit which may, in turn, cause damage and fire. Never use a jumper for anything other than temporary bypassing of components in a circuit.*

### 12 Volt Test Light

The 12 volt test light is used to check circuits and components while electrical current is flowing through them. It is used for voltage and ground tests. Twelve volt test lights come in different styles but all have three main parts; a ground clip, a probe, and a light. The most commonly used 12 volt test lights have pick-type probes. To use a 12 volt test light, connect the ground clip to a good ground and probe wherever necessary with the pick. The pick should be sharp so that it can penetrate wire insulation to make contact with the wire, without making a large hole in the insulation. The wrap-around light is handy in hard to reach areas or where it is difficult to support a wire to push a probe pick into it. To use the wrap around light, hook the wire to probed with the hook and pull the trigger. A small pick will be forced through the wire insulation into the wire core.

CAUTION: *Do not use a test light to probe electronic ignition spark plug or coil wires. Never use a pick-type test light to probe wiring on computer controlled systems unless specifically instructed to do so. Any wire insulation that is pierced by the test light probe should be taped and sealed with silicone after testing.*

Like the jumper wire, the 12 volt test light is used to isolate opens in circuits. But, whereas the jumper wire is used to bypass the open to operate the load, the 12 volt test light is used to locate the presence of voltage in a circuit. If the test light glows, you know that there is power up to that point; if the 12 volt test light does not glow when its probe is inserted into the wire or connector, you know that there is an open circuit (no power). Move the test light in successive steps back toward the power source until the light in the handle does glow. When it does glow, the open is between the probe and point previously probed.

NOTE: *The test light does not detect that 12 volts (or any particular amount of voltage) is present; it only detects that some voltage is present. It is advisable before using the test light to touch its terminals across the battery posts to make sure the light is operating properly.*

### Self-Powered Test Light

The self-powered test light usually contains a 1.5 volt penlight battery. One type of self-powered test light is similar in design to the 12 volt test light. This type has both the battery and the light in the handle and pick-type probe tip. The second type has the light toward the open tip, so that the light illuminates the contact point. The self-powered test light is dual purpose piece of test equipment. It can be used to test for either open or short circuits when power is isolated from the circuit (continuity test). A powered test light should not be used on any computer controlled system or component unless specifically instructed to do so. Many engine sensors can be destroyed by even this small amount of voltage applied directly to the terminals.

### Open Circuit Testing

To use the self-powered test light to check for open circuits, first isolate the circuit from the vehicle's 12 volt power source by disconnecting the battery or wiring harness connector. Connect the test light ground clip to a good ground and probe sections of the circuit sequentially with the test light. (start from either end of the circuit). If the light is out, the open is between the probe and the circuit ground. If the light is on, the open is between the probe and end of the circuit toward the power source.

### Short Circuit Testing

By isolating the circuit both from power and from ground, and using a self-powered test light, you can check for shorts to ground in the circuit. Isolate the circuit from power and ground. Connect the test light ground clip to a good ground and probe any easy-to-reach test point in the circuit. If the light comes on, there is a short somewhere in the circuit. To isolate the short, probe a test point at either end of the isolated circuit (the light should be on). Leave the test light probe connected and open connectors, switches, remove parts, etc., sequentially, until the light goes out. When the light goes out, the short is between the last circuit component opened and the previous circuit opened.

NOTE: *The 1.5 volt battery in the test light does not provide much current. A weak battery may not provide enough power to illuminate the test light even when a complete circuit is made (especially if there are high resistances in the circuit). Always make sure that the test battery is strong. To check the battery, briefly touch the ground clip to the probe; if the light glows brightly the battery is strong enough for testing. Never use a self-powered test light to perform checks for opens or shorts when power is applied to the electrical system under test. The 12 volt vehicle power will quickly burn out the 1.5 volt light bulb in the test light.*

### Voltmeter

A voltmeter is used to measure voltage at any point in a circuit, or to measure the voltage drop across any part of a circuit. It can also be used to check continuity in a wire or circuit by indicating current flow from one end to the other. Voltmeters usually have various scales on the meter dial and a selector switch to allow the selection of different voltages. The voltmeter has a positive and a negative lead. To avoid damage to the meter, always connect the negative lead to the negative (–) side of circuit (to ground or nearest the ground side of the circuit) and connect the positive lead to the positive ( + ) side of the circuit (to the power source or the nearest power source). Note that the negative voltmeter lead will always be black and that the positive voltmeter will always be some color other than black (usually red). Depending on how the voltmeter is connected into the circuit, it has several uses.

A voltmeter can be connected either in parallel or in series with a circuit and it has a very high resistance to current flow. When connected in parallel, only a small amount of current will flow through the voltmeter current path; the rest will flow through the normal circuit current path and the circuit will work normally. When the voltmeter is connected in series with a circuit, only a small amount of current can flow through the circuit. The circuit will not work properly, but the voltmeter reading will show if the circuit is complete or not.

### Available Voltage Measurement

Set the voltmeter selector switch to the 20V position and connect the meter negative lead to the negative post of the battery. Connect the positive meter lead to the positive post of the battery and turn the ignition switch ON to provide a load. Read the voltage on the meter or digital display. A well charged battery should register over 12 volts. If the meter reads below 11.5 volts, the battery power may be insufficient to operate the electrical system properly. This test determines voltage available from the battery and should be the first step in any electrical trouble diagnosis procedure. Many electrical problems, especially on computer controlled systems, can be caused by a low state of charge in the battery. Excessive corrosion at the battery cable terminals can cause a poor contact that will prevent proper charging and full battery current flow.

Normal battery voltage is 12 volts when fully charged. When the battery is supplying current to one or more circuits it is said to be "under load". When everything is off the electrical system is under a "no-load" condition. A fully charged battery may show about 12.5 volts at no load; will drop to 12 volts under medium load; and will drop even lower under heavy load. If the battery is partially discharged the voltage decrease under heavy load may be excessive, even though the battery shows 12 volts or more at no load. When allowed to discharge further, the battery's available voltage under load will decrease more severely. For this reason, it is important that the battery be fully charged during all testing procedures to avoid errors in diagnosis and incorrect test results.

### Voltage Drop

When current flows through a resistance, the voltage beyond the resistance is reduced (the larger the current, the greater the reduction in voltage). When no current is flowing, there is no voltage drop because there is no current flow. All points in the circuit which are connected to the power source are at the same voltage as the power source. The total voltage drop always equals the total source voltage. In a long circuit with many connectors, a series of small, unwanted voltage drops due to corrosion at the connectors can add up to a total loss of voltage which impairs the operation of the normal loads in the circuit.

#### INDIRECT COMPUTATION OF VOLTAGE DROPS

1. Set the voltmeter selector switch to the 20 volt position.

2. Connect the meter negative lead to a good ground.

3. Probe all resistances in the circuit with the positive meter lead.

4. Operate the circuit in all modes and observe the voltage readings.

*DIRECT MEASUREMENT OF VOLTAGE DROPS*

1. Set the voltmeter switch to the 20 volt position.

2. Connect the voltmeter negative lead to the ground side of the resistance load to be measured.

3. Connect the positive lead to the positive side of the resistance or load to be measured.

4. Read the voltage drop directly on the 20 volt scale.

Too high a voltage indicates too high a resistance. If, for example, a blower motor runs too slowly, you can determine if there is too high a resistance in the resistor pack. By taking voltage drop readings in all parts of the circuit, you can isolate the problem. Too low a voltage drop indicates too low a resistance. If, for example, a blower motor runs too fast in the MED and/or LOW position, the problem can be isolated in the resistor pack by taking voltage drop readings in all parts of the circuit to locate a possibly shorted resistor. The maximum allowable voltage drop under load is critical, especially if there is more than one high resistance problem in a circuit because all voltage drops are cumulative. A small drop is normal due to the resistance of the conductors.

*HIGH RESISTANCE TESTING*

1. Set the voltmeter selector switch to the 4 volt position.

2. Connect the voltmeter positive lead to the positive post of the battery.

3. Turn on the headlights and heater blower to provide a load.

4. Probe various points in the circuit with the negative voltmeter lead.

5. Read the voltage drop on the 4 volt scale. Some average maximum allowable voltage drops are:

FUSE PANEL — 7 volts
IGNITION SWITCH — 5volts
HEADLIGHT SWITCH — 7 volts
IGNITION COIL (+) — 5 volts
ANY OTHER LOAD — 1.3 volts
NOTE: *Voltage drops are all measured while a load is operating; without current flow, there will be no voltage drop.*

### Ohmmeter

The ohmmeter is designed to read resistance (ohms) in a circuit or component. Although there are several different styles of ohmmeters, all will usually have a selector switch which permits the measurement of different ranges of resistance (usually the selector switch allows the multiplication of the meter reading by 10, 100, 1,000, and 10,000). A calibration knob allows the meter to be set at zero for accurate measurement. Since all ohmmeters are powered by

an internal battery (usually 9 volts), the ohmmeter can be used as a self-powered test light. When the ohmmeter is connected, current from the ohmmeter flows through the circuit or component being tested. Since the ohmmeter's internal resistance and voltage are known values, the amount of current flow through the meter depends on the resistance of the circuit or component being tested.

The ohmmeter can be used to perform continuity test for opens or shorts (either by observation of the meter needle or as a self-powered test light), and to read actual resistance in a circuit. It should be noted that the ohmmeter is used to check the resistance of a component or wire while there is no voltage applied to the circuit. Current flow from an outside voltage source (such as the vehicle battery) can damage the ohmmeter, so the circuit or component should be isolated from the vehicle electrical system before any testing is done. Since the ohmmeter uses its own voltage source, either lead can be connected to any test point.

NOTE: *When checking diodes or other solid state components, the ohmmeter leads can only be connected one way in order to measure current flow in a single direction. Make sure the positive (+) and negative (–) terminal connections are as described in the test procedures to verify the one-way diode operation.*

In using the meter for making continuity checks, do not be concerned with the actual resistance readings. Zero resistance, or any resistance readings, indicate continuity in the circuit. Infinite resistance indicates an open in the circuit. A high resistance reading where there should be none indicates a problem in the circuit. Checks for short circuits are made in the same manner as checks for open circuits except that the circuit must be isolated from both power and normal ground. Infinite resistance indicates no continuity to ground, while zero resistance indicates a dead short to ground.

*RESISTANCE MEASUREMENT*

The batteries in an ohmmeter will weaken with age and temperature, so the ohmmeter must be calibrated or "zeroed" before taking measurements. To zero the meter, place the selector switch in its lowest range and touch the two ohmmeter leads together. Turn the calibration knob until the meter needle is exactly on zero.

NOTE: *All analog (needle) type ohmmeters must be zeroed before use, but some digital ohmmeter models are automatically calibrated when the switch is turned on. Self-calibrating digital ohmmeters do not have an ad-*

*justing knob, but its a good idea to check for a zero readout before use by touching the leads together. All computer controlled systems require the use of a digital ohmmeter with at least 10 meagohms impedance for testing. Before any test procedures are attempted, make sure the ohmmeter used is compatible with the electrical system or damage to the onboard computer could result.*

To measure resistance, first isolate the circuit from the vehicle power source by disconnecting the battery cables or the harness connector. Make sure the key is OFF when disconnecting any components or the battery. Where necessary, also isolate at least one side of the circuit to be checked to avoid reading parallel resistances. Parallel circuit resistances will always give a lower reading than the actual resistance of either of the branches. When measuring the resistance of parallel circuits, the total resistance will always be lower than the smallest resistance in the circuit. Connect the meter leads to both sides of the circuit (wire or component) and read the actual measured ohms on the meter scale. Make sure the selector switch is set to the proper ohm scale for the circuit being tested to avoid misreading the ohmmeter test value.

WARNING: *Never use an ohmmeter with power applied to the circuit. Like the self-powered test light, the ohmmeter is designed to operate on its own power supply. The normal 12 volt automotive electrical system current could damage the meter!*

### Ammeters

An ammeter measures the amount of current flowing through a circuit in units called amperes or amps. Amperes are units of electron flow which indicate how fast the electrons are flowing through the circuit. Since Ohms Law dictates that current flow in a circuit is equal to the circuit voltage divided by the total circuit resistance, increasing voltage also increases the current level (amps). Likewise, any decrease in resistance will increase the amount of amps in a circuit. At normal operating voltage, most circuits have a characteristic amount of amperes, called "current draw" which can be measured using an ammeter. By referring to a specified current draw rating, measuring the amperes, and comparing the two values, one can determine what is happening within the circuit to aid in diagnosis. An open circuit, for example, will not allow any current to flow so the ammeter reading will be zero. More current flows through a heavily loaded circuit or when the charging system is operating.

An ammeter is always connected in series with the circuit being tested. All of the current that normally flows through the circuit must also flow through the ammeter; if there is any other path for the current to follow, the ammeter reading will not be accurate. The ammeter itself has very little resistance to current flow and therefore will not affect the circuit, but it will measure current draw only when the circuit is closed and electricity is flowing. Excessive current draw can blow fuses and drain the battery, while a reduced current draw can cause motors to run slowly, lights to dim and other components to not operate properly. The ammeter can help diagnose these conditions by locating the cause of the high or low reading.

### Multimeters

Different combinations of test meters can be built into a single unit designed for specific tests. Some of the more common combination test devices are known as Volt/Amp testers, Tach/Dwell meters, or Digital Multimeters. The Volt/Amp tester is used for charging system, starting system or battery tests and consists of a voltmeter, an ammeter and a variable resistance carbon pile. The voltmeter will usually have at least two ranges for use with 6, 12 and 24 volt systems. The ammeter also has more than one range for testing various levels of battery loads and starter current draw and the carbon pile can be adjusted to offer different amounts of resistance. The Volt/Amp tester has heavy leads to carry large amounts of current and many later models have an inductive ammeter pickup that clamps around the wire to simplify test connections. On some models, the ammeter also has a zero-center scale to allow testing of charging and starting systems without switching leads or polarity. A digital multimeter is a voltmeter, ammeter and ohmmeter combined in an instrument which gives a digital readout. These are often used when testing solid state circuits because of their high input impedance (usually 10 megohms or more).

The tach/dwell meter combines a tachometer and a dwell (cam angle) meter and is a specialized kind of voltmeter. The tachometer scale is marked to show engine speed in rpm and the dwell scale is marked to show degrees of distributor shaft rotation. In most electronic ignition systems, dwell is determined by the control unit, but the dwell meter can also be used to check the duty cycle (operation) of some electronic engine control systems. Some tach/dwell meters are powered by an internal battery, while others take their power from the car battery in use. The battery powered testers usually require calibration much like an ohmmeter before testing.

### Special Test Equipment

A variety of diagnostic tools are available to help troubleshoot and repair computerized engine control systems. The most sophisticated of these devices are the console type engine analyzers that usually occupy a garage service bay, but there are several types of aftermarket electronic testers available that will allow quick circuit tests of the engine control system by plugging directly into a special connector located in the engine compartment or under the dashboard. Several tool and equipment manufacturers offer simple, hand held testers that measure various circuit voltage levels on command to check all system components for proper operation. Although these testers usually cost about $300–500, consider that the average computer control unit (or ECM) can cost just as much and the money saved by not replacing perfectly good sensors or components in an attempt to correct a problem could justify the purchase price of a special diagnostic tester the first time it's used.

These computerized testers can allow quick and easy test measurements while the engine is operating or while the car is being driven. In addition, the on-board computer memory can be read to access any stored trouble codes; in effect allowing the computer to tell you where it hurts and aid trouble diagnosis by pinpointing exactly which circuit or component is malfunctioning. In the same manner, repairs can be tested to make sure the problem has been corrected. The biggest advantage these special testers have is their relatively easy hookups that minimize or eliminate the chances of making the wrong connections and getting false voltage readings or damaging the computer accidentally.

NOTE: *It should be remembered that these testers check voltage levels in circuits; they don't detect mechanical problems or failed components if the circuit voltage falls within the preprogrammed limits stored in the tester PROM unit. Also, most of the hand held testes are designed to work only on one or two systems made by a specific manufacturer.*

A variety of aftermarket testers are available to help diagnose different computerized control systems. Owatonna Tool Company (OTC), for example, markets a device called the OTC Monitor which plugs directly into the assembly line diagnostic link (ALDL). The OTC tester makes diagnosis a simple matter of pressing the correct buttons and, by changing the internal PROM or inserting a different diagnosis cartridge, it will work on any model from full size to subcompact, over a wide range of years. An adapter is supplied with the tester to allow connection to all types of ALDL links, regardless of the number of pin terminals used. By inserting an updated PROM into the OTC tester, it can be easily updated to diagnose any new modifications of computerized control systems.

## Wiring Harnesses

The average automobile contains about ½ mile of wiring, with hundreds of individual connections. To protect the many wires from damage and to keep them from becoming a confusing tangle, they are organized into bundles, enclosed in plastic or taped together and called wire harnesses. Different wiring harnesses serve different parts of the vehicle. Individual wires are color coded to help trace them through a harness where sections are hidden from view.

A loose or corroded connection or a replacement wire that is too small for the circuit will add extra resistance and an additional voltage drop to the circuit. A ten percent voltage drop can result in slow or erratic motor operation, for example, even though the circuit is complete. Automotive wiring or circuit conductors can be in any one of three forms:

1. Single strand wire
2. Multistrand wire
3. Printed circuitry

Single strand wire has a solid metal core and is usually used inside such components as alternators, motors, relays and other devices. Multistrand wire has a core made of many small strands of wire twisted together into a single conductor. Most of the wiring in an automotive electrical system is made up of multistrand wire, either as a single conductor or grouped together in a harness. All wiring is color coded on the insulator, either as a solid color or as a colored wire with an identification stripe. A printed circuit is a thin film of copper or other conductor that is printed on an insulator backing. Occasionally, a printed circuit is sandwiched between two sheets of plastic for more protection and flexibility. A complete printed circuit, consisting of conductors, insulating material and connectors for lamps or other components is called a printed circuit board. Printed circuitry is used in place of individual wires or harnesses in places where space is limited, such as behind instrument panels.

### Wire Gauge

Since computer controlled automotive electrical systems are very sensitive to changes in resistance, the selection of properly sized wires is critical when systems are repaired. The wire gauge number is an expression of the cross section area of the conductor. The most common system for expressing wire size is the American Wire Gauge (AWG) system.

Wire cross section area is measured in circular mils. A mil is $\frac{1}{1000}''$ (0.001''); a circular mil is the area of a circle one mil in diameter. For example, a conductor ¼'' in diameter is 0.250 in. or 250 mils. The circular mil cross section area of the wire is 250 squared ($250^2$) or 62,500 circular mils. Imported car models usually use metric wire gauge designations, which is simply the cross section area of the conductor in square millimeters ($mm^2$).

Gauge numbers are assigned to conductors of various cross section areas. As gauge number increases, area decreases and the conductor becomes smaller. A 5 gauge conductor is smaller than a 1 gauge conductor and a 10 gauge is smaller than a 5 gauge. As the cross section area of a conductor decreases, resistance increases and so does the gauge number. A conductor with a higher gauge number will carry less current than a conductor with a lower gauge number.

NOTE: *Gauge wire size refers to the size of the conductor, not the size of the complete wire. It is possible to have two wires of the same gauge with different diameters because one may have thicker insulation than the other.*

12 volt automotive electrical systems generally use 10, 12, 14, 16 and 18 gauge wire. Main power distribution circuits and larger accessories usually use 10 and 12 gauge wire. Battery cables are usually 4 or 6 gauge, although 1 and 2 gauge wires are occasionally used. Wire length must also be considered when making repairs to a circuit. As conductor length increases, so does resistance. An 18 gauge wire, for example, can carry a 10 amp load for 10 feet without excessive voltage drop; however if a 15 foot wire is required for the same 10 amp load, it must be a 16 gauge wire.

An electrical schematic shows the electrical current paths when a circuit is operating properly. It is essential to understand how a circuit works before trying to figure out why it doesn't. Schematics break the entire electrical system down into individual circuits and show only one particular circuit. In a schematic, no attempt is made to represent wiring and components as they physically appear on the vehicle; switches and other components are shown as simply as possible. Face views of harness connectors show the cavity or terminal locations in all multi-pin connectors to help locate test points.

If you need to backprobe a connector while it is on the component, the order of the terminals must be mentally reversed. The wire color code can help in this situation, as well as a keyway, lock tab or other reference mark.

NOTE: *Wiring diagrams are not included in this book. As trucks have become more complex and available with longer option lists, wiring diagrams have grown in size and complexity. It has become almost impossible to provide a readable reproduction of a wiring diagram in a book this size. Information on ordering wiring diagrams from the vehicle manufacturer can be found in the owner's manual.*

## WIRING REPAIR

Soldering is a quick, efficient method of joining metals permanently. Everyone who has the occasion to make wiring repairs should know how to solder. Electrical connections that are soldered are far less likely to come apart and will conduct electricity much better than connections that are only "pig-tailed" together. The most popular (and preferred) method of soldering is with an electrical soldering gun. Soldering irons are available in many sizes and wattage ratings. Irons with higher wattage ratings deliver higher temperatures and recover lost heat faster. A small soldering iron rated for no more than 50 watts is recommended, especially on electrical systems where excess heat can damage the components being soldered.

There are three ingredients necessary for successful soldering; proper flux, good solder and sufficient heat. A soldering flux is necessary to clean the metal of tarnish, prepare it for soldering and to enable the solder to spread into tiny crevices. When soldering, always use a resin flux or resin core solder which is non-corrosive and will not attract moisture once the job is finished. Other types of flux (acid core) will leave a residue that will attract moisture and cause the wires to corrode. Tin is a unique metal with a low melting point. In a molten state, it dissolves and alloys easily with many metals. Solder is made by mixing tin with lead. The most common proportions are 40/60, 50/50 and 60/40, with the percentage of tin listed first. Low priced solders usually contain less tin, making them very difficult for a beginner to use because more heat is required to melt the solder. A common solder is 40/60 which is well suited for all-around general use, but 60/40 melts easier, has more tin for a better joint and is preferred for electrical work.

### Soldering Techniques

Successful soldering requires that the metals to be joined be heated to a temperature that will melt the solder — usually 360–460°F (182–238°C). Contrary to popular belief, the purpose of the soldering iron is not to melt the solder itself, but to heat the parts being soldered to a temperature high enough to melt the solder when it is touched to the work. Melting flux-cored solder on the soldering iron will usually destroy the effectiveness of the flux.

NOTE: *Soldering tips are made of copper for good heat conductivity, but must be "tinned" regularly for quick transference of heat to the project and to prevent the solder from sticking to the iron. To "tin" the iron, simply heat it and touch the flux-cored solder to the tip; the solder will flow over the hot tip. Wipe the excess off with a clean rag, but be careful as the iron will be hot.*

After some use, the tip may become pitted. If so, simply dress the tip smooth with a smooth file and "tin" the tip again. An old saying holds that "metals well cleaned are half soldered." Flux-cored solder will remove oxides but rust, bits of insulation and oil or grease must be removed with a wire brush or emery cloth. For maximum strength in soldered parts, the joint must start off clean and tight. Weak joints will result in gaps too wide for the solder to bridge.

If a separate soldering flux is used, it should be brushed or swabbed on only those areas that are to be soldered. Most solders contain a core of flux and separate fluxing is unnecessary. Hold the work to be soldered firmly. It is best to solder on a wooden board, because a metal vise will only rob the piece to be soldered of heat and make it difficult to melt the solder. Hold the soldering tip with the broadest face against the work to be soldered. Apply solder under the tip close to the work, using enough solder to give a heavy film between the iron and the piece being soldered, while moving slowly and making sure the solder melts properly. Keep the work level or the solder will run to the lowest part and favor the thicker parts, because these require more heat to melt the solder. If the soldering tip overheats (the solder coating on the face of the tip burns up), it should be retinned. Once the soldering is completed, let the soldered joint stand until cool. Tape and seal all soldered wire splices after the repair has cooled.

### Wire Harness and Connectors

The on-board computer (ECM) wire harness electrically connects the control unit to the various solenoids, switches and sensors used by the control system. Most connectors in the engine compartment or otherwise exposed to the elements are protected against moisture and dirt which could create oxidation and deposits on the terminals. This protection is important because of the very low voltage and current levels used by the computer and sensors. All connectors have a lock which secures the male and female terminals together, with a secondary lock holding the seal and terminal into the connec-

tor. Both terminal locks must be released when disconnecting ECM connectors.

These special connectors are weather-proof and all repairs require the use of a special terminal and the tool required to service it. This tool is used to remove the pin and sleeve terminals. If removal is attempted with an ordinary pick, there is a good chance that the terminal will be bent or deformed. Unlike standard blade type terminals, these terminals cannot be straightened once they are bent. Make certain that the connectors are properly seated and all of the sealing rings in place when connecting leads. On some models, a hinge-type flap provides a backup or secondary locking feature for the terminals. Most secondary locks are used to improve the connector reliability by retaining the terminals if the small terminal lock tangs are not positioned properly.

Molded-on connectors require complete replacement of the connection. This means splicing a new connector assembly into the harness. All splices in on-board computer systems should be soldered to insure proper contact. Use care when probing the connections or replacing terminals in them as it is possible to short between opposite terminals. If this happens to the wrong terminal pair, it is possible to damage certain components. Always use jumper wires between connectors for circuit checking and never probe through weatherproof seals.

Open circuits are often difficult to locate by sight because corrosion or terminal misalignment are hidden by the connectors. Merely wiggling a connector on a sensor or in the wiring harness may correct the open circuit condition. This should always be considered when an open circuit or a failed sensor is indicated. Intermittent problems may also be caused by oxidized or loose connections. When using a circuit tester for diagnosis, always probe connections from the wire side. Be careful not to damage sealed connectors with test probes.

All wiring harnesses should be replaced with identical parts, using the same gauge wire and connectors. When signal wires are spliced into a harness, use wire with high temperature insulation only. With the low voltage and current levels found in the system, it is important that the best possible connection at all wire splices be made by soldering the splices together. It is seldom necessary to replace a complete harness. If replacement is necessary, pay close attention to insure proper harness routing. Secure the harness with suitable plastic wire clamps to prevent vibrations from causing the harness to wear in spots or contact any hot components.

NOTE: *Weatherproof connectors cannot be replaced with standard connectors. Instruc-*

tions are provided with replacement connector and terminal packages. *Some wire harnesses have mounting indicators (usually pieces of colored tape) to mark where the harness is to be secured.*

In making wiring repairs, it's important that you always replace damaged wires with wires that are the same gauge as the wire being replaced. The heavier the wire, the smaller the gauge number. Wires are color-coded to aid in identification and whenever possible the same color coded wire should be used for replacement. A wire stripping and crimping tool is necessary to install solderless terminal connectors. Test all crimps by pulling on the wires; it should not be possible to pull the wires out of a good crimp.

Wires which are open, exposed or otherwise damaged are repaired by simple splicing. Where possible, if the wiring harness is accessible and the damaged place in the wire can be located, it is best to open the harness and check for all possible damage. In an inaccessible harness, the wire must be bypassed with a new insert, usually taped to the outside of the old harness.

When replacing fusible links, be sure to use fusible link wire, NOT ordinary automotive wire. Make sure the fusible segment is of the same gauge and construction as the one being replaced and double the stripped end when crimping the terminal connector for a good contact. The melted (open) fusible link segment of the wiring harness should be cut off as close to the harness as possible, then a new segment spliced in as described. In the case of a damaged fusible link that feeds two harness wires, the harness connections should be replaced with two fusible link wires so that each circuit will have its own separate protection.

NOTE: *Most of the problems caused in the wiring harness are due to bad ground connections. Always check all vehicle ground connections for corrosion or looseness before performing any power feed checks to eliminate the chance of a bad ground affecting the circuit.*

### Repairing Hard Shell Connectors

Unlike molded connectors, the terminal contacts in hard shell connectors can be replaced. Weatherproof hard-shell connectors with the leads molded into the shell have non-replaceable terminal ends. Replacement usually involves the use of a special terminal removal tool that depress the locking tangs (barbs) on the connector terminal and allow the connector to be removed from the rear of the shell. The connector shell should be replaced if it shows any evidence of burning, melting, cracks, or breaks.

Replace individual terminals that are burnt, corroded, distorted or loose.

NOTE: *The insulation crimp must be tight to prevent the insulation from sliding back on the wire when the wire is pulled. The insulation must be visibly compressed under the crimp tabs, and the ends of the crimp should be turned in for a firm grip on the insulation.*

The wire crimp must be made with all wire strands inside the crimp. The terminal must be fully compressed on the wire strands with the ends of the crimp tabs turned in to make a firm grip on the wire. Check all connections with an ohmmeter to insure a good contact. There should be no measurable resistance between the wire and the terminal when connected.

## Mechanical Test Equipment

### Vacuum Gauge

Most gauges are graduated in inches of mercury (in.Hg), although a device called a manometer reads vacuum in inches of water (in. $H_2O$). The normal vacuum reading usually varies between 18 and 22 in.Hg at sea level. To test engine vacuum, the vacuum gauge must be connected to a source of manifold vacuum. Many engines have a plug in the intake manifold which can be removed and replaced with an adapter fitting. Connect the vacuum gauge to the fitting with a suitable rubber hose or, if no manifold plug is available, connect the vacuum gauge to any device using manifold vacuum, such as EGR valves, etc. The vacuum gauge can be used to determine if enough vacuum is reaching a component to allow its actuation.

### Hand Vacuum Pump

Small, hand-held vacuum pumps come in a variety of designs. Most have a built-in vacuum gauge and allow the component to be tested without removing it from the vehicle. Operate the pump lever or plunger to apply the correct amount of vacuum required for the test specified in the diagnosis routines. The level of vacuum in inches of Mercury (in.Hg) is indicated on the pump gauge. For some testing, an additional vacuum gauge may be necessary.

Intake manifold vacuum is used to operate various systems and devices on late model vehicles. To correctly diagnose and solve problems in vacuum control systems, a vacuum source is necessary for testing. In some cases, vacuum can be taken from the intake manifold when the engine is running, but vacuum is normally provided by a hand vacuum pump. These hand vacuum pumps have a built-in vacuum gauge that allow testing while the device is still attached to the component. For some tests, an additional vacuum gauge may be necessary.

## HEATER AND AIR CONDITIONING

Refer to Chapter 1 for discharging and charging of the air conditioning system.

### Blower Motor

#### REMOVAL AND INSTALLATION

NOTE: *This procedure is for all cars, with or without air conditioning.*

1. Disconnect the negative cable at the battery.
2. Working inside the engine compartment, disconnect the blower motor electrical leads.
3. Remove the motor retaining screws, and remove the blower motor.
4. Reverse the removal process to install.

### Heater Core

#### REMOVAL AND INSTALLATION

#### Cars Without Air Conditioning

1. Drain the cooling system.
CAUTION: *When draining the coolant, keep in mind that cats and dogs are attracted by the ethylene glycol antifreeze, and are quite likely to drink any that is left in an uncovered container or in puddles on the ground. This will prove fatal in sufficient quantity. Always drain the coolant into a sealable container. Coolant should be reused unless it is contaminated or several years old.*

2. Remove the heater inlet and outlet hoses at the firewall, inside the engine compartment.
3. Remove the radio noise suppression strap.
4. Remove the heater core cover retaining screws. Remove the cover.
5. Remove the core. Reverse steps 1 through 5 to install.

#### Cars With Air Conditioning

1. Drain the cooling system.
CAUTION: *When draining the coolant, keep in mind that cats and dogs are attracted by the ethylene glycol antifreeze, and are quite likely to drink any that is left in an uncovered container or in puddles on the ground. This will prove fatal in sufficient quantity. Always drain the coolant into a sealable container.*

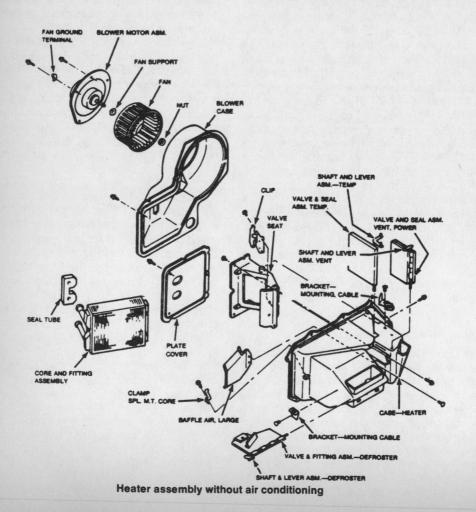

**Heater assembly without air conditioning**

*Coolant should be reused unless it is contaminated or several years old.*

2. On the diesel, raise and support the car on jackstands.

3. Disconnect the hoses at the core.

4. On the diesel, remove the instrument panel lower sound absorber.

5. Remove the heater duct and lower side covers.

6. Remove the lower heater outlet.

7. Remove the two housing cover-to-air valve housing clips.

8. Remove the housing cover.

9. Remove the core restraining straps.

10. Remove the core tubing retainers and lift out the core.

11. Reverse the above process to install the heater core.

## Control Head

### REMOVAL AND INSTALLATION

1. Disconnect the negative battery cable.

2. Remove the radio knobs (if equipped) and the clock set knob (if equipped).

3. Remove the instrument bezel retaining screws.

4. Pull the bezel out to disconnect the rear defogger switch and the remote mirror control (if equipped).

5. Remove the instrument panel.

6. Remove the control head to dash screws and pull the head out.

7. Disconnect the electrical connectors and/or control cable(s) (if equipped), then remove the control head.

8. To install, reverse steps 1 through 7.

## Evaporator Core

### REMOVAL AND INSTALLATION

1. Disconnect the negative battery cable.

2. Discharge the A/C system.

CAUTION: *When discharging, evacuating and charging the A/C system, please refer to Chapter 1 and be aware of all precautions of handling refrigerant.*

3. Remove the module's rubber seal and screen.

4. Remove the right windshield wiper arm.

5. Remove the diagnostic connector, the high blower relay and the thermostatic switch.

6. Disconnect the electrical connectors from the module.

7. Remove the module's top cover.

8. Remove the accumulator bracket screws.

9. Disconnect and tape the refrigerant lines at the accumulator and liquid line.

10. Remove the evaporator core.

11. When installing, use new sealing material.

When connecting the refrigerant lines, use new O-rings dipped in clean refrigerant oil and charge the A/C system. Refer to Chapter 1 for proper charging procedure.

## RADIO

### REMOVAL AND INSTALLATION

1. Disconnect the negative battery cable.

2. Remove the instrument panel insulator panel mounting screws enough to remove the steering column trim cover.

3. Remove the ash tray, the ash tray assembly and the fuse block, then separate the fuse block and the ash tray. Push forward to access the cigarette lighter and the rear defogger switch.

4. Disconnect the lighter and the defogger switch connectors.

5. Remove the cigarette lighter, the glove box, the instrument panel center trim panel mounting nuts and the trim panel enough to remove the radio.

6. Remove the radio mounting screws and the radio, by disconnecting the electrical connectors.

7. To install, reverse steps 1 through 6.

## WINDSHIELD WIPERS

### Blade and Arm

### REPLACEMENT

Wiper blade replacement procedures are detailed in Chapter 1.

Removal of the wiper arms requires the use of a special tool, G.M. J8966 or its equivalent. Versions of this tool are generally available in auto parts stores.

1. Insert the tool under the wiper arm and lever the arm off the shaft.

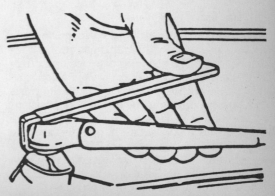

**Remove the wiper arm with the special tool**

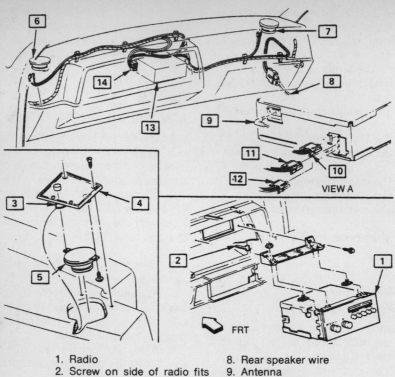

1. Radio
2. Screw on side of radio fits here
3. Retainer
4. Grille
5. Speaker
6. Front speaker assembly
7. Front speaker assembly
8. Rear speaker wire
9. Antenna
10. Rear speakers
11. Front speakers
12. I.P. harness
13. Receiver assembly
14. I.P. harness

**Typical radio removal and installation**

2. Disconnect the washer hose from the arm (if so equipped). Remove the arm.

3. Installation is in the reverse order of removal.

The proper park position is at the top of the blackout line on the glass. If the wiper arms and blades were in the proper position prior to removal, adjustment should not be required.

### ADJUSTMENT

The only adjustment for the wiper arms is to remove an arm from the transmission shaft, rotate the arm the required distance and direction and then install the arm back in position so it is in line with the blackout line on the glass. The wiper motor must be in the park position.

The correct blade-out wipe position on the driver's side is $1\frac{3}{32}''$ (28mm) from the tip of the blade to the left windshield pillar moulding. The correct blade-down wipe position on the passenger side of the car is in line with the blackout line at the bottom of the glass.

## Wiper Motor

### REMOVAL AND INSTALLATION

1. Loosen (but do not remove) the drive link-to-crank arm attaching nuts and detach the drive link from the motor crank arm.

2. Tag and disconnect all electrical leads from the wiper motor.

3. Unscrew the mounting bolts, rotate the motor up and outward and remove it.

4. Guide the crank arm through the opening in the body and then tighten the mounting bolts to 4-6 ft.lb.

5. Install the drive link to the crank arm with the motor in the park position.

6. Installation of the remaining components is in the reverse order of removal.

## Linkage

### REMOVAL AND INSTALLATION

1. Remove the wiper arms.
2. Remove the shroud top vent grille.

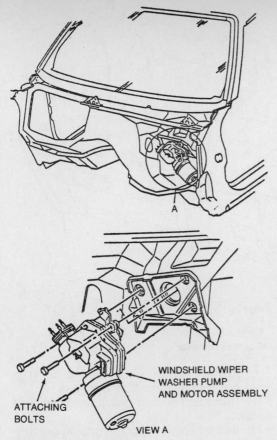

ATTACHING BOLTS

WINDSHIELD WIPER WASHER PUMP AND MOTOR ASSEMBLY

VIEW A

**Wiper motor installation**

3. Loosen (but do not remove) the drive link-to-crank arm attaching nuts.

4. Unscrew the linkage-to-cowl panel retaining screws and remove the linkage.

5. Installation is in the reverse order of removal.

## INSTRUMENTS AND SWITCHES

### Instrument Cluster

*REMOVAL AND INSTALLATION*

#### Century

1. Disconnect the battery ground.

2. Disconnect the speedometer cable and pull it through the firewall.

3. Remove the left side hush panel by removing the three 7mm screws and one 11mm nut.

4. Remove the right side hush panel by removing the five 7mm screws and two 11mm nuts.

5. Remove the shift indicator cable clip.

6. Remove the steering column trim plate.

7. Put the gear selector in LOW, remove the nine retaining screws and gently pull out the instrument panel trim plate.

8. Disconnect the parking brake cable at the lever by pushing it forward and sliding it out of its slot.

9. Unbolt and lower the steering column (3 bolts and 1 nut).

10. Remove the gauge cluster by removing the four screws and pulling the cluster out far enough to disconnect any wires, then pull the cluster out.

11. Installation is the reverse of removal.

#### Celebrity

1. Disconnect battery ground cable.

2. Remove instrument panel hush panel.

3. Remove vent control housing (heater only vehicles).

4. On non-A/C cars remove steering column trim cover screws and lower cover with vent cables attached. On A/C equipped vehicles, remove trim cover attaching screws (6) and remove cover.

5. Remove instrument cluster trim pad.

6. Remove ash tray, retainer and fuse block, disconnect wires as necessary.

7. Remove headlamp switch knob and instrument panel trim plate and disconnect electrical connectors of any accessory switches in trim plate.

8. Remove cluster assembly and disconnect speedometer cable, PRNDL and cluster electrical connectors.

9. Installation is the reverse of removal.

#### Ciera

1. Remove left instrument panel trim pad.

2. Remove instrument panel cluster trim cover.

3. Disconnect speedometer cable at transmission or cruise control transducer if equipped.

4. Remove steering column trim cover.

5. Disconnect shift indicator clip from steering column shift bowl.

6. Remove 4 screws attaching cluster assembly to instrument panel.

7. Pull assembly out far enough to reach behind cluster and disconnect speedometer cable.

8. Remove cluster assembly.

9. Installation is the reverse of removal.

#### 6000

1. Remove center and left hand lower instrument panel trim plate.

2. Remove six (6) screws holding instrument cluster to instrument panel carrier.

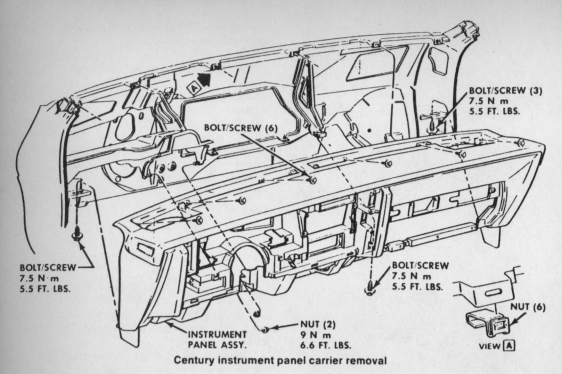

BOLT/SCREW (3)
7.5 N·m
5.5 FT. LBS.

BOLT/SCREW (6)

BOLT/SCREW
7.5 N·m
5.5 FT. LBS.

BOLT/SCREW
7.5 N·m
5.5 FT. LBS.

NUT (6)

VIEW Ⓐ

INSTRUMENT
PANEL ASSY.

NUT (2)
9 N·m
6.6 FT. LBS.

**Century instrument panel carrier removal**

3. Remove instrument cluster lens to gain access to speedometer head and instrument/gauges.

4. Disconnect negative battery cable(s).

5. Remove right hand and left hand hush panels, steering column trim cover and disconnect parking brake cable and vent cables, if so equipped.

6. Remove steering column retaining bolts and drop steering column.

7. Disconnect temperature control cable, inner to outer A/C wire harness and inner to outer A/C vacuum harness, if so equipped.

8. Disconnect chassis harness behind left lower instrument panel and ECM connectors behind glove box. Disconnect instrument panel harness at cowl.

9. Remove center instrument panel trim plate and remove radio if so equipped.

10. Disconnect neutral switch and brake light switch.

11. Remove six (6) upper instrument panel retaining screws.

12. Remove lower instrument panel retaining screws, nuts and bolts.

13. Pull instrument panel assembly out far enough to disconnect ignition switch, headlight dimmer switch and turn signal switch.

14. Disconnect all other accessory wiring, and vacuum lines necessary to remove instrument panel assembly.

15. Remove instrument panel assembly with wiring harness.

16. Installation is the reverse of removal.

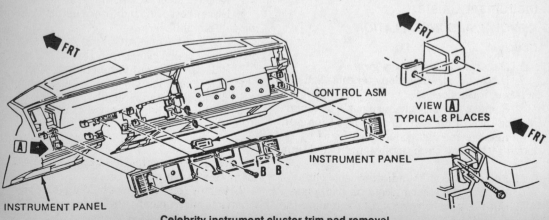

FRT

FRT

CONTROL ASM

VIEW Ⓐ
TYPICAL 8 PLACES

FRT

INSTRUMENT PANEL

B B

INSTRUMENT PANEL

**Celebrity instrument cluster trim pad removal**

## Console

### *REMOVAL AND INSTALLATION*

1. Remove the shifter knob from the shifter by removing the retaining screw at the back of the knob.

2. Remove the screws at the sides and front of the console.

3. Open the console box and remove the retaining screw inside the box.

4. Remove the ashtray at the rear of the console and remove the retaining screw behind the ashtray.

5. Slide the console rearward slightly, then lift it over the shifter.

6. To install, reverse the above process.

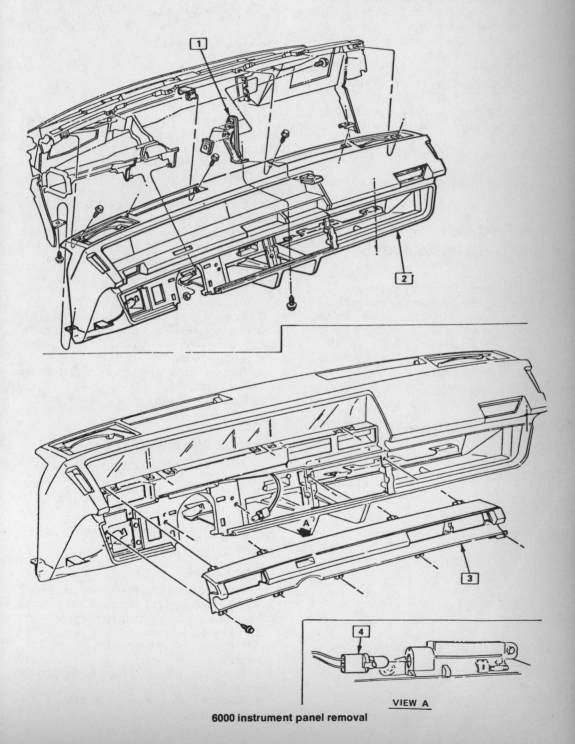

**VIEW A**

**6000 instrument panel removal**

## Wiper Switch

### REMOVAL AND INSTALLATION

1. Disconnect the negative battery cable.
2. Remove the steering wheel, the cover and the lock plate assembly.
3. Remove the turn signal actuator arm, the lever and the hazard flasher button.
4. Remove the turn signal switch screws, the lower steering column trim panel and the steering column bracket bolts.
5. Disconnect the turn signal switch and the wiper switch connectors.
6. Pull the turn signal rearward 6-8″, then remove the key buzzer switch and the cylinder lock.
7. Remove and pull the steering column housing rearward, then remove the housing cover screw.
8. Remove the wiper switch pivot and the switch.
9. To install, reverse the removal procedures.

## Headlight Switch

### REMOVAL AND INSTALLATION

#### Celebrity

1. Disconnect the battery ground.
2. Remove the headlamp switch knob.
3. Remove the instrument panel trim pad.
4. Unbolt the switch mounting plate from the instrument panel carrier.
5. Disconnect the wiring from the switch.
6. Remove the switch.
7. Installation is the reverse of removal.

#### Ciera

1. Remove the left side instrument panel trim pad.
2. Unbolt the switch from the instrument panel.
3. Pull the switch rearward and remove it.
4. Installation is the reverse of removal.

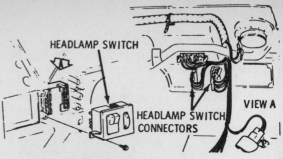

**Ciera headlight switch**

#### 6000

1. Disconnect the battery ground.
2. Remove the steering column trim cover and headlight rod and knob by reaching behind the instrument panel and depressing the lock tab with a screwdriver.
3. Remove the left instrument panel trim plate.
4. Unbolt and remove the switch and bracket assembly from the instrument panel.
5. Loosen the bezel and remove the switch from the bracket.
6. Installation is the reverse of removal.

#### Century

1. Disconnect the battery ground.
2. Remove the instrument panel trim plate.
3. Remove the left side instrument panel switch trim panel by removing the three screws and gently rocking the panel out.
4. Remove the three screws and pull the switch straight out.
5. Installation is the reverse of removal.

## Clock

### REMOVAL AND INSTALLATION

1. Remove the instrument panel cluster bezel.
2. Remove the clock retaining screws and remove the clock.

## Back-up Light Switch

### REMOVAL AND INSTALLATION

#### Column Mounted

1. Working from underneath the dashboard, locate the back-up light switch on the steering column and remove the wiring harness.
2. Then pull downward and remove the switch from the steering column.
To install:
3. Apply the parking brake and place the gear select lever in neutral.
4. Align the actuator on the switch with the hole in the shift tube.

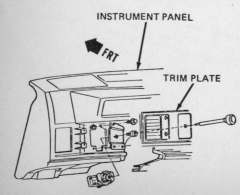

**Celebrity headlight switch**

5. Position the rearward portion of the switch (connector side) to fit into the cutout in the lower jacket.

6. Push up on the front of the switch, the two tangs on the housing back will snap into place in the rectangular holes in the jacket.

7. Adjust the switch by moving the gear selector to park. The main housing and the back should ratchet, providing proper switch adjustment.

## Speedometer Cable

### REPLACEMENT

NOTE: *Removing the instrument cluster will give better access to the speedometer cable.*

1. Remove the instrument cluster.

2. Slide the cable out from the casing. If the cable is broken, the casing will have to be unscrewed from the transaxle and the broken piece removed from that end.

3. Before installing a new cable, slip a piece of cable into the speedometer and spin it between your fingers in the direction of normal rotation. If the mechanism sticks or binds, the speedometer should be repaired or replaced.

4. Inspect the casing. If it is cracked, kinked, or broken, the casing should be replaced.

5. Slide a new cable into the casing, engaging the transaxle end securely. Sometimes it is easier to unscrew the casing at the transaxle end, install the cable into the transaxle fitting, and screw the casing back into place. Install the instrument cluster.

## LIGHTING

### Headlights

#### REMOVAL AND INSTALLATION

1. Remove the headlamp trim panel attaching screws.

2. Remove the headlamp bulb retaining screws. Do not touch the two headlamp aiming screws, at the top and side of the retaining ring,

or the headlamp aim will have to be readjusted.

3. Pull the bulb and ring forward the separate them. Unplug the electrical connector from the rear of the bulb.

4. Plug the new bulb into the electrical connector. Install the bulb into the retaining ring and install the ring and bulb. Install the trim panel.

### Signal and Marker Lights

1. Remove the headlight bezel mounting screws and the bezel.

2. Disconnect the twist lock socket from the lens housing.

3. Remove the parking light housing.

NOTE: *To remove the bulb, turn the twist lock socket at the rear of the housing) counterclockwise ¼ turn, then remove the socket with the bulb; replace the bulb if defective.*

4. To install, reverse the removal procedures.

### Side Marker Lights

1. Remove the marker light housing screws and the housing.

2. Disconnect the twist lock socket from the lens housing.

NOTE: *To remove the bulb, turn the twist lock socket (at the rear of the housing) counterclockwise ¼ turn, then remove the socket with the bulb; replace the bulb if defective.*

3. To install, reverse the removal procedures.

### Rear Turn Signal, Brake and Parking Lights

1. Remove the tail light panel screws and the panel.

2. Disconnect the twist lock socket from the lens housing.

NOTE: *To remove the bulb, turn the twist lock socket (at the rear of the housing) counterclockwise ¼ turn, then remove the socket with the bulb; replace the bulb if defective.*

3. To install, reverse the removal procedures.

## TRAILER WIRING

Wiring the car for towing is fairly easy. There are a number of good wiring kits available and these should be used, rather than trying to design your own. All trailers will need brake lights and turn signals as well as tail lights and side marker lights. Most states require extra marker lights for overly wide trailers. Also, most states have recently required back-up lights for trailers, and most trailer manufacturers have been building trailers with back-up lights for several years.

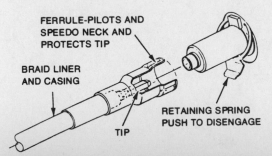

FERRULE-PILOTS AND SPEEDO NECK AND PROTECTS TIP

BRAID LINER AND CASING

RETAINING SPRING PUSH TO DISENGAGE

TIP

**Speedometer cable disengagement at the speedometer**

Additionally, some Class I, most Class II and just about all Class III trailers will have electric brakes.

Add to this number an accessories wire, to operate trailer internal equipment or to charge the trailer's battery, and you can have as many as seven wires in the harness.

Determine the equipment on your trailer and buy the wiring kit necessary. The kit will contain all the wires needed, plus a plug adapter set

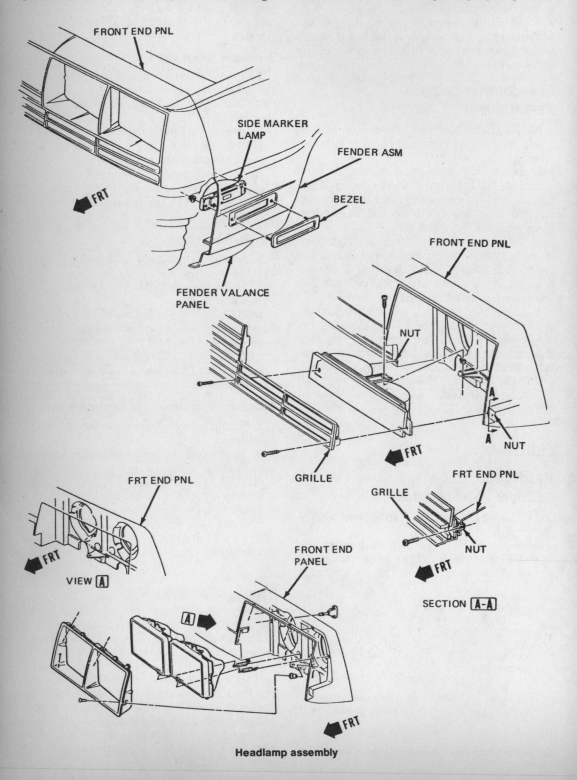

Headlamp assembly

which included the female plug, mounted on the bumper or hitch, and the male plug, wired into, or plugged into the trailer harness.

When installing the kit, follow the manufacturer's instructions. The color coding of the wires is standard throughout the industry.

One point to note, some domestic vehicles, and most imported vehicles, have separate turn signals. On most domestic vehicles, the brake lights and rear turn signals operate with the same bulb. For those vehicles with separate turn signals, you can purchase an isolation unit so that the brake lights won't blink whenever the turn signals are operated, or, you can go to your local electronics supply house and buy four diodes to wire in series with the brake and turn signal bulbs. Diodes will isolate the brake and turn signals. The choice is yours. The isolation units are simple and quick to install, but far more expensive than the diodes. The diodes, however, require more work to install properly, since they require the cutting of each bulb's wire and soldering in place of the diode.

One final point, the best kits are those with a spring loaded cover on the vehicle mounted socket. This cover prevents dirt and moisture from corroding the terminals. Never let the vehicle socket hang loosely. Always mount it securely to the bumper or hitch.

NOTE: *For more information on towing a trailer please refer to Chapter One.*

## CIRCUIT PROTECTION

### Fuses

Fuses (located on a swing down unit near the steering column or in the glove box) protect all the major electrical systems in the car. In case of an electrical overload, the fuse melts, breaking the circuit and stopping the flow of electricity.

If a fuse blows, the cause should be investigated and corrected before the installation of a new fuse. This, however, is easier to say than to do. Because each fuse protects a limited number of components, your job is narrowed down somewhat. Begin your investigation by looking for obvious fraying, loose connections, breaks in insulation, etc. Use the techniques outlined at the beginning of this chapter. Electrical problems are almost always a real headache to solve, but if you are patient and persistent, and approach the problem logically (that is, don't start replacing electrical components randomly), you will eventually find the solution.

The amperage of each fuse and the circuit it protects are marked on the fusebox, which is lo-

FUSE BLOCK

| Fuse Number | Name | Color/Size (Amps) | Circuits Protected |
|---|---|---|---|
| 1 | ECM | RED (10) | Computer Command Control |
| 2 | WIPER | WHT (25) | Wiper Washer, Wiper.Washer (Delay) |
| 3. | PWR ACC (Circuit Breaker) | (30) | Rear Window Defogger, Power Door Locks, Power Seats |
| 4 | RAD | RED (10) | Radio, Cruise Control |
| 5 | INST LMPS | TAN (5) | Lights  Instrument Panel, Lights On Reminder |
| 6 | WDO (Circuit Breaker) | (30) | Power Windows |
| 7. | CTSY/CIG | YEL (20) | Courtesy Lights, Seatbelt Warning, Digital Clock, A/C Heat, Horn, Power Door Locks, Trunk/Tailgate Release, Rear Compartment Courtesy Light, Cigar Lighter |
| 8 | GAGES | RED (10) | Warning Indicators, Gages, A/C Heat, Seatbelt Warning, Computer Command Control, Torque Converter Clutch, Rear Window Defogger, Rear Wiper/Washer |
| 9 | H A/C | LT GRN (30) | Heater, Air Conditioning |
| 10 | TAIL LMPS | YEL (20) | Lights  Rear Park/Rear Marker/License, Lights  Front Park/Front Marker, Digital Clock Radio, Twilight Sentinel |
| 11 | VAC PUMP | TAN (5) | Vacuum Pump |
| 12 | TURN B U | YEL (20) | Turn Lights, Back Up Lights |
| 13 | C/H | YEL (20) | Choke Heater, Cooling Fan |
| 14 | STP LMP | YEL (20) | Lights  Stop/Hazard |
| 15 | CCC | RED (10) | Computer Command Control |

**The fuse box is under the left side of the instrument panel**

cated under the left side (driver's side) of the instrument panel and pulls down for easy access.

### Fusible Links

The fuse link is a short length of special, Hypalon (high temperature) insulated wire, integral with the engine compartment wiring harness and should not be confused with standard wire. It is several wire gauges smaller than the circuit which it protects. Under no circumstances should a fuse link replacement repair be made using a length of standard wire cut from bulk stock or from another wiring harness.

To repair any blown fuse link use the following procedure:

1. Determine which circuit is damaged, its location and the cause of the open fuse link. If the damaged fuse link is one of three fed by a common No. 10 or 12 gauge feed wire, determine the specific affected circuit.

2. Disconnect the negative battery cable.

3. Cut the damaged fuse link from the wiring harness and discard it. If the fuse link is one of three circuits fed by a single feed wire, cut it out of the harness at each splice end and discard it.

4. Identify and procure the proper fuse link and butt connectors for attaching the fuse link to the harness.

5. To repair any fuse link in a 3-link group with one feed:

a. After cutting the open link out of the harness, cut each of the remaining undamaged fuse links close to the feed wire weld.

b. Strip approximately ½″ (13mm) of insulation from the detached ends of the two good fuse links, Then insert two wire ends into one end of a butt connector and carefully push one stripped end of the replacement fuse link into the same end of the butt connector and crimp all three firmly together.

NOTE: *Care must be taken when fitting the three fuse links into the butt connector as the internal diameter is a snug fit for three wires. Make sure to use a proper crimping tool. Pliers, side cutter, etc. will not apply the proper crimp to retain the wires and withstand a pull test.*

c. After crimping the butt connector to the three fuse links, cut the weld portion from the feed wire and strip approximately ½″ (13mm) of insulation from the cut end. Insert the stripped end into the open end of the butt connector and crimp very firmly.

d. To attach the remaining end of the replacement fuse link, strip approximately ½″ (13mm) of insulation from the wire end of the circuit from which the blown fuse link was removed, and firmly crimp a butt connector or equivalent to the stripped wire. Then, insert the end of the replacement link into the other end of the butt connector and crimp firmly.

e. Using rosin core solder with a consistency of 60 percent tin and 40 percent lead, solder the connectors and the wires at the repairs and insulate with electrical tape.

6. To replace any fuse link on a single circuit in a harness, cut out the damaged portion, strip approximately ½″ (13mm) of insulation from the two wire ends and attach the appropriate replacement fuse link to the stripped wire ends with two proper size butt connectors. Solder the connectors and wires and insulate with tape.

7. To repair any fuse link which has an eyelet terminal on one end such as the charging circuit, cut off the open fuse link behind the weld, strip approximately ½″ (13mm) of insulation from the cut end and attach the appropriate

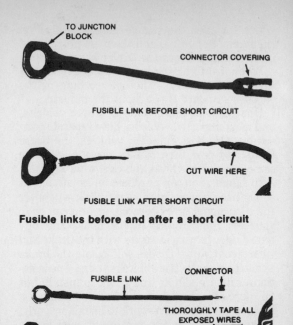

Fusible links before and after a short circuit

New fusible links are spliced to the wire

new eyelet fuse link to the cut stripped wire with an appropriate size butt connector. Solder the connectors and wires at the repair and insulate with tape.

8. Connect the negative battery cable to the battery and test the system for proper operation.

NOTE: *Do not mistake a resistor wire for a fuse link. The resistor wire is generally longer and has print stating, "Resistor-don't cut or splice".*

When attaching a single No. 16, 17, 18 or 20 gauge fuse link to a heavy gauge wire, always double the stripped wire end of the fuse link before inserting and crimping it into the butt connector for positive wire retention.

## Circuit Breakers

The headlights are protected by a circuit breaker in the headlamp switch. If the circuit breaker trips, the headlights will either flash on and off, or stay off altogether. The circuit breaker rests automatically after the overload is removed.

The windshield wipers are also protected by a circuit breaker. If the motor overheats, the circuit breaker will trip, remaining off until the motor cools or the overload is removed. One common cause of overheating is operation of the wipers in heavy snow.

The circuit breakers for the power door locks and power windows are located in the fuse box.

## Flashers

The hazard flasher is located in the convenience center', under the dash, on the left side kick panel. The horn relay and the buzzer assembly may be found here also. The turn signal flasher is installed in a clamp attached to the base of the steering column support inside the car. In all cases, replacement is made by unplugging the old unit and plugging in a new one.

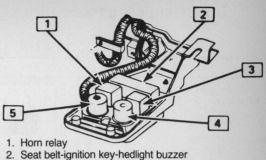

1. Horn relay
2. Seat belt-ignition key-hedlight buzzer
3. Choke relay (vacant W/EFI)
4. Hazard flasher
5. Signal flasher

**View of the convenience center and components**

## Troubleshooting Basic Turn Signal and Flasher Problems

Most problems in the turn signals or flasher system, can be reduced to defective flashers or bulbs, which are easily replaced. Occasionally, problems in the turn signals are traced to the switch in the steering column, which will require professional service.

F = Front    R = Rear    ● = Lights off    ○ = Lights on

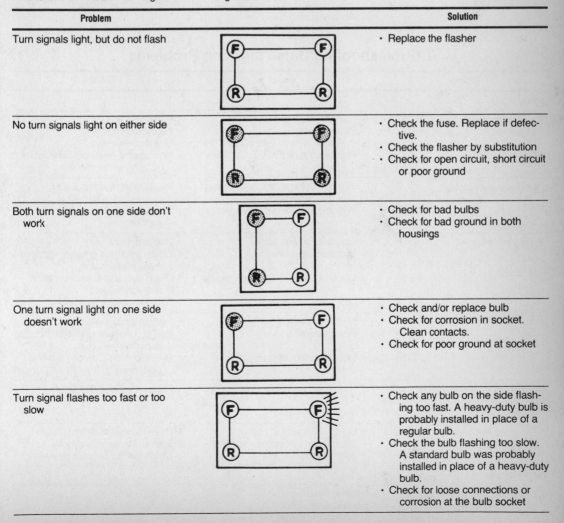

| Problem | | Solution |
|---|---|---|
| Turn signals light, but do not flash | | • Replace the flasher |
| No turn signals light on either side | | • Check the fuse. Replace if defective.<br>• Check the flasher by substitution<br>• Check for open circuit, short circuit or poor ground |
| Both turn signals on one side don't work | | • Check for bad bulbs<br>• Check for bad ground in both housings |
| One turn signal light on one side doesn't work | | • Check and/or replace bulb<br>• Check for corrosion in socket. Clean contacts.<br>• Check for poor ground at socket |
| Turn signal flashes too fast or too slow | | • Check any bulb on the side flashing too fast. A heavy-duty bulb is probably installed in place of a regular bulb.<br>• Check the bulb flashing too slow. A standard bulb was probably installed in place of a heavy-duty bulb.<br>• Check for loose connections or corrosion at the bulb socket |

## Troubleshooting Basic Turn Signal and Flasher Problems (cont.)

F = Front   R = Rear   ● = Lights off   o = Lights on

| Problem | | Solution |
|---|---|---|
| Indicator lights don't work in either direction | | • Check if the turn signals are working<br>• Check the dash indicator lights<br>• Check the flasher by substitution |
| One indicator light doesn't light | | • On systems with 1 dash indicator:<br>　See if the lights work on the same side. Often the filaments have been reversed in systems combining stoplights with taillights and turn signals.<br>　Check the flasher by substitution<br>• On systems with 2 indicators:<br>　Check the bulbs on the same side<br>　Check the indicator light bulb<br>　Check the flasher by substitution |

## Troubleshooting Basic Lighting Problems

| Problem | Cause | Solution |
|---|---|---|
| **Lights** | | |
| One or more lights don't work, but others do | • Defective bulb(s)<br>• Blown fuse(s)<br>• Dirty fuse clips or light sockets<br>• Poor ground circuit | • Replace bulb(s)<br>• Replace fuse(s)<br>• Clean connections<br>• Run ground wire from light socket housing to car frame |
| Lights burn out quickly | • Incorrect voltage regulator setting or defective regulator<br>• Poor battery/alternator connections | • Replace voltage regulator<br>• Check battery/alternator connections |
| Lights go dim | • Low/discharged battery<br>• Alternator not charging<br>• Corroded sockets or connections<br>• Low voltage output | • Check battery<br>• Check drive belt tension; repair or replace alternator<br>• Clean bulb and socket contacts and connections<br>• Replace voltage regulator |
| Lights flicker | • Loose connection<br>• Poor ground<br>• Circuit breaker operating (short circuit) | • Tighten all connections<br>• Run ground wire from light housing to car frame<br>• Check connections and look for bare wires |
| Lights "flare"—Some flare is normal on acceleration—if excessive, see "Lights Burn Out Quickly" | • High voltage setting | • Replace voltage regulator |
| Lights glare—approaching drivers are blinded | • Lights adjusted too high<br>• Rear springs or shocks sagging<br>• Rear tires soft | • Have headlights aimed<br>• Check rear springs/shocks<br>• Check/correct rear tire pressure |
| **Turn Signals** | | |
| Turn signals don't work in either direction | • Blown fuse<br>• Defective flasher<br>• Loose connection | • Replace fuse<br>• Replace flasher<br>• Check/tighten all connections |

## Troubleshooting Basic Lighting Problems (cont.)

| Problem | Cause | Solution |
|---|---|---|
| **Turn Signals** | | |
| Right (or left) turn signal only won't work | • Bulb burned out<br>• Right (or left) indicator bulb burned out<br>• Short circuit | • Replace bulb<br>• Check/replace indicator bulb<br><br>• Check/repair wiring |
| Flasher rate too slow or too fast | • Incorrect wattage bulb<br>• Incorrect flasher | • Flasher bulb<br>• Replace flasher (use a variable load flasher if you pull a trailer) |
| Indicator lights do not flash (burn steadily) | • Burned out bulb<br>• Defective flasher | • Replace bulb<br>• Replace flasher |
| Indicator lights do not light at all | • Burned out indicator bulb<br>• Defective flasher | • Replace indicator bulb<br>• Replace flasher |

## Troubleshooting Basic Dash Gauge Problems

| Problem | Cause | Solution |
|---|---|---|
| **Coolant Temperature Gauge** | | |
| Gauge reads erratically or not at all | • Loose or dirty connections<br>• Defective sending unit<br><br><br><br>• Defective gauge | • Clean/tighten connections<br>• Bi-metal gauge: remove the wire from the sending unit. Ground the wire for an instant. If the gauge registers, replace the sending unit.<br>• Magnetic gauge: disconnect the wire at the sending unit. With ignition ON gauge should register COLD. Ground the wire; gauge should register HOT. |
| **Ammeter Gauge—Turn Headlights ON (do not start engine). Note reaction** | | |
| Ammeter shows charge<br>Ammeter shows discharge<br>Ammeter does not move | • Connections reversed on gauge<br>• Ammeter is OK<br>• Loose connections or faulty wiring<br>• Defective gauge | • Reinstall connections<br>• Nothing<br>• Check/correct wiring<br>• Replace gauge |
| **Oil Pressure Gauge** | | |
| Gauge does not register or is inaccurate | • On mechanical gauge, Bourdon tube may be bent or kinked<br>• Low oil pressure<br><br><br><br>• Defective gauge<br><br><br><br><br>• Defective wiring<br><br><br><br>• Defective sending unit | • Check tube for kinks or bends preventing oil from reaching the gauge<br>• Remove sending unit. Idle the engine briefly. If no oil flows from sending unit hole, problem is in engine.<br>• Remove the wire from the sending unit and ground it for an instant with the ignition ON. A good gauge will go to the top of the scale.<br>• Check the wiring to the gauge. If it's OK and the gauge doesn't register when grounded, replace the gauge.<br>• If the wiring is OK and the gauge functions when grounded, replace the sending unit |

## Troubleshooting Basic Dash Gauge Problems (cont.)

| Problem | Cause | Solution |
|---|---|---|
| **All Gauges** | | |
| All gauges do not operate | • Blown fuse<br>• Defective instrument regulator | • Replace fuse<br>• Replace instrument voltage regulator |
| All gauges read low or erratically | • Defective or dirty instrument voltage regulator | • Clean contacts or replace |
| All gauges pegged | • Loss of ground between instrument voltage regulator and car<br>• Defective instrument regulator | • Check ground<br><br>• Replace regulator |
| **Warning Lights** | | |
| Light(s) do not come on when ignition is ON, but engine is not started | • Defective bulb<br>• Defective wire<br><br>• Defective sending unit | • Replace bulb<br>• Check wire from light to sending unit<br>• Disconnect the wire from the sending unit and ground it. Replace the sending unit if the light comes on with the ignition ON. |
| Light comes on with engine running | • Problem in individual system<br>• Defective sending unit | • Check system<br>• Check sending unit (see above) |

## Troubleshooting the Heater

| Problem | Cause | Solution |
|---|---|---|
| Blower motor will not turn at any speed | • Blown fuse<br>• Loose connection<br>• Defective ground<br>• Faulty switch<br>• Faulty motor<br>• Faulty resistor | • Replace fuse<br>• Inspect and tighten<br>• Clean and tighten<br>• Replace switch<br>• Replace motor<br>• Replace resistor |
| Blower motor turns at one speed only | • Faulty switch<br>• Faulty resistor | • Replace switch<br>• Replace resistor |
| Blower motor turns but does not circulate air | • Intake blocked<br>• Fan not secured to the motor shaft | • Clean intake<br>• Tighten security |
| Heater will not heat | • Coolant does not reach proper temperature<br>• Heater core blocked internally<br>• Heater core air-bound<br>• Blend-air door not in proper position | • Check and replace thermostat if necessary<br>• Flush or replace core if necessary<br>• Purge air from core<br>• Adjust cable |
| Heater will not defrost | • Control cable adjustment incorrect<br>• Defroster hose damaged | • Adjust control cable<br>• Replace defroster hose |

## Troubleshooting Basic Windshield Wiper Problems

| Problem | Cause | Solution |
|---------|-------|----------|
| **Electric Wipers** | | |
| Wipers do not operate— Wiper motor heats up or hums | • Internal motor defect<br>• Bent or damaged linkage<br>• Arms improperly installed on linking pivots | • Replace motor<br>• Repair or replace linkage<br>• Position linkage in park and reinstall wiper arms |
| Wipers do not operate— No current to motor | • Fuse or circuit breaker blown<br>• Loose, open or broken wiring<br>• Defective switch<br>• Defective or corroded terminals<br>• No ground circuit for motor or switch | • Replace fuse or circuit breaker<br>• Repair wiring and connections<br>• Replace switch<br>• Replace or clean terminals<br>• Repair ground circuits |
| Wipers do not operate— Motor runs | • Linkage disconnected or broken | • Connect wiper linkage or replace broken linkage |
| **Vacuum Wipers** | | |
| Wipers do not operate | • Control switch or cable inoperative<br>• Loss of engine vacuum to wiper motor (broken hoses, low engine vacuum, defective vacuum/fuel pump)<br>• Linkage broken or disconnected<br>• Defective wiper motor | • Repair or replace switch or cable<br>• Check vacuum lines, engine vacuum and fuel pump<br><br><br>• Repair linkage<br>• Replace wiper motor |
| Wipers stop on engine acceleration | • Leaking vacuum hoses<br>• Dry windshield<br>• Oversize wiper blades<br><br>• Defective vacuum/fuel pump | • Repair or replace hoses<br>• Wet windshield with washers<br>• Replace with proper size wiper blades<br>• Replace pump |

# Drive Train

**7**

## UNDERSTANDING THE MANUAL TRANSMISSION

Because of the way an internal combustion engine breathes, it can produce torque, or twisting force, only within a narrow speed range. Most modern, overhead valve engines must turn at about 2,500 rpm to produce their peak torque. By 4,500 rpm they are producing so little torque that continued increases in engine speed produce no power increases.

The torque peak on overhead camshaft engines is, generally, much higher, but much narrower.

The manual transmission and clutch are employed to vary the relationship between engine speed and the speed of the wheels so that adequate engine power can be produced under all circumstances. The clutch allows engine torque to be applied to the transmission input shaft gradually, due to mechanical slippage. The car can, consequently, be started smoothly from a full stop.

The transmission changes the ratio between the rotating speeds of the engine and the wheels by the use of gears. 4-speed or 5-speed transmissions are most common. The lower gears allow full engine power to be applied to the rear wheels during acceleration at low speeds.

The clutch drive plate is a thin disc, the center of which is splined to the transmission input shaft. Both sides of the disc are covered with a layer of material which is similar to brake lining and which is capable of allowing slippage without roughness or excessive noise.

The clutch cover is bolted to the engine flywheel and incorporates a diaphragm spring which provides the pressure to engage the clutch. The cover also houses the pressure plate. The driven disc is sandwiched between the pressure plate and the smooth surface of the flywheel when the clutch pedal is released,

thus forcing it to turn at the same speed as the engine crankshaft.

The transmission contains a mainshaft which passes all the way through the transmission, from the clutch to the driveshaft. This shaft is separated at one point, so that front and rear portions can turn at different speeds.

Power is transmitted by a countershaft in the lower gears and reverse. The gears of the countershaft mesh with gears on the mainshaft, allowing power to be carried from one to the other. All the countershaft gears are integral with that shaft, while several of the mainshaft gears can either rotate independently of the shaft or be locked to it. Shifting from one gear to the next causes one of the gears to be freed from rotating with the shaft and locks another to it. Gears are locked and unlocked by internal dog clutches which slide between the center of the gear and the shaft. The forward gears usually employ synchronizers; friction members which smoothly bring gear and shaft to the same speed before the toothed dog clutches are engaged.

The clutch is operating properly if:

1. It will stall the engine when released with the vehicle held stationary.

2. The shift lever can be moved freely between first and reverse gears when the vehicle is stationary and the clutch disengaged.

A clutch pedal free-play adjustment is incorporated in the linkage. If there is about 1–2" (25-50mm) of motion before the pedal begins to release the clutch, it is adjusted properly. Inadequate free-play wears all parts of the clutch releasing mechanisms and may cause slippage. Excessive free-play may cause inadequate release and hard shifting of gears.

Some clutches use a hydraulic system in place of mechanical linkage. If the clutch fails to release, fill the clutch master cylinder with fluid to the proper level and pump the clutch pedal to fill the system with fluid. Bleed the system in the same way as a brake system. If leaks are located, tighten loose connections or overhaul the master or slave cylinder as necessary.

## MANUAL TRANSAXLE

Transaxle is the term used to identify a unit which combines the transmission and drive axle into one component. All 1982-86 models were equipped with MT-125 manual four speed

transaxles. In 1987-88 Muncie five speed transaxles were used. The 4-speed transaxles use cable actuated clutches while the five speed clutches are hydraulically controlled utilizing a clutch master and slave cylinder.

All forward gears in this design are in constant mesh. Final drive from the transmission is taken from the output gear, which is an integral part of the output shaft; the output gear transfers power to the differential ring gear and differential assembly. The differential is of conventional design.

## Troubleshooting the Manual Transmission and Transfer Case

| Problem | Cause | Solution |
|---|---|---|
| Transmission shifts hard | • Clutch adjustment incorrect<br>• Clutch linkage or cable binding<br>• Shift rail binding | • Adjust clutch<br>• Lubricate or repair as necessary<br>• Check for mispositioned selector arm roll pin, loose cover bolts, worn shift rail bores, worn shift rail, distorted oil seal, or extension housing not aligned with case. Repair as necessary. |
| | • Internal bind in transmission caused by shift forks, selector plates, or synchronizer assemblies<br>• Clutch housing misalignment<br><br>• Incorrect lubricant<br>• Block rings and/or cone seats worn | • Remove, dissemble and inspect transmission. Replace worn or damaged components as necessary.<br>• Check runout at rear face of clutch housing<br>• Drain and refill transmission<br>• Blocking ring to gear clutch tooth face clearance must be 0.030 inch or greater. If clearance is correct it may still be necessary to inspect blocking rings and cone seats for excessive wear. Repair as necessary. |
| Gear clash when shifting from one gear to another | • Clutch adjustment incorrect<br>• Clutch linkage or cable binding<br>• Clutch housing misalignment<br><br>• Lubricant level low or incorrect lubricant<br><br>• Gearshift components, or synchronizer assemblies worn or damaged | • Adjust clutch<br>• Lubricate or repair as necessary<br>• Check runout at rear of clutch housing<br>• Drain and refill transmission and check for lubricant leaks if level was low. Repair as necessary.<br>• Remove, disassemble and inspect transmission. Replace worn or damaged components as necessary. |
| Transmission noisy | • Lubricant level low or incorrect lubricant<br><br><br>• Clutch housing-to-engine, or transmission-to-clutch housing bolts loose<br>• Dirt, chips, foreign material in transmission<br>• Gearshift mechanism, transmission gears, or bearing components worn or damaged<br><br>• Clutch housing misalignment | • Drain and refill transmission. If lubricant level was low, check for leaks and repair as necessary.<br>• Check and correct bolt torque as necessary<br><br>• Drain, flush, and refill transmission<br>• Remove, disassemble and inspect transmission. Replace worn or damaged components as necessary.<br>• Check runout at rear face of clutch housing |

## Troubleshooting the Manual Transmission and Transfer Case (cont.)

| Problem | Cause | Solution |
|---|---|---|
| Jumps out of gear | • Clutch housing misalignment | • Check runout at rear face of clutch housing |
| | • Gearshift lever loose | • Check lever for worn fork. Tighten loose attaching bolts. |
| | • Offset lever nylon insert worn or lever attaching nut loose | • Remove gearshift lever and check for loose offset lever nut or worn insert. Repair or replace as necessary. |
| | • Gearshift mechanism, shift forks, selector plates, interlock plate, selector arm, shift rail, detent plugs, springs or shift cover worn or damaged | • Remove, disassemble and inspect transmission cover assembly. Replace worn or damaged components as necessary. |
| | • Clutch shaft or roller bearings worn or damaged | • Replace clutch shaft or roller bearings as necessary |
| | • Gear teeth worn or tapered, synchronizer assemblies worn or damaged, excessive end play caused by worn thrust washers or output shaft gears | • Remove, disassemble, and inspect transmission. Replace worn or damaged components as necessary. |
| | • Pilot bushing worn | • Replace pilot bushing |
| Will not shift into one gear | • Gearshift selector plates, interlock plate, or selector arm, worn, damaged, or incorrectly assembled | • Remove, disassemble, and inspect transmission cover assembly. Repair or replace components as necessary. |
| | • Shift rail detent plunger worn, spring broken, or plug loose | • Tighten plug or replace worn or damaged components as necessary |
| | • Gearshift lever worn or damaged | • Replace gearshift lever |
| | • Synchronizer sleeves or hubs, damaged or worn | • Remove, disassemble and inspect transmission. Replace worn or damaged components. |
| Locked in one gear—cannot be shifted out | • Shift rail(s) worn or broken, shifter fork bent, setscrew loose, center detent plug missing or worn | • Inspect and replace worn or damaged parts |
| | • Broken gear teeth on countershaft gear, clutch shaft, or reverse idler gear | • Inspect and replace damaged part |
| | Gearshift lever broken or worn, shift mechanism in cover incorrectly assembled or broken, worn damaged gear train components | • Disassemble transmission. Replace damaged parts or assemble correctly. |
| Transfer case difficult to shift or will not shift into desired range | • Vehicle speed too great to permit shifting | • Stop vehicle and shift into desired range. Or reduce speed to 3–4 km/h (2–3 mph) before attempting to shift. |
| | • If vehicle was operated for extended period in 4H mode on dry paved surface, driveline torque load may cause difficult shifting | • Stop vehicle, shift transmission to neutral, shift transfer case to 2H mode and operate vehicle in 2H on dry paved surfaces |
| | • Transfer case external shift linkage binding | • Lubricate or repair or replace linkage, or tighten loose components as necessary |
| | • Insufficient or incorrect lubricant | • Drain and refill to edge of fill hole with SAE 85W-90 gear lubricant only |
| | • Internal components binding, worn, or damaged | • Disassemble unit and replace worn or damaged components as necessary |
| Transfer case noisy in all drive modes | • Insufficient or incorrect lubricant | • Drain and refill to edge of fill hole with SAE 85W-90 gear lubricant |

# Troubleshooting the Manual Transmission and Transfer Case (cont.)

| Problem | Cause | Solution |
|---|---|---|
| Transfer case noisy in all drive modes (cont.) | | only. Check for leaks and repair if necessary.<br>Note: If unit is still noisy after drain and refill, disassembly and inspection may be required to locate source of noise. |
| Noisy in—or jumps out of four wheel drive low range | • Transfer case not completely engaged in 4L position<br><br>• Shift linkage loose or binding<br><br>• Shift fork cracked, inserts worn, or fork is binding on shift rail | • Stop vehicle, shift transfer case in Neutral, then shift back into 4L position<br>• Tighten, lubricate, or repair linkage as necessary<br>• Disassemble unit and repair as necessary |
| Lubricant leaking from output shaft seals or from vent | • Transfer case overfilled<br>• Vent closed or restricted<br>• Output shaft seals damaged or installed incorrectly | • Drain to correct level<br>• Clear or replace vent if necessary<br>• Replace seals. Be sure seal lip faces interior of case when installed. Also be sure yoke seal surfaces are not scored or nicked. Remove scores, nicks with fine sandpaper or replace yoke(s) if necessary. |
| Abnormal tire wear | • Extended operation on dry hard surface (paved) roads in 4H range | • Operate in 2H on hard surface (paved) roads |

# Adjustments

## SHIFT LINKAGE

### MT-125

1. Disconnect the negative battery cable. Remove the shifter boot, the console and retainer inside the car. Shift into first gear, then loosen the shift cable mounting nuts at the transaxle.

2. Install two No. 22 drill bits, or two $5/32''$ rods, into the two alignment holes in the shifter assembly to hold it in first gear.

3. Place the transaxle into first gear by pushing the rail selector shaft down just to the point of feeling the resistance of the inhibitor spring. Then rotate the shift lever all the way counterclockwise.

4. Install the stud, with the cable attached, into the slotted area of the select lever, while gently pulling on the lever to remove all lash.

5. Remove the two drill bits or pins from the shifter.

6. Check the shifter for proper operation. It may be necessary to fine tune the adjustment after road testing.

## Neutral Safety/Back-up Light Switch

### REMOVAL AND INSTALLATION

1. Remove the shifter knob from the shifter by removing the retaining screw at the back of the knob.

2. Remove the screws at the sides and front of the console.

3. Open the console box and remove the retaining screw inside the box.

4. Remove the ashtray at the rear of the console and remove the retaining screw behind the ashtray.

5. Slide the console rearward slightly, then lift it over the shifter.

6. Disconnect the wiring harness at the back-up light switch.

7. Remove the switch from the base of the shifter.

8. Reverse steps 1 through 7 to install the switch.

## Transaxle

### REMOVAL AND INSTALLATION

#### 1982-83

*MT-125*

1. Disconnect the negative battery cable from the transaxle case.

2. Remove the two transaxle strut bracket bolts on the left side of the engine compartment, if equipped.

3. Remove the top four engine-to-transaxle bolts, and the one at the rear near the firewall. The one at the rear is installed from the engine side.

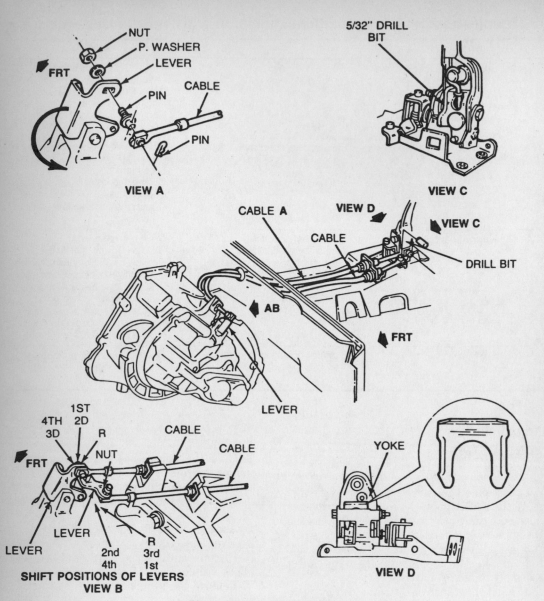

**VIEW A**

**VIEW C**

**SHIFT POSITIONS OF LEVERS
VIEW B**

**VIEW D**

**Manual transaxle shift linkage**

4. Loosen the engine-to-transaxle bolt near the starter, but do not remove.

5. Disconnect the speedometer cable at the transaxle, or at the speed control transducer on cars so equipped.

6. Remove the retaining clip and washer from the shift linkage at the transaxle. Remove the clips holding the cables to the mounting bosses on the case.

7. Support the engine with a lifting chain.

8. Unlock the steering column and raise and support the car. Drain the transaxle. Remove the two nuts attaching the stabilizer bar to the left lower control arm. Remove the four bolts which attach the left retaining plate to the en-gine cradle. The retaining plate covers and holds the stabilizer bar.

9. Loosen the four bolts holding the right stabilizer bracket.

10. Disconnect and remove the exhaust pipe and crossover if necessary.

11. Pull the stabilizer bar down on the left side.

12. Remove the four nuts and disconnect the front and rear transaxle mounts from the en-gine cradle. Remove the two rear center cross-member bolts.

13. Remove the three right side front cradle attaching bolts. They are accessible under the splash shield.

14. Remove the top bolt from the lower front transaxle shock absorber if equipped.

15. Remove the left front wheel. Remove the front cradle-to-body bolts on the left side, and the rear cradle-to-body bolts.

16. Pull the left side driveshaft from the transaxle using G. M. special tool J-28468 or the equivalent. The right side axle shaft will simply disconnect from the cage. When the transaxle is removed, the right shaft can be swung out of the way. A boot protector should be used when disconnecting the driveshafts.

17. Swing the cradle to the left side. Secure out of the way, outboard of the fender well.

18. Remove the flywheel and starter shield bolts, and remove the shields.

19. Remove the two transaxle extension bolts from the engine-to-transaxle bracket, if equipped.

20. Place a jack under the transaxle case. Remove the last engine-to-transaxle bolt. Pull the transaxle to the left, away from the engine, then down and out from under the car.

**To install:**

21. Place the transaxle on a jack and raise it into position. Position the right axle shaft into its bore as the transaxle is bolted to the engine.

22. Swing the cradle into position and install the cradle-to-body bolts immediately. Be sure to guide the left axle shaft into place as the cradle is moved back into position.

23. Install the two transaxle extension bolts into the engine-to-transaxle bracket.

24. Install the lower engine-to-transaxle bolts.

25. Install the flywheel to starter shield and retaining bolts.

26. Remove the boot protectors from the driveshafts.

27. Install the top bolt to the lower front transaxle shock absorber.

28. Install the four nuts and connect the front and rear transaxle mounts to the engine cradle. Install the two rear center crossmember bolts.

29. Install the stabilizer bar.

30. Install the exhaust pipe and crossover.

31. Install the four bolts holding the right stabilizer bracket.

32. Install the two nuts attaching the stabilizer bar to the left lower control arm. Install the four bolts which attach the left retaining plate to the engine cradle.

33. Remove the transaxle jack, disconnect the engine lifting chain and lower the vehicle.

34. Fill the transaxle with the recommended fluid.

35. Install the retaining clip and washer to the shift linkage at the transaxle. Install the clips holding the cables to the mounting bosses on the case.

36. Connect the speedometer cable at the transaxle, or at the speed control transducer on cars so equipped.

37. Tighten the engine-to-transaxle bolt near the starter.

38. Install the top four engine-to-transaxle bolts, and the one at the rear near the firewall. The one at the rear is installed from the engine side.

39. Remove the two transaxle strut bracket bolts on the left side of the engine compartment, if equipped.

40. Connect the negative battery cable to the transaxle case.

**1984-86**

*MT-125*

1. Disconnect the battery ground cable from the transaxle and support it with a wire.

2. Disconnect the horn's electrical lead and remove the horn's mounting bolt. Remove the air cleaner.

3. Support the clutch pedal upward against the bumper stop to release the pawl from the quadrant. Disconnect the clutch cable from the release lever at the transaxle.

CAUTION: *DO NOT allow the clutch cable to snap rapidly toward the rear of the vehicle, for the quadrant in the adjusting mechanism can be damaged.*

4. Lift the locking pawl away from the quadrant and slide the cable out to the right side of the quadrant.

5. At the right side of the cowl, disconnect the cable retainer-to-upper stud nuts. Disconnect the cable from the transaxle bracket and remove the cable.

6. If equipped with a V6 engine, disconnect the fuel lines and clamps from the clutch cable bracket, then remove the exhaust crossover pipe.

7. At the transaxle, remove the shift linkage retaining clips and the shift cable retaining clips from the transaxle bosses.

8. Disconnect the speedometer cable at the transaxle. Remove the top engine-to-transaxle bolts.

9. Install and support the engine with tool J-22825-1. Raise the vehicle and drain the transaxle fluid.

10. Install the drive axle boot protector tool J-33162 to the drive axle boot. Remove the left front wheel and tire assembly.

11. Turn the steering wheel so that the intermediate shaft-to-steering gear stub shaft is in the upward position, then remove the bolt.

12. Position a floor jack under the engine to act as a support. Remove the power steering pressure line brackets.

13. Remove the steering gear mounting bolts,

then support the steering gear. Disconnect the drive line vibration absorber, the front stabilizer from the left side lower control arm and the left side lower ball joint from the steering knuckle.

14. Remove both sides of the stabilizer bar reinforcements.

15. Using a ½″ drill bit, drill through the spot weld (located between the rear holes of the left side front stabilizer bar mounting).

16. Disconnect the engine/transaxle mounts from the cradle. Remove the crossmember side bolts and the left side body bolts.

17. Remove the left side and the front crossmember assembly.

18. Using tools J-33008, J-29794 and J-261901, remove the left drive axle from the transaxle and the support.

NOTE: *The right drive axle can be removed when the transaxle is removed from the vehicle.*

19. Remove the flywheel/starter shield bolts. Connect a transaxle jack to the transaxle, then remove the last engine-to-transaxle bolt.

20. Slide the transaxle away from the engine, lower the jack and move the transaxle away from the vehicle.

**To install:**

21. Place the transaxle on a jack and raise it into position. Position the right axle shaft into its bore as the transaxle is bolted to the engine.

22. Swing the cradle into position and install the cradle-to-body bolts immediately. Be sure to guide the left axle shaft into place as the cradle is moved back into position.

23. Install the flywheel/starter shield and bolts.

24. Install the left side and front crossmember assembly.

25. Install the crossmember side bolts and the left side body bolts.

26. Connect the engine/transaxle mounts to the cradle.

27. Connect the left side lower ball joint to the steering knuckle.

28. Connect the front stabilizer to the left lower control arm.

29. Connect the drive line vibration absorber.

30. Install the stabilizer bar reinforcements, and the steering gear.

31. Install the power steering pressure line brackets.

32. Turn the steering wheel so that the intermediate shaft-to-steering gear stub shaft is in the upward position, then install the bolt.

33. Remove the drive axle boot protector tool J-33162 from the drive axle boot. Install the left front wheel and tire assembly.

34. Remove the engine support tool J-22825-

1. Lower the vehicle and fill the transaxle with fluid.

35. Connect the speedometer cable at the transaxle. Install the top engine-to-transaxle bolts.

36. Install the shift linkage retaining clips and the shift cable retaining clips to the transaxle bosses.

37. If equipped with a V6 engine, connect the fuel lines and clamps to the clutch cable bracket, then install the exhaust crossover pipe.

38. At the right side of the cowl, connect the cable retainer-to-upper stud nuts. Install the cable to the transaxle bracket.

39. Lift the locking pawl away from the quadrant and slide the cable into the right side of the quadrant.

40. Connect the clutch cable to the release lever at the transaxle. Return the clutch pedal to its normal position.

41. Connect the horn's electrical lead and install the mounting bolt. Install the air cleaner.

42. Connect the battery ground cable to the transaxle.

**1987-88**

*MUNCIE*

1. Disconnect the negative battery cable.

2. Remove the air cleaner and air intake duct assembly.

3. Remove the sound insulator from inside the car.

4. Remove the clutch master cylinder push rod from the clutch pedal.

5. Remove the clutch slave cylinder from the transaxle.

6. Disconnect the exhaust crossover pipe.

7. Disconnect the shift cables at the transaxle.

8. Install the engine support fixture J-28467.

9. Remove the top engine to transaxle bolts.

10. Raise the car and suitably support it.

11. Remove the L.H. and R.H. front wheel and tire.

12. Install the drive axle boot seal protectors, Tool J-34754.

13. Remove the L.H. side frame and disconnect the rear transaxle mount from the bracket.

14. Drain the transaxle.

15. Disengage the R.H. and L.H. drive axles from the transaxle.

16. Remove the clutch housing cover bolts.

17. Disconnect the speedometer cable.

18. Attach a jack to the transaxle case.

19. Remove the remaining transaxle to engine bolts.

20. Slide the transaxle away from the engine. Carefully lower the jack while guiding the R.H. drive axle out of the transaxle.

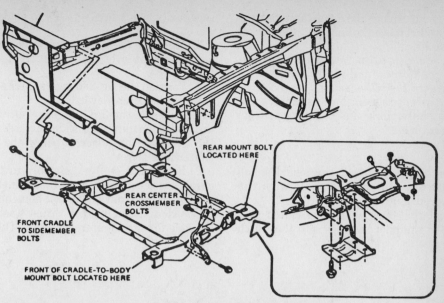

REAR MOUNT BOLT
LOCATED HERE

REAR CENTER
CROSSMEMBER
BOLTS

FRONT CRADLE
TO SIDEMEMBER
BOLTS

FRONT OF CRADLE-TO-BODY
MOUNT BOLT LOCATED HERE

Typical engine/transaxle cradle

## To install:

21. Place the transaxle on a jack and guide it into the vehicle, position the right drive axle shaft into its bore as the transaxle is being installed. The R.H. shaft CANNOT be readily installed after the transaxle is connected to the engine.

22. Install the transaxle to engine bolts.

23. After the transaxle is fastened to the engine and the left drive axle is installed at the transaxle, position the left side frame and install the frame to body bolts.

24. Connect the transaxle to the front and rear mounts.

25. Connect the speedometer cable.

26. Install the clutch housing cover bolts.

27. Remove the drive axle boot seal protectors, Tool J-34754.

28. Fill the transaxle with the proper fluid.

29. Install the left side frame and connect the rear transaxle mount to the bracket (if not already done).

30. Install the left and right front wheel and tire.

31. Remove the jack and safety supports and lower the car.

32. Install the top engine to transaxle bolts.

33. Remove the engine support fixture J-28467.

34. Connect the shift cables at the transaxle.

35. Connect the exhaust crossover pipe.

36. Install the clutch slave cylinder to the transaxle.

37. Install the clutch master cylinder push rod from the clutch pedal.

38. Install the sound insulator inside the car.

39. Install the air intake duct assembly and the air cleaner.

40. Connect the negative battery cable.

### MT-125 TRANSAXLE OVERHAUL

#### Transaxle Case

*DISASSEMBLY*

1. Place the transmission so that it is resting on the bell housing.

2. Drive the spring pin from the shifter shaft arm assembly and the shifter shaft, then remove the shifter shaft arm assembly.

3. Remove the five extension housing-to-case bolts and the extension housing.

4. Press down on the speedometer gear retainer, then remove the gear and the retainer from the mainshaft.

5. Remove the snaprings from the shifter shaft, then the Reverse shifter shaft cover, the shifter shaft detent cap, the spring, the ball and the interlock lock pin.

6. Pull the Reverse lever shaft outward to disengage the Reverse idler, then remove the idler shaft with the gear attached.

7. Remove the Reverse gear snapring, the Reverse countershaft gear and the gears.

8. Turn the case on its side and remove the clutch gear bearing retainer bolts, the retainer and the gasket.

9. Remove the clutch gear ball bearing-to-bell housing snapring, then the bell housing-to-case bolts.

10. Turn the case so that it rests on the bell

housing, then expand the mainshaft bearing snapring and remove the case by lifting it off the mainshaft.

NOTE: *Make sure that the mainshaft assembly, the countergear and shifter shaft assembly stay with the bell housing.*

11. Lift the entire mainshaft assembly complete with shifter forks and countergear from the bell housing.

### ASSEMBLY

1. Using a press, install the shielded ball bearing to the clutch gear shaft with the snapring groove up.

2. Install the snapring on the clutch gear shaft. Place the pilot bearings into the clutch gear cavity, using heavy grease to hold them in place.

3. Assemble the clutch gear to the mainshaft and the detent lever to the shift shaft with the roll pin.

4. Position the 1st-2nd gear shifter so that it engages the detent lever.

5. Assemble the 3rd-4th gear shifter fork to the detent bushing and slide the assembly on the shift shaft to place it below the 1st-2nd shifter fork arm.

6. Install the shifter assembly to the synchronizer sleeve grooves on the mainshaft.

5. With the front of the bell housing resting on wooden blocks, place a thrust washer over the hole for the countergear shaft. The thrust

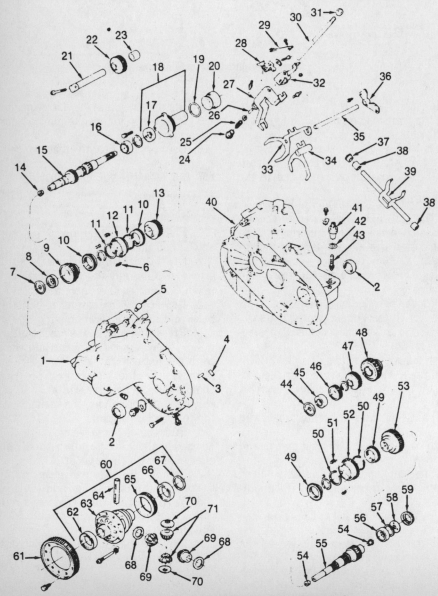

Exploded view of the GM125-4 4-speed transaxle

washer must be placed in the holes in the bellhousing.

6. Mesh the countershaft gears to the mainshaft gears and install this assembly into the bellhousing.

7. Turn the bellhousing on its side, then install the snapring to the ball bearing on the clutch gear and the bearing retainer to the bell housing. Use sealant on the four retaining bolts.

8. Turn the bell housing (so that it is resting on the blocks) and install the Reverse lever to the case using grease to hold it in place. When installing the Reverse lever, the screwdriver slot should be parallel to the front of the case.

9. Install the Reverse lever snapring and the roller bearing-to-countergear opening with the snapring groove inside of the case.

10. Using rubber cement, install the gasket on the bell housing. Before installing the case, make sure the synchronizers are in the Neutral position, the detent bushing slot is facing outward and the Reverse lever is flush with the inside wall of the case.

11. Expand the snapring in the mainshaft case opening and let it slide over the bearing.

12. Install the interlock lock pin with locking

compound to hold the shifter shaft in place and the idler shaft so it engages with the Reverse lever inside the shaft.

13. Install the cover over the screwdriver arm to hold the Reverse lever in place.

14. Install the detent ball, the spring and the cap in the case, then the Reverse gear (with the chamfer on the gear teeth facing up). Push the Reverse gear onto the splines and secure with a snapring.

15. Install the smaller Reverse gear on the countergear shaft (with the shoulder resting against the countergear bearing) and secure with a snapring.

16. Install the snapring, the thrust washer and the Reverse idler gear (with the gear teeth chamfer facing down) to the idler shaft, then secure with the thrust washer and the snapring.

17. Install the shifter shaft snaprings and engage the speedometer gear retainer in the hole in the mainshaft (with the retainer loop toward the front), then slide the speedometer gear over the mainshaft and into position.

NOTE: *Before installation, heat the gear to 175°F; use an oven or heat lamp, not a torch.*

18. Place the extension housing and the gasket on the case, then loosely install the two pilot

1. Case assembly
2. Axle shaft seal assembly
3. Case locating pin
4. Chip collecting magnet
5. Vent assembly
6. Synchronizer key
7. Oil shield
8. Bearing assembly
9. 4th speed input gear
10. Blocking ring
11. Synchronizer spring
12. Synchronizer assembly
13. 3rd speed input gear
14. Oil shield sleeve
15. Input cluster gear
16. Input gear bearing
17. Input gear seal
18. Input gear retainer assembly
19. Retainer seal
20. Throwout bearing assembly
21. Reverse idler shaft
22. Reverse idler shaft
23. Reverse idler shaft gear
24. Reverse inhibitor spring seat
25. Reverse inhibitor spring
26. Reverse inhibitor spring pin
27. Reverse shift lever
28. Detent lever assembly
29. Detent spring
30. Shift shaft
31. Shift shaft seal assembly
32. Shift interlock
33. 3rd-4th shift fork
34. 1st-2nd shift fork
35. Shift fork shaft
36. Oil guide
37. Clutch fork shaft seal assembly
38. Clutch fork shaft bearing
39. Clutch fork shaft assembly
40. Clutch and differential housing assembly
41. Speedometer driven gear sleeve
42. Speedometer driven gear sleeve seal
43. Speedometer driven gear
44. Case bearing oil shield
45. Case bearing assembly
46. 4th speed gear
47. 3rd speed output gear
48. 2nd speed output gear
49. Synchronizer blocking ring
50. Synchronizer spring
51. Synchronizer key
52. 1st-2nd synchronizer assembly
53. 1st speed output gear
54. Oil shield sleeve
55. Output gear
56. Output bearing assembly
57. Output gear bearing shim
58. Output gear bearing oil shield
59. Output gear bearing oil shield retainer
60. Differential assembly
61. Differential ring gear
62. Differential bearing assembly
63. Differential case
64. Differential pinion shaft
65. Speedometer drive gear
66. Differential bearing assembly
67. Housing bearing shim
68. Side gear thrust washer
69. Differential side gear
70. Pinion thrust washer
71. Differential pinion gear

**Exploded view of the GM125-4 4-speed transaxle**

bolts (one in the top right hand corner and the other in the bottom left hand corner) and the other three bolts. The pilot bolts must be installed in the right holes to prevent splitting the case.

19. Assemble the shifter shaft arm over the shifter shaft, align with the drilled hole near the end of the shaft, then drive the spring pin into the shifter shaft arm and shaft.

20. Turn the case on its side and loosely install the two pilot bolts through the bell housing and then the four retaining bolts.

### Mainshaft
*DISASSEMBLY*

1. Separate the shift shaft assembly and countergear from the mainshaft.

2. Remove the clutch gear and the blocking ring from the mainshaft; make sure you don't lose any of the clutch gear roller bearings.

3. Remove the 3rd-4th gear synchronizer hub snapring and the hub, using an arbor press (if necessary).

4. Remove the blocking ring and the 3rd speed gear. Using an arbor press and press plates, remove the ball bearing from the rear of the mainshaft. Remove the remaining parts from the mainshaft keeping them in order for later reassembly.

*ASSEMBLY*

1. With the rear of the mainshaft turned up, install the 2nd speed gear with the clutching teeth facing upward; the rear face of the gear will butt against the flange of the mainshaft.

2. Install a blocking ring (with the clutching teeth down) over the 2nd speed gear.

3. Install the 1st-2nd synchronizer assembly (with the fork slot down), then press it onto the splines on the mainshaft until it bottoms.

NOTE: *Make sure the notches of the blocking ring align with the keys of the synchronizer assembly.*

4. Install the synchronizer hub-to-mainshaft snapring, then install a blocking ring (with the notches facing down) so they align with the keys of the 1st-2nd gear synchronizer assembly.

5. Install the 1st speed gear (with the clutching teeth down), then the rear ball bearing (with the snapring groove down) and press it into place on the mainshaft.

6. Turn the mainshaft up and install the 3rd speed gear (with the clutching teeth facing up); the front face of the gear will butt against the flange on the mainshaft.

7. Install a blocking ring (with the clutching teeth facing down) over the synchronizer surface of the 3rd speed gear.

8. Install the 3rd-4th gear synchronizer assembly (with the fork slot facing down); make sure the notches of the blocking ring align with the keys of the synchronizer assembly.

9. Install the synchronizer hub-to-mainshaft snapring and a blocking ring (with the notches facing down) so that they align with the keys of the 3rd-4th gear synchronizer assembly.

### Synchronizer Keys And Springs
*REPLACEMENT*

1. The synchronizer hubs and the sliding sleeves are an assembly which should be kept together as an assembly; the keys and the springs can be replaced.

2. Mark the position of the hub and the sleeve for reassembly.

3. Push the hub from the sliding sleeve; the keys will fall out and the springs can be easily removed.

4. Place the new springs in position (with one on each side of the hub) so that the three keys are engaged by both springs.

5. Place and hold the keys in position, then slide the sleeve into the hub aligning the marks made during disassembly.

### Extension Oil Seal
*REPLACEMENT*

1. Pry the oil seal and drive the bushing from rear of the extension housing.

2. Coat the inside diameter of the seal and bushing with transmission fluid and install them.

### Drive Gear Bearing Oil Seal
*REPLACEMENT*

Pry out the old seal and install a new one making sure that it bottoms properly in its bore.

## MUNCIE TRANSAXLE OVERHAUL
### Transaxle Case
*DISASSEMBLY*

1. Using a 10mm wrench, remove the ten cover bolts and lift off the cover.

2. Drain the lubricant.

3. Using a pencil size magnet, remove the shift rail detent plug, the spring and the plunger from the upper left side of the case.

4. Working through the shift turret opening in the extension housing, remove the access plug from the rear of the housing.

5. After shifting into Reverse gear, remove

the roll pin from the gear shift shaft offset lever, then slide the offset lever and bushing off the shaft.

6. Remove the 5th speed interlock pilot bolt from the front top of the extension housing.

7. Remove the 6 extension housing bolts, then slide the housing and the gasket off the output shaft.

8. Remove the snapring, the speedometer drive gear and the drive ball from the output shaft.

9. Remove the 5th gear synchronizer snapring from the output shaft, then slide the retaining spacer off the output shaft.

10. Shift the transmission into 1st gear. Using a hammer and a punch, drive out the roll pin located inside the case, which secures the 1st, 2nd, 3rd, 4th and Reverse selector pin, then remove the selector pin.

11. Slide the shifter shaft, the 5th speed shift fork and the synchronizer from the output shaft as an assembly.

12. Remove the interlock sleeve bolt from the right side of the case.

13. Remove the interlock sleeve, the 3rd-4th speed shift fork and the 1st-2nd speed shift fork from the case.

14. Working inside the case, remove the C-clip from the Reverse gear selector fork pivot pin. Remove the pivot pin, then lift the Reverse gear selector fork relay lever, the spring and the Reverse gearshift fork from the case.

15. Slide the 5th speed main drive gear off the output shaft.

16. Remove the snapring located at the rear of the 5th speed cluster gear.

17. Using a puller, remove the 5th speed cluster gear.

18. Remove the output shaft rear bearing snapring and the bearing cup.

19. Remove the 4 input shaft bearing retainer bolts, the bearing retainer, the seal, the shim and the O-ring from the case.

20. Without loosing the roller bearings, the thrust washers and the thrust bearing, rotate the input shaft so that the teeth recess face the countershaft gear, then lift the input gear from the case.

21. Remove the output shaft assembly through the top of the transmission case.

22. Remove the snapring from the rear of the case and the countershaft gear rear bearing cup from the case.

23. Remove the three bolts, the bearing retainer, the gasket, the shim and the front bearing cup from the case.

24. Lift the countershaft gear through the top of the case.

25. Remove the Reverse idler gear and shaft by removing the roll pin that secures the shaft to the case.

*ASSEMBLY*

NOTE: *Coat the bolts and plugs used throughout the case with a thread sealant to prevent leakage.*

1. Hold the Reverse idler gear into position with the long end of the hub facing to the rear of the case. Slide the idler gear shaft through the case and gear and align the roll pin holes, then secure the shaft with the roll pin.

2. Lower the countershaft and bearings into place and install the rear bearing cup, then secure with the snapring.

3. Position the front bearing cup, the shim, a new gasket and the bearing retainer to the front of the case. Install the bearing retainer cap bolts and torque to 7-10 ft.lb. (while rotating the gear). If the gear rotating effort increases while torquing the bearing retainer, replace the shim with a thinner one.

4. The correct end play is 0.001-0.005″.

NOTE: *Decrease the shim thickness to increase the end play and increase the shim thickness to reduce end play.*

5. Lower the main shaft into the case through the case cover opening.

6. Apply a coat of polyethylene grease to the thrust washers and the thrust bearing. Place the thrust washer on the 3rd-4th speed synchronization thrust surface. Place the thrust bearing and the remaining thrust washer on the 3rd-4th speed synchronizer.

7. Without disturbing the roller bearings, carefully install the input shaft assembly in the case with the blank portion of the teeth facing the countershaft gear.

8. Coat a new input shaft O-ring with polyethylene grease and position it in the bearing retainer groove.

9. Install the output shaft bearing cup and the snapring into the rear of the case.

10. Position the shim and bearing retainer into the case. Install the bearing retainer bolts and torque to 8-10 ft.lb. (while rotating the input shaft).

NOTE: *If the input shaft turning effort increases when torquing the bearing retainer bolts, replace the shim with a thicker one.*

11. Install a dial indicator on the case. Pry the output shaft toward the dial indicator and zero the indicator. Pry the output shaft in the opposite direction. The end play should be between 0.001-0.005″. Increase shim thickness to decrease end play or decrease shim thickness to increase end play. Remove the dial indicator.

12. Install the spring and the Reverse fork on the relay lever. Position the relay lever assem-

bly in the case, then install the pivot pin in the case and lever assembly. Secure the lever with a C-clip.

13. Install the 5th speed cluster gear and secure with a snapring.

14. Slide the 5th speed main drive gear onto the output shaft. Coat the blocking ring with polyethylene grease and position it on the main drive gear.

15. Position the 1st-2nd and the 3rd-4th shift forks onto the main shaft assembly.

16. Place the interlock gear selector sleeve between the 2 shifter forks and install the interlock pilot bolt in the right side of the case.

17. With the synchronizer thrust surface facing the rear of the output shaft, install the shifter shaft, the 5th speed shift fork and the 5th speed synchronizer as an assembly.

18. Working through the cover opening in the case, install the gearshift selector pin in the shifter shaft and secure with a roll pin.

19. Slide the 5th speed synchronizer retaining plate onto the output shaft and secure with a snapring.

20. Secure the speedometer drive gear ball to the output shaft with polyethylene grease then slide the speedometer drive gear onto the shaft over the ball and secure with a snapring.

21. Using a new gasket, position the extension housing on the case. Install the two pilot bolts, one in the upper left side of the housing and the other in the lower right corner. Install

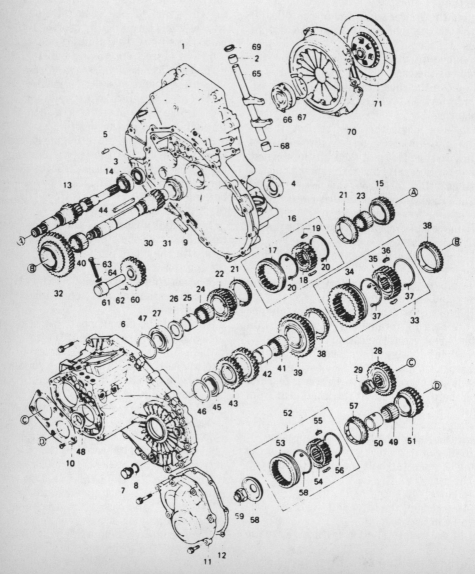

**Exploded view of the 5-speed (76mm) transaxle**

the four remaining bolts and torque to 40-60 ft.lb.

22. Install the 5th gear pilot bolt in the top of the extension housing.

23. Shift the into Reverse gear. Install the offset lever on the rear of the shifter shaft and secure with a roll pin.

24. Install the detent plunger, the spring and the plug in the upper right side of the case, then torque the plug to 12-14 ft.lb.

25. Install the access plug in the rear of the extension housing.

26. Using a new gasket place the cover on the case and torque the bolts to 8-10 ft.lb.

## Output Shaft
*DISASSEMBLY*

1. Slide the 3rd-4th speed synchronizer off the front end of the output shaft.

2. Slide the 3rd speed gear off the front of the output shaft.

3. Remove the snapring and the 2nd speed gear thrust washer from the output shaft. Slide the 2nd speed gear and the synchronizer blocking ring off the output shaft.

4. Remove the 1st-2nd speed synchronizer

snapring from the output shaft, then press the synchronizer off the output shaft.

5. Remove the snapring from the rear of the output shaft. Place the output shaft in a press, then remove the 1st speed gear, the thrust washer and the output shaft rear bearing.

*ASSEMBLY*

1. Position the 1st gear thrust washer and the bearing on the rear of the output shaft. Apply pressure on the bearing inner race until the bearing is bottomed on the spacer and shaft.

2. Select a snapring that will not allow any clearance between the bearing race and the ring groove. Then press the 1st-2nd gear synchronizer and the Reverse sliding gear into place, then secure with the snapring.

3. Slide the 2nd gear and the thrust washer into position, then secure with the snapring.

4. Slide the 3rd gear and the 3rd-4th synchronizer into place. Make sure the thrust surface of the synchronizer hub is facing forward.

## Input Shaft
*DISASSEMBLY*

1. If not previously removed, remove the roller bearings from the input shaft.

| | | | |
|---|---|---|---|
| 1. | Clutch and diff. housing | 37. | Insert spring |
| 2. | Clutch shaft bushing | 38. | 1st/2nd blocker ring |
| 3. | Input shaft oil seal | 39. | 2nd gear assembly |
| 4. | Drive shaft oil seal | 40. | 1st needle bearing |
| 5. | Straight knock pin | 41. | 2nd needle bearing |
| 6. | Transaxle case | 42. | 2nd collar |
| 7. | Drain plug | 43. | 3rd/4th output gear |
| 8. | Gasket | 44. | Key |
| 9. | Magnet | 45. | Output shaft rear bearing |
| 10. | Bearing retainer | 46. | Input shaft bearing shim |
| 11. | Rear cover | 47. | Output shaft bearing shim |
| 12. | Gasket | 48. | 5th gear thrust washer |
| 13. | Input shaft | 49. | 5th needle bearing |
| 14. | Input shaft front bearing | 50. | 5th collar |
| 15. | 3rd gear assembly | 51. | 5th gear assembly |
| 16. | 3rd/4th synchronizer asm. | 52. | 5th synchronizer assembly |
| 17. | Synchronizer sleeve | 53. | Synchronizer sleeve |
| 18. | Clutch hub | 54. | Clutch hub |
| 19. | Insert | 55. | Insert |
| 20. | Insert spring | 56. | Insert spring |
| 21. | 3rd/4th blocker ring | 57. | 5th blocker ring |
| 22. | 4th gear assembly | 58. | Insert stopper plate |
| 23. | 3rd needle bearing | 59. | Output shaft end nut |
| 24. | 4th needle bearing | 60. | Reverse idler gear asm. |
| 25. | 4th collar | 61. | Reverse idler shaft |
| 26. | 4th gear thrust washer | 62. | Straight pin |
| 27. | Input shaft rear bearing | 63. | Reverse idler shaft bolt |
| 28. | 5th gear | 64. | Gasket |
| 29. | Input shaft end nut | 65. | Clutch fork shaft asm. |
| 30. | Output shaft | 66. | Clutch release bearing |
| 31. | Output shaft front bearing | 67. | Release bearing spring |
| 32. | 1st gear assembly | 68. | Clutch shaft bushing |
| 33. | 1st/2nd synchronizer assembly | 69. | Clutch shaft seal |
| 34. | Reverse gear | 70. | Clutch pressure plate asm. |
| 35. | Clutch hub | 71. | Clutch disk assembly |
| 36. | Insert | | |

**Exploded view of the 5-speed (76mm) transaxle**

2. Place the input gear in a press and press the input gear from the bearing.

*ASSEMBLY*

1. With the taper toward the front of the gear, apply pressure on the inner race and press the bearing onto the input gear until it is bottomed.

2. Apply a heavy coat of polyethylene on the inner bearing surface of the gear. Insert the 15 roller bearings into the gear.

### Countershaft Gear

*DISASSEMBLY*

1. Place the countershaft gear in a press and remove the rear bearing.

2. Place the countershaft in a vise protected with wood blocks and pry the front bearing from the countershaft.

*ASSEMBLY*

1. With the taper facing outward, exert pressure on the inner race of the front bearing and press the bearing until it is bottomed on the gear.

2. Install the rear bearing in the same manner.

### Input Shaft Gear Bearing Retainer

*DISASSEMBLY*

1. Place the bearing retainer in a vise.

2. Using a slide impact type puller, remove the seal from the bearing retainer.

*ASSEMBLY*

Install the seal in the retainer with the lip facing forward. Make sure the seal is bottomed in the retainer.

### Extension Housing

*DISASSEMBLY*

1. Carefully remove the seal from the extension housing.

2. Using a suitable driver, remove the bushing.

*ASSEMBLY*

Install the bushing and the seal using a suitable driver.

## Halfshafts

### REMOVAL AND INSTALLATION

CAUTION: *Use care when removing the drive axle. Tri-pots can be damaged if the drive axle is over extended.*

1. Remove the hub nut.

2. Raise the front of the car. Remove the wheel and tire.

3. Install an axle shaft boot seal protector, G.M. special tool no. J-28712 or the equivalent, onto the seal.

4. Disconnect the brake hose clip from the MacPherson strut, but do not disconnect the hose from the caliper. Remove the brake caliper from the spindle, and hang the caliper out of the way by a length of wire. Do not allow the caliper to hang by the brake hose.

5. Mark the camber alignment cam bolt for reassembly. Remove the cam bolt and the upper attaching bolt from the strut and spindle.

6. Pull the steering knuckle assembly from the strut bracket.

7. Using G.M. special tool J-28468 or the equivalent, remove the axle shaft from the transaxle.

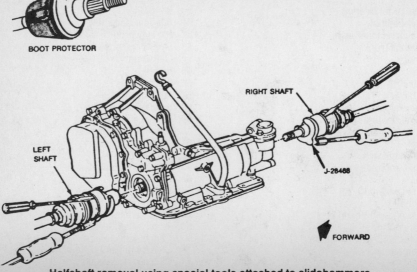

BOOT PROTECTOR

RIGHT SHAFT

LEFT SHAFT

J-28468

FORWARD

**Halfshaft removal using special tools attached to slidehammers**

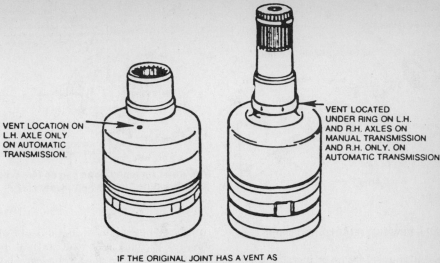

VENT LOCATION ON L.H. AXLE ONLY ON AUTOMATIC TRANSMISSION.

VENT LOCATED UNDER RING ON L.H. AND R.H. AXLES ON MANUAL TRANSMISSION AND R.H. ONLY, ON AUTOMATIC TRANSMISSION

IF THE ORIGINAL JOINT HAS A VENT AS SHOWN ABOVE A NEW SEAL IS REQUIRED.

**Comparison of old and new CV joints**

8. Using G.M. special tool J-28733 or the equivalent spindle remover, remove the axle shaft from the hub and bearing assembly.

**To install:**

1. If a new drive axle is to be installed, a new knuckle seal should be installed first.

2. Loosely install the drive axle into the transaxle and steering knuckle.

3. Loosely attach the steering knuckle to the suspension strut.

4. The drive axle is an interference fit in the steering knuckle. Press the axle into place, then install the hub nut. When the shaft begins to turn with the hub, insert a drift through the caliper into one of the cooling slots in the rotor to keep it from turning. Insert a long bolt in the hub flange to prevent the shaft from turning. Tighten the hub nut to 70 ft.lb. to completely seat the shaft.

5. Install the brake caliper. Tighten the bolts to 30 ft.lb.

6. Load the hub assembly by lowering it onto a jackstand. Align the camber cam bolt marks made during removal, install the bolt and tighten to 140 ft.lb. Tighten the upper nut to the same value.

7. Install the axle shaft all the way into the transaxle using a screwdriver inserted into the groove provided on the inner retainer. Tap the screwdriver until the shaft seats in the transaxle. Remove the boot seal protector.

## OVERHAUL

### Outer Joint

1. Remove the axle shaft.

2. Cut off the seal retaining clamp. Using a brass drift and a hammer, lightly tap the seal retainer from the outside toward the inside of the shaft to remove from the joint.

3. Use a pair of snapring pliers to spread the retaining ring apart. Pull the axle shaft from the joint.

4. Using a brass drift and a hammer, lightly tap on the inner race cage until it has tilted sufficiently to remove one of the balls. Remove the other balls in the same manner.

5. Pivot the cage 90 degrees and, with the cage ball windows aligned with the outer joint windows, lift out the cage and the inner race.

6. The inner race can be removed from the cage by pivoting it 90 degrees and lifting out. Clean all parts thoroughly and inspect for wear.

7. To install, put a light coat of the grease provided in the rebuilding kit onto the ball grooves of the inner race and outer joint.

8. Install the balls into the inner race cage.

9. Install the inner race into the cage onto the axle joint.

10. Install the axle shaft into the joint.

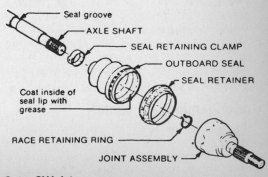

Seal groove

AXLE SHAFT

SEAL RETAINING CLAMP

OUTBOARD SEAL

SEAL RETAINER

Coat inside of seal lip with grease

RACE RETAINING RING

JOINT ASSEMBLY

**Outer CV joint**

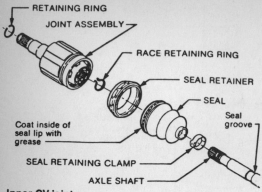

**Inner CV joint**

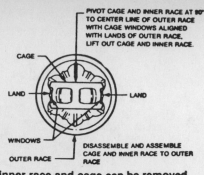

**The inner race and cage can be removed from the outer race when pivoted 90°**

11. Install a new seal retainer and clamp onto the joint.

12. To install the seal retainer, install the axle shaft assembly into an arbor press. Support the seal retainer on blocks, and press the axle shaft down until the seal retainer seats on the outer joint. When assembling, apply half the grease provided in the rebuilding kit to the joint; fill the seal (boot) with the rest of the grease. Install the axle shaft.

### Inner Joint

1. The joint seal is removed in the same manner as the outer joint seal. Follow Steps 1-3 of the outer joint procedure.

2. To disassemble the inner joint, remove the ball retaining ring from the joint. Pull the cage and inner race from the joint. The balls will come out with the race.

3. Center the inner race lobes in the cage windows, pivot the race 90 degrees, and lift the race from the cage.

4. Reverse steps 1, 2 and 3 to assembly the joint. The inner joint seal retainer must be pressed onto the joint. See Step 12 of the outer joint procedure.

## CLUTCH

CAUTION: *The clutch driven disc contains asbestos, which has been determined to be a cancer causing agent. Never clean clutch surfaces with compressed air! Avoid inhaling any dust from any clutch surface! When cleaning clutch surfaces, use a commercially available brake cleaning fluid.*

### Understanding the Clutch

The purpose of the clutch is to disconnect and connect engine power from the transmission. A car at rest requires a lot of engine torque to get all that weight moving. An internal combustion engine does not develop a high starting torque (unlike steam engines), so it must be allowed to operate without any load until it builds up enough torque to move the car. Torque increases with engine rpm. The clutch allows the engine to build up torque by physically disconnecting the engine from the transmission, relieving the engine of any load or resistance. The transfer of engine power to the transmission (the load) must be smooth and gradual; if it weren't, drive line components would wear out or break quickly. This gradual power transfer is made possible by gradually releasing the clutch pedal. The clutch disc and pressure plate are the connecting link between the engine and transmission. When the clutch pedal is released, the disc and plate contact each other (clutch engagement), physically joining the engine and transmission. When the pedal is pushed in, the disc and plate separate (the clutch is disengaged), disconnecting the engine from the transmission.

The clutch assembly consists of the flywheel, the clutch disc, the clutch pressure plate, the throwout bearing and fork, the actuating linkage and the pedal. The flywheel and clutch pressure plate (driving members) are connected to the engine crankshaft and rotate with it. The clutch disc is located between the flywheel and pressure plate, and splined to the transmission shaft. A driving member is one that is attached to the engine and transfers engine power to a driven member (clutch disc) on the transmission shaft. A driving member (pressure plate) rotates (drives) a driven member (clutch disc) on contact and, in so doing, turns the transmission shaft. There is a circular diaphragm spring within the pressure plate cover (transmission side). In a relaxed state (when the clutch pedal is fully released), this spring is convex; that it, it is dished outward toward the transmission. Pushing in the clutch pedal actuates an attached linkage rod. Connected to the other end of this rod is the throwout bearing fork. The throwout bearing is attached to the fork. When

## Troubleshooting Basic Clutch Problems

| Problem | Cause |
|---|---|
| Excessive clutch noise | Throwout bearing noises are more audible at the lower end of pedal travel. The usual causes are:<br>• Riding the clutch<br>• Too little pedal free-play<br>• Lack of bearing lubrication<br>A bad clutch shaft pilot bearing will make a high pitched squeal, when the clutch is disengaged and the transmission is in gear or within the first 2″ of pedal travel. The bearing must be replaced.<br>Noise from the clutch linkage is a clicking or snapping that can be heard or felt as the pedal is moved completely up or down. This usually requires lubrication.<br>Transmitted engine noises are amplified by the clutch housing and heard in the passenger compartment. They are usually the result of insufficient pedal free-play and can be changed by manipulating the clutch pedal. |
| Clutch slips (the car does not move as it should when the clutch is engaged) | This is usually most noticeable when pulling away from a standing start. A severe test is to start the engine, apply the brakes, shift into high gear and SLOWLY release the clutch pedal. A healthy clutch will stall the engine. If it slips it may be due to:<br>• A worn pressure plate or clutch plate<br>• Oil soaked clutch plate<br>• Insufficient pedal free-play |
| Clutch drags or fails to release | The clutch disc and some transmission gears spin briefly after clutch disengagement. Under normal conditions in average temperatures, 3 seconds is maximum spin-time. Failure to release properly can be caused by:<br>• Too light transmission lubricant or low lubricant level<br>• Improperly adjusted clutch linkage |
| Low clutch life | Low clutch life is usually a result of poor driving habits or heavy duty use. Riding the clutch, pulling heavy loads, holding the car on a grade with the clutch instead of the brakes and rapid clutch engagement all contribute to low clutch life. |

the clutch pedal is depressed, the clutch linkage pushes the fork and bearing forward to contact the diaphragm spring of the pressure plate. The outer edges of the spring are secured to the pressure plate and are pivoted on rings so that when the center of the spring is compressed by the throwout bearing, the outer edges bow outward and, by so doing, pull the pressure plate in the same direction - away from the clutch disc. This action separates the disc from the plate, disengaging the clutch and allowing the transmission to be shifted into another gear. A coil type clutch return spring attached to the clutch pedal arm permits full release of the pedal. Releasing the pedal pulls the throwout bearing away from the diaphragm spring resulting in a reversal of spring position. As bearing pressure is gradually released from the spring center, the outer edges of the spring bow outward, pushing the pressure plate into closer contact with the clutch disc. As the disc and plate move closer together, friction between the two increases and slippage is reduced until, when full spring pressure is applied (by fully releasing the pedal), The speed of the disc and plate are the same.

This stops all slipping, creating a direct connection between the plate and disc which results in the transfer of power from the engine to the transmission. The clutch disc is now rotating with the pressure plate at engine speed and, because it is splined to the transmission shaft, the shaft now turns at the same engine speed. Understanding clutch operation can be rather difficult at first; if you're still confused after reading this, consider the following analogy. The action of the diaphragm spring can be compared to that of an oil can bottom. The bottom of an oil can is shaped very much like the clutch diaphragm spring and pushing in on the can bottom and then releasing it produces a similar effect. As mentioned earlier, the clutch pedal return spring permits full release of the pedal and reduces linkage slack due to wear. As the linkage wears, clutch free-pedal travel will increase and free-travel will decrease as the clutch wears. Free-travel is actually throwout bearing lash.

The diaphragm spring type clutches used are available in two different designs: flat diaphragm springs or bent spring. The bent fingers are bent back to create a centrifugal boost ensuring quick re-engagement at higher engine speeds. This design enables pressure plate load to increase as the clutch disc wears and makes low pedal effort possible even with a heavy-duty clutch. The throwout bearing used with the bent finger design is 1¼" long and is shorter than the bearing used with the flat finger design. These bearings are not interchangeable. If the longer bearing is used with the bent finger clutch, free-pedal travel will not exist. This results in clutch slippage and rapid wear.

The transmission varies the gear ratio between the engine and rear wheels. It can be shifted to change engine speed as driving conditions and loads change. The transmission allows disengaging and reversing power from the engine to the wheels.

## Adjustments

On 1982-86 models the only service adjustment necessary on the clutch is to maintain the correct pedal free play. Clutch pedal free play, or throwout bearing lash, decreases with driven disc wear. On 1987-88 models a hydraulic clutch system provides automatic clutch adjustment.

### CLUTCH LINKAGE AND PEDAL HEIGHT/ FREE – PLAY ADJUSTMENT

#### 1982-86 Models

All cars use a self-adjusting clutch mechanism which may be checked as follows:

As the clutch friction material wears, the cable must be lengthened. This is accomplished by simply pulling the clutch pedal up to its rubber bumper. This action forces the pawl against its stop and rotates it out of mesh with the quadrant teeth, allowing the cable to play out until the quadrant spring load is balanced against the load applied by the release bearing. This adjustment procedure is required every 5,000 miles or less.

1. With engine running and brake on, hold the clutch pedal approximately ½" from floor mat and move shift lever between first and reverse several times. If this can be done smoothly without clashing into reverse, the clutch is fully releasing. If shift is not smooth, clutch is not fully releasing and linkage should be inspected and corrected as necessary.

2. Check clutch pedal bushings for sticking or excessive wear.

3. Have an assistant sit in the driver's seat and fully apply the clutch pedal to the floor. Observe the clutch fork lever travel at the transaxle. The end of the clutch fork lever should have a total travel of approximately 1.5-1.7".

4. If fork lever is not correct, check the adjusting mechanism by depressing the clutch pedal and looking for pawl to firmly engage with the teeth in the quadrant.

## Clutch Cable

### REMOVAL

1. Support the clutch pedal upward against the bumper stop to release the pawl from the quadrant. Disconnect the end of the cable from the clutch release lever at the transaxle. Be careful to prevent the cable from snapping rapidly toward the rear of the car. The quadrant in the adjusting mechanism can be damaged by allowing the cable to snap back.

2. Disconnect the clutch cable from the quadrant. Lift the locking pawl away from the quadrant, then slide the cable out on the right side of the quadrant.

3. From the engine side of the cowl disconnect the two upper nuts holding the cable re-

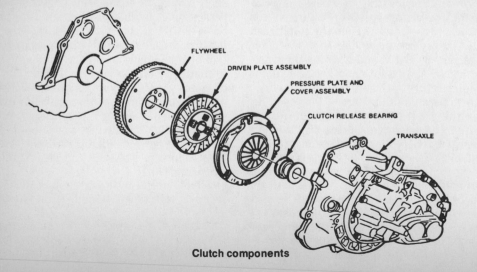

FLYWHEEL

DRIVEN PLATE ASSEMBLY

PRESSURE PLATE AND COVER ASSEMBLY

CLUTCH RELEASE BEARING

TRANSAXLE

**Clutch components**

tainer to the upper studs. Disconnect the cable from the bracket mounted to the transaxle, and remove the cable.

4. Inspect the clutch cable for frayed wires, kinks, worn ends and excessive friction. If any of these conditions exist, replace the cable.

### INSTALLATION

1. With the gasket in position on the two upper studs, position a new cable with the retaining flange against the bracket.

2. Attach the end of the cable to the quadrant, being sure to route the cable underneath the pawl.

3. Attach the two upper nuts to the retainer mounting studs, and torque to specifications.

4. Attach the cable to the bracket mounted to the transaxle.

5. Support the clutch pedal upward against the bumper stop to release the pawl from the quadrant. Attach the outer end of the cable to the clutch release lever. Be sure not to yank on the cable, since overloading the cable could damage the quadrant.

6. Check clutch operation and adjust by lifting the clutch pedal up to allow the mechanism to adjust the cable length. Depress the pedal slowly several times to set the pawl into mesh with the quadrant teeth.

## Driven Disc and Pressure Plate

### REMOVAL AND INSTALLATION

1. On 1987-88 models disconnect the negative battery cable, remove the hush panel from inside the vehicle then disconnect the clutch master cylinder push rod from the clutch pedal.

2. Remove the transaxle.

3. Mark the pressure plate assembly and the flywheel so that they can be assembled in the same position. They were balanced as an assembly at the factory.

4. Loosen the attaching bolts one turn at a time until spring tension is relieved.

5. Support the pressure plate and remove the bolts. Remove the pressure plate and clutch disc. Do not disassemble the pressure plate assembly; replace it if defective.

6. Inspect the flywheel, clutch disc, pressure plate, throwout bearing and the clutch fork and pivot shaft assembly for wear. Replace the parts as required. If the flywheel shows any signs of overheating, or if it is badly grooved or scored, it should be replaced.

7. Clean the pressure plate and flywheel mating surfaces thoroughly. Position the clutch disc and pressure plate into the installed position, and support with a dummy shaft or clutch aligning tool. The clutch plate is assembled with the damper springs offset toward the

transaxle. One side of the factory supplied clutch disc is stamped "Flywheel side".

8. Install the pressure plate-to-flywheel bolts. Tighten them gradually in a crisscross pattern.

9. Lubricate the outside groove and the inside recess of the release bearing with high temperature grease. Wipe off any excess. Install the release bearing.

10. Install the transaxle.

11. On 1987-88 models connect the clutch master cylinder push rod to the clutch pedal and install the retaining clip.

12. On 1987-88 models, if equipped with cruise control, check the switch adjustment at the clutch pedal bracket.

NOTE: *When adjusting the cruise control switch, do not exert an upward force on the clutch pedal pad of more than 20 lbs. or damage to the master cylinder push rod retaining ring may result.*

13. On 1987-88 models, install the hush panel and reconnect the negative battery cable.

## Clutch Master & Slave Cylinder

NOTE: *The clutch hydraulic system is serviced as a complete unit, it has been bled of air and filled with fluid.*

### REMOVAL AND INSTALLATION

**1987-88**

1. Disconnect the negative battery cable.

2. Remove the hush panel from inside the vehicle.

3. Remove the clutch master cylinder retaining nuts at the front of the dash.

4. Remove the slave cylinder retaining nuts at the transaxle.

5. Remove the hydraulic system as a unit from the vehicle.

6. Install the slave cylinder to the transmission support bracket aligning the push rod into the pocket on the clutch fork outer lever. Tighten the retaining nuts evenly to prevent damage to the slave cylinder. Torque the nuts to 40 ft.lb.

NOTE: *Do not remove the plastic push rod retainer from the slave cylinder. The straps will break on the first clutch pedal application.*

7. Position the clutch master cylinder to the front of the dash. Torque the nuts evenly to 20 ft.lb.

8. Remove the pedal restrictor from the push rod. Lube the push rod bushing on the clutch pedal. Connect the push rod to the clutch pedal and install the retaining clip.

9. If equipped with cruise control, check the switch adjustment at the clutch pedal bracket.

NOTE: *When adjusting the cruise control switch, do not exert an upward force on the clutch pedal pad of more than 20 lbs. or damage to the master cylinder push rod retaining ring may result.*

10. Install the hush panel.

11. Press the clutch pedal down several times. This will break the plastic retaining straps on the slave cylinder push rod. Do not remove the plastic button on the end of the push rod.

12. Connect the negative battery cable.

### OVERHAUL

This is a tedious, time consuming job. You can save yourself a lot of trouble by buying a rebuilt master cylinder from your dealer or parts supply house. The small difference in price between a rebuilding kit and a rebuilt part usually makes it more economical, in terms of time and work, to buy the rebuilt part.

1. Remove the master cylinder.

2. Remove the reservoir cover and drain the fluid.

3. Remove the pushrod and the rubber boot on non-power models.

4. Unbolt the proportioners and the failure warning switch from the side of the master cylinder body. Discard the O-rings found under the proportioners. Use new ones on installation. There may or may not be an O-ring under the original equipment failure warning switch. If there is, discard it. In either case, use a new O-ring upon assembly.

5. Clamp the master cylinder body in a vise, taking care not to crush it. Depress the primary piston with a wooden dowel and remove the lock ring with a pair of snapring pliers.

6. The primary and secondary pistons can be removed by applying compressed air into one of the outlets at the end of the cylinder and plugging the other three outlets. The primary piston must be replaced as an assembly if the seals are bad. The secondary piston seals are replaceable. Install these new seals with the lips facing outwards.

7. Inspect the bore for corrosion. If any corrosion is evident, the master cylinder body must be replaced. Do not attempt to polish the bore with crocus cloth, sandpaper or anything else. The body is aluminum; polishing the bore won't work.

8. To remove the failure warning switch piston assembly, remove the allen head plug from the end of the bore and withdraw the assembly with a pair of needlenosed pliers. The switch piston assembly seals are replaceable.

9. The reservoir can be removed from the master cylinder if necessary. Clamp the body in a vise by its mounting flange. Use a pry bar to remove the reservoir. If the reservoir is removed, remove the reservoir grommets and discard them. The quick take-up valves under the grommets are accessible after the retaining snaprings are removed. Use snapring pliers; no other tool will work.

10. Clean all parts in denatured alcohol and allow to air dry. Do not use anything else to clean and do not wipe dry with a rag, which will leaves bits of lint behind. Inspect all parts for corrosion or wear. Generally, it is best to replace all rubber parts whenever the master cylinder is disassembled and replace any metal part which shows any sign of wear or corrosion.

11. Lubricate all parts with fresh brake fluid before assembly.

12. Install the quick take-up valves into the master cylinder body and secure with the snaprings. Make sure the snaprings are properly seated in their grooves. Lubricate the new reservoir grommets with fresh brake fluid and press them into the master cylinder.

13. Install the reservoir into the grommets by placing the reservoir on its lid and pressing the master cylinder body down onto it with a rocking motion.

14. Lubricate the switch piston assembly. Install new O-rings and retainers on the piston. Install the piston assembly into the master cylinder and secure with the plug, using a new O-ring on the plug. Torque is 40-140 in.lb. (5-16 Nm.).

15. Assemble the new secondary piston seals onto the piston. Lubricate the parts, then install the spring, spring retainer and secondary piston into the cylinder. Install the primary piston, depress and install the lock ring.

16. Install new O-rings on the proportioners and the failure warning switch. Install the proportioners and torque to 18-30 ft.lb. (25-40 Nm.). Install the failure warning switch and torque to 15-50 in.lb. (2-6 Nm.).

17. Clamp the master cylinder body upright into a vise by one of the mounting flanges. Fill the reservoir with fresh fluid. Pump the piston with a dowel until fluid squirts from the outlet ports. Continue pumping until the expelled fluid is free of air bubbles.

18. Install the master cylinder and bleed the clutch. Check the clutch system for proper operation.

### BLEEDING THE HYDRAULIC CLUTCH SYSTEM

Bleeding air from the system is necessary any time part of the system has been disconnected, or the fluid level in the reservoir has been allowed to fall so low that air has been drawn into the master cylinder.

CAUTION: *Never under any circumstance use fluid that has been bled from the system as it could be contaminated with air or moisture.*

1. Clean the cap then remove the cap and diaphragm and fill the reservoir to the top with certified DOT 3 brake fluid.

2. Fully loosen the bleed screw which is in the slave cylinder body next to the inlet connection. Fluid will now begin to move from the master cylinder down the tube to the slave. It is important that for efficient gravity fill, the reservoir must be filled at all times.

3. At this point bubbles will be noticeable at the bleed screw outlet showing air is being expelled. When the slave is full, a steady stream of fluid will come from the slave outlet. At this point, tighten the bleed screw.

4. Install the diaphragm and cap to the reservoir. The fluid in the reservoir should be level with the step.

5. The hydraulic system should now be fully bled and should release the clutch. Check the vehicle by starting, then push the clutch pedal to the floor and selecting reverse gear. There should be no grinding of gears, if there is, the hydraulic system still contains air. If so, bleed the system again.

## AUTOMATIC TRANSAXLE

## Understanding Automatic Transmissions

The automatic transmission allows engine torque and power to be transmitted to the rear wheels within a narrow range of engine operating speeds. The transmission will allow the engine to turn fast enough to produce plenty of power and torque at very low speeds, while keeping it at a sensible rpm at high vehicle speeds. The transmission performs this job entirely without driver assistance. The transmission uses a light fluid as the medium for the transmission of power. This fluid also works in the operation of various hydraulic control circuits and as a lubricant. Because the transmission fluid performs all of these three functions, trouble within the unit can easily travel from one part to another. For this reason, and because of the complexity and unusual operating principles of the transmission, a very sound understanding of the basic principles of operation will simplify troubleshooting.

### THE TORQUE CONVERTER

The torque converter replaces the conventional clutch. It has three functions:

1. It allows the engine to idle with the vehicle at a standstill, even with the transmission in gear.

2. It allows the transmission to shift from range to range smoothly, without requiring that the driver close the throttle during the shift.

3. It multiplies engine torque to an increasing extent as vehicle speed drops and throttle opening is increased. This has the effect of making the transmission more responsive and reduces the amount of shifting required.

The torque converter is a metal case which is shaped like a sphere that has been flattened on opposite sides. It is bolted to the rear end of the engine's crankshaft. Generally, the entire metal case rotates at engine speed and serves as the engine's flywheel.

The case contains three sets of blades. One set is attached directly to the case. This set forms the torus or pump. Another set is directly connected to the output shaft, and forms the turbine. The third set is mounted on a hub which, in turn, is mounted on a stationary shaft through a one-way clutch. This third set is known as the stator.

A pump, which is driven by the converter hub at engine speed, keeps the torque converter full of transmission fluid at all times. Fluid flows continuously through the unit to provide cooling.

Under low speed acceleration, the torque converter functions as follows:

The torus is turning faster than the turbine. It picks up fluid at the center of the converter and, through centrifugal force, slings it outward. Since the outer edge of the converter moves faster than the portions at the center, the fluid picks up speed.

The fluid then enters the outer edge of the turbine blades. It then travels back toward the center of the converter case along the turbine blades. In impinging upon the turbine blades, the fluid loses the energy picked up in the torus.

If the fluid were now to immediately be returned directly into the torus, both halves of the converter would have to turn at approximately the same speed at all times, and torque input and output would both be the same.

In flowing through the torus and turbine, the fluid picks up two types of flow, or flow in two separate directions. It flows through the turbine blades, and it spins with the engine. The stator, whose blades are stationary when the vehicle is being accelerated at low speeds, converts one type of flow into another. Instead of allowing the fluid to flow straight back into the torus, the stator's curved blades turn the fluid almost 90° toward the direction of rotation of the engine. Thus the fluid does not flow as fast toward the torus, but is already spinning when the torus picks it up. This has the effect of allowing the torus to turn much faster than the turbine. This difference in speed may be compared to the difference in speed between the smaller and larger gears in any gear train. The result is that engine power output is higher, and engine torque is multiplied.

As the speed of the turbine increases, the fluid spins faster and faster in the direction of engine rotation. As a result, the ability of the stator to redirect the fluid flow is reduced. Under cruising conditions, the stator is eventually forced to rotate on its one-way clutch in the direction of engine rotation. Under these conditions, the torque converter begins to behave almost like a solid shaft, with the torus and turbine speeds being almost equal.

### THE PLANETARY GEARBOX

The ability of the torque converter to multiply engine torque is limited. Also, the unit tends to be more efficient when the turbine is rotating at relatively high speeds. Therefore, a planetary gearbox is used to carry the power output of the turbine to the driveshaft.

Planetary gears function very similarly to conventional transmission gears. However, their construction is different in that three elements make up one gear system, and, in that all three elements are different from one another. The three elements are: an outer gear that is shaped like a hoop, with teeth cut into the inner surface; a sun gear, mounted on a shaft and located at the very center of the outer gear; and a set of three planet gears, held by pins in a ring-like planet carrier, meshing with both the sun gear and the outer gear. Either the outer gear or the sun gear may be held stationary, providing more than one possible torque multiplication factor for each set of gears. Also, if all three gears are forced to rotate at the same speed, the gearset forms, in effect, a solid shaft.

Most modern automatics use the planetary gears to provide either a single reduction ratio of about 1.8:1, or two reduction gears: a low of about 2.5:1, and an intermediate of about 1.5:1. Bands and clutches are used to hold various portions of the gearsets to the transmission case or to the shaft on which they are mounted. Shifting is accomplished, then, by changing the portion of each planetary gearset which is held to the transmission case or to the shaft.

### THE SERVOS AND ACCUMULATORS

The servos are hydraulic pistons and cylinders. They resemble the hydraulic actuators used on many familiar machines, such as bulldozers. Hydraulic fluid enters the cylinder, under pressure, and forces the piston to move to engage the band or clutches.

The accumulators are used to cushion the engagement of the servos. The transmission fluid must pass through the accumulator on the way to the servo. The accumulator housing contains a thin piston which is sprung away from the discharge passage of the accumulator. When fluid passes through the accumulator on the way to the servo, it must move the piston against spring pressure, and this action smooths out the action of the servo.

### THE HYDRAULIC CONTROL SYSTEM

The hydraulic pressure used to operate the servos comes from the main transmission oil pump. This fluid is channeled to the various servos through the shift valves. There is generally a manual shift valve which is operated by the transmission selector lever and an automatic shift valve for each automatic upshift the transmission provides: i.e., 2-speed automatics have a low/high shift valve, while 3-speeds have a 1–2 valve, and a 2–3 valve.

There are two pressures which effect the operation of these valves. One is the governor pressure which is affected by vehicle speed. The other is the modulator pressure which is affected by intake manifold vacuum or throttle position. Governor pressure rises with an increase in vehicle speed, and modulator pressure rises as the throttle is opened wider. By responding to these two pressures, the shift valves cause the upshift points to be delayed with increased throttle opening to make the best use of the engine's power output.

Most transmissions also make use of an auxiliary circuit for downshifting. This circuit may be actuated by the throttle linkage or the vacuum line which actuates the modulator, or by a cable or solenoid. It applies pressure to a special downshift surface on the shift valve or valves.

The transmission modulator also governs the line pressure, used to actuate the servos. In this way, the clutches and bands will be actuated with a force matching the torque output of the engine.

## Identification

All models use a 125C or 440-T4 automatic transmission. The 125C is equipped with a torque converter clutch (TCC) which under certain conditions mechanically couples the engine to the transaxle for greater power transfer efficiency and increased fuel mileage. The 440-T4 provides an overdrive feature, for greater fuel efficiency. A cable operated throttle valve linkage is used. Automatic transaxle operation is provided through a conventional three element torque converter, a compound planetary gear set, and a dual sprocket and drive link assembly.

No overhaul procedures are given in this book because of the complexity of the transaxle.

## Lockup Torque Converter Service Diagnosis

| Problem | Cause | Solution |
|---|---|---|
| No lockup | • Faulty oil pump<br>• Sticking governor valve<br>• Valve body malfunction<br>　(a) Stuck switch valve<br>　(b) Stuck lockup valve<br>　(c) Stuck fail-safe valve<br>• Failed locking clutch<br>• Leaking turbine hub seal<br>• Faulty input shaft or seal ring | • Replace oil pump<br>• Repair or replace as necessary<br>• Repair or replace valve body or its internal components as necessary<br><br><br>• Replace torque converter<br>• Replace torque converter<br>• Repair or replace as necessary |
| Will not unlock | • Sticking governor valve<br>• Valve body malfunction<br>　(a) Stuck switch valve<br>　(b) Stuck lockup valve<br>　(c) Stuck fail-safe valve | • Repair or replace as necessary<br>• Repair or replace valve body or its internal components as necessary |
| Stays locked up at too low a speed in direct | • Sticking governor valve<br>• Valve body malfunction<br>　(a) Stuck switch valve<br>　(b) Stuck lockup valve<br>　(c) Stuck fail-safe valve | • Repair or replace as necessary<br>• Repair or replace valve body or its internal components as necessary |
| Locks up or drags in low or second | • Faulty oil pump<br>• Valve body malfunction<br>　(a) Stuck switch valve<br>　(b) Stuck fail-safe valve | • Replace oil pump<br>• Repair or replace valve body or its internal components as necessary |
| Sluggish or stalls in reverse | • Faulty oil pump<br>• Plugged cooler, cooler lines or fittings<br>• Valve body malfunction<br>　(a) Stuck switch valve<br>　(b) Faulty input shaft or seal ring | • Replace oil pump as necessary<br>• Flush or replace cooler and flush lines and fittings<br>• Repair or replace valve body or its internal components as necessary |
| Loud chatter during lockup engagement (cold) | • Faulty torque converter<br>• Failed locking clutch<br>• Leaking turbine hub seal | • Replace torque converter<br>• Replace torque converter<br>• Replace torque converter |
| Vibration or shudder during lockup engagement | • Faulty oil pump<br><br>• Valve body malfunction<br><br><br>• Faulty torque converter<br>• Engine needs tune-up | • Repair or replace oil pump as necessary<br>• Repair or replace valve body or its internal components as necessary<br>• Replace torque converter<br>• Tune engine |
| Vibration after lockup engagement | • Faulty torque converter<br>• Exhaust system strikes underbody<br>• Engine needs tune-up<br>• Throttle linkage misadjusted | • Replace torque converter<br>• Align exhaust system<br>• Tune engine<br>• Adjust throttle linkage |
| Vibration when revved in neutral Overheating: oil blows out of dip stick tube or pump seal | • Torque converter out of balance<br>• Plugged cooler, cooler lines or fittings<br>• Stuck switch valve | • Replace torque converter<br>• Flush or replace cooler and flush lines and fittings<br>• Repair switch valve in valve body or replace valve body |
| Shudder after lockup engagement | • Faulty oil pump<br>• Plugged cooler, cooler lines or fittings<br>• Valve body malfunction<br><br><br>• Faulty torque converter<br>• Fail locking clutch<br>• Exhaust system strikes underbody<br>• Engine needs tune-up<br>• Throttle linkage misadjusted | • Replace oil pump<br>• Flush or replace cooler and flush lines and fittings<br>• Repair or replace valve body or its internal components as necessary<br>• Replace torque converter<br>• Replace torque converter<br>• Align exhaust system<br>• Tune engine<br>• Adjust throttle linkage |

## Troubleshooting Basic Automatic Transmission Problems

| Problem | Cause | Solution |
|---|---|---|
| Fluid leakage | • Defective pan gasket | • Replace gasket or tighten pan bolts |
| | • Loose filler tube | • Tighten tube nut |
| | • Loose extension housing to transmission case | • Tighten bolts |
| | • Converter housing area leakage | • Have transmission checked professionally |
| Fluid flows out the oil filler tube | • High fluid level | • Check and correct fluid level |
| | • Breather vent clogged | • Open breather vent |
| | • Clogged oil filter or screen | • Replace filter or clean screen (change fluid also) |
| | • Internal fluid leakage | • Have transmission checked professionally |
| Transmission overheats (this is usually accompanied by a strong burned odor to the fluid) | • Low fluid level | • Check and correct fluid level |
| | • Fluid cooler lines clogged | • Drain and refill transmission. If this doesn't cure the problem, have cooler lines cleared or replaced. |
| | • Heavy pulling or hauling with insufficient cooling | • Install a transmission oil cooler |
| | • Faulty oil pump, internal slippage | • Have transmission checked professionally |
| Buzzing or whining noise | • Low fluid level | • Check and correct fluid level |
| | • Defective torque converter, scored gears | • Have transmission checked professionally |
| No forward or reverse gears or slippage in one or more gears | • Low fluid level | • Check and correct fluid level |
| | • Defective vacuum or linkage controls, internal clutch or band failure | • Have unit checked professionally |
| Delayed or erratic shift | • Low fluid level | • Check and correct fluid level |
| | • Broken vacuum lines | • Repair or replace lines |
| | • Internal malfunction | • Have transmission checked professionally |

## Transmission Fluid Indications

The appearance and odor of the transmission fluid can give valuable clues to the overall condition of the transmission. Always note the appearance of the fluid when you check the fluid level or change the fluid. Rub a small amount of fluid between your fingers to feel for grit and smell the fluid on the dipstick.

| If the fluid appears: | It indicates: |
|---|---|
| Clear and red colored | • Normal operation |
| Discolored (extremely dark red or brownish) or smells burned | • Band or clutch pack failure, usually caused by an overheated transmission. Hauling very heavy loads with insufficient power or failure to change the fluid, often result in overheating.<br>Do not confuse this appearance with newer fluids that have a darker red color and a strong odor (though not a burned odor). |
| Foamy or aerated (light in color and full of bubbles) | • The level is too high (gear train is churning oil)<br>• An internal air leak (air is mixing with the fluid). Have the transmission checked professionally. |
| Solid residue in the fluid | • Defective bands, clutch pack or bearings. Bits of band material or metal abrasives are clinging to the dipstick. Have the transmission checked professionally. |
| Varnish coating on the dipstick | • The transmission fluid is overheating |

Transaxle removal and installation, adjustment, and halfshaft removal, installation, and overhaul procedures are covered.

## Pan and Filter
### REMOVAL AND INSTALLATION

1. Raise and support the vehicle on jackstands.
2. Loosen the pan bolts and drain the fluid.
3. Remove the pan and the filter.
4. Clean the gasket mounting surfaces.
5. To install, use a new gasket and filter, then reverse the removal procedures. Refill the transaxle. Torque the pan bolts to 10 ft.lb.

## Adjustments

The only adjustment required on the 125C transaxle is the shift linkage (cable) adjustment. The neutral start switch and throttle valve are self-adjusting. The transaxle has only one band, with no provision for periodic adjustment. Pan removal, fluid and filter changes are covered in Chapter 1.

### T.V. CABLE

1. Depress and hold down the metal adjustment tab at the engine end of the TV cable.
2. Move the slider up until it stops against the fitting.
3. Release the adjusting tab.

### SHIFT LINKAGE

1. Place the shift lever into Neutral.
2. Disconnect the shift cable from the transaxle lever. Place the transaxle lever in Neutral, by moving the lever clockwise to the Low (L) detent, then counterclockwise through the Second (S) and Drive (D) detents to the Neutral detent.
3. Attach and torque the shift cable to the pin on the transaxle lever. Check the shift operation.

CAUTION: *Any inaccuracies in shift linkage adjustments may result in premature failure of the transmission due to operation without the controls in full detent. Such operation results in reduced fluid pressure and in turn, partial engagement of the affected clutches. Partial engagement of the clutches, with sufficient pressure to permit apparently normal vehicle operation will result in failure of the clutches and/or other internal parts after only a few miles of operation.*

## Neutral Safety/Back-Up Light Switch
### REMOVAL AND INSTALLATION

1. Remove the shifter knob from the shifter by removing the retaining screw at the back of the knob.

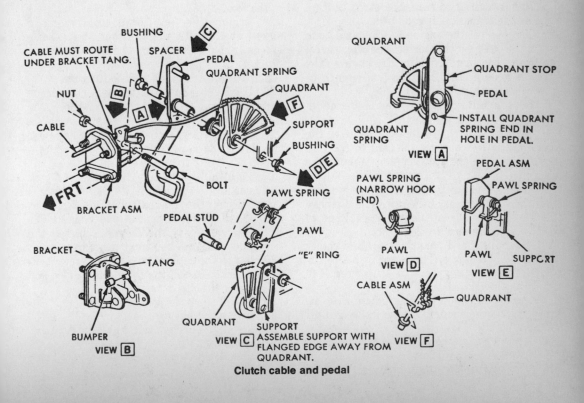

**Clutch cable and pedal**

2. Remove the screws at the sides and front of the console.

3. Open the console box and remove the retaining screw inside the box.

4. Remove the ashtray at the rear of the console and remove the retaining screw behind the ashtray.

5. Slide the console rearward slightly, then lift it over the shifter.

6. Disconnect the wiring harness at the back-up light switch.

7. Remove the switch from the base of the shifter.

8. Reverse steps 1 through 7 to install the switch.

## Transaxle

### REMOVAL AND INSTALLATION

#### 125C

1. Disconnect the negative battery cable from the transaxle. Tape the wire to the upper radiator hose to keep it out of the way.

2. Remove the air cleaner and disconnect the detent cable. Slide the detent cable in the opposite direction of the cable to remove it from the carburetor.

3. Unbolt the detent cable attaching bracket at the transaxle.

4. Pull up on the detent cable cover at the transaxle until the cable is exposed. Disconnect the cable from the rod.

5. Remove the two transaxle strut bracket bolts at the transaxle, if equipped.

6. Remove all the engine-to-transaxle bolts except the one near the starter. The one nearest the firewall is installed from the engine side; you will need a short handled box wrench or ratchet to reach it.

7. Loosen, but do not remove the engine-to-transaxle bolt near the starter.

8. Disconnect the speedometer cable at the upper and lower coupling. On cars with cruise control, remove the speedometer cable at the transducer.

9. Remove the retaining clip and washer from the shift linkage at the transaxle. Remove the two shift linkage at the transaxle. Remove the two shift linkage bracket bolts.

10. Disconnect and plug the two fluid cooler lines at the transaxle. These are inch-size fittings ($\frac{1}{2}$" and $\frac{11}{16}$"); use a back-up wrench to avoid twisting the lines.

11. Install an engine holding chain or hoist. Raise the engine enough to take its weight off the mounts.

12. Unlock the steering column and raise the car.

13. Remove the two nuts holding the anti-

sway (stabilizer) bar to the left lower control arm (driver's side).

14. Remove the four bolts attaching the covering plate over the stabilizer bar to the engine cradle on the left side (driver's side).

15. Loosen but do not remove the four bolts holding the stabilizer bar bracket to the right side (passenger's side) of the engine cradle. Pull the bar down on the driver's side.

16. Disconnect the front and rear transaxle mounts at the engine cradle.

17. Remove the two rear center crossmember bolts.

18. Remove the three right (passenger) side front engine cradle attaching bolts. The nuts are accessible under the splash shield next to the frame rail.

19. Remove the top bolt from the lower front transaxle shock absorber, if equipped (V6 engine only).

20. Remove the left (driver) side front and rear cradle-to-body bolts.

21. Remove the left front wheel. Attach an axle shaft removing tool (G.M. part no. J-28468 or the equivalent) to a slide hammer. Place the tool behind the axle shaft cones and pull the cones out away from the transaxle. Remove the right shaft in the same manner. Set the shafts out of the way. Plug the openings in the transaxle to prevent fluid leakage and the entry of dirt.

22. Swing the partial engine cradle to the left (driver) side and wire it out of the way outboard of the fender well.

23. Remove the four torque converter and starter shield bolts. Remove the two transaxle extension bolts from the engine-to-transaxle bracket.

24. Attach a transaxle jack to the case.

25. Use a felt pen to matchmark the torque converter and flywheel. Remove the three torque converter-to-flywheel bolts.

26. Remove the transaxle-to-engine bolt near the starter. Remove the transaxle by sliding it to the left, away from the engine.

27. To install, place the transaxle on a jack and raise it into the vehicle. As the transaxle is installed, slide the right axle shaft into the case.

28. Align the matchmarks and connect the torque converter to the flywheel. Install the transaxle-to-engine bolt near the starter.

29. Install the engine-to-transaxle bracket extension bolts. Install the torque converter and starter shield bolts.

30. Install the partial engine cradle.

31. Install the left axle shaft.

32. Install the drivers side front and rear cradle to body bolts.

33. Install the top bolt tr the lower front

transaxle shock absorber, if equipped (V6 engine only).

34. Install the three right (passenger) side front engine cradle attaching bolts.

35. Install the two rear center crossmember bolts.

36. Connect the front and rear transaxle mounts at the engine cradle.

37. Install the stabilizer bar. Tighten the four bolts holding the stabilizer bar bracket to the right side (passenger's side) of the engine cradle.

NOTE: *To aid in stabilizer bar installation, a pry hole has been provided in the engine cradle.*

38. Install the four bolts attaching the covering plate over the stabilizer bar to the engine cradle on the left side (driver's side).

39. Install the two nuts holding the anti-sway (stabilizer) bar to the left lower control arm (driver's side).

40. Lower the vehicle and remove the engine support device.

41. Connect the two fluid cooler lines at the transaxle.

42. Install the two shift linkage bracket bolts.

43. Connect the two shift linkages at the transaxle and install the retaining clips and washers.

44. Connect the speedometer cable at the upper and lower coupling. On cars with cruise control, connect the speedometer cable at the transducer.

45. Tighten the engine-to-transaxle bolt near the starter.

46. Install all remaining engine-to-transaxle bolts. The one nearest the firewall is installed from the engine side; you will need a short handled box wrench or ratchet to reach it.

47. Install the two transaxle strut bracket bolts at the transaxle, if equipped.

48. Install the detent cable and air cleaner.

49. Connect the negative battery cable to the transaxle.

**440-T4**

1. Disconnect the negative battery cable. Remove the air cleaner and the TV cable from the carburetor, then the shift linkage from the transaxle.

2. Install the Engine Support Fixture tool J-28467 to the engine and support it.

3. Disconnect the converter clutch electrical connector and the vacuum line from the modulator.

4. Remove the transaxle-to-engine bolts, then raise and support the vehicle on jackstands.

5. Remove the left front wheel and the pinch bolt from the lower ball joint.

6. Remove the brake line bracket from the strut and the drive axles from the transaxle.

7. Remove the cradle-to-stabilizer bolts, the stabilizer-to-control arm bolts and the left front cradle assembly.

8. Remove the speedometer cable from the transaxle, the extension housing-to-engine block support bracket and the oil cooler lines from the transaxle.

9. Remove the right and the left insulator mounting bolts, the flexplate splash shield and the converter-to-flexplate bolts.

10. Remove the remaining bellhousing bolts, except one, then position a jack under the transaxle.

11. Secure the transaxle to the jack and remove the remaining bellhousing bolt.

12. Lower the transaxle from the engine.

13. To install, place the transaxle on a jack and raise it into the vehicle.

14. Install the lower bellhousing bolts. Torque the bellhousing-to-engine bolts to 55 ft.lb.

15. Install the right and the left insulator mounting bolts, the flexplate splash shield and the converter-to-flexplate bolts.

16. Install the speedometer cable to the transaxle, the extension housing-to-engine block support bracket and the oil cooler lines to the transaxle.

17. Install the cradle-to-stabilizer bolts, the stabilizer-to-control arm bolts and the left front cradle assembly.

18. Install the drive axles to the transaxle and the brake line bracket to the strut.

19. Install the lower ball joint and the pinch bolt. Install the left front wheel.

20. Remove the jack stands. Lower the vehicle and install the upper bellhousing-to-engine bolts. Torque the bellhousing-to-engine bolts to 55 ft.lb.

21. Connect the converter clutch electrical connector and the vacuum line to the modulator.

22. Remove the Engine Support Fixture tool J-28467 from the engine.

23. Connect the negative battery cable. Install the shift linkage to the transaxle, and the TV cable and air cleaner to the carburetor. Check the fluid level. Adjust the TV cable and the shift linkage.

## Halfshafts

### REMOVAL AND INSTALLATION

CAUTION: *Use care when removing the drive axle. Tri-pots can be damaged if the drive axle is over-extended.*

1. Remove the hub nut.

2. Raise the front of the car. Remove the wheel and tire.

3. Install an axle shaft boot seal protector, GM special tool No. J-28712 or equivalent, onto the seal.

4. Disconnect the brake hose clip from the MacPherson strut, but do not disconnect the hose from the caliper. Remove the brake caliper from the spindle, and hang the caliper out of the way by a length of wire. Do not allow the caliper to hang by the brake hose.

5. Mark the camber alignment cam bolt for reassembly. Remove the cam bolt and the upper attaching bolt from the strut and spindle.

6. Pull the steering knuckle assembly from the strut bracket.

7. Using GM special tool J-28733 or the equivalent spindle remover, remove the axle shaft from the hub and bearing assembly.

8. If a new drive axle is to be installed, a new knuckle seal should be installed first.

9. Loosely install the drive axle into the transaxle and steering knuckle.

10. Loosely attach the steering knuckle to the suspension strut.

11. The drive axle is an interference fit in the steering knuckle. Press the axle into place, then install the hub nut. When the shaft begins to turn with the hub, insert a drift through the caliper into one of the cooling slots in the rotor to keep it from turning. Insert a long bolt in the hub flange to prevent the shaft from turning. Tighten the hub nut to 70 ft.lb. to completely seat the shaft.

12. Install the brake caliper. Tighten the bolts to 30 ft.lb.

13. Load the hub assembly by lowering it onto a jackstand. Align the camber cam bolt marks made during removal, install the bolt and tighten to 140 ft.lb. Tighten the upper nut to the same value.

14. Install the axle shaft all the way into the transaxle using a screwdriver inserted into the groove provided on the inner retainer. Tap the screwdriver until the shaft seats in the transaxle. Remove the boot seal protector.

15. Connect the brake hose clip to the strut. Install the tire and wheel, lower the car, and tighten the hub nut to 225 ft.lb. (1982); 185 ft.lb. (1983-88).

### OVERHAUL

**Inner And Outer Boots**

*OUTER BOOT*

1. Raise and support the vehicle safely.
2. Remove the front tire and wheel.
3. Remove the caliper bolts and wire the caliper off to the side.

4. Remove the hub nut, washer and wheel bearing.

5. Using a brass drift, lightly tap around the seal retainer to loosen it. Remove the seal retainer.

6. Remove the seal retaining clamp or ring and discard.

7. Using snapring pliers, remove the race retaining ring from the axle shaft.

8. Pull the outer joint assembly and the outboard seal away from the axle shaft.

9. Installation is the reverse of the removal procedure. Pack the joint assembly with half of the grease provided. Put the remainder of the grease in the seal.

*INNER BOOT*

1. Raise and support the vehicle safely.
2. Remove the front tire and wheel.
3. Remove the caliper bolts and wire the caliper off to the side of the vehicle.
4. Remove the hub nut, washer and wheel bearing.

5. Remove the front drive axle as outlined earlier in this section. Place in a suitable holding fixture being careful not place undue pressure on the axle shaft.

6. Remove the joint assembly retaining ring. Remove the joint assembly.

7. Remove the race retaining ring and remove the seal retainer.

8. Remove the inner seal retaining clamp. Remove the inner joint seal.

9. Installation is the reverse of the removal procedure. Pack the joint assembly with half of the grease provided. Place remainder of the grease in the seal.

## REAR AXLE

### Hub and Bearing Assembly
#### REMOVAL AND INSTALLATION

1. Raise and support the car on a hoist.
2. Remove the wheel and brake drum.

CAUTION: *Do not hammer on the brake drum as damage to the bearing could result.*

3. Remove the hub and bearing assembly to rear axle attaching bolts and remove the hub and bearing assembly.

NOTE: *The bolts which attach the hub and bearing assembly also support the brake assembly. When removing these bolts, support the brake assembly with a wire or other means. Do not let the brake line support the brake assembly.*

4. Install the hub and bearing assembly to

the rear axle and torque the hub and bearing bolts to 45 ft.lb.

5. Install the brake drum, tire and wheel assembly and lower the car.

### ADJUSTMENT

There is no necessary adjustment to the rear wheel bearing and hub assembly.

## Axle Housing

### REMOVAL AND INSTALLATION

1. Raise and support the rear end on jackstands.

2. Remove the rear wheels. Remove the rear brake drums. Disconnect the parking brake from the rear axle.

3. Remove the brake brackets from the vehicle frame.

4. Remove the rear shock absorbers. Remove the track bar.

5. Disconnect the rear brake hoses.

6. Lower the axle assembly and remove the coil springs and insulators.

7. Remove the hub attaching bolts. Remove the hub and bearing assembly.

8. Remove the control arm bracket attaching bolts. Remove the control arms. Lower the axle from the vehicle.

9. To install:

10. Install the control arms and bracket bolts.

11. Install the hub and bearing assemblies and bracket bolts.

12. Install the coil springs and insulators.

13. Rraise the axle into the vehicle.

14. Connect the rear brake hoses.

15. Install the shock absorbers and track bar.

16. Install the brake brackets to the vehicle frame.

17. Connect the parking brake, install the brake drums and rear wheels.

18. Remove the safety stands anmd lower the vehicle.

# Suspension and Steering

## 8

## FRONT SUSPENSION

The A-Bodies use a MacPherson strut front suspension design. A MacPherson strut combines the functions of a shock absorber and an upper suspension member (upper arm) into one unit. The strut is surrounded by a coil spring, which provides normal front suspension functions.

The strut bolts to the body shell at its upper end, and to the steering knuckle at the lower end. The strut pivots with the steering knuckle by means of a sealed mounting assembly at the upper end which contains a preloaded, non-adjustable bearing.

The steering knuckle is connected to the chassis at the lower end by a conventional lower control arm, and pivots in the arm in a preloaded ball joint of standard design. The knuckle is fastened to the ball joint stud by means of a castellated nut and cotter pin.

Advantages of the MacPherson strut design, aside from its relative simplicity, include reduced weight and friction, minimal intrusion

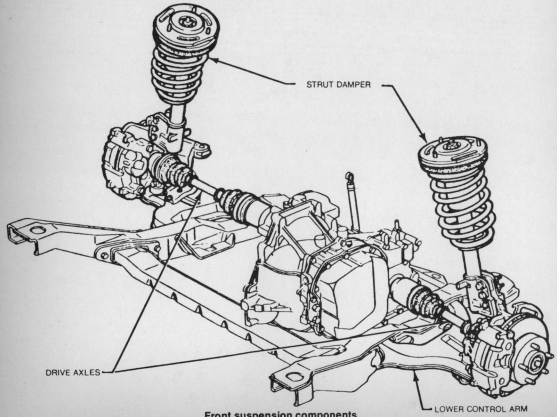

STRUT DAMPER

DRIVE AXLES

LOWER CONTROL ARM

**Front suspension components**

into the engine and passenger compartments, and ease of service.

## MacPherson Struts
## Springs and Shock Absorbers
### TESTING

The function of the shock absorber is to dampen harsh spring movement and provide a means of dissipating the motion of the wheels so that the shocks encountered by the wheels are not totally transmitted to the body and, therefore, to you and your passengers. As the wheel moves up and down, the shock absorber shortens and lengthens, thereby imposing a restraint on movement by its hydraulic action.

A good way to see if your shock absorbers are functioning correctly is to push one corner of the car until it is moving up and down for almost the full suspension travel, then release it

## Troubleshooting Basic Driveshaft and Rear Axle Problems

When abnormal vibrations or noises are detected in the driveshaft area, this chart can be used to help diagnose possible causes. Remember that other components such as wheels, tires, rear axle and suspension can also produce similar conditions.

## BASIC DRIVESHAFT PROBLEMS

| Problem | Cause | Solution |
|---|---|---|
| Shudder as car accelerates from stop or low speed | • Loose U-joint<br>• Defective center bearing | • Replace U-joint<br>• Replace center bearing |
| Loud clunk in driveshaft when shifting gears | • Worn U-joints | • Replace U-joints |
| Roughness or vibration at any speed | • Out-of-balance, bent or dented driveshaft<br>• Worn U-joints<br>• U-joint clamp bolts loose | • Balance or replace driveshaft<br>• Replace U-joints<br>• Tighten U-joint clamp bolts |
| Squeaking noise at low speeds | • Lack of U-joint lubrication | • Lubricate U-joint; if problem persists, replace U-joint |
| Knock or clicking noise | • U-joint or driveshaft hitting frame tunnel<br>• Worn CV joint | • Correct overloaded condition<br>• Replace CV joint |

## BASIC REAR AXLE PROBLEMS

First, determine when the noise is most noticeable.

Drive Noise: Produced under vehicle acceleration.

Coast Noise: Produced while the car coasts with a closed throttle.

Float Noise: Occurs while maintaining constant car speed (just enough to keep speed constant) on a level road.

## Road Noise

Brick or rough surfaced concrete roads produce noises that seem to come from the rear axle. Road noise is usually identical in Drive or Coast and driving on a different type of road will tell whether the road is the problem.

## Tire Noise

Tire noises are often mistaken for rear axle problems. Snow treads or unevenly worn tires produce vibrations seeming to originate elsewhere. **Temporarily** inflating the tires to 40 lbs will significantly alter tire noise, but will have no effect on rear axle noises (which normally cease below about 30 mph).

## Engine/Transmission Noise

Determine at what speed the noise is most pronounced, then stop the car in a quiet place. With the transmission in Neutral, run the engine through speeds corresponding to road speeds where the noise was noticed. Noises produced with the car standing still are coming from the engine or transmission.

## Front Wheel Bearings

While holding the car speed steady, lightly apply the footbrake; this will often decease bearing noise, as some of the load is taken from the bearing.

## Rear Axle Noises

Eliminating other possible sources can narrow the cause to the rear axle, which normally produces noise from worn gears or bearings. Gear noises tend to peak in a narrow speed range, while bearing noises will usually vary in pitch with engine speeds.

## NOISE DIAGNOSIS

| The Noise Is | Most Probably Produced By |
|---|---|
| • Identical under Drive or Coast | • Road surface, tires or front wheel bearings |
| • Different depending on road surface | • Road surface or tires |
| • Lower as the car speed is lowered | • Tires |
| • Similar with car standing or moving | • Engine or transmission |
| • A vibration | • Unbalanced tires, rear wheel bearing, unbalanced driveshaft or worn U-joint |
| • A knock or click about every 2 tire revolutions | • Rear wheel bearing |
| • Most pronounced on turns | • Damaged differential gears |
| • A steady low-pitched whirring or scraping, starting at low speeds | • Damaged or worn pinion bearing |
| • A chattering vibration on turns | • Wrong differential lubricant or worn clutch plates (limited slip rear axle) |
| • Noticed only in Drive, Coast or Float conditions | • Worn ring gear and/or pinion gear |

and watch its recovery. If the car bounces slightly about one more time and comes to a rest, the shock is all right. If the car continues to bounce excessively, the shocks will probably require replacement.

### REMOVAL

1. Remove the top strut-to-body mounting nuts.
2. Loosen the wheel nuts, then raise and support the vehicle on jackstands.
3. Remove the brake line clip from the strut, then the wheel and the tire assembly.
4. Install the boot protector tool J-28712 (Double-Offset joint) or J-33162 (Tri-Pot joint) over the drive axle boot.
NOTE: *If equipped with a Tri-Pot joint, disconnect the drive axle from the transaxle before separating the strut from the steering knuckle.*
5. Before separating the strut from the steering knuckle, perform the following:
   a. Refer to view A, then using a sharp tool, scribe the steering knuckle along the lower outboard strut radius.
   b. Refer to view B, then scribe the strut flange on the inboard side, along the curve of the steering knuckle.
   c. Refer to view C, then using a chisel, mark the strut-to-steering knuckle interface.
6. Remove the steering knuckle-to-strut bolts.
7. Remove the strut.

### OVERHAUL

A MacPherson strut compressor tool J-26584 or the equivalent must be used.
1. Clamp the strut compressor in a vise.
2. Install the strut in the compressor. Install the compressor adapters, if used.
3. Compress the spring approximately ½". Do not bottom the spring or the strut rod.

4. Remove the strut shaft top nut and the top mount and bearing assembly from the strut.
5. Unscrew the compressor until all spring tension is relieved. Remove the spring.
6. Place the strut into the compressor. Rotate the strut until the spindle mounting flange is facing out, away from the compressor.
7. Place the spring on the strut. Make sure it is properly seated on the strut bottom plate.
8. Install the strut assembly on the spring. Install the compressor adapters, if used.
9. Tighten the strut compressor until it just contacts the spring seat, or the adapters if a tool with adapters is being used.
10. Thread on alignment rod tool J-26584-27 (1982-83) or J-34013-27 (1984-88), onto the strut damper shaft, hand tight.
11. Compress the spring until approximately 1½" of the damper rod can be pulled up through the top spring seat. Do not compress the spring until it bottoms.
12. Remove the alignment rod and install the top mount and nut. Tighten the nut to 65 ft.lb. (88 Nm.).
13. Unscrew the compressor and remove the strut.

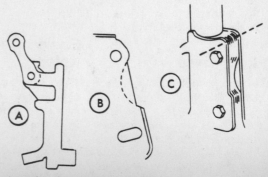

**Locating the camber eccentric**

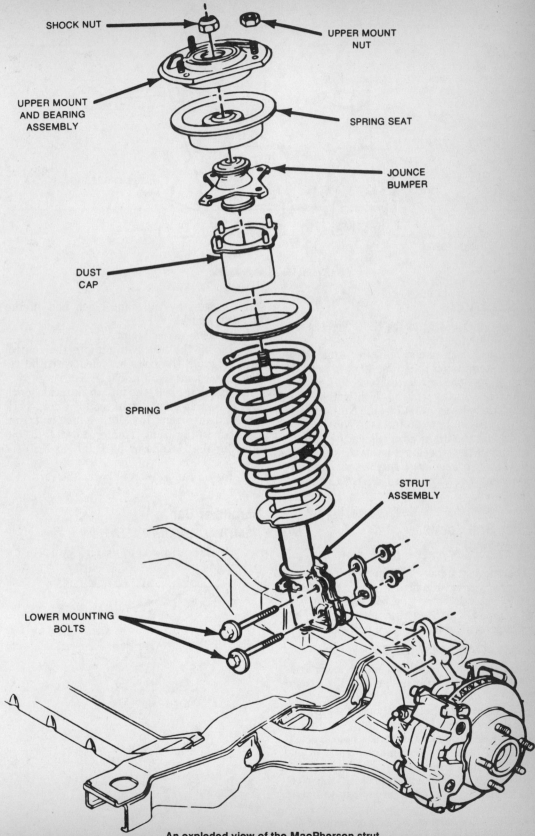

SHOCK NUT

UPPER MOUNT
NUT

UPPER MOUNT
AND BEARING
ASSEMBLY

SPRING SEAT

JOUNCE
BUMPER

DUST
CAP

SPRING

STRUT
ASSEMBLY

LOWER MOUNTING
BOLTS

**An exploded view of the MacPherson strut**

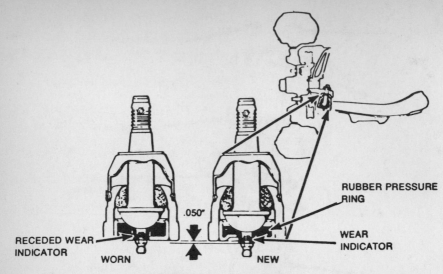

**Ball joint wear indicators**

## INSTALLATION

1. Install the strut to the body. Tighten the upper nuts hand tight.

2. Place a jack under the lower arm. Raise the arm and install the lower strut-to-knuckle bolts. Align the strut-to-steering knuckle marks made during removal. Tighten the strut-to-knuckle bolts to 140 ft.lb. (190 Nm), and the strut-to-body nuts to 18 ft.lb. (24 Nm).

3. Install the brake hose clip on the strut.

4. Install the wheel and lower the car.

NOTE: *If a new strut damper has been installed, the front end will have to be realigned.*

## Lower Ball Joints

### INSPECTION

The ball joints have built-in wear indicators. As long as the wear indicator (part of the grease nipple) extends below the ball joint seat, the ball joint is OK. When the indicator recedes beneath the seat, replacement if necessary.

### REMOVAL AND INSTALLATION

Only one ball joint is used in each lower arm. The MacPherson strut design does not use an upper ball joint.

1. Loosen the wheel nuts, raise the car, and remove the wheel.

2. Use an ⅛″ drill bit to drill a hole approximately ¼″ deep in the center of each of the three ball joint rivets.

3. Use a ½″ drill bit to drill off the rivet heads. Drill only enough to remove the rivet head.

4. Use a hammer and punch to remove the rivets. Drive them out from the bottom.

5. Loosen the ball joint pinch bolt in the steering knuckle.

6. Remove the ball joint.

7. Install the new ball joint in the control arm. Tighten the bolts supplied with the replacement joint to 13 ft.lb. (18 Nm).

8. Install the ball stud into the knuckle pinch bolt fitting. It should go in easily; if not, check the stud alignment. Install the pinch bolt from the rear to the front. Tighten to 40 ft.lb. (50 Nm) for for 1982-84 or 33 ft.lb. (45 Nm) for 1985-88.

9. Install the wheel and lower the car.

## Stabilizer Bar

### REMOVAL AND INSTALLATION

1. Raise and support the vehicle on jackstands.

**Drill out the ball joint rivets**

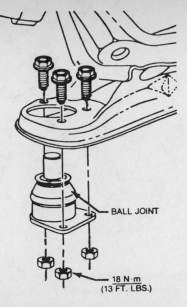

BALL JOINT

18 N·m
(13 FT. LBS.)

**Ball joint installation**

2. Remove the two nuts attaching the stabilizer bar to the left lower control arm. Remove the four bolts which attach the left retaining plate to the engine cradle. The retaining plate covers and holds the stabilizer bar.

3. Loosen the four bolts holding the right stabilizer bracket.

4. Disconnect and remove the exhaust pipe and crossover if necessary.

5. Pull the stabilizer bar down on the left side.

6. Reverse steps 1 through 5 to install the stabilizer bar

NOTE: *To aid in stabilizer bar installation, a pry hole has been provided in the engine cradle.*

7. Install the stabilizer bar attachment. Tighten to 35 ft.lb.

## Lower Control Arm
### REMOVAL AND INSTALLATION

1. Loosen the wheel nuts, raise the car, and remove the wheel.

2. Remove the stabilizer bar from the control arm.

3. Remove the ball joint pinch bolt in the steering knuckle.

4. Remove the control arm pivot bolts and the control arm.

5. To install, insert the control arm into its fittings. Install the pivot bolts from the rear to the front. Tighten the bolts to 66 ft.lb. (90 Nm).

6. Insert the ball stud into the knuckle pinch bolt fitting. It should go in easily; if not, check the ball joint stud alignment.

7. Install the pinch bolt from the rear to the front. Tighten to 40 ft.lb. (50 Nm) for 1982-84 or 33 ft.lb. (45 Nm) for 1985-88.

8. Install the stabilizer bar clamp. Tighten to 33 ft.lb. (45 Nm).

9. Install the wheel and lower the car.

## Knuckle
### REMOVAL AND INSTALLATION

1. Remove the hub nut.

2. Raise the front of the car. Remove the wheel and tire.

3. Install an axle shaft boot seal protector, GM special tool No. J-28712 or equivalent, onto the seal.

4. Disconnect the brake hose clip from the MacPherson strut, but do not disconnect the hose from the caliper. Remove the brake caliper, rotor and shield from the spindle, and hang the caliper out of the way by a length of wire. Do not allow the caliper to hang by the brake hose.

5. Mark the camber alignment cam bolt for reassembly. Remove the cam bolt and the upper attaching bolt from the strut and spindle.

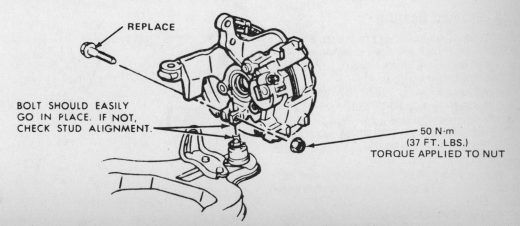

REPLACE

BOLT SHOULD EASILY
GO IN PLACE. IF NOT,
CHECK STUD ALIGNMENT.

50 N·m
(37 FT. LBS.)
TORQUE APPLIED TO NUT

**Installing the ball joint stud to the steering knuckle**

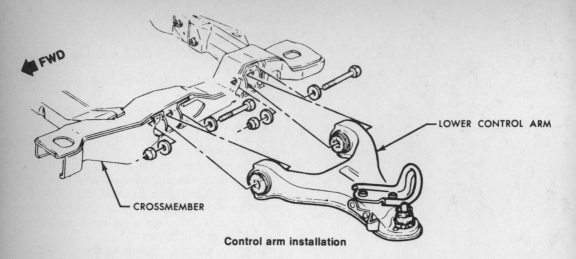

**Control arm installation**

6. Pull the steering knuckle assembly from the strut bracket.

Prior to installation, a new knuckle seal should be installed on the steering knuckle.

7. Loosely attach the steering knuckle to the suspension strut, then install the rotor and the hub nut. When the shaft begins to turn with the hub, insert a drift through the caliper into one of the cooling slots in the rotor to keep it from turning. Insert a long bolt in the hub flange to prevent the shaft from turning. Tighten the hub nut to 70 ft.lb.

8. Tighten the brake caliper bolts to 30 ft.lb.

9. Load the hub assembly by lowering it onto a jackstand. Align the camber cam bolt marks made during removal, install the bolt and tighten to 140 ft.lb. Tighten the upper nut to the same value.

10. Remove the boot seal protector.

11. Connect the brake hose clip to the strut. Install the tire and wheel, lower the car, and tighten the hub nut to 225 ft.lb. (1981-82); 185 ft.lb. (1983-88).

## Front Hub and Bearing

The front wheel bearings are sealed, non-adjustable units which require no periodic attention. They are bolted to the steering knuckle by means of an integral flange.

You will need a special tool to pull the bearing free of the halfshaft tool J-28733 or the equivalent. You should also use a halfshaft boot protector tool J-28712 (Double-Offset joint) or J-33162 (Tri-Pot joint) to protect the parts from damage.

1. Remove the wheel cover, loosen the hub nut, and raise and support the car. Remove the front wheel.

2. Install the boot cover, tool J-28712 (Double-Offset joint) or J-33162 (Tri-Pot joint).

3. Remove and discard the hub nut. Be sure to use a new one on assembly, not the old one.

4. Remove the brake caliper and rotor:

a. Remove the allen head caliper mounting bolts;

b. Remove the caliper from the knuckle and suspend from a length of wire. Do not allow the caliper to hang from the brake hose. Pull the rotor from the knuckle.

5. Remove the three hub and bearing attaching bolts and remove the hub. If the old bearing is to be reused, match mark the bolts and holes for installation. The brake rotor splash shield will have to come off, too.

6. Attach a puller, tool J-28733 or the equivalent, and remove the bearing. If corrosion is present, make sure the bearing is loose in the knuckle before using the puller.

7. Clean the mating surfaces of all dirt and corrosion. Check the knuckle bore and knuckle seal for damage. If a new bearing is to be installed, remove the old knuckle seal and install a new one. Grease the lips of the new seal before installation; install with a seal driver made for

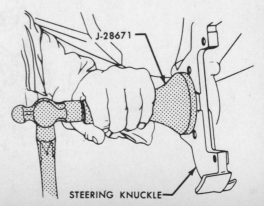

**Use a seal driver when installing a new seal into the knuckle**

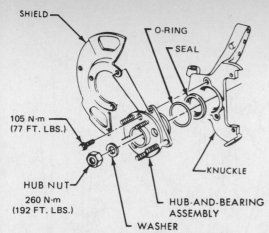

**Exploded view of the hub and bearing attachment to the steering knuckle**

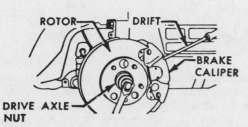

**Insert a drift pin into the rotor when installing the hub nut**

the purpose, tool J-28671 (1982-84) or J-34657 (1985-88).

8. Push the bearing onto the halfshaft. Install a new washer and hub nut.

9. Tighten the new hub nut on the halfshaft until the bearing is seated. If the rotor and hub start to rotate as the hub nut is tightened, insert a drift through the caliper and into the rotor cooling fins to prevent rotation. Do not apply full torque to the hub nut at this time—just seat the bearing.

10. Install the brake shield and the bearing retaining bolts. Tighten the bolts evenly to 63 ft.lb. (85 Nm).

11. Install the caliper and rotor. Be sure that the caliper hose isn't twisted. Install the caliper bolts and tighten to 28 ft.lb. (38 Nm) for 1982-84 or 38 ft.lb. (51 Nm) for 1985-88.

12. Install the wheel. Lower the car. Tighten the hub nut to 214 ft.lb. (290 Nm) for '82 or 192 ft.lb. (260 Nm) for 1983-88.

## Front End Alignment

Only camber and toe are adjustable on the A-Body cars; caster is preset and non-adjustable.

### CAMBER

Camber is the inward or outward tilt from the vertical, measured in degrees, of the front wheels at the top. An outward tilt gives the wheel positive camber, an inward tilt is called negative camber. Proper camber is critical to assure even tire wear.

Camber angle is adjusted on the A-Bodies by loosening the through bolts which attach the MacPherson strut to the steering knuckle in or out. The bolts must be tightened to 140 ft.lb. (190 Nm) afterwards. The bolts must be seated properly between the inner and outer guide surfaces on the strut flange. Measurement of the camber angle requires special alignment equipment; thus the adjustment of camber is not a do-it-yourself job, and not covered here.

### TOE

Toe is the amount, measured in a fraction of a millimeter, that the wheels are closer together at one end than the other. Toe-in means that the front wheels are closer together at the front than the rear; toe-out means the rear of the front wheels are closer together than the front. A-Body cars are designed to have a slight amount of toe-in.

Toe is adjusted by turning the tie rods. It must be checked after camber has been adjusted, but it can be adjusted without disturbing the camber setting. you can make this adjustment without special equipment if you make very careful measurements. The wheels must be straight ahead.

1. Toe can be determined by measuring the distance between the centers of the tire treads, at the front of the tire and at the rear. If the tread pattern makes this impossible, you can measure between the edges of the wheel rims, but make sure to move the car forward and

## Wheel Alignment Specifications

| Year | Model | Caster* | | Camber | | Toe-In (in.) | Steering Axis (deg) Inclination |
|---|---|---|---|---|---|---|---|
| | | Range (deg) | Pref Setting (deg) | Range (deg) | Pref Setting (deg) | | |
| '82–'85 | All | — | — | ½N–½P | 0 | 1⁄16 out–1⁄16 in | 14.5 |

*Caster is not adjustable

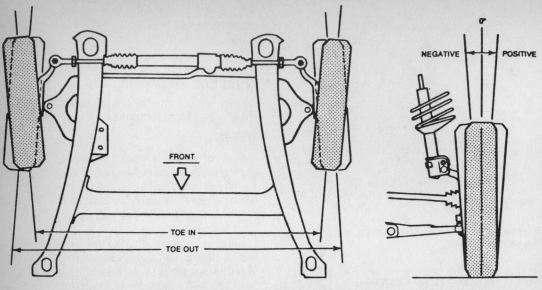

**Wheel alignment: toe (left) and camber (right)**

measure in a couple of places to avoid errors caused by bent rims or wheel runout.

2. If the measurement is not within specifications, loosen the nuts at the steering knuckle end of the tie rod, and remove the tie rod boot clamps. Rotate the tie rods to align the toe to specifications. Rotate the tie rods evenly, or the steering wheel will be crooked when you're done.

3. When the adjustment is correct, tighten the nuts to 44 ft.lb. (60 Nm). Adjust the boots and tighten the clamps.

## REAR SUSPENSION

Rear suspension consists of a solid rear axle tube containing an integral, welded-in stabiliz-

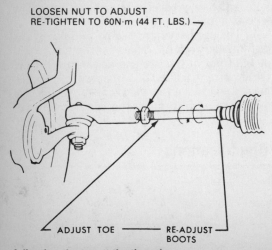

**Adjusting the toe at the tie rods**

er bar, coil springs, shock absorbers, a lateral track bar, and trailing arms. The trailing arms (control arms) are welded to the axle, and pivot at the frame. Fore and after movement is controlled by the trailing arms; lateral movement is controlled by the track bar. A permanently lubricated and sealed hub and bearing assembly is bolted to each end of the axle tube, it is a non-adjustable unit which must be replaced as an assembly if defective.

## Coil Springs

### REMOVAL AND INSTALLATION

CAUTION: *The coil springs are under a considerable amount of tension. Be very careful when removing or installing them; they can exert enough force to cause very serious injuries.*

1. Raise and support the car on a hoist. Do not use twin-post hoist. The swing arc of the axle may cause it to slip from the hoist when the bolts are removed. If a suitable hoist is not available, raise and support the car on jackstands, and use a jack under the axle.

2. Support the axle with a jack that can be raised and lowered.

3. Remove the brake hose attaching brackets (right and left), allowing the hoses to hang freely. Do not disconnect the hoses.

4. Remove the track bar attaching bolts from the rear axle.

5. Remove both shock absorber lower attaching bolts from the axle.

6. Lower the axle. Remove the coil spring and insulator.

7. To install, position the spring and insulator on the axle. The leg on the upper coil of the

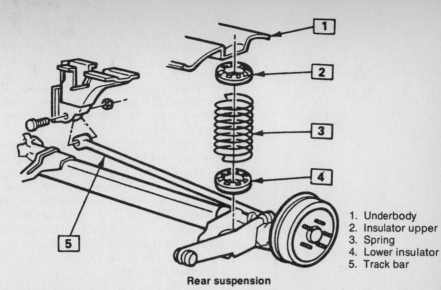

1. Underbody
2. Insulator upper
3. Spring
4. Lower insulator
5. Track bar

**Rear suspension**

spring must be parallel to the axle, facing the left hand side of the car.

8. Install the shock absorber bolts. Tighten to 43 ft.lb. (58 Nm) for 1982-84 or 35 ft.lb. (47 Nm) for 1985-88. Install the track bar, tightening to 44 ft.lb. (60 Nm). Install the brake line brackets. Tighten to 8 ft.lb. (11 Nm).

## Track Bar

### REMOVAL AND INSTALLATION

1. Raise the vehicle on a hoist and support the rear axle.

2. Remove the nut and bolt from both the axle and body attachments and remove the bar.

3. To install: Position the track bar at the axle mounting bracket and loosely install the bolt and nut.

4. Place the other end of the track bar into the body reinforcement and install the bolt and nut. Torque the nut at the axle bracket to 44 ft.lb. (60 Nm). Torque the nut at the body reinforcement to 35 ft.lb. (47 Nm).

5. Remove the rear axle support and lower the vehicle.

## Shock Absorbers

### REMOVAL AND INSTALLATION

1. Open the hatch or trunk lid, remove the trim cover if present, and remove the upper shock absorber nut.

2. Raise and support the car at a convenient

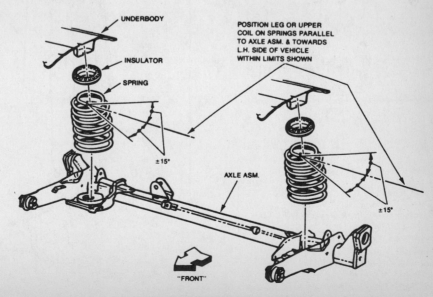

**Spring installation**

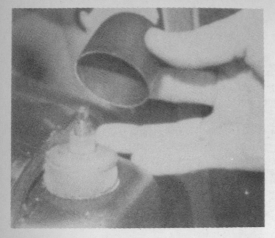

The upper shock absorber mounts are accessible in the trunk

to 43 ft.lb. (58 Nm) for 1982-84 or 38 ft.lb. (51 Nm) for 1985-88, the upper to 13 ft.lb. (17 Nm) for 1982-83 or 28 ft.lb. (37 Nm) for 1984-88.

### TESTING

Visually inspect the shock absorber. If there is evidence of leakage and the shock absorber is covered with oil, the shock is defective and should be replaced.

If there is no sign of excessive leakage (a small amount of weeping is normal) bounce the car at one corner by pressing down on the fender or bumper and releasing. When you have the car bouncing as much as you can, release the fender or bumper. The car should stop bouncing after the first rebound. If the bouncing continues past the center point of the bounce more than once, the shock absorbers are worn and should be replaced.

working height if you desire. It is not necessary to remove the weight of the car from the shock absorbers, however, so you can leave the car on the ground if you prefer.

3. If the car is equipped with superlift shock absorbers, disconnect the air line.

4. Remove the lower attaching bolt and remove the shock.

5. If new shock absorbers are being installed, repeatedly compress them while inverted and extend them in their normal upright position. This will purge them of air.

6. Install the shocks in the reverse order of removal. Tighten the lower mount nut and bolt

## Rear Hub and Bearing

### REMOVAL AND INSTALLATION

1. Loosen the wheel lug nuts. Raise and support the car and remove the wheel.

2. Remove the brake drum. Removal procedures are covered in the next chapter, if needed.

NOTE: *Do not hammer on the brake drum to remove; damage to the bearing will result.*

3. Remove the four hub and bearing retaining bolts and remove the assembly from the axle.

4. Installation is the reverse. Hub and bearing bolt torque is 45 ft.lb. (60 Nm).

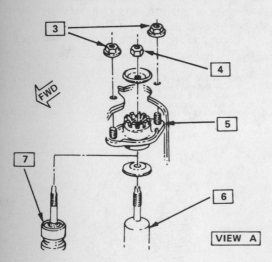

VIEW A

1. Body shock tower mounting bracket
2. 58 N·m (43 ft. lb.)
3. 17 N·m (13 ft. lb.)
4. 37 N·m (28 ft. lb.)
5. Upper shock absorber mount
6. Air lift shock absorber
7. Standard shock absorber

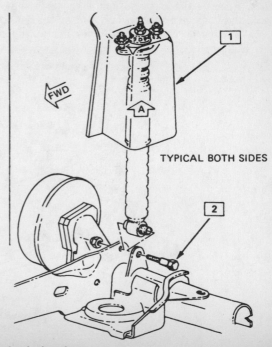

TYPICAL BOTH SIDES

**Installation of the shock absorbers**

## Troubleshooting the Steering Column

| Problem | Cause | Solution |
|---|---|---|
| Will not lock | • Lockbolt spring broken or defective | • Replace lock bolt spring |
| High effort (required to turn ignition key and lock cylinder) | • Lock cylinder defective<br>• Ignition switch defective<br>• Rack preload spring broken or deformed<br>• Burr on lock sector, lock rack, housing, support or remote rod coupling<br>• Bent sector shaft<br>• Defective lock rack<br>• Remote rod bent, deformed<br>• Ignition switch mounting bracket bent<br>• Distorted coupling slot in lock rack (tilt column) | • Replace lock cylinder<br>• Replace ignition switch<br>• Replace preload spring<br><br>• Remove burr<br><br><br>• Replace shaft<br>• Replace lock rack<br>• Replace rod<br>• Straighten or replace<br><br>• Replace lock rack |
| Will stick in "start" | • Remote rod deformed<br>• Ignition switch mounting bracket bent | • Straighten or replace<br>• Straighten or replace |
| Key cannot be removed in "off-lock" | • Ignition switch is not adjusted correctly<br>• Defective lock cylinder | • Adjust switch<br>• Replace lock cylinder |
| Lock cylinder can be removed without depressing retainer | • Lock cylinder with defective retainer<br>• Burr over retainer slot in housing cover or on cylinder retainer | • Replace lock cylinder<br><br>• Remove burr |
| High effort on lock cylinder between "off" and "off-lock" | • Distorted lock rack<br>• Burr on tang of shift gate (automatic column)<br>• Gearshift linkage not adjusted | • Replace lock rack<br>• Remove burr<br><br>• Adjust linkage |
| Noise in column | • One click when in "off-lock" position and the steering wheel is moved (all except automatic column)<br>• Coupling bolts not tightened<br>• Lack of grease on bearings or bearing surfaces<br>• Upper shaft bearing worn or broken<br>• Lower shaft bearing worn or broken<br>• Column not correctly aligned<br>• Coupling pulled apart<br>• Broken coupling lower joint<br><br>• Steering shaft snap ring not seated<br><br>• Shroud loose on shift bowl. Housing loose on jacket—will be noticed with ignition in "off-lock" and when torque is applied to steering wheel. | • Normal—lock bolt is seating<br><br><br><br>• Tighten pinch bolts<br>• Lubricate with chassis grease<br><br>• Replace bearing assembly<br><br>• Replace bearing. Check shaft and replace if scored.<br>• Align column<br>• Replace coupling<br>• Repair or replace joint and align column<br>• Replace ring. Check for proper seating in groove.<br>• Position shroud over lugs on shift bowl. Tighten mounting screws. |
| High steering shaft effort | • Column misaligned<br>• Defective upper or lower bearing<br>• Tight steering shaft universal joint<br>• Flash on I.D. of shift tube at plastic joint (tilt column only)<br>• Upper or lower bearing seized | • Align column<br>• Replace as required<br>• Repair or replace<br>• Replace shift tube<br><br>• Replace bearings |
| Lash in mounted column assembly | • Column mounting bracket bolts loose<br>• Broken weld nuts on column jacket<br>• Column capsule bracket sheared | • Tighten bolts<br><br>• Replace column jacket<br>• Replace bracket assembly |

## Troubleshooting the Steering Column (cont.)

| Problem | Cause | Solution |
|---|---|---|
| Lash in mounted column assembly (cont.) | • Column bracket to column jacket mounting bolts loose | • Tighten to specified torque |
| | • Loose lock shoes in housing (tilt column only) | • Replace shoes |
| | • Loose pivot pins (tilt column only) | • Replace pivot pins and support |
| | • Loose lock shoe pin (tilt column only) | • Replace pin and housing |
| | • Loose support screws (tilt column only) | • Tighten screws |
| Housing loose (tilt column only) | • Excessive clearance between holes in support or housing and pivot pin diameters | • Replace pivot pins and support |
| | • Housing support-screws loose | • Tighten screws |
| Steering wheel loose—every other tilt position (tilt column only) | • Loose fit between lock shoe and lock shoe pivot pin | • Replace lock shoes and pivot pin |
| Steering column not locking in any tilt position (tilt column only) | • Lock shoe seized on pivot pin | • Replace lock shoes and pin |
| | • Lock shoe grooves have burrs or are filled with foreign material | • Clean or replace lock shoes |
| | • Lock shoe springs weak or broken | • Replace springs |
| Noise when tilting column (tilt column only) | • Upper tilt bumpers worn | • Replace tilt bumper |
| | • Tilt spring rubbing in housing | • Lubricate with chassis grease |
| One click when in "off-lock" position and the steering wheel is moved | • Seating of lock bolt | • None. Click is normal characteristic sound produced by lock bolt as it seats. |
| High shift effort (automatic and tilt column only) | • Column not correctly aligned | • Align column |
| | • Lower bearing not aligned correctly | • Assemble correctly |
| | • Lack of grease on seal or lower bearing areas | • Lubricate with chassis grease |
| Improper transmission shifting— automatic and tilt column only | • Sheared shift tube joint | • Replace shift tube |
| | • Improper transmission gearshift linkage adjustment | • Adjust linkage |
| | • Loose lower shift lever | • Replace shift tube |

## Troubleshooting the Ignition Switch

| Problem | Cause | Solution |
|---|---|---|
| Ignition switch electrically inoperative | • Loose or defective switch connector | • Tighten or replace connector |
| | • Feed wire open (fusible link) | • Repair or replace |
| | • Defective ignition switch | • Replace ignition switch |
| Engine will not crank | • Ignition switch not adjusted properly | • Adjust switch |
| Ignition switch wil not actuate mechanically | • Defective ignition switch | • Replace switch |
| | • Defective lock sector | • Replace lock sector |
| | • Defective remote rod | • Replace remote rod |
| Ignition switch cannot be adjusted correctly | • Remote rod deformed | • Repair, straighten or replace |

## Troubleshooting the Turn Signal Switch

| Problem | Cause | Solution |
|---|---|---|
| Turn signal will not cancel | • Loose switch mounting screws<br>• Switch or anchor bosses broken<br>• Broken, missing or out of position detent, or cancelling spring | • Tighten screws<br>• Replace switch<br>• Reposition springs or replace switch as required |
| Turn signal difficult to operate | • Turn signal lever loose<br>• Switch yoke broken or distorted<br>• Loose or misplaced springs<br><br>• Foreign parts and/or materials in switch<br>• Switch mounted loosely | • Tighten mounting screws<br>• Replace switch<br>• Reposition springs or replace switch<br>• Remove foreign parts and/or material<br>• Tighten mounting screws |
| Turn signal will not indicate lane change | • Broken lane change pressure pad or spring hanger<br>• Broken, missing or misplaced lane change spring<br>• Jammed wires | • Replace switch<br><br>• Replace or reposition as required<br><br>• Loosen mounting screws, reposition wires and retighten screws |
| Turn signal will not stay in turn position | • Foreign material or loose parts impeding movement of switch yoke<br>• Defective switch | • Remove material and/or parts<br><br>• Replace switch |
| Hazard switch cannot be pulled out | • Foreign material between hazard support cancelling leg and yoke | • Remove foreign material. No foreign material impeding function of hazard switch—replace turn signal switch. |
| No turn signal lights | • Inoperative turn signal flasher<br>• Defective or blown fuse<br>• Loose chassis to column harness connector<br>• Disconnect column to chassis connector. Connect new switch to chassis and operate switch by hand.<br>If vehicle lights now operate normally, signal switch is inoperative<br>• If vehicle lights do not operate, check chassis wiring for opens, grounds, etc. | • Replace turn signal flasher<br>• Replace fuse<br>• Connect securely<br><br>• Replace signal switch<br><br><br><br><br>• Repair chassis wiring as required |
| Instrument panel turn indicator lights on but not flashing | • Burned out or damaged front or rear turn signal bulb<br>• If vehicle lights do not operate, check light sockets for high resistance connections, the chassis wiring for opens, grounds, etc.<br>• Inoperative flasher<br>• Loose chassis to column harness connection<br>• Inoperative turn signal switch<br>• To determine if turn signal switch is defective, substitute new switch into circuit and operate switch by hand. If the vehicle's lights operate normally, signal switch is inoperative. | • Replace bulb<br><br>• Repair chassis wiring as required<br><br><br><br>• Replace flasher<br>• Connect securely<br><br>• Replace turn signal switch<br>• Replace turn signal switch |
| Stop light not on when turn indicated | • Loose column to chassis connection<br>• Disconnect column to chassis connector. Connect new switch into system without removing old. | • Connect securely<br><br>• Replace signal switch |

## Troubleshooting the Turn Signal Switch (cont.)

| Problem | Cause | Solution |
|---|---|---|
| Stop light not on when turn indicated (cont.) | Operate switch by hand. If brake lights work with switch in the turn position, signal switch is defective. | |
| | · If brake lights do not work, check connector to stop light sockets for grounds, opens, etc. | · Repair connector to stop light circuits using service manual as guide |
| Turn indicator panel lights not flashing | · Burned out bulbs<br>· High resistance to ground at bulb socket | · Replace bulbs<br>· Replace socket |
| | · Opens, ground in wiring harness from front turn signal bulb socket to indicator lights | · Locate and repair as required |
| Turn signal lights flash very slowly | · High resistance ground at light sockets | · Repair high resistance grounds at light sockets |
| | · Incorrect capacity turn signal flasher or bulb | · Replace turn signal flasher or bulb |
| | · If flashing rate is still extremely slow, check chassis wiring harness from the connector to light sockets for high resistance | · Locate and repair as required |
| | · Loose chassis to column harness connection | · Connect securely |
| | · Disconnect column to chassis connector. Connect new switch into system without removing old. Operate switch by hand. If flashing occurs at normal rate, the signal switch is defective. | · Replace turn signal switch |
| Hazard signal lights will not flash—turn signal functions normally | · Blow fuse<br>· Inoperative hazard warning flasher | · Replace fuse<br>· Replace hazard warning flasher in fuse panel |
| | · Loose chassis-to-column harness connection | · Conect securely |
| | · Disconnect column to chassis connector. Connect new switch into system without removing old. Depress the hazard warning lights. If they now work normally, turn signal switch is defective. | · Replace turn signal switch |
| | · If lights do not flash, check wiring harness "K" lead for open between hazard flasher and connector. If open, fuse block is defective | · Repair or replace brown wire or connector as required |

## Troubleshooting the Manual Steering Gear

| Problem | Cause | Solution |
|---|---|---|
| Hard or erratic steering | · Incorrect tire pressure | · Inflate tires to recommended pressures |
| | · Insufficient or incorrect lubrication | · Lubricate as required (refer to Maintenance Section) |
| | · Suspension, or steering linkage parts damaged or misaligned | · Repair or replace parts as necessary |
| | · Improper front wheel alignment | · Adjust incorrect wheel alignment angles |
| | · Incorrect steering gear adjustment | · Adjust steering gear |
| | · Sagging springs | · Replace springs |

## Troubleshooting the Manual Steering Gear (cont.)

| Problem | Cause | Solution |
|---|---|---|
| Play or looseness in steering | • Steering wheel loose | • Inspect shaft spines and repair as necessary. Tighten attaching nut and stake in place. |
| | • Steering linkage or attaching parts loose or worn | • Tighten, adjust, or replace faulty components |
| | • Pitman arm loose | • Inspect shaft splines and repair as necessary. Tighten attaching nut and stake in place |
| | • Steering gear attaching bolts loose | • Tighten bolts |
| | • Loose or worn wheel bearings | • Adjust or replace bearings |
| | • Steering gear adjustment incorrect or parts badly worn | • Adjust gear or replace defective parts |
| Wheel shimmy or tramp | • Improper tire pressure | • Inflate tires to recommended pressures |
| | • Wheels, tires, or brake rotors out-of-balance or out-of-round | • Inspect and replace or balance parts |
| | • Inoperative, worn, or loose shock absorbers or mounting parts | • Repair or replace shocks or mountings |
| | • Loose or worn steering or suspension parts | • Tighten or replace as necessary |
| | • Loose or worn wheel bearings | • Adjust or replace bearings |
| | • Incorrect steering gear adjustments | • Adjust steering gear |
| | • Incorrect front wheel alignment | • Correct front wheel alignment |
| Tire wear | • Improper tire pressure | • Inflate tires to recommended pressures |
| | • Failure to rotate tires | • Rotate tires |
| | • Brakes grabbing | • Adjust or repair brakes |
| | • Incorrect front wheel alignment | • Align incorrect angles |
| | • Broken or damaged steering and suspension parts | • Repair or replace defective parts |
| | • Wheel runout | • Replace faulty wheel |
| | • Excessive speed on turns | • Make driver aware of conditions |
| Vehicle leads to one side | • Improper tire pressures | • Inflate tires to recommended pressures |
| | • Front tires with uneven tread depth, wear pattern, or different cord design (i.e., one bias ply and one belted or radial tire on front wheels) | • Install tires of same cord construction and reasonably even tread depth, design, and wear pattern |
| | • Incorrect front wheel alignment | • Align incorrect angles |
| | • Brakes dragging | • Adjust or repair brakes |
| | • Pulling due to uneven tire construction | • Replace faulty tire |

## Troubleshooting the Power Steering Gear

| Problem | Cause | Solution |
|---|---|---|
| Hissing noise in steering gear | • There is some noise in all power steering systems. One of the most common is a hissing sound most evident at standstill parking. There is no relationship between this noise and performance of the steering. Hiss may be expected when steering wheel is at end of travel or when slowly turning at standstill. | • Slight hiss is normal and in no way affects steering. Do not replace valve unless hiss is extremely objectionable. A replacement valve will also exhibit slight noise and is not always a cure. Investigate clearance around flexible coupling rivets. Be sure steering shaft and gear are aligned so flexible coupling rotates in a flat plane and is not distorted as |

## Troubleshooting the Power Steering Gear (cont.)

| Problem | Cause | Solution |
|---|---|---|
| Hissing noise in steering gear (cont.) | | shaft rotates. Any metal-to-metal contacts through flexible coupling will transmit valve hiss into passenger compartment through the steering column. |
| Rattle or chuckle noise in steering gear | • Gear loose on frame<br><br><br>• Steering linkage looseness<br><br>• Pressure hose touching other parts of car<br>• Loose pitman shaft over center adjustment<br>**NOTE:** A slight rattle may occur on turns because of increased clearance off the "high point." This is normal and clearance must not be reduced below specified limits to eliminate this slight rattle.<br>• Loose pitman arm | • Check gear-to-frame mounting screws. Tighten screws to 88 N·m (65 foot pounds) torque.<br>• Check linkage pivot points for wear. Replace if necessary.<br>• Adjust hose position. Do not bend tubing by hand.<br>• Adjust to specifications<br><br><br><br><br><br>• Tighten pitman arm nut to specifications |
| Squawk noise in steering gear when turning or recovering from a turn | • Damper O-ring on valve spool cut | • Replace damper O-ring |
| Poor return of steering wheel to center | • Tires not properly inflated<br>• Lack of lubrication in linkage and ball joints<br>• Lower coupling flange rubbing against steering gear adjuster plug<br>• Steering gear to column misalignment<br>• Improper front wheel alignment<br>• Steering linkage binding<br>• Ball joints binding<br>• Steering wheel rubbing against housing<br>• Tight or frozen steering shaft bearings<br>• Sticking or plugged valve spool<br><br>• Steering gear adjustments over specifications<br>• Kink in return hose | • Inflate to specified pressure<br>• Lube linkage and ball joints<br><br>• Loosen pinch bolt and assemble properly<br><br>• Align steering column<br><br>• Check and adjust as necessary<br>• Replace pivots<br>• Replace ball joints<br>• Align housing<br><br>• Replace bearings<br><br>• Remove and clean or replace valve<br>• Check adjustment with gear out of car. Adjust as required.<br>• Replace hose |
| Car leads to one side or the other (keep in mind road condition and wind. Test car in both directions on flat road) | • Front end misaligned<br>• Unbalanced steering gear valve<br>**NOTE:** If this is cause, steering effort will be very light in direction of lead and normal or heavier in opposite direction | • Adjust to specifications<br>• Replace valve |
| Momentary increase in effort when turning wheel fast to right or left | • Low oil level<br>• Pump belt slipping<br>• High internal leakage | • Add power steering fluid as required<br>• Tighten or replace belt<br>• Check pump pressure. (See pressure test) |

## Troubleshooting the Power Steering Gear (cont.)

| Problem | Cause | Solution |
| --- | --- | --- |
| Steering wheel surges or jerks when turning with engine running especially during parking | • Low oil level<br>• Loose pump belt<br>• Steering linkage hitting engine oil pan at full turn<br>• Insufficient pump pressure<br><br>• Pump flow control valve sticking | • Fill as required<br>• Adjust tension to specification<br>• Correct clearance<br><br>• Check pump pressure. (See pressure test). Replace relief valve if defective.<br>• Inspect for varnish or damage, replace if necessary |
| Excessive wheel kickback or loose steering | • Air in system<br><br><br><br><br>• Steering gear loose on frame<br><br>• Steering linkage joints worn enough to be loose<br>• Worn poppet valve<br>• Loose thrust bearing preload adjustment<br>• Excessive overcenter lash | • Add oil to pump reservoir and bleed by operating steering. Check hose connectors for proper torque and adjust as required.<br>• Tighten attaching screws to specified torque<br>• Replace loose pivots<br><br>• Replace poppet valve<br>• Adjust to specification with gear out of vehicle<br>• Adjust to specification with gear out of car |
| Hard steering or lack of assist | • Loose pump belt<br>• Low oil level<br>**NOTE:** Low oil level will also result in excessive pump noise<br><br>• Steering gear to column misalignment<br>• Lower coupling flange rubbing against steering gear adjuster plug<br>• Tires not properly inflated | • Adjust belt tension to specification<br>• Fill to proper level. If excessively low, check all lines and joints for evidence of external leakage. Tighten loose connectors.<br>• Align steering column<br><br>• Loosen pinch bolt and assemble properly<br><br>• Inflate to recommended pressure |
| Foamy milky power steering fluid, low fluid level and possible low pressure | • Air in the fluid, and loss of fluid due to internal pump leakage causing overflow | • Check for leak and correct. Bleed system. Extremely cold temperatures will cause system aeriation should the oil level be low. If oil level is correct and pump still foams, remove pump from vehicle and separate reservoir from housing. Check welsh plug and housing for cracks. If plug is loose or housing is cracked, replace housing. |
| Low pressure due to steering pump | • Flow control valve stuck or inoperative<br>• Pressure plate not flat against cam ring | • Remove burrs or dirt or replace. Flush system.<br>• Correct |
| Low pressure due to steering gear | • Pressure loss in cylinder due to worn piston ring or badly worn housing bore<br>• Leakage at valve rings, valve body-to-worm seal | • Remove gear from car for disassembly and inspection of ring and housing bore<br>• Remove gear from car for disassembly and replace seals |

## Troubleshooting the Power Steering Pump

| Problem | Cause | Solution |
|---|---|---|
| Chirp noise in steering pump | • Loose belt | • Adjust belt tension to specification |
| Belt squeal (particularly noticeable at full wheel travel and stand still parking) | • Loose belt | • Adjust belt tension to specification |
| Growl noise in steering pump | • Excessive back pressure in hoses or steering gear caused by restriction | • Locate restriction and correct. Replace part if necessary. |
| Growl noise in steering pump (particularly noticeable at stand still parking) | • Scored pressure plates, thrust plate or rotor<br>• Extreme wear of cam ring | • Replace parts and flush system<br><br>• Replace parts |
| Groan noise in steering pump | • Low oil level<br>• Air in the oil. Poor pressure hose connection. | • Fill reservoir to proper level<br>• Tighten connector to specified torque. Bleed system by operating steering from right to left—full turn. |
| Rattle noise in steering pump | • Vanes not installed properly<br>• Vanes sticking in rotor slots | • Install properly<br>• Free up by removing burrs, varnish, or dirt |
| Swish noise in steering pump | • Defective flow control valve | • Replace part |
| Whine noise in steering pump | • Pump shaft bearing scored | • Replace housing and shaft. Flush system. |
| Hard steering or lack of assist | • Loose pump belt<br>• Low oil level in reservoir<br>**NOTE:** Low oil level will also result in excessive pump noise<br><br>• Steering gear to column misalignment<br>• Lower coupling flange rubbing against steering gear adjuster plug<br>• Tires not properly inflated | • Adjust belt tension to specification<br>• Fill to proper level. If excessively low, check all lines and joints for evidence of external leakage. Tighten loose connectors.<br>• Align steering column<br><br>• Loosen pinch bolt and assemble properly<br><br>• Inflate to recommended pressure |
| Foaming milky power steering fluid, low fluid level and possible low pressure | • Air in the fluid, and loss of fluid due to internal pump leakage causing overflow | • Check for leaks and correct. Bleed system. Extremely cold temperatures will cause system aeration should the oil level be low. If oil level is correct and pump still foams, remove pump from vehicle and separate reservoir from body. Check welsh plug and body for cracks. If plug is loose or body is cracked, replace body. |
| Low pump pressure | • Flow control valve stuck or inoperative<br>• Pressure plate not flat against cam ring | • Remove burrs or dirt or replace. Flush system.<br>• Correct |
| Momentary increase in effort when turning wheel fast to right or left | • Low oil level in pump<br><br>• Pump belt slipping<br>• High internal leakage | • Add power steering fluid as required<br>• Tighten or replace belt<br>• Check pump pressure. (See pressure test) |
| Steering wheel surges or jerks when turning with engine running especially during parking | • Low oil level<br>• Loose pump belt<br>• Steering linkage hitting engine oil pan at full turn<br>• Insufficient pump pressure | • Fill as required<br>• Adjust tension to specification<br>• Correct clearance<br><br>• Check pump pressure. (See pressure test). Replace flow control valve if defective. |

## Troubleshooting the Power Steering Pump (cont.)

| Problem | Cause | Solution |
| --- | --- | --- |
| Steering wheel surges or jerks when turning with engine running especially during parking (cont.) | • Sticking flow control valve | • Inspect for varnish or damage, replace if necessary |
| Excessive wheel kickback or loose steering | • Air in system | • Add oil to pump reservoir and bleed by operating steering. Check hose connectors for proper torque and adjust as required. |
| Low pump pressure | • Extreme wear of cam ring<br>• Scored pressure plate, thrust plate, or rotor<br>• Vanes not installed properly<br>• Vanes sticking in rotor slots<br><br>• Cracked or broken thrust or pressure plate | • Replace parts. Flush system.<br>• Replace parts. Flush system.<br><br>• Install properly<br>• Freeup by removing burrs, varnish, or dirt<br>• Replace part |

## Troubleshooting Basic Steering and Suspension Problems

| Problem | Cause | Solution |
| --- | --- | --- |
| Hard steering (steering wheel is hard to turn) | • Low or uneven tire pressure<br>• Loose power steering pump drive belt<br>• Low or incorrect power steering fluid<br>• Incorrect front end alignment<br><br>• Defective power steering pump<br>• Bent or poorly lubricated front end parts | • Inflate tires to correct pressure<br>• Adjust belt<br><br>• Add fluid as necessary<br><br>• Have front end alignment checked/adjusted<br>• Check pump<br>• Lubricate and/or replace defective parts |
| Loose steering (too much play in the steering wheel) | • Loose wheel bearings<br>• Loose or worn steering linkage<br>• Faulty shocks<br>• Worn ball joints | • Adjust wheel bearings<br>• Replace worn parts<br>• Replace shocks<br>• Replace ball joints |
| Car veers or wanders (car pulls to one side with hands off the steering wheel) | • Incorrect tire pressure<br>• Improper front end alignment<br><br>• Loose wheel bearings<br>• Loose or bent front end components<br>• Faulty shocks | • Inflate tires to correct pressure<br>• Have front end alignment checked/adjusted<br>• Adjust wheel bearings<br>• Replace worn components<br><br>• Replace shocks |
| Wheel oscillation or vibration transmitted through steering wheel | • Improper tire pressures<br>• Tires out of balance<br>• Loose wheel bearings<br>• Improper front end alignment<br><br>• Worn or bent front end components | • Inflate tires to correct pressure<br>• Have tires balanced<br>• Adjust wheel bearings<br>• Have front end alignment checked/adjusted<br>• Replace worn parts |
| Uneven tire wear | • Incorrect tire pressure<br>• Front end out of alignment<br><br>• Tires out of balance | • Inflate tires to correct pressure<br>• Have front end alignment checked/adjusted<br>• Have tires balanced |

## STEERING

The A-Body cars use an aluminum-housed Saginaw manual rack and pinion steering gear as standard equipment. The pinion is supported by and turns in a sealed ball bearing at the top and a pressed-in roller bearing at the bottom. The rack moves in bushings pressed into each end of the rack housing.

Wear compensation occurs through the action of an adjuster spring which forces the rack against the pinion teeth. This adjuster eliminates the need for periodic pinion preload adjustments. Preload is adjustable only at overhaul.

The inner tie rod assemblies are both threaded and staked to the rack. A special joint is used, allowing both rocking and rotating motion of the tie rods. The inner tie rod assemblies are lubricated for life and require no periodic attention.

Any service other than replacement of the outer tie rods or the boots requires removal of the unit from the car.

The optional power rack and pinion steering gear is an integral unit, and shares most features with the manual gear. A rotary control valve directs the hydraulic fluid to either side of the rack piston. The integral rack piston is attached to the rack and converts the hydraulic pressure into left or right linear motion. A vane-type constant displacement pump with integral reservoir provides hydraulic pressure. No in-car adjustments are necessary or possible on the system, except for periodic belt tension checks and adjustments for the pump.

### Steering Wheel
#### REMOVAL AND INSTALLATION

CAUTION: *Disconnect the battery ground cable before removing the steering wheel. When installing a steering wheel, always make sure that the turn signal lever is in the neutral position.*

1. Remove the trim retaining screws from behind the wheel. On wheels with a center cap, pull off the cap.
2. Lift the trim off and pull the horn wires from the turn signal canceling cam.
3. Remove the retainer and the steering wheel nut.
4. Mark the wheel-to-shaft relationship, and then remove the wheel with a puller.
5. Install the wheel on the shaft aligning the previously made marks. Tighten the nut.
6. Insert the horn wires into the canceling cam.
7. Install the center trim and reconnect the battery cable.

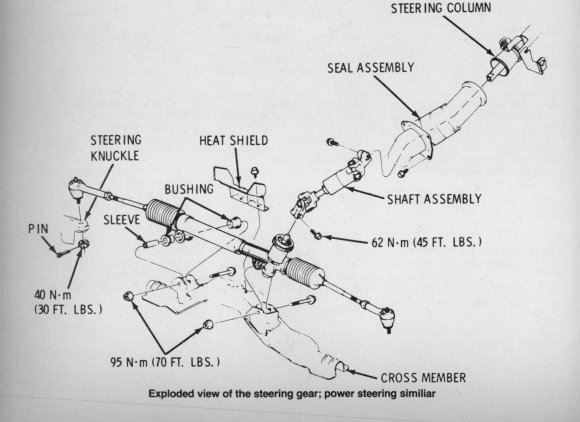

Exploded view of the steering gear; power steering similiar

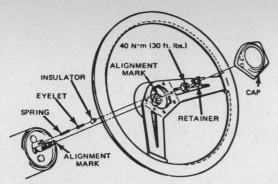

**Sport steering wheel removal**

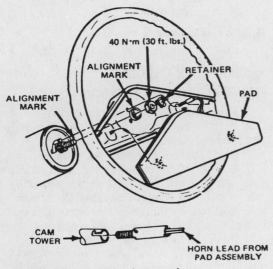

**Standard steering wheel removal**

the turn signal switch connector. When install-ing the turn signal switch, feed this wire through the column first, and then use this wire to pull the switch connector into position. On tilt wheels, place the turn signal and shifter housing in low position and remove the harness cover.

8. Remove the three switch mounting screws. Remove the switch by pulling it straight up while guiding the wiring harness cover through the column.

9. Install the replacement switch by working the connector and cover down through the housing and under the bracket. On tilt models, the connector is worked down through the housing, under the bracket, and then the cover is installed on the harness.

10. Install the switch mounting screws and

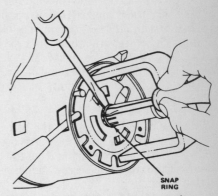

**Depress the lockplate and remove the snapring**

## Turn Signal Switch
### REMOVAL AND INSTALLATION

1. Remove the steering wheel as previously outlined. Remove the trim cover.

2. Loosen the cover screws. Pry the cover off with a screwdriver, and lift the cover off the shaft.

3. Position the U-shaped lockplate compress-ing tool on the end of the steering shaft and compress the lock plate by turning the shaft nut clockwise. Pry the wire snapring out of the shaft groove.

4. Remove the tool and lift the lock plate off the shaft.

5. Slip the canceling cam, upper bearing pre-load spring, and thrust washer off the shaft.

6. Remove the turn signal lever. Push the flasher knob in and unscrew it. Remove the button retaining screw and remove the button, spring and knob.

7. Pull the switch connector out the mast jacket and tape the upper part to facilitate switch removal. Attach a long piece of wire to

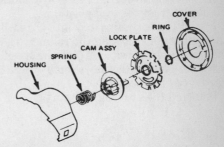

**Remove these parts for access to the turn signal switch**

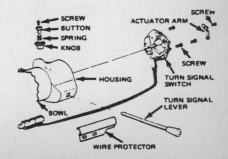

**Turn signal switch**

the connector on the mast jacket bracket. Install the column-to-dash trim plate.

11. Install the flasher knob and the turn signal lever.

12. With the turn signal lever in neutral and the flasher know out, slide the thrust washer, upper bearing preload spring, and canceling cam onto the shaft.

13. Position the lock plate on the shaft and press it down until a new snapring can be inserted in the shaft groove. Always use a new snapring when assembling.

14. Install the cover and the steering wheel.

## Ignition Switch
### REMOVAL AND INSTALLATION

The switch is located inside the channel section of the brake pedal support and is completely inaccessible without first lowering the steering column. The switch is actuated by a rod and rack assembly. A gear on the end of the lock cylinder engages the toothed upper end of the rod.

1. Lower the steering column; be sure to properly support it.

2. Put the switch in the Off-Unlocked position. With the cylinder removed, the rod is in Lock when it is in the next to the uppermost detent. Off-Unlocked is two detents from the top.

3. Remove the two switch screws and remove the switch assembly.

4. Before installing, place the new switch in Off-Unlocked position and make sure the lock cylinder and actuating rod are in Off-Unlocked (third detent from the top) position.

5. Install the activating rod into the switch and assemble the switch on the column. Tighten the mounting screws. Use only the specified screws since overlength screws could impair the collapsibility of the column.

6. Reinstall the steering column.

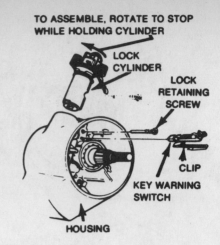

**Ignition lock cylinder**

## Ignition Lock Cylinder
### REMOVAL AND INSTALLATION

1. Place the lock in the Run position.

2. Remove the lock plate, turn signal switch and buzzer switch.

3. Remove the screw and lock cylinder.

CAUTION: *If the screw is dropped on removal, it could fall into the column, requiring complete disassembly to retrieve the screw.*

4. Rotate the cylinder clockwise to align cylinder key with the keyway in the housing.

5. Push the lock all the way in.

6. Install the screw. Tighten the screw to 14 inch lb. for adjustable columns and 25 inch lb. for standard columns.

## Steering Column

NOTE: *Once the steering column is removed from the car, the column is extremely susceptible to damage. Dropping the column assembly on its end could collapse the steering shaft or loosen the plastic injections which main-*

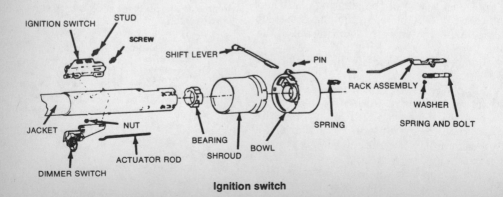

**Ignition switch**

*tain column rigidity. Leaning on the column assembly could cause the jacket to bend or deform. Any of the above damage could impair the column's collapsible design. If it is necessary to remove the steering wheel, use a standard wheel puller. Under no condition should the end of the shaft be hammered upon, as hammering could loosen the plastic injection which maintains column rigidity.*

### REMOVAL AND INSTALLATION

1. Disconnect the negative battery cable.
2. If column repairs are to be made, remove the steering wheel.
3. Remove the nuts and bolts attaching the flexible coupling to the bottom of the steering column. Remove the safety strap and bolt if equipped.
4. Remove the steering column trim shrouds and column covers.
5. Disconnect all wiring harness connectors. Remove the dust boot mounting screws and column mounting bracket bolts.
6. Lower the column to clear the mounting bracket and carefully remove from the car.

**To install:**

7. Install the column into the vehicle and raise it into the mounting bracket.
8. Loosely install the column mounting bolts and connect all wiring harness connectors.
9. Tighten the column mounting bolts and install the trim shrouds and column covers.
10. Install and tighten the nuts and bolts in the flexible coupling at the bottom of the steering shaft.
11. Install the steering wheel and connect the battery cable.

## Steering Linkage
### REMOVAL AND INSTALLATION

**Tie Rod Ends**

1. Loosen the jam nut on the steering rack (inner tie rod).
2. Remove the tie rod end nut. Separate the tie rod end from the steering knuckle using a puller tool J-6627 or BT-7101.
3. Unscrew the tie rod end, counting the number of turns.
4. To install, screw the tie rod end onto the steering rack (inner tie rod) the same number of turns as counted for removal. This will give approximately correct toe.
5. Install the tie rod end into the knuckle. Install the nut and tighten to 40 ft.lb. (1982-84) or 30 ft.lb. (1985-88).
6. If the toe must be adjusted, use pliers to

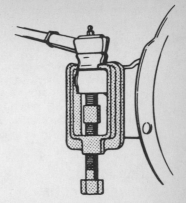

Separate the tie-rod end from the knuckle with a puller

expand the boot clamp. Turn the inner tie rod to adjust. Replace the clamp.

7. Tighten the jam nut to 44 ft.lb.

## Power Rack and Pinion Steering Gear
### REMOVAL AND INSTALLATION

1. Raise the intermediate shaft seal and remove intermediate shaft-to-stub shaft pinch bolt.
2. If equipped with power steering, remove the air cleaner and disconnect the pressure hoses from the steering gear.
3. Raise and support the vehicle on jackstands, then remove both front wheel and tire assemblies.
4. Remove the cotter pins and nuts from both tie rod ends. Using tool J-6627 or BT-7101, press the tie rod ends from the steering knuckle.
5. If equipped with an Air Management pipe, remove the bracket bolt from the crossmember.
6. Remove the 2 rear cradle mounting bolts and lower the rear of the cradle about 4-5".

CAUTION: *If the rear of the cradle is lowered to far, the engine components nearest the cowl may be damaged.*

7. If equipped, remove the rack and pinion heat shield.
8. Remove the rack and pinion mounting bolts, then the gear assembly through the left wheel opening.
9. To install:
10. Install the gear assembly through the left wheel opening and install the mounting bolts.
11. Install the heat shield.
12. Raise the rear of the cradle and install the mounting bolts.
13. Install the bracket bolt to the crossmember under the air management pipe.
14. Install the tie rod ends to the steering

knuckles, install the retaining nuts and insert new cotter pins.

15. Install the front wheels and lower the vehicle.

16. Install the high pressure hoses to the steering gear and install the air cleaner.

17. Install the intermediate shaft seal and the intermediate shaft-to-stub shaft pinch bolt.

NOTE: *If equipped with power steering, reconnect the pressure hoses and bleed the system.*

## Power Steering Pump
### REMOVAL AND INSTALLATION
#### Gasoline Engines

All models use integral rack and pinion power steering. A pump delivers hydraulic pressure through two hoses to the steering gear itself.

1. Remove the hoses at the pump and tape the openings shut to prevent contamination. Position the disconnected lines in a raised position to prevent leakage.

2. Remove the pump belt.

3. On the four cylinder, remove the radiator hose clamp bolt. On the 6-173, disconnect the negative battery cable, disconnect the electrical connector at the blower motor, drain the cooling system, and remove the heater hose at the water pump. On the 6-183, remove the alternator.

4. Loosen the retaining bolts and any braces, and remove the pump.

5. Install the pump on the engine with the retaining bolts handtight.

6. Connect and tighten the hose fittings.

7. Refill the pump with fluid and bleed the system.

8. Install the pump belt on the pulley and adjust the tension.

9. Remove the tape and install the power steering pump hoses.

#### Diesel Engine

1. Remove the drive belt.

2. Siphon the fluid from the power steering reservoir.

NOTE: *On some models, it may be necessary to remove the right front wheel.*

3. Disconnect the hoses from the pump.

4. Remove the three bolts from the front of the pump through the access holes in the pulley.

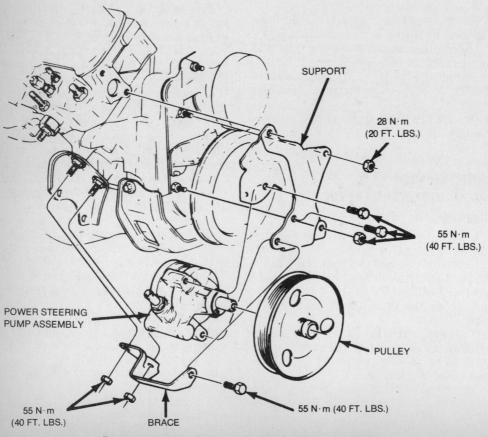

SUPPORT

28 N·m
(20 FT. LBS.)

55 N·m
(40 FT. LBS.)

POWER STEERING
PUMP ASSEMBLY

PULLEY

55 N·m
(40 FT. LBS.)

BRACE

55 N·m (40 FT. LBS.)

**Power steering pump removal, 6-183—others are similiar**

5. Remove the two nuts holding the lower brace to the engine. Remove the brace.

6. Remove the pump.

7. To install, reverse steps 1 through 6. Torque the brace nuts to 40 ft.lb.; the pump bolt to 40 ft.lb.

### BLEEDING

1. Fill the fluid reservoir.

2. Let the fluid stand undisturbed for two minutes, then crank the engine for about two seconds. Refill reservoir if necessary.

3. Repeat Steps 1 and 2 above until the fluid level remains constant after cranking the engine.

4. Raise the front of the car until the wheels are off the ground, then start the engine. Increase the engine speed to about 1,500 rpm.

5. Turn the wheels lightly against the stops to the left and right, checking the fluid level and refilling if necessary.

# Brakes

## BRAKE SYSTEM

## UNDERSTANDING THE BRAKE SYSTEM

### Hydraulic System

A hydraulic system is used to actuate the brakes. The system transports the power required to force the frictional surfaces of the braking system together from the pedal to the individual braking units at each wheel. A hydraulic system is used for three reasons. First, fluid under pressure can be carried to all parts of the automobile by small hoses, some of which are flexible, without taking up a significant amount of room or posing routine problems. Second, liquid is non-compressible; a hydraulic system can transport force without modifying or reducing that force. Third, a great mechanical advantage can be given to the brake pedal end of the system, and the foot pressure required to actuate the brakes can be reduced by making the surface area of the master cylinder pistons smaller than that of any of the pistons in the wheel cylinders or calipers.

The master cylinder consists of a fluid reservoir, a double cylinder and a piston assembly. Double type master cylinders are designed to separate the front and rear braking systems hydraulically in case of a leak.

Steel lines carry the brake fluid to a point on the vehicle's frame near each of the vehicle's wheels. The fluid is then carried to the slave cylinder by flexible tubes in order to allow for suspension and steering movements.

In drum brake systems, the slave cylinders are called wheel cylinders. Each wheel cylinder contains two pistons, one at either end, which push outward in opposite directions.

In disc brake systems, the slave cylinders are part of the calipers. One large cylinder is used to force the brake pads against the disc. All slave cylinder pistons employ some type of seal, usually made of rubber, to minimize the leakage of fluid around the piston. A rubber dust boot seals the outer end of the cylinder against dust and dirt. The boot fits around the outer end of the piston on disc brake calipers and around the brake actuating rod on wheel cylinders.

The hydraulic system operates as follows: When at rest, the entire system, from the pistons in the master cylinder to those in the wheel cylinders or calipers, is full of brake fluid. Upon application of the brake pedal, fluid trapped in front of the master cylinder pistons is forced through the lines to the slave cylinders. Here, it forces the pistons outward, in the case of drum brakes, and inward toward the disc, in the case of disc brakes. The motion of the pistons is opposed by return springs mounted outside the cylinders in drum brakes.

Upon release of the brake pedal, a spring located inside the master cylinder immediately returns the master cylinder pistons to the normal position. The pistons contain check valves and the master cylinder has compensating ports drilled in it. These are uncovered as the pistons reach their normal position. The piston check valves allow fluid to flow toward the wheel cylinders or calipers as the master cylinder pistons withdraw. Then, as the return springs force the shoes into the released position, the excess fluid returns to the master cylinder fluid reservoir through the compensating ports. It is during the time the pedal is in the released position that any fluid that has leaked out of the system will be replaced through the compensating ports.

Dual circuit master cylinders employ two pistons, located one behind the other, in the same cylinder. The primary piston is actuated by fluid trapped between the two pistons. If a leak develops in front of the secondary piston, it moves forward until it bottoms against the front of the

# Troubleshooting the Brake System

| Problem | Cause | Solution |
|---|---|---|
| Low brake pedal (excessive pedal travel required for braking action.) | • Excessive clearance between rear linings and drums caused by in-operative automatic adjusters | • Make 10 to 15 alternate forward and reverse brake stops to adjust brakes. If brake pedal does not come up, repair or replace adjuster parts as necessary. |
| | • Worn rear brakelining | • Inspect and replace lining if worn beyond minimum thickness specification |
| | • Bent, distorted brakeshoes, front or rear | • Replace brakeshoes in axle sets |
| | • Air in hydraulic system | • Remove air from system. Refer to Brake Bleeding. |
| Low brake pedal (pedal may go to floor with steady pressure applied.) | • Fluid leak in hydraulic system | • Fill master cylinder to fill line; have helper apply brakes and check calipers, wheel cylinders, differential valve tubes, hoses and fittings for leaks. Repair or replace as necessary. |
| | • Air in hydraulic system | • Remove air from system. Refer to Brake Bleeding. |
| | • Incorrect or non-recommended brake fluid (fluid evaporates at below normal temp). | • Flush hydraulic system with clean brake fluid. Refill with correct-type fluid. |
| | • Master cylinder piston seals worn, or master cylinder bore is scored, worn or corroded | • Repair or replace master cylinder |
| Low brake pedal (pedal goes to floor on first application—o.k. on subsequent applications.) | • Disc brake pads sticking on abutment surfaces of anchor plate. Caused by a build-up of dirt, rust, or corrosion on abutment surfaces | • Clean abutment surfaces |
| Fading brake pedal (pedal height decreases with steady pressure applied.) | • Fluid leak in hydraulic system | • Fill master cylinder reservoirs to fill mark, have helper apply brakes, check calipers, wheel cylinders, differential valve, tubes, hoses, and fittings for fluid leaks. Repair or replace parts as necessary. |
| | • Master cylinder piston seals worn, or master cylinder bore is scored, worn or corroded | • Repair or replace master cylinder |
| Decreasing brake pedal travel (pedal travel required for braking action decreases and may be accompanied by a hard pedal.) | • Caliper or wheel cylinder pistons sticking or seized | • Repair or replace the calipers, or wheel cylinders |
| | • Master cylinder compensator ports blocked (preventing fluid return to reservoirs) or pistons sticking or seized in master cylinder bore | • Repair or replace the master cylinder |
| | • Power brake unit binding internally | • Test unit according to the following procedure:<br>(a) Shift transmission into neutral and start engine<br>(b) Increase engine speed to 1500 rpm, close throttle and fully depress brake pedal<br>(c) Slow release brake pedal and stop engine<br>(d) Have helper remove vacuum check valve and hose from power unit. Observe for backward movement of brake pedal.<br>(e) If the pedal moves backward, the power unit has an internal bind—replace power unit |

## Troubleshooting the Brake System (cont.)

| Problem | Cause | Solution |
|---|---|---|
| Spongy brake pedal (pedal has abnormally soft, springy, spongy feel when depressed.) | • Air in hydraulic system<br><br>• Brakeshoes bent or distorted<br>• Brakelining not yet seated with drums and rotors<br>• Rear drum brakes not properly adjusted | • Remove air from system. Refer to Brake Bleeding.<br>• Replace brakeshoes<br>• Burnish brakes<br><br>• Adjust brakes |
| Hard brake pedal (excessive pedal pressure required to stop vehicle. May be accompanied by brake fade.) | • Loose or leaking power brake unit vacuum hose<br>• Incorrect or poor quality brakelining<br>• Bent, broken, distorted brakeshoes<br>• Calipers binding or dragging on mounting pins. Rear brakeshoes dragging on support plate.<br><br><br><br><br><br><br><br>• Caliper, wheel cylinder, or master cylinder pistons sticking or seized<br>• Power brake unit vacuum check valve malfunction<br><br><br><br><br><br><br><br>• Power brake unit has internal bind<br><br><br><br><br><br><br><br><br><br><br><br><br><br>• Master cylinder compensator ports (at bottom of reservoirs) blocked by dirt, scale, rust, or have small burrs (blocked ports prevent fluid return to reservoirs).<br>• Brake hoses, tubes, fittings clogged or restricted<br><br>• Brake fluid contaminated with improper fluids (motor oil, transmission fluid, causing rubber components to swell and stick in bores<br>• Low engine vacuum | • Tighten connections or replace leaking hose<br>• Replace with lining in axle sets<br><br>• Replace brakeshoes<br>• Replace mounting pins and bushings. Clean rust or burrs from rear brake support plate ledges and lubricate ledges with molydisulfide grease.<br>**NOTE:** If ledges are deeply grooved or scored, do not attempt to sand or grind them smooth—replace support plate.<br>• Repair or replace parts as necessary<br><br>• Test valve according to the following procedure:<br>(a) Start engine, increase engine speed to 1500 rpm, close throttle and immediately stop engine<br>(b) Wait at least 90 seconds then depress brake pedal<br>(c) If brakes are not vacuum assisted for 2 or more applications, check valve is faulty<br>• Test unit according to the following procedure:<br>(a) With engine stopped, apply brakes several times to exhaust all vacuum in system<br>(b) Shift transmission into neutral, depress brake pedal and start engine<br>(c) If pedal height decreases with foot pressure and less pressure is required to hold pedal in applied position, power unit vacuum system is operating normally. Test power unit. If power unit exhibits a bind condition, replace the power unit.<br>• Repair or replace master cylinder<br>**CAUTION:** Do not attempt to clean blocked ports with wire, pencils, or similar implements. Use compressed air only.<br>• Use compressed air to check or unclog parts. Replace any damaged parts.<br>• Replace all rubber components, combination valve and hoses. Flush entire brake system with DOT 3 brake fluid or equivalent.<br>• Adjust or repair engine |

## Troubleshooting the Brake System (cont.)

| Problem | Cause | Solution |
|---|---|---|
| Grabbing brakes (severe reaction to brake pedal pressure.) | • Brakelining(s) contaminated by grease or brake fluid | • Determine and correct cause of contamination and replace brakeshoes in axle sets |
| | • Parking brake cables incorrectly adjusted or seized | • Adjust cables. Replace seized cables. |
| | • Incorrect brakelining or lining loose on brakeshoes | • Replace brakeshoes in axle sets |
| | • Caliper anchor plate bolts loose | • Tighten bolts |
| | • Rear brakeshoes binding on support plate ledges | • Clean and lubricate ledges. Replace support plate(s) if ledges are deeply grooved. Do not attempt to smooth ledges by grinding. |
| | • Incorrect or missing power brake reaction disc | • Install correct disc |
| | • Rear brake support plates loose | • Tighten mounting bolts |
| Dragging brakes (slow or incomplete release of brakes) | • Brake pedal binding at pivot | • Loosen and lubricate |
| | • Power brake unit has internal bind | • Inspect for internal bind. Replace unit if internal bind exists. |
| | • Parking brake cables incorrrectly adjusted or seized | • Adjust cables. Replace seized cables. |
| | • Rear brakeshoe return springs weak or broken | • Replace return springs. Replace brakeshoe if necessary in axle sets. |
| | • Automatic adjusters malfunctioning | • Repair or replace adjuster parts as required |
| | • Caliper, wheel cylinder or master cylinder pistons sticking or seized | • Repair or replace parts as necessary |
| | • Master cylinder compensating ports blocked (fluid does not return to reservoirs). | • Use compressed air to clear ports. Do not use wire, pencils, or similar objects to open blocked ports. |
| Vehicle moves to one side when brakes are applied | • Incorrect front tire pressure | • Inflate to recommended cold (reduced load) inflation pressure |
| | • Worn or damaged wheel bearings | • Replace worn or damaged bearings |
| | • Brakelining on one side contaminated | • Determine and correct cause of contamination and replace brakelining in axle sets |
| | • Brakeshoes on one side bent, distorted, or lining loose on shoe | • Replace brakeshoes in axle sets |
| | • Support plate bent or loose on one side | • Tighten or replace support plate |
| | • Brakelining not yet seated with drums or rotors | • Burnish brakelining |
| | • Caliper anchor plate loose on one side | • Tighten anchor plate bolts |
| | • Caliper piston sticking or seized | • Repair or replace caliper |
| | • Brakelinings water soaked | • Drive vehicle with brakes lightly applied to dry linings |
| | • Loose suspension component attaching or mounting bolts | • Tighten suspension bolts. Replace worn suspension components. |
| | • Brake combination valve failure | • Replace combination valve |
| Chatter or shudder when brakes are applied (pedal pulsation and roughness may also occur.) | • Brakeshoes distorted, bent, contaminated, or worn | • Replace brakeshoes in axle sets |
| | • Caliper anchor plate or support plate loose | • Tighten mounting bolts |
| | • Excessive thickness variation of rotor(s) | • Refinish or replace rotors in axle sets |
| Noisy brakes (squealing, clicking, scraping sound when brakes are applied.) | • Bent, broken, distorted brakeshoes | • Replace brakeshoes in axle sets |
| | • Excessive rust on outer edge of rotor braking surface | • Remove rust |

## Troubleshooting the Brake System (cont.)

| Problem | Cause | Solution |
|---|---|---|
| Noisy brakes (squealing, clicking, scraping sound when brakes are applied.) (cont.) | • Brakelining worn out—shoes contacting drum of rotor | • Replace brakeshoes and lining in axle sets. Refinish or replace drums or rotors. |
| | • Broken or loose holdown or return springs | • Replace parts as necessary |
| | • Rough or dry drum brake support plate ledges | • Lubricate support plate ledges |
| | • Cracked, grooved, or scored rotor(s) or drum(s) | • Replace rotor(s) or drum(s). Replace brakeshoes and lining in axle sets if necessary. |
| | • Incorrect brakelining and/or shoes (front or rear). | • Install specified shoe and lining assemblies |
| Pulsating brake pedal | • Out of round drums or excessive lateral runout in disc brake rotor(s) | • Refinish or replace drums, re-index rotors or replace |

master cylinder and the fluid trapped between the pistons will operate the rear brakes. If the rear brakes develop a leak, the primary piston will move forward until direct contact with the secondary piston takes place and it will force the secondary piston to actuate the front brakes. In either case, the brake pedal moves farther when the brakes are applied and less braking power is available.

All dual circuit systems use a distributor switch to warn the driver when only half of the brake system is operational. This switch is located in a valve body which is mounted on the master cylinder. A hydraulic piston receives pressure from both circuits, each circuit's pressure being applied to one end of the piston. When the pressures are in balance, the piston remains stationary. When one circuit has a leak, however, the greater pressure in that circuit during application of the brakes will push the piston to one side, closing the distributor switch and activating the brake warning light.

In disc brake systems, this valve body also contains a metering valve and, in some cases, a proportioning valve. The metering valve keeps pressure from traveling to the disc brakes on the front wheels until the brake shoes on the rear wheels have contacted the drums, ensuring that the front brakes will never be used alone. The proportioning valve throttles the pressure to the rear brakes so as to avoid rear wheel lock-up during very hard braking.

These valves may be tested by removing the lines to the front and rear brake systems and installing special brake pressure testing gauge. Front and rear system pressures are then compared as the pedal is gradually depressed. Specifications vary with the manufacturer and design of the brake systems.

Brake warning lights may be tested by depressing the brake pedal and holding it while opening one of the wheel cylinder bleeder screws. If this does not cause the light to go on, substitute a new lamp, make continuity checks, and finally, replace the switch as necessary.

The hydraulic system may be checked for leaks by applying pressure to the pedal gradually and steadily. If the pedal sinks very slowly to the floor, the system has a leak. This is not to be confused with a springy or spongy feel due to the compression of air within the lines. If the system leaks, there will be a gradual change in the position of the pedal with a constant pressure.

Check for leaks along all lines and at wheel cylinder. If no external leaks are apparent, the problem is inside the master cylinder.

### Disc Brakes

Instead of the traditional expanding brakes that press outward against a circular drum, disc brake systems utilize a cast iron disc with brake pads positioned on either side of it. Braking effect is achieved in a manner similar to the way you would squeeze a spinning phonograph record between your fingers. The disc (rotor) is a one-piece casting with cooling fins between the two braking surfaces. This enables air to circulate between the braking surfaces making them less sensitive to heat buildup and more resistant to fade. Dirt and water do not affect braking action since contaminants are thrown off by the centrifugal action of the rotor or scraped off by the pads. Also, the equal clamp action of the two brake pads tends to ensure uniform, straightline stops. All disc brakes are self-adjusting.

### Drum Brakes

Drum brakes employ two brake shoes mounted on a stationary backing plate. These shoes are positioned inside a circular cast iron drum which rotates with the wheel assembly. The shoes are held in place by springs; this allows them to slide toward the drums (when they are applied) while keeping the linings and drums in alignment. The shoes are actuated by a wheel cylinder which is mounted at the top of the backing plate. When the brakes are applied, hydraulic pressure forces the wheel cylinder's two actuating links outward. Since these links bear directly against the top of the brake shoes, the tops of the shoes are then forced outward against the inner side of the drum. This action forces the bottoms of the two shoes to contact the brake drum by rotating the entire assembly slightly (known as servo action). When pressure within the wheel cylinder is relaxed, return springs pull the shoes back away from the drum.

The drum brakes are designed to self-adjust during application when the car is moving in reverse. This motion causes both shoes to rotate very slightly with the drum, rocking an adjusting lever, thereby causing rotation of the adjusting screw by means of an actuating lever.

## Power Brake Boosters

Power brakes operate just as standard brake systems except in the actuation of the master cylinder pistons. A vacuum diaphragm is located on the front of the master cylinder and assists the driver in applying the brakes, reducing both the effort and travel he must put into moving the brake pedal.

The vacuum diaphragm housing is connected to the intake manifold by a vacuum hose. A check valve is placed at the point where the hose enters the diaphragm housing, so that during periods of low manifold vacuum brake assist vacuum will not be lost.

Depressing the brake pedal closes off the vacuum source and allows atmospheric pressure to enter on one side of the diaphragm. This causes the master cylinder pistons to move and apply the brakes. When the brake pedal is released, vacuum is applied to both sides of the diaphragm, the return springs return the diaphragm and master cylinder pistons to the released position. If the vacuum fails, the brake pedal rod will butt against the end of the master cylinder actuating rod and direct mechanical application will occur as the pedal is depressed.

The hydraulic and mechanical problems that apply to conventional brake systems also apply to power brakes and should be checked if the following tests do not reveal the problem.

The hydraulic and mechanical problems that apply to conventional brake systems also apply to power brakes and should be checked if the following tests do not reveal the problem.

Test for a system vacuum leak as described below:

1. Operate the engine at idle with the transaxle in Neutral without touching the brake pedal for at least one minute.
2. Turn off the engine and wait one minute.
3. Test for the presence of assist vacuum by depressing the brake pedal and releasing it several times. Light application will produce less and less pedal travel, if vacuum was present. If there is no vacuum air is leaking into the system.

Test for system operation as follows:

1. Pump the brake pedal (with engine off) until the supply vacuum is entirely gone.
2. Put a light, steady pressure on the pedal.
3. Start the engine and operate it at idle with the transaxle in Neutral. If the system is operating, the brake pedal should fall toward the floor if constant pressure is maintained on the pedal. Power brake systems may be tested for hydraulic leaks just as ordinary systems are tested, except that the engine should be idling with the transaxle in neutral throughout the test.

## BRAKE SYSTEM

The A-Body cars have a diagonally split hydraulic system. This differs from conventional practice in that the left front and right rear brakes are on one hydraulic circuit, and the right front and left rear are on the other.

A diagonally split system necessitates the use of a special master cylinder design. The A-Body master cylinder incorporates the functions of a standard tandem master cylinder, plus a warning light switch and proportioning valves. Additionally, the master cylinder is designed with a quick take-up feature which provides a large volume of fluid to the brakes at low pressure when the brakes are initially applied. The lower pressure fluid acts to quickly fill the large displacement requirements of the system.

The front disc brakes are single piston sliding caliper units. Fluid pressure acts equally against the piston and the bottom of the piston bore in the caliper. This forces the piston outward until the pad contacts the caliper to slide over, carrying the other pad into contact with the other side of the rotor. The disc brakes are self-adjusting.

Rear drum brakes are conventional duo-servo units. A dual piston wheel cylinder mounted to the top of the backing plate, actuates both brake shoes. Wheel cylinder force to the shoes is supplemented by the tendency of the shoes to wrap into the drum (servo action). An actuating link, pivot and lever serve to automatically engage the adjuster as the brakes are applied when the car is moving in reverse. Provisions for manual adjustment are also provided. The rear brakes also serve as the parking brakes; linkage is mechanical. Vacuum boost is an option. The booster is a conventional tandem vacuum unit.

## Adjustment

### DISC BRAKES

The front disc brakes are self-adjusting. No adjustments are either necessary or possible.

### DRUM BRAKES

The drum brakes are designed to self-adjust when applied with the car moving in reverse. however, they can also be adjusted manually. This manual adjustment should also be performed whenever the linings are replaced.

1. Use a punch to knock out the stamped area on the brake drum. If this is done with the drum installed on the car, the drum must then be removed to clean out all metal pieces. After adjustments are complete, obtain a hole cover from your dealer (Part no. 4874119 or the equivalent) to present entry of dirt and water into the brakes.

2. Use an adjusting tool especially made for the purpose to turn the brake adjusting screw star wheel. Expand the shoes until the drum can just barely be turned by hand.

3. Back off the adjusting screw a few notches. If the shoes still are dragging lightly, back off the adjusting screw one or two additional notches. If the brakes still drag, the parking brake adjustment is incorrect or the parking brake is applied. Fix and start over.

4. Install the hole cover into the drum.

5. Check the parking brake adjustment.

On some models, no marked area or stamped area is present on the drum. In this case, a hole must be drilled in the backing plate:

1. All backing plates have two round flat areas in the lower half through which the parking brake cable is installed. Drill a ½" hole into the round flat area on the backing plate opposite the parking brake cable. This will allow access to the star wheel.

2. After drilling the hole, remove the drum and remove all metal particles. Install a hole plug (Part no. 4874119 or the equivalent) to prevent the entry of water or dirt.

## Brake Light Switch

### REMOVAL AND INSTALLATION

1. Disconnect the wiring connectors from the brake light switch.

2. Unscrew the brake light switch from the tubular retaining clip.

3. Insert the new switch into the retainer until the switch body seats against the clip.

4. Connect the wiring connectors.

5. Pull the brake pedal rearward against the internal pedal stop. The switch will be moved in the tubular clip providing proper adjustment.

## Master Cylinder

### REMOVAL AND INSTALLATION

1. If your car does not have power brakes, disconnect the master cylinder pushrod at the brake pedal inside the car. The pushrod is retained to the brake pedal by a clip; there is a washer under the clip, and a spring washer on the other side of the pushrod.

2. Unplug the electrical connector from the master cylinder.

3. Place a number of cloths or a container under the master cylinder to catch the brake fluid. Disconnect the brake tubes from the master cylinder; use a flare nut wrench if one is available. Tape over the open ends of the tubes.

NOTE: *Brake fluid eats paint. Wipe up any spilled fluid immediately, then flush the area with clean water.*

4. Remove the two nuts attaching the master cylinder to the booster or firewall.

5. Remove the master cylinder.

6. To install, attach the master cylinder to the firewall or the booster with the nuts. Torque to 29 ft.lb. (40 Nm) for 1982-84 or 22 ft.lb. (27 Nm) for 1985-88.

7. Reconnect the pushrod to the brake pedal with non-power brakes.

8. Remove the tape from the lines and connect to the master cylinder. Torque to 12 ft.lb.

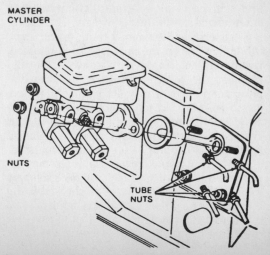

MASTER CYLINDER

NUTS

TUBE NUTS

**Master cylinder removal; power brakes similar**

(17 Nm) for 1982-84 or 18 ft.lb. (24 Nm) for 1985-88. Connect the electrical lead.

9. Bleed the brakes.

## OVERHAUL

This is a tedious, time consuming job. You can save yourself a lot of trouble by buying a rebuilt master cylinder from your dealer or parts supply house. The small difference in price between a rebuilding kit and a rebuilt part usually makes it more economical, in terms of time and work, to buy the rebuilt part.

1. Remove the master cylinder.

2. Remove the reservoir cover and drain the fluid.

3. Remove the pushrod and the rubber boot on non-power models.

4. Unbolt the proportioners and the failure warning switch from the side of the master cylinder body. Discard the O-rings found under the proportioners. Use new ones on installation. There may or may not be an O-ring under the original equipment failure warning switch. If there is, discard it. In either case, use a new O-ring upon assembly.

5. Clamp the master cylinder body in a vise, taking care not to crush it. Depress the primary piston with a wooden dowel and remove the lock ring with a pair of snapring pliers.

6. The primary and secondary pistons can be removed by applying compressed air into one of the outlets at the end of the cylinder and plugging the other three outlets. The primary piston must be replaced as an assembly if the seals are bad. The secondary piston seals are replaceable. Install these new seals with the lips facing outwards.

7. Inspect the bore for corrosion. If any corrosion is evident, the master cylinder body must be replaced. Do not attempt to polish the bore with crocus cloth, sandpaper or anything else. The body is aluminum; polishing the bore won't work.

8. To remove the failure warning switch piston assembly, remove the allen head plug from the end of the bore and withdraw the assembly with a pair of needlenosed pliers. The switch piston assembly seals are replaceable.

9. The reservoir can be removed from the master cylinder if necessary. Clamp the body in a vise by its mounting flange. Use a pry bar to remove the reservoir. If the reservoir is removed, remove the reservoir grommets and discard them. The quick take-up valves under the grommets are accessible after the retaining snaprings are removed. Use snapring pliers; no other tool will work.

10. Clean all parts in denatured alcohol and allow to air dry. Do not use anything else to clean and do not wipe dry with a rag, which will leaves bits of lint behind. Inspect all parts for corrosion or wear. Generally, it is best to replace all rubber parts whenever the master cylinder is disassembled and replace any metal part which shows any sign of wear or corrosion.

11. Lubricate all parts with clean brake fluid before assembly.

12. Install the quick take-up valves into the master cylinder body and secure with the snaprings. Make sure the snaprings are properly seated in their grooves. Lubricate the new reservoir grommets with clean brake fluid and press them into the master cylinder.

13. Install the reservoir into the grommets by placing the reservoir on its lid and pressing the master cylinder body down onto it with a rocking motion.

14. Lubricate the switch piston assembly with clean brake fluid. Install new O-rings and retainers on the piston. Install the piston assembly into the master cylinder and secure with the plug, using a new O-ring on the plug. Torque is 40-140 in.lb. (5-16 Nm).

15. Assemble the new secondary piston seals onto the piston. Lubricate the parts with clean brake fluid, then install the spring, spring retainer and secondary piston into the cylinder. Install the primary piston, depress and install the lock ring.

16. Install new O-rings on the proportioners and the failure warning switch. Install the proportioners and torque to 18-30 ft.lb. (25-40 Nm). Install the failure warning switch and torque to 15-50 in.lb. (2-6 Nm).

17. Clamp the master cylinder body upright into a vise by one of the mounting flanges. Fill the reservoir with fresh brake fluid. Pump the piston with a dowel until fluid squirts from the outlet ports. Continue pumping until the expelled fluid is free of air bubbles.

18. Install the master cylinder and bleed the brakes. Check the brake system for proper operation. Do not move the car until a "hard" brake pedal is obtained and the brake system has been thoroughly checked for soundness.

## Power Brake Booster

### REMOVAL AND INSTALLATION

1. Remove the master cylinder from the booster. It is not necessary to disconnect the lines from the master cylinder. Just move the cylinder aside.

2. Disconnect the vacuum booster pushrod from the brake pedal inside the car. It is retained by a bolt. A spring washer lies under the bolt head, and a flat washer goes on the other side of the pushrod eye, next to the pedal arm.

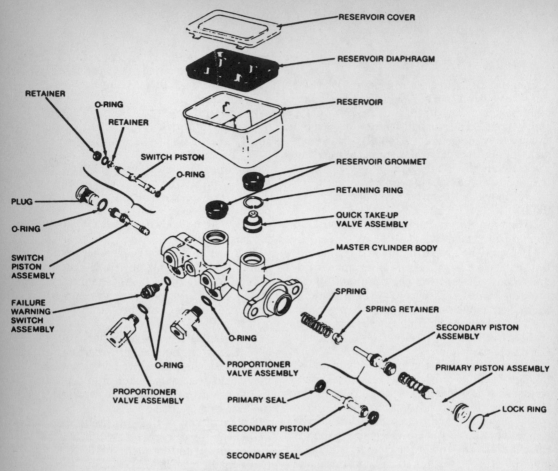

**Exploded view of the master cylinder**

3. Remove the four attaching nuts from inside the car. Remove the booster.

4. Install the booster on the firewall. Tighten the mounting nuts to 22 ft.lb. (30 Nm) for 1982-84 or 15 ft.lb. (21 Nm) for 1985-88.

5. Connect the pushrod to the brake pedal.

6. Install the master cylinder. Mounting torque is 29 ft.lb. (40 Nm) for 1982-84 or 22 ft.lb. (27 Nm) for 1985-88.

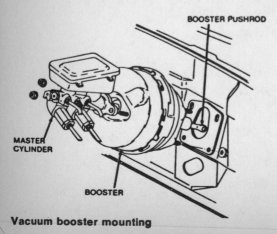

**Vacuum booster mounting**

### OVERHAUL

This job is not difficult, but requires a number of special tools which are expensive, especially if they're to be used only once. Generally, it's better to leave this job to your dealer, or buy a rebuilt vacuum booster and install it yourself.

## Hydro-Boost

Hydro-Boost differs from conventional power brake systems, in that it operates from power steering pump fluid pressure rather than intake manifold vacuum.

The Hydro-Boost unit contains a spool valve with an open center which controls the strength of the pump pressure when braking occurs. A lever assembly controls the valve's position. A boost piston provides the force necessary to operate the conventional master cylinder on the front of the booster.

A reserve of at least two assisted brake applications is supplied by an pneumatic accumulator. The accumulator is an integral part of the Hydro-Boost II unit. The brakes can be applied manually if the reserve system is depleted.

All system checks, tests and troubleshooting procedure are the same for the two systems.

1. Turn the engine off and pump the brake pedal 4 or 5 times to deplete the accumulator.

2. Remove the nuts from the master cylinder, then move the master cylinder away from the booster, with brake lines still attached.

3. Remove the hydraulic lines from the booster.

4. Remove the retainer and washer at the brake pedal.

5. Remove the attaching nuts retaining the booster fastened to the cowl and the booster.

6. To install, place the booster into position, reconnect the hydraulic lines, reconnect the booster rod to the brake pedal and torque the booster-to-cowl nuts to 15 ft.lb., and the master cylinder-to-booster nuts to 20 ft.lb. Bleed the power steering and hydro-booster system.

## Proportioning Valves and Failure Warning Switch

These parts are installed in the master cylinder body. No separate proportioning or metering valve is used. Replacement of these parts requires disassembly of the master cylinder.

## Brake Hoses

Brake hoses are rubber covered flex hoses designed to transmit brake pressure from the metal tubes running along the frame to the calipers in front and wheel cylinders in the rear. The calipers and wheel cylinders are unsprung (ride along with the wheels) and the metal brake lines coming from the master cylinder are suspended by the vehicle's springs, along with the frame and body. The flex hoses permit the hydraulic force of the brake fluid to be transmitted to the wheels even though they are moving up and down in relation to the frame. The flexing can cause the hoses to wear, especially if the surface of a hose should rub against the frame or a suspension component. Inspect the hoses frequently and replace them if the rubber cover has cracked or deteriorated, or if there is any sign of leakage.

### REMOVAL AND INSTALLATION

#### Front

1. Remove the through bolt that fastens the hose to the caliper. Remove the washers, noting that there is one on either side of the fitting at the caliper end of the hose, and disconnect the hose.

2. If there is a clip retaining the connection at the frame, remove it. Then, unscrew the flare fitting located on the pipe running along the frame, using a backup wrench on the flats of

the fitting at the end of the brake hose. Remove the brake line.

3. Install in reverse order, using new washers and torquing the connection at the caliper to 33 ft.lb. Bleed the system.

#### Rear

1. Remove the clips at either end of the hose. Unscrew the flared fitting located on the pipe running along the frame, using a backup wrench on the flats of the fitting at the end of the brake hose. Do the same with the flared fitting on the wheel cylinder end.

2. Install in reverse order. Bleed the system.

## Bleeding

The purpose of bleeding the brakes is to expel air trapped in the hydraulic system. The system must be bled whenever the pedal feels spongy, indicating that compressible air has entered the system. It must also be bled whenever the system has been opened or repaired. You will need a helper for this job.

CAUTION: *Never reuse brake fluid which has been bled from the brake system.*

1. The sequence for bleeding is right rear, left front, left rear and right front. If the car has power brakes, remove the vacuum by applying the brakes several times. Do not run the engine while bleeding the brakes.

2. Clean all the bleeder screws. You may want to give each one a shot of penetrating solvent to loosen it up; seizure is a common problem with bleeder screws, which then break off, sometimes requiring replacement of the part to which they are attached.

3. Fill the master cylinder with DOT 3 brake fluid.

NOTE: *Brake fluid absorbs moisture from the air. Don't leave the master cylinder or the fluid container uncovered any longer than necessary. Be careful handling the fluid, it eats paint.*

Check the level of the fluid often when bleeding, and refill the reservoirs as necessary. Don't let them run dry, or you will have to repeat the process.

4. Attach a length of clear vinyl tubing to the bleeder screw on the wheel cylinder. Insert the other end of the tube into a clear, clean jar half filled with brake fluid.

5. Have your assistant slowly depress the brake pedal. As this is done, open the bleeder screw 1/3-1/2 of a turn and allow the fluid to run through the tube. Then close the bleeder screw before the pedal reaches the end of its travel. Have your assistant slowly release the pedal. Repeat this process until no air bubbles appear in the expelled fluid.

6. Repeat the procedure on the other three

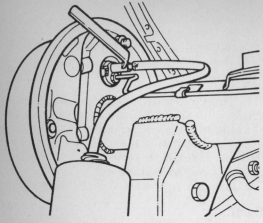

**Bleeding the brakes**

brakes, checking the level of fluid in the master cylinder reservoir often.

After you're done, there should be no in the brake pedal feel. If there is, either there is still air in the line, in which case the process should be repeated or there is a leak somewhere, which of course must be corrected before the car is moved.

## FRONT DISC BRAKES

CAUTION: *Brake shoes contain asbestos, which has been determined to be a cancer causing agent. Never clean the brake surfaces with compressed air! Avoid inhaling any dust from any brake surface! When cleaning brake surfaces, use a commercially available brake cleaning fluid.*

## Brake Pads
### INSPECTION

The pad thickness should be inspected every time that the tires are removed for rotation. The outer pad can be checked by looking in at each end, which is the point at which the highest rate of wear occurs. The inner pad can be checked by looking down through the inspection hole in the top of the caliper. If the thickness of the pad is worn to within 0.030" (0.76mm) of the rivet at either end of the pad, all the pads should be replaced. This is the factory recommended measurement; your state's automobile inspection laws may not agree with this.

NOTE: *Always replace all pads on both front wheels at the same time. Failure to do so will result in uneven braking action and premature wear.*

### REMOVAL AND INSTALLATION

1. Siphon ⅔ of the brake fluid from the master cylinder reservoir. Loosen the wheel lug nuts and raise the car. Remove the wheel.

2. Position a C-clamp across the caliper so that it presses on the pads and tighten it until the caliper bottoms in its bore.

NOTE: *If you haven't removed some brake fluid from the master cylinder, it will overflow when the piston is retracted.*

3. Remove the C-clamp.

4. Remove the allen head caliper mounting bolts. Inspect the bolts for corrosion and replace as necessary.

5. Remove the caliper from the steering knuckle and suspend it from the body of the car with a length of wire. Do not allow the caliper to hang by its hose.

6. Remove the pad retaining springs and the pads from the caliper.

7. Remove the plastic sleeves and the rubber bushings from the mounting bolt holes.

8. Install new sleeves and bushings. Lubricate the sleeves with a light coating of silicone grease before installation. These parts must always be replaced when the pads are replaced. The parts are usually included in the pad replacement kits.

9. Install the outboard pad into the caliper.

10. Install the retainer spring on the inboard pad. A new spring should be included in the pad replacement kit.

11. Install the new inboard into the caliper. The retention lugs fit into the piston.

12. Use a large pair of slip joint pliers to bend the outer pad ears down over the caliper.

13. Install the caliper onto the steering knuckle. Tighten the mounting bolts to 28 ft.lb.

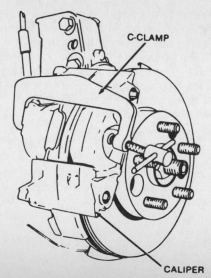

**Install a C-clamp to retract the disc brake pads**

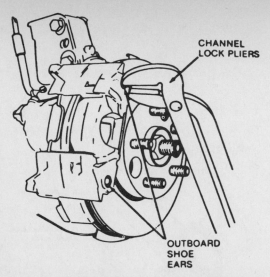

Bend the outboard pad ears into place with a large pair of slip joint pliers

(38 Nm) for 1982-84 or 48 ft.lb. (51 Nm) for 1985-88. Install the wheel and lower the car. Fill the master cylinder to its proper level with fresh brake fluid meeting DOT 3 specifications. Since the brake hose wasn't disconnected it isn't really necessary to bleed the brakes, although most mechanics do this as a matter of course.

## Brake Caliper

### REMOVAL AND INSTALLATION

1. Follow Steps 1, 2 and 3 of the pad replacement procedure.
2. Before removing the caliper mounting bolts, remove the bolt holding the brake hose to the caliper.
3. Remove the allen head caliper mounting bolts. Inspect them for corrosion and replace them if necessary.
4. Install the caliper and brake pads over the rotor. Mounting bolt torque is 28 ft.lb. (38 Nm) for 1982-84 or 38 ft.lb. (51 Nm) for 1985-88 for the caliper.
5. Install the brake hose to the caliper. The brake hose fitting should be tightened to 33 ft.lb. (45 Nm).
6. Install the wheel and tire and lower the vehicle.

### OVERHAUL

1. Remove the caliper.
2. Remove the pads.
3. Place some cloths or a slat of wood in front of the piston. Remove the piston by applying compressed air to the fluid inlet fitting. Use just enough air pressure to ease the piston from the bore.

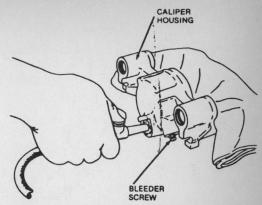

Use air pressure to remove the piston from the bore

CAUTION: *Do not try to catch the piston with your fingers, which can result in serious injury.*

4. Remove the piston boot with a screwdriver, working carefully so that the piston bore is not scratched.
5. Remove the bleeder screw.
6. Inspect the piston for scoring, nicks, corrosion, wear, etc., and damaged or worn chrome plating. Replace the piston if any defects are found.
7. Remove the piston seal from the caliper bore groove using a piece of pointed wood or plastic. Do not use a screwdriver, which will damage the bore. Inspect the caliper bore for nicks, corrosion and so on. Very light wear can be cleaned up with crocus cloth. Use finger pressure to rub the crocus cloth around the circumference of the bore; do not slide it in and out. More extensive wear or corrosion warrants replacement of the part.
8. Clean any parts which are to be reused in denatured alcohol. Dry them with compressed or allow to air dry. Don't wipe the parts dry with a cloth, which will leave behind bits of lint.
9. Lubricate the new seal, provided in the repair kit, with clean brake fluid. Install the seal in its groove, making sure it is fully seated and not twisted.

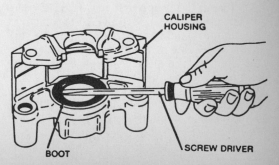

Remove the piston boot with a screwdriver

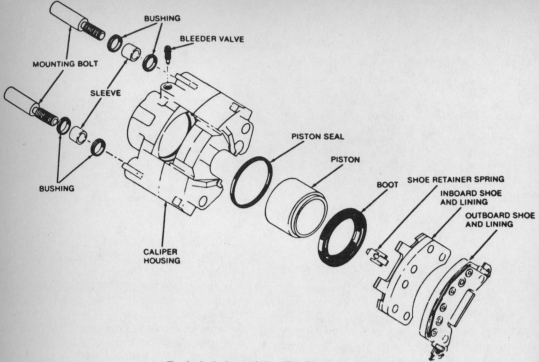

MOUNTING BOLT

BUSHING

BLEEDER VALVE

SLEEVE

BUSHING

PISTON SEAL

PISTON

BOOT

SHOE RETAINER SPRING

INBOARD SHOE AND LINING

OUTBOARD SHOE AND LINING

CALIPER HOUSING

**Exploded view of the disc brake caliper**

10. Install the new dust boot on the piston. Lubricate the bore of the caliper with clean brake fluid and insert the piston into its bore. Position the boot in the caliper housing and seat with a seal driver of the appropriate size, or G.M. tool N. J-29077.

11. Install the bleeder screw, tightening to 110 in.lb. (13 Nm) for 1982-84 or 120 in.lb. (14 Nm) for 1985-88. Do not overtighten.

12. Install the pads, the caliper and bleed the brakes.

## Brake Disc (Rotor)

### REMOVAL AND INSTALLATION

1. Remove the wheel cover, loosen the hub nut, and raise and support the car. Remove the front wheel.

2. Install the boot cover, tool J-28712 (Double-Offset joint) or J-33162 (Tri-Pot joint).

3. Remove and discard the hub nut. Be sure to use a new one on assembly, not the old one.

4. Remove the allen head caliper mounting bolts and remove the brake caliper.

5. Remove the caliper from the knuckle and suspend from a length of wire. Do not allow the caliper to hang from the brake hose.

6. Pull the rotor from the knuckle.

7. To install, place the rotor onto the steering knuckle, then install the hub nut. When the shaft begins to turn with the hub, insert a drift

through the caliper into one of the cooling slots in the rotor to keep it from turning. Insert a long bolt in the hub flange to prevent the shaft from turning. Tighten the hub nut to 70 ft.lb.

8. Tighten the brake caliper bolts to 30 ft.lb.

9. Remove the boot seal protector.

10. Connect the brake hose clip to the strut. Install the tire and wheel, lower the car, and tighten the hub nut to 225 ft.lb. (1981-82); 185 ft.lb. (1983-88).

### INSPECTION

1. Check the rotor surface for wear or scoring. Deep scoring, grooves or rust pitting can be removed by refacing, a job to be referred to your local machine shop or garage. Minimum thickness is stamped on the rotor 0.030″ (0.76mm) or 0.972″ (24.69mm) for heavy duty. If the rotor will be thinner than this after refinishing, it must be replaced.

2. Check the rotor parallelism; it must vary less than 0.0005″ (0.0127mm) measured at four or more points around the circumference. Make all measurements at the same distance in from the edge of the rotor. Refinish the rotor if it fails to meet this specification.

3. Measure the disc runout with a dial indicator. If runout exceeds 0.002″ (0.051mm) for 1982-84 or 0.004″ (0.10mm) for 1985-88 and the wheel bearings are OK (if runout is being measured with the disc on the car), the rotor must be refaced or replaced as necessary.

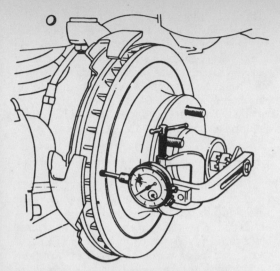

Check the rotor runout with a dial indicator

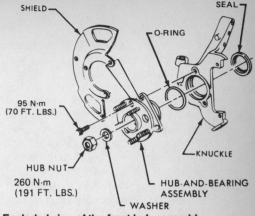

SHIELD

SEAL

O-RING

95 N·m
(70 FT. LBS.)

KNUCKLE

HUB NUT
260 N·m
(191 FT. LBS.)

HUB-AND-BEARING
ASSEMBLY

WASHER

**Exploded view of the front hub assembly**

## Wheel Bearing

### REMOVAL AND INSTALLATION

1. Loosen the hub nut, then raise and support the vehicle on jackstands. Remove the wheel and tire assembly.

2. Using tool J-28712 (Double-Offset Joint) or J-33162 (Tri-Pot Joint), install it over the drive axle joint boot.

3. Remove the hub nut, the caliper (support it on a wire) and the rotor.

4. Remove the hub/bearing assembly-to-steering knuckle mounting bolts and the bearing assembly, then the splash shield.

NOTE: *If the bearing assembly is to be re-used, mark the assembly and the steering knuckle so that the assembly can be reinstalled in the same position.*

*To prevent damage to the bearing, DO NOT use heat or a hammer.*

5. Install tool J-28733 to the bearing assembly and press the assembly from the drive axle.

6. Remove the steering knuckle seal from the inboard side and cut it off the drive axle.

NOTE: *On the 1985 and later models with a*

standard bearing, it will be necessary to remove the steering knuckle from the vehicle. Disconnect the stabilizer bar from the lower control arm, using tool J-29330, separate the ball joint from the steering knuckle, then disconnect the steering knuckle from the strut. Support the drive axle (out of the way) on a wire. Using a brass drift, drive the inner knuckle seal from the steering knuckle.

7. Clean the gasket and the seal mounting surfaces.

8. Using tool J-28671 (1982-84) or J-34657 (1985-88 heavy duty), install the new steering knuckle seal from the outboard side; use tool J-34658 (1985-88 standard duty) to install the seal from the inboard side. Grease the lip of the seal with wheel bearing grease.

9. Install a new O-ring between the steering knuckle and the bearing assembly.

10. To complete the installation, reverse the removal procedures. Torque the bearing assembly-to-steering knuckle bolts to 63 ft.lb. (85 Nm) for 1982-85 standard duty or 77 ft.lb. (104 Nm) for 1985-88 heavy duty.

11. Install the hub/bearing assembly-to-drive axle nut and partially torque to 74 ft.lb. (100 Nm), then lower the vehicle and torque the hub nut to 214 ft.lb. (289 Nm) for 1982 or 192 ft.lb. (260 Nm) for 1983-88.

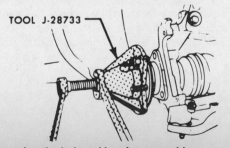

TOOL J-28733

**Removing the hub and bearing assembly**

## REAR DRUM BRAKES

CAUTION: *Brake shoes contain asbestos, which has been determined to be a cancer causing agent. Never clean the brake surfaces with compressed air! Avoid inhaling any dust from any brake surface! When cleaning brake surfaces, use a commercially available brake cleaning fluid.*

## Brake Drums
### REMOVAL AND INSTALLATION

1. Loosen the wheel lug nuts. Raise and support the car. Mark the relationship of the wheel to the axle and remove the wheel.

2. Mark the relationship of the drum to the axle and remove the drum. If it cannot be slipped off easily, check to see that the parking brake is fully released. If so, the brake shoes are probably locked against the drum. See the "Adjustment" section earlier in this chapter for details on how to back off the adjuster.

3. Installation is the reverse. Be sure to align the matchmarks made during removal. Lug nut torque is 102 ft.lb. (140 Nm).

### INSPECTION

1. After removing the brake drum, wipe out the accumulated dust with a damp cloth.

WARNING: *Do not blow the brake dust out of the drums with compressed air or lung-power. Brake linings contain asbestos, a known cancer causing substance. Dispose of the cloth used to clean the parts after use.*

2. Inspect the drums for cracks, deep grooves, roughness, scoring, or out-of-roundness. Replace any drum which is cracked; do not try to weld it up.

3. Smooth any slight scores by polishing the friction surface with fine emery cloth. Heavy or extensive scoring will cause excessive lining wear and should be removed from the drum through resurfacing, a job to be referred to your local machine shop or garage. The maximum finished diameter of the drums is 7.894" (200.51mm) for 1982-84 or 8.92" (226.57mm) for 1985-88. The drum must be replaced if the diameter is 7.929" (201.40mm) for 1982-84 or 8.95" (227.33mm) for 1985-88 or greater.

## Brake Shoes
### INSPECTION

After removing the brake drum, inspect the brake shoes. If the lining is worn down to within $\frac{1}{32}$" (0.79mm) of a rivet, the shoes must be replaced.

NOTE: *This figure may disagree with your state's automobile inspection laws. If the brake lining is soaked with brake fluid or grease, it must be replaced. If this is the case, the brake drum should be sanded with crocus cloth to remove all traces of brake fluid, and the wheel cylinders should be rebuilt. Clean all grit from the friction surface of the drum before replacing it.*

If the lining is chipped, cracked or otherwise damaged, it must be replaced with a new lining.

NOTE: *Always replace the brake linings in* sets of two on both ends of the axle. Never replace just one shoe or both shoes on one side.

Check the condition of the shoes, retracting springs and holddown springs for signs of overheating. If the shoes or springs have a slight blue color, this indicates overheating, then replacement of the shoes and springs is recommended. The wheel cylinders should be rebuilt as a precaution against future problems.

### REMOVAL AND INSTALLATION

1. Loosen the lug nuts on the wheel to be serviced, raise and support the car, and remove the wheel and brake drum.

NOTE: *It is not really necessary to remove the hub and wheel bearing assembly from the axle, but it does make the job easier. If you can work with the hub and bearing assembly in place, skip down to Step 3.*

2. Remove the four hub and bearing assembly retaining bolts and remove the assembly from the axle.

3. Remove the return springs from the shoes with a pair of needle nose pliers. There are also special brake spring pliers for this job.

4. Remove the hold down springs by gripping them with a pair of pliers, then pressing down and turning 90 degrees. There are special tools to grab and turn these parts, but pliers work fairly well.

5. Remove the shoe holddown pins from behind the brake backing plate. They will simply slide out once the holddown spring tension is relieved.

6. Lift up the actuator lever for the self-adjusting mechanism and remove the actuating link. Remove the actuator lever, pivot and the pivot return spring.

7. Spread the shoes apart to clear the wheel cylinder pistons, then remove the parking brake strut and spring.

8. If the hub and bearing assembly is still in place, spread the shoes far enough apart to clear it.

9. Disconnect the parking brake cable from the lever. Remove the shoes, still connected by their adjusting screw spring, from the car.

10. With the shoes removed, note the position of the adjusting spring, then remove the spring and adjusting screw.

11. Remove the C-clip from the parking brake lever and the lever from the secondary shoe.

12. Use a damp cloth to remove all dirt and dust from the backing plate and brake parts.

13. Check the wheel cylinder by carefully pulling the lower edges of the wheel cylinder boots away from the cylinders. If there is excessive leakage, the inside of the cylinder will be moist with fluid. If leakage exists, a wheel cylin-

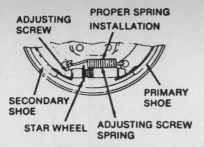

**Proper spring installation is with the coils over the adjuster, not the star wheel**

der overhaul is in order. Do not delay, because brake failure could result.

NOTE: *A small amount of fluid will be present to act as a lubricant for the wheel cylinder pistons. Fluid spilling from the boot center hole, after the piston is removed, indicates cup leakage and the necessity for cylinder overhaul.*

14. Check the backing plate attaching bolts to make sure that they are tight. Use fine emery cloth to clean all rust and dirt from the shoe contact surfaces on the plate.

15. Lubricate the fulcrum end of the parking brake lever with brake grease specially made for the purpose. Install the lever on the secondary shoe and secure with the C-clip.

16. Install the adjusting screw and spring on the shoes, connecting them together. The coils of the spring must not be over the star wheel on the adjuster. The left and right hand springs are not interchangeable. Do not mix them up.

17. Lubricate the shoe contact surfaces on the backing plate with the brake grease. Be certain when you are using this stuff that none of it actually gets on the linings or drums. Apply the same grease to the point where the parking brake cable contacts the plate. Use the grease sparingly.

18. Spread the shoe assemblies apart and connect the parking brake cable. Install the shoes on the backing plate, engaging the shoes at the top temporarily with the wheel cylinder pistons. Make sure that the star wheel on the adjuster is lined up with the adjusting hole in the backing plate, if the hole is back there.

19. Spread the shoes apart slightly and install the parking brake strut and spring. Make sure

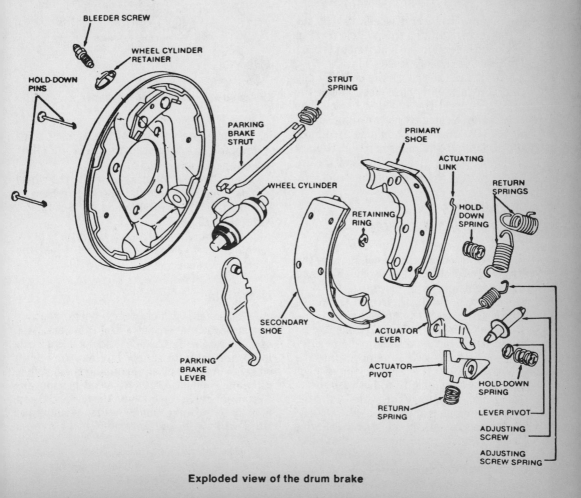

**Exploded view of the drum brake**

that the end of the strut without the spring engages the parking brake lever. The end with the spring engages the primary shoe (the one with the shorter lining).

20. Install the actuator pivot, lever and return spring. Install the actuating link in the shoe retainer. Lift up the actuator lever and hook the link into the lever.

21. Install the holddown pins through the back of the plate, install the lever pivots and holddown springs. Install the shoe return springs with a pair of pliers. Be very careful not to stretch or otherwise distort these springs.

22. Take a look at everything. Make sure the linings are in the right place, the self-adjusting mechanism is correctly installed and the parking brake parts are all hooked up. if in doubt, remove the other wheel and take a look at that one for comparison.

23. Measure the width of the linings, then measure the inside width of the drum. Adjust the linings by means of the adjuster so that the drum will fit onto the linings.

24. Install the hub and bearing assembly onto the axle if removed. Tighten the retaining bolts to 45 ft.lb. (60 Nm).

25. Install the drum and wheel. Adjust the brakes. Be sure to install a rubber hole cover in the knock-out hole after the adjustment is complete. Adjust the parking brake.

26. Lower the car and check the pedal for any sponginess or lack of a "hard" feel. Check the braking action and the parking brake. The brakes must not be applied severely immediately after installation. They should be used moderately for the first 200 miles of city driving or 1000 miles of highway driving, to allow the linings to conform to the shape of the drum.

## Wheel Cylinders
### REMOVAL AND INSTALLATION

1. Loosen the wheel lug nuts, raise and support the car, and remove the wheel. Remove the drum and brake shoes. Leave the hub and wheel bearing assembly in place.

2. Remove any dirt from around the brake line fitting. Disconnect the brake line.

3. Remove the wheel cylinder retainer by using two awls or punches with a tip diameter of 1/8″ or less. Insert the awls or punches into the access slots between the wheel cylinder pilot and retainer locking tabs. Bend both tabs away simultaneously. Remove the wheel cylinder from the backing plate.

4. To install, position the wheel cylinder against the backing plate and hold it in place with a wooden block between the wheel cylinder and the hub and bearing assembly.

5. Install a new retainer over the wheel cylin-

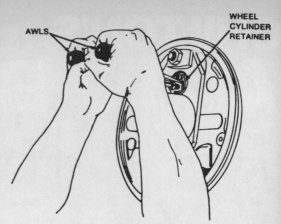

Remove the wheel cylinder retainer from the backing plate with a pair of awls or punches

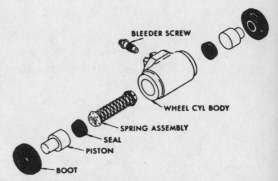

Exploded view of the wheel cylinder

der abutment on the rear of the backing plate by pressing it into place with a 1⅛″ 12-point socket and an extension.

6. Install a new bleeder screw into the wheel cylinder. Install the brake line and tighten to 12.5 ft.lb. (17 Nm) for 1982-84 or 18 ft.lb. (24 Nm) for 1985-88.

7. The rest of installation is the reverse of removal. After the drum is installed, bleed the brakes.

### OVERHAUL

As is the case with master cylinders, overhaul kits are available for the wheel cylinders. And, as is the case with master cylinders, it is usually more profitable to simply buy new or rebuilt wheel cylinders rather rebuilding them. When rebuilding wheel cylinders, avoid getting any contaminants in the system. Always install new high quality brake fluid; the use of improper fluid will swell and deteriorate the rubber parts.

1. Remove the wheel cylinders.

2. Remove the rubber boots from the cylinder ends. Discard the boots.

# CHILTON'S
# AUTO BODY
# REPAIR TIPS

**EASY STEP-BY-STEP TIPS FROM PROS**

**Tools and Materials • Step-by-Step Illustrated Procedures**
**How To Repair Dents, Scratches and Rust Holes**
**Spray Painting and Refinishing Tips**

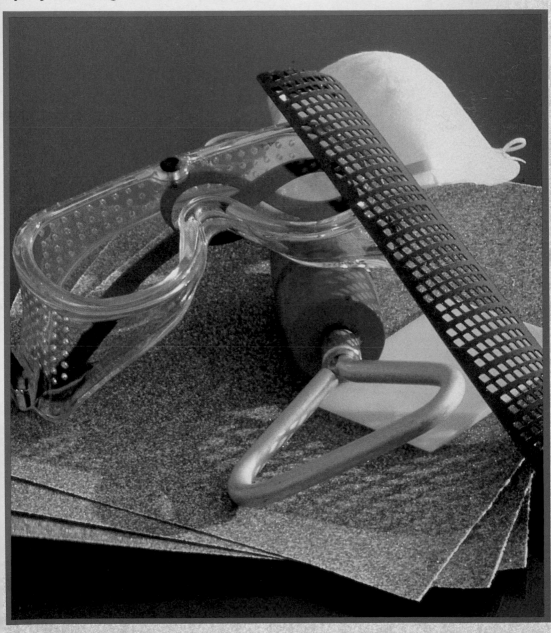

**W**ith a little practice, basic body repair procedures can be mastered by any do-it-yourself mechanic. The step-by-step repairs shown here can be applied to almost any type of auto body repair.

# TOOLS & MATERIALS

**Y**ou may already have basic tools, such as hammers and electric drills. Other tools unique to body repair — body hammers, grinding attachments, sanding blocks, dent puller, half-round plastic file and plastic spreaders — are relatively inexpensive and can be obtained wherever auto parts or auto body repair parts are sold. Portable air compressors and paint spray guns can be purchased or rented.

## Auto Body Repair Kits

**T**he best and most often used products are available to the do-it-yourselfer in kit form, from major manufacturers of auto body repair products. The same manufacturers also merchandise the individual products for use by pros.

Kits are available to make a wide variety of repairs, including holes, dents and scratches and fiberglass, and offer the advantage of buying the materials you'll need for the job. There is little waste or chance of materials going bad from not being used. Many kits may also contain basic body-working tools such as body files, sanding blocks and spreaders. Check the contents of the kit before buying your tools.

# BODY REPAIR TIPS

## Safety

**M**any of the products associated with auto body repair and refinishing contain toxic chemicals. Read all labels before opening containers and store them in a safe place and manner.

• Wear eye protection (safety goggles) when using power tools or when performing any operation that involves

the removal of any type of material.

• Wear lung protection (disposable mask or respirator) when grinding, sanding or painting.

## Sanding

**1** Sand off paint before using a dent puller. When using a non-adhesive sanding disc, cover the back of the disc with an overlapping layer or two of masking tape and trim the edges. The disc will last considerably longer.

**2** Use the circular motion of the sanding disc to grind *into* the edge of the repair. Grinding or sanding away from the jagged edge will only tear the sandpaper.

**3** Use the palm of your hand flat on the panel to detect high and low spots. Do not use your fingertips. Slide your hand slowly back and forth.

# WORKING WITH BODY FILLER

## Mixing The Filler

**C**leanliness and proper mixing and application are extremely important. Use a clean piece of plastic or glass or a disposable artist's palette to mix body filler.

**1** Allow plenty of time and follow directions. No useful purpose will be served by adding more hardener to make it cure (set-up) faster. Less hardener means more curing time, but the mixture dries harder; more hardener means less curing time but a softer mixture.

**2** Both the hardener and the filler should be thoroughly kneaded or stirred before mixing. Hardener should be a solid paste and dispense like thin toothpaste. Body filler should be smooth, and free of lumps or thick spots.

Getting the proper amount of hardener in the filler is the trickiest part of preparing the filler. Use the same amount of hardener in cold or warm weather. For contour filler (thick coats), a bead of hardener twice the diameter of the filler is about right. There's about a 15% margin on either side, but, if in doubt use less hardener.

**3** Mix the body filler and hardener by wiping across the mixing surface, picking the mixture up and wiping it again. Colder weather requires longer mixing times. Do not mix in a circular motion; this will trap air bubbles which will become holes in the cured filler.

## Applying The Filler

**1** For best results, filler should not be applied over ¼" thick.

Apply the filler in several coats. Build it up to above the level of the repair surface so that it can be sanded or grated down.

The first coat of filler must be pressed on with a firm wiping motion.

Apply the filler in one direction only. Working the filler back and forth will either pull it off the metal or trap air bubbles.

# REPAIRING DENTS

**B**efore you start, take a few minutes to study the damaged area. Try to visualize the shape of the panel before it was damaged. If the damage is on the left fender, look at the right fender and use it as a guide. If there is access to the panel from behind, you can reshape it with a body hammer. If not, you'll have to use a dent puller. Go slowly and work the metal a little at a time. Get the panel as straight as possible before applying filler.

**1** This dent is typical of one that can be pulled out or hammered out from behind. Remove the headlight cover, headlight assembly and turn signal housing.

**2** Drill a series of holes ½ the size of the end of the dent puller along the stress line. Make some trial pulls and assess the results. If necessary, drill more holes and try again. Do not hurry.

**3** If possible, use a body hammer and block to shape the metal back to its original contours. Get the metal back as close to its original shape as possible. Don't depend on body filler to fill dents.

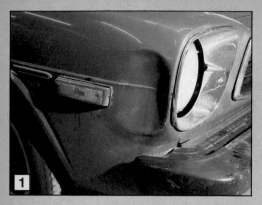

**4** Using an 80-grit grinding disc on an electric drill, grind the paint from the surrounding area down to bare metal. Use a new grinding pad to prevent heat buildup that will warp metal.

**5** The area should look like this when you're finished grinding. Knock the drill holes in and tape over small openings to keep plastic filler out.

**6** Mix the body filler (see Body Repair Tips). Spread the body filler evenly over the entire area (see Body Repair Tips). Be sure to cover the area completely.

**7** Let the body filler dry until the surface can just be scratched with your fingernail. Knock the high spots from the body filler with a body file ("Cheesegrater"). Check frequently with the palm of your hand for high and low spots.

**8** Check to be sure that trim pieces that will be installed later will fit exactly. Sand the area with 40-grit paper.

**9** If you wind up with low spots, you may have to apply another layer of filler.

**10** Knock the high spots off with 40-grit paper. When you are satisfied with the contours of the repair, apply a thin coat of filler to cover pin holes and scratches.

**11** Block sand the area with 40-grit paper to a smooth finish. Pay particular attention to body lines and ridges that must be well-defined.

**12** Sand the area with 400 paper and then finish with a scuff pad. The finished repair is ready for priming and painting (see Painting Tips).

Materials and photos courtesy of Ritt Jones Auto Body, Prospect Park, PA.

# REPAIRING RUST HOLES

There are many ways to repair rust holes. The fiberglass cloth kit shown here is one of the most cost efficient for the owner because it provides a strong repair that resists cracking and moisture and is relatively easy to use. It can be used on large and small holes (with or without backing) and can be applied over contoured areas. Remember, however, that short of replacing an entire panel, no repair is a guarantee that the rust will not return.

**1** Remove any trim that will be in the way. Clean away all loose debris. Cut away all the rusted metal. But be sure to leave enough metal to retain the contour or body shape.

**2** Grind away all traces of rust with a 24-grit grinding disc. Be sure to grind back 3-4 inches from the edge of the hole down to bare metal and be sure all traces of paint, primer and rust are removed.

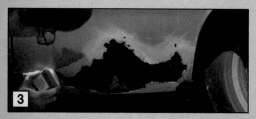

**3** Block sand the area with 80 or 100 grit sandpaper to get a clear, shiny surface and feathered paint edge. Tap the edges of the hole inward with a ball peen hammer.

**4** If you are going to use release film, cut a piece about 2-3″ larger than the area you have sanded. Place the film over the repair and mark the sanded area on the film. Avoid any unnecessary wrinkling of the film.

**5** Cut 2 pieces of fiberglass matte to match the shape of the repair. One piece should be about 1″ smaller than the sanded area and the second piece should be 1″ smaller than the first. Mix enough filler and hardener to saturate the fiberglass material (see Body Repair Tips).

**6** Lay the release sheet on a flat surface and spread an even layer of filler, large enough to cover the repair. Lay the smaller piece of fiberglass cloth in the center of the sheet and spread another layer of filler over the fiberglass cloth. Repeat the operation for the larger piece of cloth.

**7** Place the repair material over the repair area, with the release film facing outward. Use a spreader and work from the center outward to smooth the material, following the body contours. Be sure to remove all air bubbles.

**8** Wait until the repair has dried tack-free and peel off the release sheet. The ideal working temperature is 60°-90° F. Cooler or warmer temperatures or high humidity may require additional curing time. Wait longer, if in doubt.

**9** Sand and feather-edge the entire area. The initial sanding can be done with a sanding disc on an electric drill if care is used. Finish the sanding with a block sander. Low spots can be filled with body filler; this may require several applications.

**10** When the filler can just be scratched with a fingernail, knock the high spots down with a body file and smooth the entire area with 80-grit. Feather the filled areas into the surrounding areas.

**11** When the area is sanded smooth, mix some topcoat and hardener and apply it directly with a spreader. This will give a smooth finish and prevent the glass matte from showing through the paint.

**12** Block sand the topcoat smooth with finishing sandpaper (200 grit), and 400 grit. The repair is ready for masking, priming and painting (see Painting Tips).

Materials and photos courtesy Marson Corporation, Chelsea, Massachusetts

# PAINTING TIPS

## Preparation

**1** SANDING — Use a 400 or 600 grit wet or dry sandpaper. Wet-sand the area with a 1/4 sheet of sandpaper soaked in clean water. Keep the paper wet while sanding. Sand the area until the repaired area tapers into the original finish.

**2** CLEANING — Wash the area to be painted thoroughly with water and a clean rag. Rinse it thoroughly and wipe the surface dry until you're sure it's completely free of dirt, dust, fingerprints, wax, detergent or other foreign matter.

**3** MASKING — Protect any areas you don't want to overspray by covering them with masking tape and newspaper. Be careful not get fingerprints on the area to be painted.

**4** PRIMING — All exposed metal should be primed before painting. Primer protects the metal and provides an excellent surface for paint adhesion. When the primer is dry, wet-sand the area again with 600 grit wet-sandpaper. Clean the area again after sanding.

## Painting Techniques

**P** aint applied from either a spray gun or a spray can (for small areas) will provide good results. Experiment on an old piece of metal to get the right combination before you begin painting.

**SPRAYING VISCOSITY (SPRAY GUN ONLY)** — Paint should be thinned to spraying viscosity according to the directions on the can. Use only the recommended thinner or reducer and the same amount of reduction regardless of temperature.

**AIR PRESSURE (SPRAY GUN ONLY)** — This is extremely important. Be sure you are using the proper recommended pressure.

**TEMPERATURE** — The surface to be painted should be approximately the same temperature as the surrounding air. Applying warm paint to a cold surface, or vice versa, will completely upset the paint characteristics.

**THICKNESS** — Spray with smooth strokes. In general, the thicker the coat of paint, the longer the drying time. Apply several thin coats about 30 seconds apart. The paint should remain wet long enough to flow out and no longer; heavier coats will only produce sags or wrinkles. Spray a light (fog) coat, followed by heavier color coats.

**DISTANCE** — The ideal spraying distance is 8″-12″ from the gun or can to the surface. Shorter distances will produce ripples, while greater distances will result in orange peel, dry film and poor color match and loss of material due to overspray.

**OVERLAPPING** — The gun or can should be kept at right angles to the surface at all times. Work to a wet edge at an even speed, using a 50% overlap and direct the center of the spray at the lower or nearest edge of the previous stroke.

**RUBBING OUT (BLENDING) FRESH PAINT** — Let the paint dry thoroughly. Runs or imperfections can be sanded out, primed and repainted.

Don't be in too big a hurry to remove the masking. This only produces paint ridges. When the finish has dried for at least a week, apply a small amount of fine grade rubbing compound with a clean, wet cloth. Use lots of water and blend the new paint with the surrounding area.

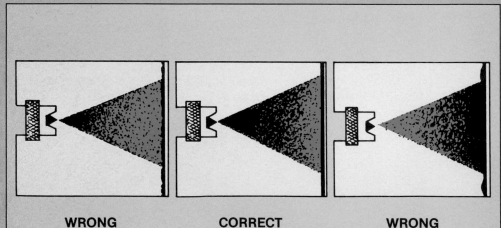

| WRONG | CORRECT | WRONG |
|---|---|---|
| *Thin coat. Stroke too fast, not enough overlap, gun too far away.* | *Medium coat. Proper distance, good stroke, proper overlap.* | *Heavy coat. Stroke too slow, too much overlap, gun too close.* |

3. Remove and discard the pistons and cups.

4. Wash the cylinder and metal parts in denatured alcohol.

CAUTION: *Never use mineral based solvents to clean the brake parts.*

5. Allow the parts to air dry and inspect the cylinder bore for corrosion or wear. Light corrosion can be cleaned up with crocus cloth; use finger pressure and rotate the cloth around the circumference of the bore. Do not move the cloth in and out. Any deep corrosion can be cleaned up with crocus cloth; use finger pressure and rotate the cloth around the circumference of the bore. Do not move the cloth in and out. Any deep corrosion or pitting or wear warrants replacement of the parts.

6. Rinse the parts and allow to dry. Do not dry with a rag, which will leave bits of line behind.

7. Lubricate the cylinder bore with clean brake fluid. Insert the spring assembly.

8. Install new cups. Do not lubricate prior to assembly.

9. Install the new pistons.

10. Press the new boots onto the cylinders by hand. Do not lubricate prior to assembly.

11. Install the wheel cylinders. Bleed the brakes after installation of the drum.

# PARKING BRAKE

## Cables

### *REMOVAL AND INSTALLATION*

**Front Cable**

1. Loosen the cable at the equalizer nut, then disconnect it from the lever assembly.

2. While depressing the retaining tangs, remove the conduit fitting from the lever assembly.

3. While lifting the carpet, in the cable and the grommet area, remove the screw and the retainer.

4. Lift the cable retaining clips and unseat the grommet by pushing it towards the passenger compartment.

5. Remove the front cable conduit fitting from the equalizer, then the cable end button from the connector.

6. Pull the cable forward, through the floor pan hole.

7. To install, reverse the removal procedures.

**Left Rear Cable**

1. Raise and support the rear of the vehicle on jackstands.

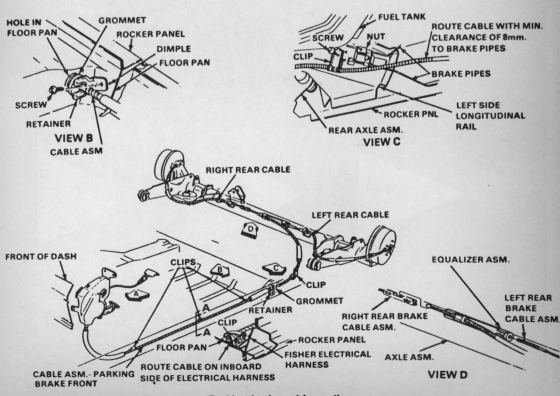

**Parking brake cable routing**

## Brake Specifications

| Model | Lug Nut Torque (ft. lb.) | Master Cylinder Bore | Bake Disc | | Brake Drum | | | Minimum Lining Thickness | |
|---|---|---|---|---|---|---|---|---|---|
| | | | Minimum Thickness | Maximum Run-Out | Diameter | Max Machine O/S | Max Wear Limit | Front | Rear |
| All | 102 | 0.874 | 0.830 ② ③ | 0.0005 | 7.874 | 7.900 | 7.930 | ① | ① |

① Minimum lining thickness is to 1/32 of rivet
② *Minimum lining thickness is as recommended by the manufacturer. Because of variations in state inspection regulations, the minimum allowable thickness may be different than recommended by the manufacturer.*
③ Heavy Duty: 0.972

2. Loosen the equalizer nut to relieve the cable tension, then remove the wheel and tire assembly.

3. Remove the brake drum, then insert a screwdriver between the brake shoe and the top of the brake adjuster bracket.

4. Push the bracket forward and release the top adjuster bracket rod. Remove the rear holddown spring, the actuator lever and the lever return spring.

5. Remove the adjuster screw spring and the top rear brake shoe return spring.

6. Remove the parking brake cable from the parking brake lever.

7. Depress the conduit fitting retaining tangs and remove the fitting from the backing plate.

8. Back off the equalizer nut and remove the left cable from the equalizer.

9. Depress the conduit fitting retaining tangs and remove the fitting from the axle bracket.

10. To install, reverse the removal procedures.

**Right Rear Cable**

1. Refer to the "Left Rear Cable, Removal and Installation" procedures, then follow steps 1-7.

2. Remove the cable button end from the connector.

3. Depress the conduit fitting retaining tangs and remove the fitting from the axle bracket.

4. To install, reverse the removal procedures.

### ADJUSTMENT

1. Raise and support the car with both rear wheels off the ground.

2. Depress the parking brake pedal exactly three ratchet clicks.

3. Loosen the equalizer locknut, then tighten the adjusting nut until the left rear wheel can just be turned backward using two hands, but is locked in forward rotation.

4. Tighten the locknut.

5. Release the parking brake. Rotate the rear wheels; there should be no drag.

6. Lower the car.

## EXTERIOR

### Doors

#### REMOVAL AND INSTALLATION

1. Open the door and support it securely.
2. On doors equipped with power operated components, proceed as follows.

    a. Remove the door trim panel, insulator pad (if so equipped) and inner panel water deflector.

    b. Disconnect the wiring harness from all components in door.

    c. Remove rubber conduit from door, then remove wire harness from door through conduit access hole.

3. Tape the area around the door pillar and body pillar (below the upper hinge) with cloth backed body tape.

CAUTION: *Before performing the following step, cover the door spring with a towel to prevent the spring from flying out and possibly causing personal injury or damaging the car.*

4. Insert a long flat-bladed lever underneath the pivot point of the hold-open link and over top of the spring. The lever should be positioned so as not to apply pressure to the hold-open link. Cover spring with shop cloth and lift screwdriver to disengage spring. Spring can also be removed using tool No. J-28625, door hinge spring compressor tool, or equivalent. Proceed as follows:

    a. Install two jaws of tool over spring. Jaw with slot slides over spring at hold-open link. Jaw with hole fits over spring at bubble on door hinge pillar.

    b. Install bolt to jaws of tool and tighten to compress spring.

    c. Remove tool and spring from door hinge assembly. Do not remove spring from tool.

5. If replacement hinge pin barrel clips are not available, save the clips as follows:

    a. Using two small flat-bladed tools, spread each clip just enough to move clip over recess, toward the pointed end of the pin.

    b. As pin is removed, clip will ride the shank of the pin and fall free.

    c. Reinstall clips onto pins before installing the door.

6. With the aid of an assistant, to support the door, remove the lower hinge pin using soft

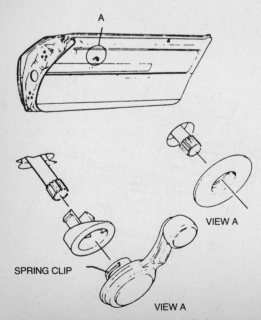

**Typical window regulator handle installation**

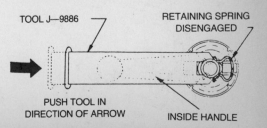

**Removing clip retained door inside handle**

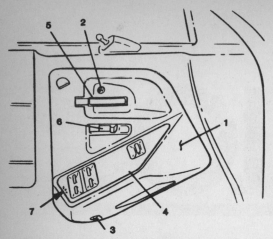

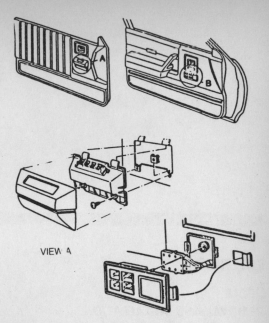

1. Inside remote handle escutcheon
2. Screw
3. Screw
4. Switch plate
5. Inside handle
6. Door lock knob
7. Insert screwdriver at this location

**Front door remote handle escutcheon**

VIEW A

VIEW B

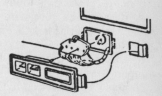

headed hammer and locking type pliers. Assistant can aid in removal of hinge pins by raising and lowering rear of door.

7. Insert 1¼" x 1½" bolt into upper hole of lower hinge to maintain door attachment during upper hinge pin removal.

8. Remove upper hinge pin in same manner as lower. Remove screw from lower hinge and remove door from body.

VIEW B

**Power window control switch assembly**

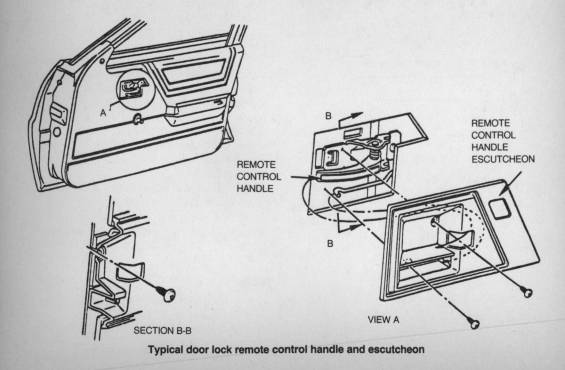

REMOTE
CONTROL
HANDLE

REMOTE
CONTROL
HANDLE
ESCUTCHEON

SECTION B-B

VIEW A

**Typical door lock remote control handle and escutcheon**

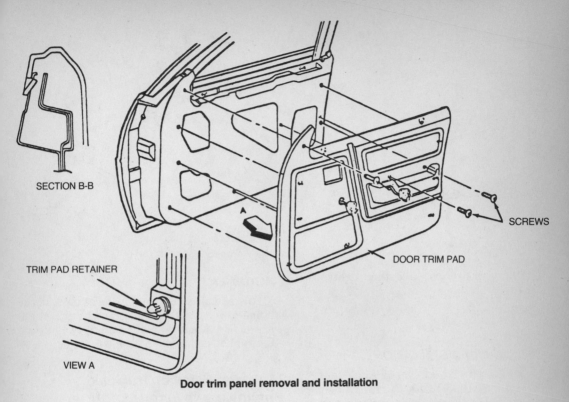

SECTION B-B

TRIM PAD RETAINER

VIEW A

SCREWS

DOOR TRIM PAD

**Door trim panel removal and installation**

NOTE: *Before installing door, replace hinge pin clips or reuse old clips as explained in the removal procedure.*

9. With the aid of an assistant, position the door and insert a small bolt in the upper hole of the lower hinge.

10. The upper hinge pin is installed with the pointed end up. The lower hinge pin is installed with the pointed end down. With the door in the full open position, install the upper hinge pin using locking type pliers and a soft-headed hammer. Use a drift punch and hammer to complete installation.

11. Remove the screw from the lower hinge and install the lower hinge pin. Use of tool No. J-28625 or equivalent is the recommended method for installing the hinge spring.

NOTE: *If spring is installed before installing upper hinge pin, hinge bushings may be damaged.*

12. If spring was removed using a screwdriver, install as follows:

a. Place spring in tool No. J-28625 or equivalent.

b. Place tool and spring in a bench vise.

c. Compress tool in vise and install bolt until spring is fully compressed.

d. Remove tool (with compressed spring) from vise and install in proper position in door upper hinge. Slot in one jaw of tool fits over hold-open link. Hole on other jaw fits over bubble on hinge.

e. Remove bolt from tool to install the spring.

f. Remove the tool from the door hinge (tool will fall out in three pieces). Open and close door to check for proper operation of the spring.

NOTE: *If tool No. J-28625 or equivalent was used to remove spring, follow steps d, e and f to install the spring.*

13. Remove the tape from the door and body pillars.

14. On doors with power operated components, install the wire harness to the door through conduit access hole and install the rubber conduit to the door.

15. Connect the wiring harness to each component in the door.

16. Install the inner panel water deflector.

17. Install the insulator pad and the door trim panel.

### STRIKER ADJUSTMENT

The striker has provisions for fore and aft adjustment only.

1. Insert tool No. J-23457, BT7107 or equivalent into the star shaped recess in the head of the striker and loosen the bolt.

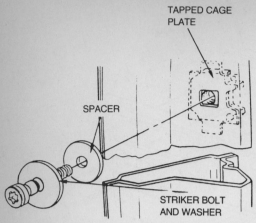

TAPPED CAGE PLATE

SPACER

STRIKER BOLT AND WASHER

**Installing door lock striker**

2. Shift striker as required, then tighten the bolt 34-46 ft.lb.

## Hood

### REMOVAL AND INSTALLATION

1. Raise the hood. Install protective coverings over the fenders, to prevent damage to paint and moldings when removing or installing the hood.

2. Disconnect the underhood lamp wire.

3. Mark the position of the hinge on the hood to Lid in alignment when hood is reinstalled.

4. With the hood supported, remove the hinge to hood screws on each side of the hood.

5. Remove the hood.

**To install:**

6. Align the hood with the marks made during removal.

7. Install the hood to hinge screws on each side of the hood and torque to 20 ft.lb.

8. Connect the underhood lamp wire.

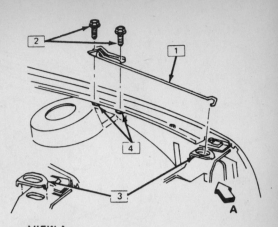

VIEW A

**Hood prop rod**

### ALIGNMENT

Fore and aft adjustment made be made at the hinge-to-hood attaching screws. Vertical adjustment at the front may be made by adjusting the rubber bumpers up or down.

## Tailgate, Hatch or Trunk Lid

### REMOVAL AND INSTALLATION

1. Prop the lid open and place protective covering along the edges of the rear compartment opening to prevent damage to the painted areas.

2. Where necessary, disconnect the wiring harness from the lid.

3. Mark the location of the hinge strap attaching bolts to lid.

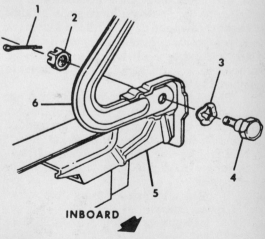

INBOARD

1. Pin
2. Nut
3. Washer
4. Bolt
5. Hinge bracket
6. Hinge strap

**Hood hinge replacement**

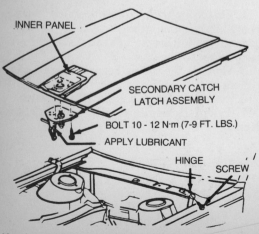

INNER PANEL

SECONDARY CATCH LATCH ASSEMBLY

BOLT 10 - 12 N·m (7-9 FT. LBS.)

APPLY LUBRICANT

HINGE

SCREW

**Hood assembly**

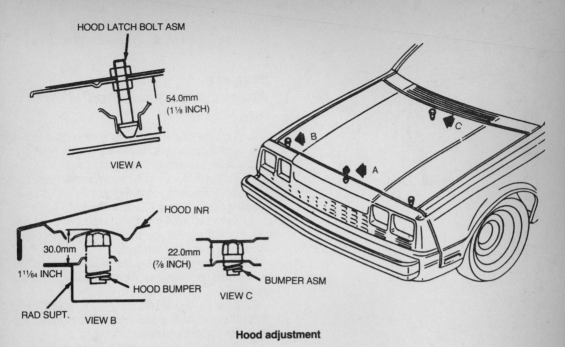

VIEW A

HOOD LATCH BOLT ASM

54.0mm
(1⅛ INCH)

HOOD INR

30.0mm

1¹¹⁄₆₄ INCH

HOOD BUMPER

22.0mm
(⅞ INCH)

BUMPER ASM

VIEW C

RAD SUPT.   VIEW B

**Hood adjustment**

4. While a helper supports the lid, remove the hinge to lid bolts and remove the lid.

5. Reverse steps 1 through 4 to install the lid.

6. Torque the hinge-to-lid attaching bolts to 20 ft.lb.

### ADJUSTMENT

Fore and aft adjustment of the lid assembly is controlled by the hinge-to-lid attaching bolts. To adjust the lid, loosen the hinge-to-lid attaching bolts and shift the lid to the desired position; then tighten the bolts to 20 ft.lb.

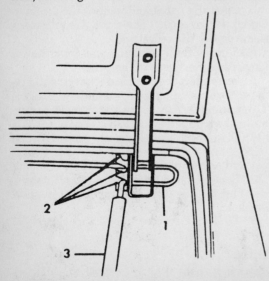

1. Torque rod
2. Adjusting notches
3. Length of ⅜″ inside diameter pipe

**Trunk torque rod adjustment**

## Lift Gate/Hatch

### REMOVAL AND INSTALLATION

1. Open and support the lift gate in the full open position.

2. Remove the lid and body side retaining clips from the ends of the gas support assemblies.

3. Disengage the attachment at each end of the support and remove from body.

4. On styles with heated glass or rear wiper-washer system, disconnect the wiring harness and hose from the washer assembly.

5. Using a $\frac{5}{32}$″ diameter rod, place the end of the rod against the pointed end of the hinge pin; then strike rod firmly to shear retaining clip tabs and drive pin through hinge. Repeat opera-

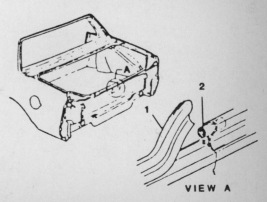

VIEW A

1. Weatherstrip
2. Plug

**Rear compartment weatherstrip**

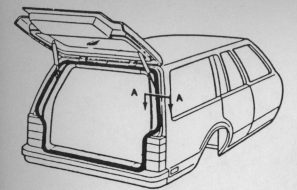

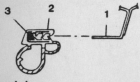

Section A-A

1. Pinchweld Flange
2. Weatherstrip
3. Adhesive

**Back body opening weatherstrip**

tion on the opposite side hinge and with the aid of a helper remove the lift gate from the body.

6. To install, reverse the above process. Prior to installing hinge pins, install new retaining

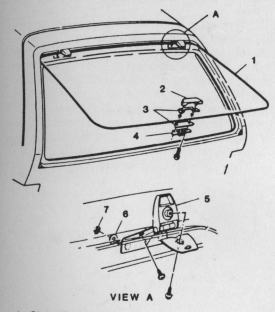

VIEW A

1. Glass-lift gate pivot
2. Handle
3. Gaskets
4. Striker
5. Hinge assembly
6. Gasket
7. Retaining nut

**Lift gate pivot glass handle and striker assembly**

clips in notches provided in hinge pins. Position retaining clips so that tabs point toward head of pin.

## Bumpers

### REMOVAL AND INSTALLATION

**Front**

1. Remove the 4 retaining screws in each of the head light bezels and remove the bezels.
2. Raise the car and support it securely.
3. Remove the 6 push-on retainers from the bottom of the bumper and remove the 6 screws holding the retainer to each fender.
4. Remove the 4 push-on retainers from the outer molding and partially remove the outer moulding from the fenders.
5. Remove the 2 sheet metal screws from the center bumper retainer, then remove the front bumper.
6. Remove the 8 retaining screws and bolts from the impact bar and remove the impact bar from its reinforcements.
7. To install, reverse steps 1 through 6.

**Rear**

1. Remove the 2 push-on retainer clips from each end of the molding, then remove the molding.
2. Remove the 4 wing nuts and electrical connectors from each of the tail lamp assemblies and remove the left and right tail lamp assemblies.
3. Remove the 5 wing nuts, disconnect the electrical connector and remove the backup light assembly.
4. Open the trunk and remove the 2 retaining nuts from the left and right side reflectors, then remove the reflectors.
5. Remove the 7 retaining pins from the valance panel and remove the panel.
6. Disconnect the electrical connector and remove the 8 retaining nuts, 4 retaining bolts and 11 retaining pins from the rear bumper and remove the bumper.
7. Disconnect the electrical connector, and remove the 8 retaining nuts from the impact bar and energy absorber.
8. Remove the 8 retaining clips and remove the impact bar from the mounting support bracket.
9. To install, reverse steps 1 through 8.

## Grille

### REMOVAL AND INSTALLATION

1. Remove the 8 retaining screws from the grille assembly.
2. Remove the grille from the front end panel.

3. To install; position the grille in the front end panel and install the retaining screws.

## Mirrors

### REMOVAL AND INSTALLATION

#### Standard

1. Remove the door trim panel and detach the inner panel water deflector. With the glass in the down position, pull out the front portion of the glass run weather strip.

2. Remove the attaching bolts and screws from the front glass run channel lower retainer to filler and rotate retainer rearward.

3. Remove the noise control patch to gain access to the 7mm screw at the belt and remove the screw.

4. Remove the filler attaching screws at the top front of the window frame and remove the mirror and filler from the door.

5. Remove the attaching nuts from the mirror base studs and remove the mirror.

6. To install, reverse steps 1 through 5. Be sure that the mirror gasket is aligned.

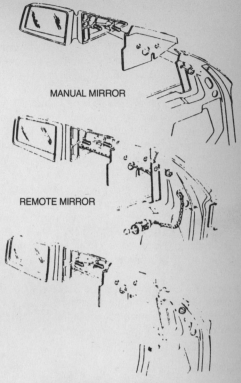

MANUAL MIRROR

REMOTE MIRROR

ELECTRIC REMOTE MIRROR

**Left-hand outside mirror—remote and manual**

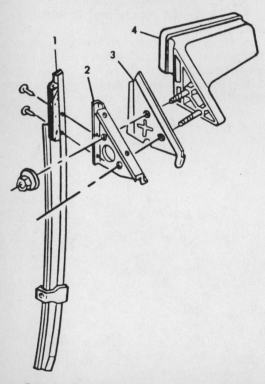

1. Front run channel retainer
2. Filler
3. Mirror gasket
4. Mirror

**Run channel to mirror filler assembly**

#### Manual Remote Control

1. Remove the mirror remote control escutcheon and door trim panel. Detach the inner panel water deflector.

NOTE: *Right side remote mirror may require detaching part of the instrument panel.*

2. With the glass in the down position, pull out the front portion of the glass run weather strip.

3. Remove the attaching bolts and screws from the front glass run channel lower retainer to filler and rotate retainer rearward.

4. Remove the noise control patch to gain access to the 7mm screw at the belt and remove the screw.

5. Remove the filler attaching screws at the top front of the window frame.

6. Remove the mirror base with mirror and cable assembly from the door.

7. Remove the mirror to filler attaching nuts and remove the mirror and cable from filler.

8. To install, reverse steps 1 through 6. Be sure cable is routed around front glass run channel retainer and installed to clip. Torque nuts to 72 in.lb.

#### Electric Remote Control

1. Remove the mirror remote control escutcheon and door trim panel. Detach the inner

panel water deflector and the electrical connector for the mirror.

NOTE: *Right side remote mirror may require detaching part of the instrument panel.*

2. With the glass in the down position, pull out the front portion of the glass run weather strip.

3. Remove the attaching bolts and screws from the front glass run channel lower retainer to filler and rotate retainer rearward.

4. Remove the noise control patch to gain access to the 7mm screw at the belt and remove the screw.

5. Remove the filler attaching screws at the top front of the window frame.

6. Remove the mirror base with mirror and electric connector from the door.

7. Remove the mirror to filler attaching nuts and remove the mirror and electric wire from filler.

8. To install, reverse steps 1 through 6. Be sure electric wire is routed around front glass run channel retainer and installed to the clip. Torque nuts to 72 in.lb.

## Antenna

### REMOVAL AND INSTALLATION

#### Manual

1. Working from underneath the dash, disconnect the antenna cable from the radio.

2. Unscrew the antenna from the fender and remove it, with the cable, from the car.

3. To install, reverse the above process.

#### Power

1. Remove the screw securing the antenna bracket to the support bracket.

2. Disconnect the antenna lead wire to antenna wire.

3. Disconnect the ground lead from the harness assembly by removing the attaching screw.

4. Disconnect the rear quarter harness assembly wiring feed relay.

5. Remove nut, bezel and gasket over top of antenna. Remove the antenna through the bottom of the hole in the quarter panel.

6. To install, reverse steps 1 through 5.

## INTERIOR

## Door Panels

### REMOVAL AND INSTALLATION

1. Remove all door inside handles.
2. Remove door inside locking rod knob.
3. Remove screws inserted through door

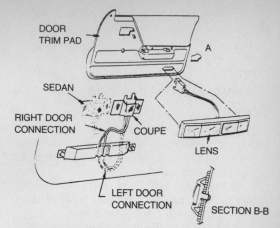

**Front door courtesy and warning lamp assembly coupe shown**

armrest and pull handle assembly into door inner panel or armrest hanger support bracket.

4. On styles with remote control mirror assemblies, remove remote mirror escutcheon and disengage end of mirror control cable from escutcheon.

5. On styles with power window controls located in the door trim assembly, disconnect the wire harness at the switch assembly.

6. Remove the remote control handle escutcheon screws.

7. On styles with integral armrests, remove the screws inserted through the pull cup into the armrest hanger support.

8. Remove screws and plastic retainers from the perimeter of the door trim pad using tool

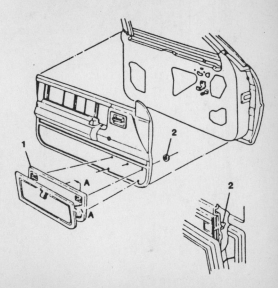

1. Map pocket
2. Nut

**Removing door trim panel map pocket**

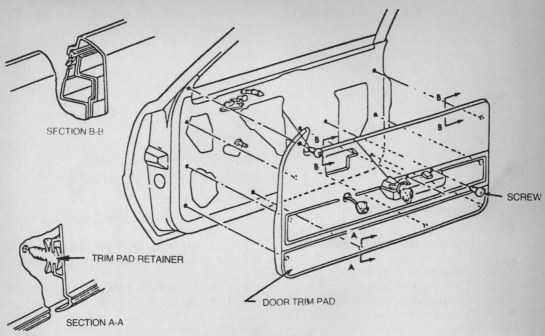

SECTION B-B

SECTION A-A

TRIM PAD RETAINER

DOOR TRIM PAD

SCREW

**Door trim panel fasteners**

BT-7323A or equivalent and a screwdriver. To remove the door trim panel, push trim upward and outboard to disengage it from the door inner panel at the belt line.

9. On styles with courtesy lamps located in the lower area of the trim panel, disconnect the wiring harness at the lamp assembly.

NOTE: *Before installing the door trim panel, check that all trim retainers are securely installed to the panel and are not damaged. Replace damaged retainers as required.*

10. Connect electrical components where present.

11. To install the door trim panel, pull door inside handle inward; then position the trim panel to the inner panel, inserting door handle through hole in panel.

12. Position the trim panel to the door inner panel so trim retainers are aligned with the attaching holes in the panel and tap the retainers into the holes with a clean rubber mallet. Install all previously removed items.

## Door Locks

### REMOVAL AND INSTALLATION

1. Raise door window. Remove door trim panel and inner panel water deflector.

2. Disengage the inside lock rod, the inside handle to lock rod, the lock cylinder to lock rod

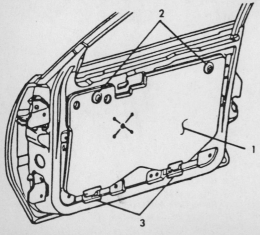

1. Water deflector
2. Plastic nails
3. Tape

**Front door water deflector installation**

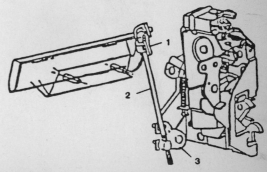

1. Clip
2. Lock rod
3. Lever

**Adjusting lift bar handle lock rod**

and the power lock actuator rod (power locks only) from the lock assembly.

3. On 2AG19 styles, remove the screw holding door ajar switch to lock and disconnect the connector from the lock.

4. Remove the lock screws and lower the lock to disengage the outside handle to lock rod. Remove the lock from the door.

5. To install, first install the spring clips to the lock assembly, then reverse steps 1 through 4. Torque the door lock attaching screws to 80-100 in.lb.

## Power Lock Actuator

### REMOVAL AND INSTALLATION

1. Remove the door trim panel and inner panel water deflector. Raise door window. Locate actuator rivets on inner panel.

2. Remove the electrical connector.

3. Drive out rivet center pins.

4. Drill out rivets using ¼" drill bit.

5. Remove the actuator from the actuator to lock rod and remove the actuator from the door.

6. To install, first install the actuator to the actuator to lock rod.

7. Using hand rivet tool J-29002 or equivalent, install the actuator to the inner panel using ¼" x ½" aluminum peel type rivets, part No. 9436175 or equivalent.

8. If hand rivet tool is not available, attach actuator to inner panel using ¼"-20 x ½" nuts and bolts. Torque bolts 90-125 in.lb.

9. Install the electrical connector to the actuator.

10. Install the water deflector and the door trim.

## Door Glass and Regulator

### REMOVAL AND INSTALLATION

#### Door Glass (Coupe)

1. Remove the door trim panel and inner panel water deflector.

2. Raise the window to the full up position and tape glass to door frame using cloth-backed tape.

3. Remove the bolts holding the lower sash channel to the regulator sash.

4. Remove the rubber down stop at the bottom of the door by pulling carefully.

5. Attach the regulator handle and run the regulator to the full down position. Remove the regulator sash by rotating 90° and pulling outboard.

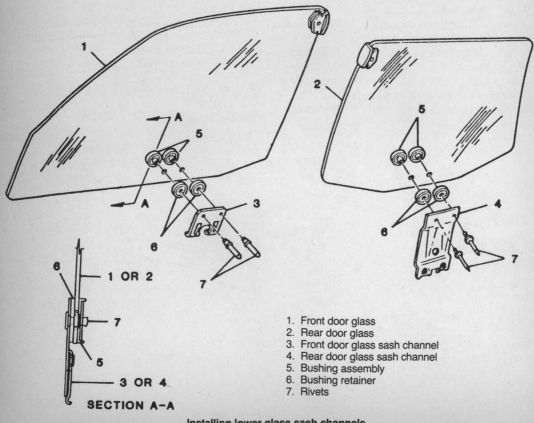

1. Front door glass
2. Rear door glass
3. Front door glass sash channel
4. Rear door glass sash channel
5. Bushing assembly
6. Bushing retainer
7. Rivets

SECTION A–A

**Installing lower glass sash channels**

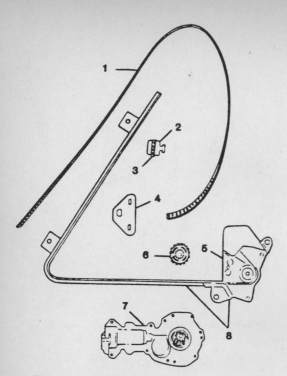

1. Tape
2. Guide
3. Block
4. Sash
5. Fishmouth
6. Gear (electric only)
7. Motor
8. Regulator complete

**Tape drive regulator service parts—electric shown, manual similar**

6. While supporting the glass, remove the tape and lower the window to the full down position. Disengage the front edge of the glass from the glass run channel retainer. Slide the glass forward and tilt slightly to remove the guide from the retainer in the run channel.

7. Using care, raise the glass while tilting forward and remove glass inboard of the upper frame.

8. To install, reverse steps 1 through 7. Use liquid soap solution on the rubber down stop before installing the trim parts, check the window for proper operation and alignment.

**Door Glass (Sedan)**

1. Remove the door trim panel and inner panel water deflector.

2. Raise the window to the full up position and tape glass to door frame using cloth-backed tape.

3. Remove the bolts holding the lower sash channel to the regulator sash.

4. Attach the regulator handle and run the regulator to the full down position.

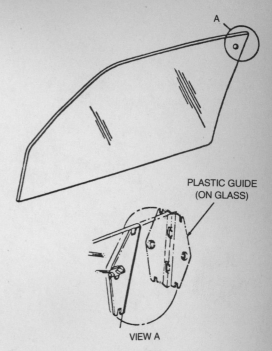

**Installing front door glass guide**

5. While supporting the glass, remove the tape and lower the window to the half down position.

6. Wrap tape around the blade of tool BT-7323A or equivalent. Insert tool between the guide and glass at the fastener and carefully pry apart.

7. Using care, raise the glass while tilting forward and remove glass inboard of the upper frame.

8. Remove guide from the rear of the run channel weatherstrip metal retainer and discard guide.

9. Replace guide on glass in the following manner:

    a. Heat guide with hot air gun or soak in hot water for about one minute.

    b. Install guide to glass by aligning to hole in glass and carefully press guide together at fastener location.

10. Install glass and lower about halfway.

11. With one hand on bottom edge, rotate glass rearward to snap guide into retainer.

12. To complete installation, reverse the remainder of the removal process.

**Regulator**

1. Remove the door trim panel and inner panel water deflector.

2. Raise the window to the full up position and tape glass to door frame using cloth-backed tape.

3. Remove the lower sash bolts.

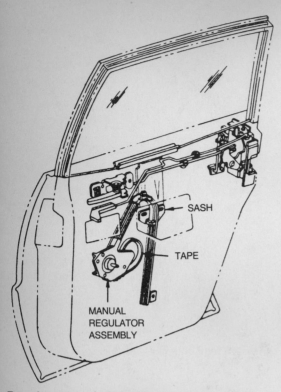

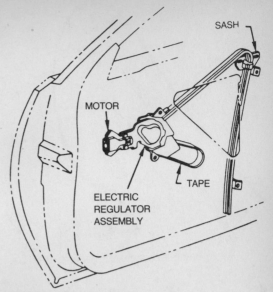

Front door window electric regulator assembly

Rear door manual window regulator, electric regulator similar

4. Punch out center pins of regulator rivet. Drill out rivets using ¼″ drill bit.

5. For manual regulators, remove the regulator through the rear access hole. For electric regulator, remove the glass as stated previously. Move the regulator and motor assembly rearward and remove the electric connector. Remove the regulator and motor assembly through the rear access hole.

6. To install, use hand rivet tool J-29002 or equivalent and install the regulator to the inner panel using ¼″ x ½″ aluminum peel type rivets, part No. 9436175 or equivalent.

7. If hand rivet tool is not available, install U-clips on regulator at three attaching locations. Be sure to install clips with cinch nuts on outboard side of retainers.

8. Slide the regulator through the rear access hole and align the regulator attaching clips with the holes in the inner panel. Attach regulator metal retainers with ¼″-20 x ½″ screws. Attach housing part of regulator with ¼″-20 x ½″ screws into ¼″ nuts with integral washers! Torque bolts 90-125 in.lb.

9. Install the lower sash bolts.

10. Remove the tape from the door glass and frame.

11. Install the inner panel water deflector and door trim panel.

## Electric Window Motor
### REMOVAL AND INSTALLATION

1. Remove the door trim panel and inner panel water deflector.

2. Raise the window to the full up position and tape glass to door frame using cloth-backed tape.

3. Remove the lower sash bolts.

4. Punch out center pins of regulator rivet. Drill out rivets using ¼″ drill bit.

5. Move regulator and motor assembly rearward and remove electrical connector.

6. With the regulator in the door, drill out the regulator to motor rivets using a ³⁄₁₆″ drill bit and remove the motor.

7. To install, reverse steps 1 through 6. Use ³⁄₁₆″ rivets or ³⁄₁₆″ nuts and bolts to install the motor to the regulator.

## Inside Rear View Mirror
### REPLACEMENT

The inside rear view mirror is permanently attached to the windshield. Should replacement become necessary, refer to your local dealer or a qualified technician for service.

## Seats
### REMOVAL AND INSTALLATION
#### Front

1. Position the seat in the full forward position. If the car is equipped with six-way power

seats, place the seat in the full forward and up position. When necessary to gain access to the adjuster-to-floor pan attaching nuts, remove the adjuster rear foot covers and or carpet retainers.

2. Remove the track covers where necessary; then remove the adjuster-to-floor pan rear attaching nuts. Position the seat in the full rearward position.

3. Remove the adjuster front foot covers; then remove the adjuster to floor pan front attaching nuts. Tilt the seat rearward and disconnect the feed wire connector.

4. Remove the seat assembly from the car.

5. To install, reverse steps 1 through 4 and check for proper seat operation. Torque the bolts to 40 ft.lb.

### Rear

1. Push the lower forward edge of the seat cushion rearward.

2. Lift upward and pull forward on the seat cushion frame to disengage the cushion frame wires from the retainers on the rear seat pan.

3. Remove the lower seat cushion from the vehicle.

4. At the bottom of the seatback, remove the anchor bolts securing the rear seat wire retainers.

5. Grasp the bottom of the seatback and swing toward to disengage the offsets on the upper frame bar from the hangers.

6. Lift the seatback upward and remove from vehicle.

7. To install, reverse the above process. Torque the bolts to 40 ft.lb.

## Power Seat Motor

### REMOVAL AND INSTALLATION

1. Position the seat in the full forward position. If the car is equipped with six-way power seats, place the seat in the full forward and up position. When necessary to gain access to the adjuster-to-floor pan attaching nuts, remove the adjuster rear foot covers and or carpet retainers.

2. Remove the track covers where necessary; then remove the adjuster-to-floor pan rear attaching nuts. Position the seat in the full rearward position.

3. Remove the adjuster front foot covers; then remove the adjuster to floor pan front attaching nuts. Tilt the seat rearward and disconnect the feed wire connector.

4. Remove the seat assembly from the car.

5. Place the seat up side down on a clean surface.

6. Disconnect the vertical and horizontal drive cables from the motor.

7. Remove the retainer nut from the motor support bracket.

8. Remove the motor from the seat.

**To install:**

9. Position the motor in the motor support bracket.

10. Connect the vertical and hortizontal drive cables.

11. Place the seat into the vehicle and connect the feed wire.

12. Position the seat in the position that makes installation of the retaining nuts easiest. Install the adjuster to floor pan attaching nuts and torque to 15-21 ft.lbs. Install the foot covers.

## How to Remove Stains from Fabric Interior

For rest results, spots and stains should be removed as soon as possible. Never use gasoline, lacquer thinner, acetone, nail polish remover or bleach. Use a 3' x 3" piece of cheesecloth. Squeeze most of the liquid from the fabric and wipe the stained fabric from the outside of the stain toward the center with a lifting motion. Turn the cheesecloth as soon as one side becomes soiled. When using water to remove a stain, be sure to wash the entire section after the spot has been removed to avoid water stains. Encrusted spots can be broken up with a dull knife and vacuumed before removing the stain.

| Type of Stain | How to Remove It |
| --- | --- |
| Surface spots | Brush the spots out with a small hand brush or use a commercial preparation such as K2R to lift the stain. |
| Mildew | Clean around the mildew with warm suds. Rinse in cold water and soak the mildew area in a solution of 1 part table salt and 2 parts water. Wash with upholstery cleaner. |
| Water stains | Water stains in fabric materials can be removed with a solution made from 1 cup of table salt dissolved in 1 quart of water. Vigorously scrub the solution into the stain and rinse with clear water. Water stains in nylon or other synthetic fabrics should be removed with a commercial type spot remover. |

## How to Remove Stains from Fabric Interior (cont.)

| Type of Stain | How to Remove It |
|---|---|
| Chewing gum, tar, crayons, shoe polish (greasy stains) | Do not use a cleaner that will soften gum or tar. Harden the deposit with an ice cube and scrape away as much as possible with a dull knife. Moisten the remainder with cleaning fluid and scrub clean. |
| Ice cream, candy | Most candy has a sugar base and can be removed with a cloth wrung out in warm water. Oily candy, after cleaning with warm water, should be cleaned with upholstery cleaner. Rinse with warm water and clean the remainder with cleaning fluid. |
| Wine, alcohol, egg, milk, soft drink (non-greasy stains) | Do not use soap. Scrub the stain with a cloth wrung out in warm water. Remove the remainder with cleaning fluid. |
| Grease, oil, lipstick, butter and related stains | Use a spot remover to avoid leaving a ring. Work from the outisde of the stain to the center and dry with a clean cloth when the spot is gone. |
| Headliners (cloth) | Mix a solution of warm water and foam upholstery cleaner to give thick suds. Use only foam—liquid may streak or spot. Clean the entire headliner in one operation using a circular motion with a natural sponge. |
| Headliner (vinyl) | Use a vinyl cleaner with a sponge and wipe clean with a dry cloth. |
| Seats and door panels | Mix 1 pint upholstery cleaner in 1 gallon of water. Do not soak the fabric around the buttons. |
| Leather or vinyl fabric | Use a multi-purpose cleaner full strength and a stiff brush. Let stand 2 minutes and scrub thoroughly. Wipe with a clean, soft rag. |
| Nylon or synthetic fabrics | For normal stains, use the same procedures you would for washing cloth upholstery. If the fabric is extremely dirty, use a multi-purpose cleaner full strength with a stiff scrub brush. Scrub thoroughly in all directions and wipe with a cotton towel or soft rag. |

# Mechanic's Data

**11**

## General Conversion Table

| Multiply By | To Convert | To | |
|---|---|---|---|
| | | LENGTH | |
| 2.54 | Inches | Centimeters | .3937 |
| 25.4 | Inches | Millimeters | .03937 |
| 30.48 | Feet | Centimeters | .0328 |
| .304 | Feet | Meters | 3.28 |
| .914 | Yards | Meters | 1.094 |
| 1.609 | Miles | Kilometers | .621 |
| | | VOLUME | |
| .473 | Pints | Liters | 2.11 |
| .946 | Quarts | Liters | 1.06 |
| 3.785 | Gallons | Liters | .264 |
| .016 | Cubic inches | Liters | 61.02 |
| 16.39 | Cubic inches | Cubic cms. | .061 |
| 28.3 | Cubic feet | Liters | .0353 |
| | | MASS (Weight) | |
| 28.35 | Ounces | Grams | .035 |
| .4536 | Pounds | Kilograms | 2.20 |
| — | To obtain | From | Multiply by |

| Multiply By | To Convert | To | |
|---|---|---|---|
| | | AREA | |
| .645 | Square inches | Square cms. | .155 |
| .836 | Square yds. | Square meters | 1.196 |
| | | FORCE | |
| 4.448 | Pounds | Newtons | .225 |
| .138 | Ft./lbs. | Kilogram/meters | 7.23 |
| 1.36 | Ft./lbs. | Newton-meters | .737 |
| .112 | In./lbs. | Newton-meters | 8.844 |
| | | PRESSURE | |
| .068 | Psi | Atmospheres | 14.7 |
| 6.89 | Psi | Kilopascals | .145 |
| | | OTHER | |
| 1.104 | Horsepower (DIN) | Horsepower (SAE) | .9861 |
| .746 | Horsepower (SAE) | Kilowatts (KW) | 1.34 |
| 1.60 | Mph | Km/h | .625 |
| .425 | Mpg | Km/1 | 2.35 |
| — | To obtain | From | Multiply by |

## Tap Drill Sizes

### National Coarse or U.S.S.

| Screw & Tap Size | Threads Per Inch | Use Drill Number |
|---|---|---|
| No. 5 | 40 | 39 |
| No. 6 | 32 | 36 |
| No. 8 | 32 | 29 |
| No. 10 | 24 | 25 |
| No. 12 | 24 | 17 |
| 1/4 | 20 | 8 |
| 5/16 | 18 | F |
| 3/8 | 16 | 5/16 |
| 7/16 | 14 | U |
| 1/2 | 13 | 27/64 |
| 9/16 | 12 | 31/64 |
| 5/8 | 11 | 17/32 |
| 3/4 | 10 | 21/32 |
| 7/8 | 9 | 49/64 |

### National Coarse or U.S.S.

| Screw & Tap Size | Threads Per Inch | Use Drill Number |
|---|---|---|
| 1 | 8 | 7/8 |
| 1 1/8 | 7 | 63/64 |
| 1 1/4 | 7 | 1 7/64 |
| 1 1/2 | 6 | 1 11/32 |

### National Fine or S.A.E.

| Screw & Tap Size | Threads Per Inch | Use Drill Number |
|---|---|---|
| No. 5 | 44 | 37 |
| No. 6 | 40 | 33 |
| No. 8 | 36 | 29 |
| No. 10 | 32 | 21 |

### National Fine or S.A.E.

| Screw & Tap Size | Threads Per Inch | Use Drill Number |
|---|---|---|
| No. 12 | 28 | 15 |
| 1/4 | 28 | 3 |
| 6/16 | 24 | 1 |
| 3/8 | 24 | Q |
| 7/16 | 20 | W |
| 1/2 | 20 | 29/64 |
| 9/16 | 18 | 33/64 |
| 5/8 | 18 | 37/64 |
| 3/4 | 16 | 11/16 |
| 7/8 | 14 | 13/16 |
| 1 1/8 | 12 | 1 3/64 |
| 1 1/4 | 12 | 1 11/64 |
| 1 1/2 | 12 | 1 27/64 |

# GLOSSARY OF TERMS

**AIR/FUEL RATIO**: The ratio of air to gasoline by weight in the fuel mixture drawn into the engine.

**AIR INJECTION**: One method of reducing harmful exhaust emissions by injecting air into each of the exhaust ports of an engine. The fresh air entering the hot exhaust manifold causes any remaining fuel to be burned before it can exit the tailpipe.

**ALTERNATOR**: A device used for converting mechanical energy into electrical energy.

**AMMETER**: An instrument, calibrated in amperes, used to measure the flow of an electrical current in a circuit. Ammeters are always connected in series with the circuit being tested.

**AMPERE**: The rate of flow of electrical current present when one volt of electrical pressure is applied against one ohm of electrical resistance.

**ANALOG COMPUTER**: Any microprocessor that uses similar (analogous) electrical signals to make its calculations.

**ARMATURE**: A laminated, soft iron core wrapped by a wire that converts electrical energy to mechanical energy as in a motor or relay. When rotated in a magnetic field, it changes mechanical energy into electrical energy as in a generator.

**ATMOSPHERIC PRESSURE**: The pressure on the Earth's surface caused by the weight of the air in the atmosphere. At sea level, this pressure is 14.7 psi at 32°F (101 kPa at 0°C).

**ATOMIZATION**: The breaking down of a liquid into a fine mist that can be suspended in air.

**AXIAL PLAY**: Movement parallel to a shaft or bearing bore.

**BACKFIRE**: The sudden combustion of gases in the intake or exhaust system that results in a loud explosion.

**BACKLASH**: The clearance or play between two parts, such as meshed gears.

**BACKPRESSURE**: Restrictions in the exhaust system that slow the exit of exhaust gases from the combustion chamber.

**BAKELITE**: A heat resistant, plastic insulator material commonly used in printed circuit boards and transistorized components.

**BALL BEARING**: A bearing made up of hardened inner and outer races between which hardened steel ball roll.

**BALLAST RESISTOR**: A resistor in the primary ignition circuit that lowers voltage after the engine is started to reduce wear on ignition components.

**BEARING**: A friction reducing, supportive device usually located between a stationary part and a moving part.

**BIMETAL TEMPERATURE SENSOR**: Any sensor or switch made of two dissimilar types of metal that bend when heated or cooled due to the different expansion rates of the alloys. These types of sensors usually function as an on/off switch.

**BLOWBY**: Combustion gases, composed of water vapor and unburned fuel, that leak past the piston rings into the crankcase during normal engine operation. These gases are removed by the PCV system to prevent the buildup of harmful acids in the crankcase.

**BRAKE PAD**: A brake shoe and lining assembly used with disc brakes.

**BRAKE SHOE**: The backing for the brake lining. The term is, however, usually applied to the assembly of the brake backing and lining.

**BUSHING**: A liner, usually removable, for a bearing; an anti-friction liner used in place of a bearing.

**BYPASS**: System used to bypass ballast resistor during engine cranking to increase voltage supplied to the coil.

**CALIPER**: A hydraulically activated device in a disc brake system, which is mounted straddling the brake rotor (disc). The caliper contains at least one piston and two brake pads. Hydraulic pressure on the piston(s) forces the pads against the rotor.

**CAMSHAFT**: A shaft in the engine on which are the lobes (cams) which operate the valves. The camshaft is driven by the crankshaft, via a belt, chain or gears, at one half the crankshaft speed.

**CAPACITOR**: A device which stores an electrical charge.

**CARBON MONOXIDE (CO)**: a colorless, odorless gas given off as a normal byproduct of combustion. It is poisonous and extremely dangerous in confined areas, building up slowly to toxic levels without warning if adequate ventilation is not available.

**CARBURETOR**: A device, usually mounted on the intake manifold of an engine, which mixes the air and fuel in the proper proportion to allow even combustion.

**CATALYTIC CONVERTER**: A device installed in the exhaust system, like a muffler, that converts harmful byproducts of combustion into carbon dioxide and water vapor by means of a heat-producing chemical reaction.

**CENTRIFUGAL ADVANCE**: A mechanical method of advancing the spark timing by using flyweights in the distributor that react to centrifugal force generated by the distributor shaft rotation.

**CHECK VALVE**: Any one-way valve installed to permit the flow of air, fuel or vacuum in one direction only.

**CHOKE**: A device, usually a moveable valve, placed in the intake path of a carburetor to restrict the flow of air.

**CIRCUIT**: Any unbroken path through which an electrical current can flow. Also used to describe fuel flow in some instances.

**CIRCUIT BREAKER**: A switch which protects an electrical circuit from overload by opening the circuit when the current flow exceeds a predetermined level. Some circuit breakers must be reset manually, while other reset automatically

**COIL (IGNITION)**: A transformer in the ignition circuit which steps of the voltage provided to the spark plugs.

**COMBINATION MANIFOLD**: An assembly which includes both the intake and exhaust manifolds in one casting.

**COMBINATION VALVE**: A device used in some fuel systems that routes fuel vapors to a charcoal storage canister instead of venting them into the atmosphere. The valve relieves fuel tank pressure and allows fresh air into the tank as fuel level drops to prevent a vapor lock situation.

**COMPRESSION RATIO**: The comparison of the total volume of the cylinder and combustion chamber with the piston at BDC and the piston at TDC.

**CONDENSER**: 1. An electrical device which acts to store an electrical charge, preventing voltage surges.
 2. A radiator-like device in the air conditioning system in which refrigerant gas condenses into a liquid, giving off heat.

**CONDUCTOR**: Any material through which an electrical current can be transmitted easily.

**CONTINUITY**: Continuous or complete circuit. Can be checked with an ohmmeter.

**COUNTERSHAFT**: An intermediate shaft which is rotated by a mainshaft and transmits, in turn, that rotation to a working part.

**CRANKCASE**: The lower part of an engine in which the crankshaft and related parts operate.

**CRANKSHAFT**: The main driving shaft of an engine which receives reciprocating motion from the pistons and converts it to rotary motion.

**CYLINDER**: In an engine, the round hole in the engine block in which the piston(s) ride.

**CYLINDER BLOCK**: The main structural member of an engine in which is found the cylinders, crankshaft and other principal parts.

**CYLINDER HEAD**: The detachable portion of the engine, fastened, usually, to the top of the cylinder block, containing all or most of the combustion chambers. On overhead valve engines, it contains the valves and their operating parts. On overhead cam engines, it contains the camshaft as well.

**DEAD CENTER**: The extreme top or bottom of the piston stroke.

**DETONATION**: An unwanted explosion of the air fuel mixture in the combustion chamber caused by excess heat and compression, advanced timing, or an overly lean mixture. Also referred to as "ping".

**DIAPHRAGM**: A thin, flexible wall separating two cavities, such as in a vacuum advance unit.

**DIESELING**: A condition in which hot spots in the combustion chamber cause the engine to run on after the key is turned off.

**DIFFERENTIAL**: A geared assembly which allows the transmission of motion between drive axles, giving one axle the ability to turn faster than the other.

**DIODE**: An electrical device that will allow current to flow in one direction only.

**DISC BRAKE**: A hydraulic braking assembly consisting of a brake disc, or rotor, mounted on an axle, and a caliper assembly containing, usually two brake pads which are activated by hydraulic pressure. The pads are forced against the sides of the disc, creating friction which slows the vehicle.

**DISTRIBUTOR**: A mechanically driven device on an engine which is responsible for electrically firing the spark plug at a predetermined point of the piston stroke.

**DOWEL PIN**: A pin, inserted in mating holes in two different parts allowing those parts to maintain a fixed relationship.

**DRUM BRAKE**: A braking system which consists of two brake shoes and one or two wheel cylinders, mounted on a fixed backing plate, and a brake drum, mounted on an axle, which revolves around the assembly. Hydraulic action applied to the wheel cylinders forces the shoes outward against the drum, creating friction and slowing the vehicle.

**DWELL**: The rate, measured in degrees of shaft rotation, at which an electrical circuit cycles on and off.

**ELECTRONIC CONTROL UNIT (ECU)**: Ignition module, module, amplifier or igniter. See Module for definition.

**ELECTRONIC IGNITION**: A system in which the timing and firing of the spark plugs is controlled by an electronic control unit, usually called a module. These systems have not points or condenser.

**ENDPLAY**: The measured amount of axial movement in a shaft.

**ENGINE**: A device that converts heat into mechanical energy.

**EXHAUST MANIFOLD**: A set of cast passages or pipes which conduct exhaust gases from the engine.

**FEELER GAUGE**: A blade, usually metal, of precisely predetermined thickness, used to measure the clearance between two parts. These blades usually are available in sets of assorted thicknesses.

**F-Head**: An engine configuration in which the intake valves are in the cylinder head, while the camshaft and exhaust valves are located in the cylinder block. The camshaft operates the intake valves via lifters and pushrods, while it operates the exhaust valves directly.

**FIRING ORDER**: The order in which combustion occurs in the cylinders of an engine. Also the order in which spark is distributed to the plugs by the distributor.

**FLATHEAD**: An engine configuration in which the camshaft and all the valves are located in the cylinder block.

**FLOODING**: The presence of too much fuel in the intake manifold and combustion chamber which prevents the air/fuel mixture from firing, thereby causing a no-start situation.

**FLYWHEEL**: A disc shaped part bolted to the rear end of the crankshaft. Around the outer perimeter is affixed the ring gear. The starter drive engages the ring gear, turning the flywheel, which rotates the crankshaft, imparting the initial starting motion to the engine.

**FOOT POUND (ft.lb. or sometimes, ft. lbs.)**: The amount of energy or work needed to raise an item weighing one pound, a distance of one foot.

**FUSE**: A protective device in a circuit which prevents circuit overload by breaking the circuit when a specific amperage is present. The device is constructed around a strip or wire of a lower amperage rating than the circuit it is designed to protect. When an amperage higher than that stamped on the fuse is present in the circuit, the strip or wire melts, opening the circuit.

**GEAR RATIO**: The ratio between the number of teeth on meshing gears.

**GENERATOR**: A device which converts mechanical energy into electrical energy.

**HEAT RANGE**: The measure of a spark plug's ability to dissipate heat from its firing end. The higher the heat range, the hotter the plug fires.

**HUB**: The center part of a wheel or gear.

**HYDROCARBON (HC)**: Any chemical compound made up of hydrogen and carbon. A major pollutant formed by the engine as a byproduct of combustion.

**HYDROMETER**: An instrument used to measure the specific gravity of a solution.

**INCH POUND (in.lb. or sometimes, in. lbs.)**: One twelfth of a foot pound.

**INDUCTION**: A means of transferring electrical energy in the form of a magnetic field. Principle used in the ignition coil to increase voltage.

**INJECTION PUMP**: A device, usually mechanically operated, which meters and delivers fuel under pressure to the fuel injector.

**INJECTOR**: A device which receives metered fuel under relatively low pressure and is activated to inject the fuel into the engine under relatively high pressure at a predetermined time.

**INPUT SHAFT**: The shaft to which torque is applied, usually carrying the driving gear or gears.

**INTAKE MANIFOLD**: A casting of passages or pipes used to conduct air or a fuel/air mixture to the cylinders.

**JOURNAL**: The bearing surface within which a shaft operates.

**KEY**: A small block usually fitted in a notch between a shaft and a hub to prevent slippage of the two parts.

**MANIFOLD**: A casting of passages or set of pipes which connect the cylinders to an inlet or outlet source.

**MANIFOLD VACUUM**: Low pressure in an engine intake manifold formed just below the throttle plates. Manifold vacuum is highest at idle and drops under acceleration.

**MASTER CYLINDER**: The primary fluid pressurizing device in a hydraulic system. In automotive use, it is found in brake and hydraulic clutch systems and is pedal activated, either directly or, in a power brake system, through the power booster.

**MODULE**: Electronic control unit, amplifier or igniter of solid state or integrated design which controls the current flow in the ignition primary circuit based on input from the pickup coil. When the module opens the primary circuit, the high secondary voltage is induced in the coil.

**NEEDLE BEARING**: A bearing which consists of a number (usually a large number) of long, thin rollers.

**OHM**: ($\Omega$) The unit used to measure the resistance of conductor to electrical flow. One ohm is the amount of resistance that limits current flow to one ampere in a circuit with one volt of pressure.

**OHMMETER**: An instrument used for measuring the resistance, in ohms, in an electrical circuit.

**OUTPUT SHAFT**: The shaft which transmits torque from a device, such as a transmission.

**OVERDRIVE**: A gear assembly which produces more shaft revolutions than that transmitted to it.

**OVERHEAD CAMSHAFT (OHC)**: An engine configuration in which the camshaft is mounted on top of the cylinder head and operates the valve either directly or by means of rocker arms.

**OVERHEAD VALVE (OHV)**: An engine configuration in which all of the valves are located in the cylinder head and the camshaft is located in the cylinder block. The camshaft operates the valves via lifters and pushrods.

**OXIDES OF NITROGEN (NOx)**: Chemical compounds of nitrogen produced as a byproduct of combustion. They combine with hydrocarbons to produce smog.

**OXYGEN SENSOR**: Used with the feedback system to sense the presence of oxygen in the exhaust gas and signal the computer which can reference the voltage signal to an air/fuel ratio.

**PINION**: The smaller of two meshing gears.

**PISTON RING**: An open ended ring which fits into a groove on the outer diameter of the piston. Its chief function is to form a seal between the piston and cylinder wall. Most automotive pistons have three rings: two for compression sealing; one for oil sealing.

**PRELOAD**: A predetermined load placed on a bearing during assembly or by adjustment.

**PRIMARY CIRCUIT**: Is the low voltage side of the ignition system which consists of the ignition switch, ballast resistor or resistance wire, bypass, coil, electronic control unit and pick-up coil as well as the connecting wires and harnesses.

**PRESS FIT**: The mating of two parts under pressure, due to the inner diameter of one being smaller than the outer diameter of the other, or vice versa; an interference fit.

**RACE**: The surface on the inner or outer ring of a bearing on which the balls, needles or rollers move.

**REGULATOR**: A device which maintains the amperage and/or voltage levels of a circuit at predetermined values.

**RELAY**: A switch which automatically opens and/or closes a circuit.

**RESISTANCE**: The opposition to the flow of current through a circuit or electrical device, and is measured in ohms. Resistance is equal to the voltage divided by the amperage.

**RESISTOR**: A device, usually made of wire, which offers a preset amount of resistance in an electrical circuit.

**RING GEAR**: The name given to a ring-shaped gear attached to a differential case, or affixed to a flywheel or as part a planetary gear set.

**ROLLER BEARING**: A bearing made up of hardened inner and outer races between which hardened steel rollers move.

**ROTOR**: 1. The disc-shaped part of a disc brake assembly, upon which the brake pads bear; also called, brake disc.
2. The device mounted atop the distributor shaft, which passes current to the distributor cap tower contacts.

**SECONDARY CIRCUIT**: The high voltage side of the ignition system, usually above 20,000 volts. The secondary includes the ignition coil, coil wire, distributor cap and rotor, spark plug wires and spark plugs.

**SENDING UNIT**: A mechanical, electrical, hydraulic or electromagnetic device which transmits information to a gauge.

**SENSOR**: Any device designed to measure engine operating conditions or ambient pressures and temperatures. Usually electronic in nature and designed to send a voltage signal to an on-board computer, some sensors may operate as a simple on/off switch or they may provide a variable voltage signal (like a potentiometer) as conditions or measured parameters change.

**SHIM**: Spacers of precise, predetermined thickness used between parts to establish a proper working relationship.

**SLAVE CYLINDER**: In automotive use, a device in the hydraulic clutch system which is activated by hydraulic force, disengaging the clutch.

**SOLENOID**: A coil used to produce a magnetic field, the effect of which is produce work.

**SPARK PLUG**: A device screwed into the combustion chamber of a spark ignition engine. The basic construction is a conductive core inside of a ceramic insulator, mounted in an outer conductive base. An electrical charge from the spark plug wire travels along the conductive core and jumps a preset air gap to a grounding point or points at the end of the conductive base. The resultant spark ignites the fuel/air mixture in the combustion chamber.

**SPLINES**: Ridges machined or cast onto the outer diameter of a shaft or inner diameter of a bore to enable parts to mate without rotation.

**TACHOMETER**: A device used to measure the rotary speed of an engine, shaft, gear, etc., usually in rotations per minute.

**THERMOSTAT**: A valve, located in the cooling system of an engine, which is closed when cold and opens gradually in response to engine heating, controlling the temperature of the coolant and rate of coolant flow.

**TOP DEAD CENTER (TDC)**: The point at which the piston reaches the top of its travel on the compression stroke.

**TORQUE**: The twisting force applied to an object.

**TORQUE CONVERTER**: A turbine used to transmit power from a driving member to a driven member via hydraulic action, providing changes in drive ratio and torque. In automotive use, it links the driveplate at the rear of the engine to the automatic transmission.

**TRANSDUCER**: A device used to change a force into an electrical signal.

**TRANSISTOR**: A semi-conductor component which can be actuated by a small voltage to perform an electrical switching function.

**TUNE-UP**: A regular maintenance function, usually associated with the replacement and adjustment of parts and components in the electrical and fuel systems of a vehicle for the purpose of attaining optimum performance.

**TURBOCHARGER**: An exhaust driven pump which compresses intake air and forces it into the combustion chambers at higher than atmospheric pressures. The increased air pressure allows more fuel to be burned and results in increased horsepower being produced.

**VACUUM ADVANCE**: A device which advances the ignition timing in response to increased engine vacuum.

**VACUUM GAUGE**: An instrument used to measure the presence of vacuum in a chamber.

**VALVE**: A device which control the pressure, direction of flow or rate of flow of a liquid or gas.

**VALVE CLEARANCE**: The measured gap between the end of the valve stem and the rocker arm, cam lobe or follower that activates the valve.

**VISCOSITY**: The rating of a liquid's internal resistance to flow.

**VOLTMETER**: An instrument used for measuring electrical force in units called volts. Voltmeters are always connected parallel with the circuit being tested.

**WHEEL CYLINDER**: Found in the automotive drum brake assembly, it is a device, actuated by hydraulic pressure, which, through internal pistons, pushes the brake shoes outward against the drums.

# ABBREVIATIONS AND SYMBOLS

A: Ampere

AC: Alternating current

A/C: Air conditioning

A-h: Ampere hour

AT: Automatic transmission

ATDC: After top dead center

$\mu$A: Microampere

bbl: Barrel

BDC: Bottom dead center

bhp: Brake horsepower

BTDC: Before top dead center

BTU: British thermal unit

C: Celsius (Centigrade)

CCA: Cold cranking amps

cd: Candela

$cm^2$: Square centimeter

$cm^3$, cc: Cubic centimeter

CO: Carbon monoxide

$CO_2$: Carbon dioxide

cu.in., $in^3$: Cubic inch

CV: Constant velocity

Cyl.: Cylinder

DC: Direct current

ECM: Electronic control module

EFE: Early fuel evaporation

EFI: Electronic fuel injection

EGR: Exhaust gas recirculation

Exh.: Exhaust

F: Fahrenheit

F: Farad

pF: Picofarad

$\mu$F: Microfarad

FI: Fuel injection

ft.lb., ft. lb., ft. lbs.: foot pound(s)

gal: Gallon

g: Gram

HC: Hydrocarbon

HEI: High energy ignition

HO: High output

hp: Horsepower

Hyd.: Hydraulic

Hz: Hertz

ID: Inside diameter

in.lb.; in. lb.; in. lbs: inch pound(s)

Int.: Intake

K: Kelvin

kg: Kilogram

kHz: Kilohertz

km: Kilometer

km/h: Kilometers per hour

k$\Omega$: Kilohm

kPa: Kilopascal

kV: Kilovolt

kW: Kilowatt

l: Liter

l/s: Liters per second

m: Meter

mA: Milliampere

mg: Milligram

mHz: Megahertz

mm: Millimeter

$mm^2$: Square millimeter

$m^3$: Cubic meter

$M\Omega$: Megohm

m/s: Meters per second

MT: Manual transmission

mV: Millivolt

$\mu$m: Micrometer

N: Newton

N-m: Newton meter

NOx: Nitrous oxide

OD: Outside diameter

OHC: Over head camshaft

OHV: Over head valve

$\Omega$: Ohm

PCV: Positive crankcase ventilation

psi: Pounds per square inch

pts: Pints

qts: Quarts

rpm: Rotations per minute

rps: Rotations per second

R-12: A refrigerant gas (Freon)

SAE: Society of Automotive Engineers

$SO_2$: Sulfur dioxide

T: Ton

t: Megagram

TBI: Throttle Body Injection

TPS: Throttle Position Sensor

V: 1. Volt; 2. Venturi

$\mu$V: Microvolt

W: Watt

$\infty$: Infinity

<: Less than

>: Greater than

# Index

# Chilton's Repair & Tune-Up Guides

## The Complete line covers domestic cars, imports, trucks, vans, RV's and 4-wheel drive vehicles.

| RTUG Title | Part No. |
|---|---|
| **AMC 1975-82** | 7199 |
| Covers all U.S. and Canadian models | |
| **Aspen/Volare 1976-80** | 6637 |
| Covers all U.S. and Canadian models | |
| **Audi 1970-73** | 5902 |
| Covers all U.S. and Canadian models. | |
| **Audi 4000/5000 1978-81** | 7028 |
| Covers all U.S. and Canadian models including turbocharged and diesel engines | |
| **Barracuda/Challenger 1965-72** | 5807 |
| Covers all U.S. and Canadian models | |
| **Blazer/Jimmy 1969-82** | 6931 |
| Covers all U.S. and Canadian 2- and 4-wheel drive models, including diesel engines | |
| **BMW 1970-82** | 6844 |
| Covers U.S. and Canadian models | |
| **Buick/Olds/Pontiac 1975-85** | 7308 |
| Covers all U.S. and Canadian full size rear wheel drive models | |
| **Cadillac 1967-84** | 7462 |
| Covers all U.S. and Canadian rear wheel drive models | |
| **Camaro 1967-81** | 6735 |
| Covers all U.S. and Canadian models | |
| **Camaro 1982-85** | 7317 |
| Covers all U.S. and Canadian models | |
| **Capri 1970-77** | 6695 |
| Covers all U.S. and Canadian models | |
| **Caravan/Voyager 1984-85** | 7482 |
| Covers all U.S. and Canadian models | |
| **Century/Regal 1975-85** | 7307 |
| Covers all U.S. and Canadian rear wheel drive models, including turbocharged engines | |
| **Champ/Arrow/Sapporo 1978-83** | 7041 |
| Covers all U.S. and Canadian models | |
| **Chevette/1000 1976-86** | 6836 |
| Covers all U.S. and Canadian models | |
| **Chevrolet 1968-85** | 7135 |
| Covers all U.S. and Canadian models | |
| **Chevrolet 1968-79 Spanish** | 7082 |
| **Chevrolet/GMC Pick-Ups 1970-82 Spanish** | 7468 |
| **Chevrolet/GMC Pick-Ups and Suburban 1970-86** | 6936 |
| Covers all U.S. and Canadian $^{1}/_{2}$, $^{3}/_{4}$ and 1 ton models, including 4-wheel drive and diesel engines | |
| **Chevrolet LUV 1972-81** | 6815 |
| Covers all U.S. and Canadian models | |
| **Chevrolet Mid-Size 1964-86** | 6840 |
| Covers all U.S. and Canadian models of 1964-77 Chevelle, Malibu and Malibu SS; 1974-85 Laguna; 1978-85 Malibu; 1970-86 Monte Carlo; 1964-84 El Camino, including diesel engines | |
| **Chevrolet Nova 1986** | 7658 |
| Covers all U.S. and Canadian models | |
| **Chevy/GMC Vans 1967-84** | 6930 |
| Covers all U.S. and Canadian models of $^{1}/_{2}$, $^{3}/_{4}$, and 1 ton vans, cutaways, and motor home chassis, including diesel engines | |
| **Chevy S-10 Blazer/GMC S-15 Jimmy 1982-85** | 7383 |
| Covers all U.S. and Canadian models | |
| **Chevy S-10/GMC S-15 Pick-Ups 1982-85** | 7310 |
| Covers all U.S. and Canadian models | |
| **Chevy II/Nova 1962-79** | 6841 |
| Covers all U.S. and Canadian models | |
| **Chrysler K- and E-Car 1981-85** | 7163 |
| Covers all U.S. and Canadian front wheel drive models | |
| **Colt/Challenger/Vista/Conquest 1971-85** | 7037 |
| Covers all U.S. and Canadian models | |
| **Corolla/Carina/Tercel/Starlet 1970-85** | 7036 |
| Covers all U.S. and Canadian models | |
| **Corona/Cressida/Crown/Mk.II/Camry/Van 1970-84** | 7044 |
| Covers all U.S. and Canadian models | |

| RTUG Title | Part No. |
|---|---|
| **Corvair 1960-69** | 6691 |
| Covers all U.S. and Canadian models | |
| **Corvette 1953-62** | 6576 |
| Covers all U.S. and Canadian models | |
| **Corvette 1963-84** | 6843 |
| Covers all U.S. and Canadian models | |
| **Cutlass 1970-85** | 6933 |
| Covers all U.S. and Canadian models | |
| **Dart/Demon 1968-76** | 6324 |
| Covers all U.S. and Canadian models | |
| **Datsun 1961-72** | 5790 |
| Covers all U.S. and Canadian models of Nissan Patrol; 1500, 1600 and 2000 sports cars; Pick-Ups; 410, 411, 510, 1200 and 240Z | |
| **Datsun 1973-80 Spanish** | 7083 |
| **Datsun/Nissan F-10, 310, Stanza, Pulsar 1977-86** | 7196 |
| Covers all U.S. and Canadian models | |
| **Datsun/Nissan Pick-Ups 1970-84** | 6816 |
| Covers all U.S. and Canadian models | |
| **Datsun/Nissan Z & ZX 1970-86** | 6932 |
| Covers all U.S. and Canadian models | |
| **Datsun/Nissan 1200, 210, Sentra 1973-86** | 7197 |
| Covers all U.S. and Canadian models | |
| **Datsun/Nissan 200SX, 510, 610, 710, 810, Maxima 1973-84** | 7170 |
| Covers all U.S. and Canadian models | |
| **Dodge 1968-77** | 6554 |
| Covers all U.S. and Canadian models | |
| **Dodge Charger 1967-70** | 6486 |
| Covers all U.S. and Canadian models | |
| **Dodge/Plymouth Trucks 1967-84** | 7459 |
| Covers all $^{1}/_{2}$, $^{3}/_{4}$, and 1 ton 2- and 4-wheel drive U.S. and Canadian models, including diesel engines | |
| **Dodge/Plymouth Vans 1967-84** | 6934 |
| Covers all $^{1}/_{2}$, $^{3}/_{4}$, and 1 ton U.S. and Canadian models of vans, cutaways and motor home chassis | |
| **D-50/Arrow Pick-Up 1979-81** | 7032 |
| Covers all U.S. and Canadian models | |
| **Fairlane/Torino 1962-75** | 6320 |
| Covers all U.S. and Canadian models | |
| **Fairmont/Zephyr 1978-83** | 6965 |
| Covers all U.S. and Canadian models | |
| **Fiat 1969-81** | 7042 |
| Covers all U.S. and Canadian models | |
| **Fiesta 1978-80** | 6846 |
| Covers all U.S. and Canadian models | |
| **Firebird 1967-81** | 5996 |
| Covers all U.S. and Canadian models | |
| **Firebird 1982-85** | 7345 |
| Covers all U.S. and Canadian models | |
| **Ford 1968-79 Spanish** | 7084 |
| **Ford Bronco 1966-83** | 7140 |
| Covers all U.S. and Canadian models | |
| **Ford Bronco II 1984** | 7408 |
| Covers all U.S. and Canadian models | |
| **Ford Courier 1972-82** | 6983 |
| Covers all U.S. and Canadian models | |
| **Ford/Mercury Front Wheel Drive 1981-85** | 7055 |
| Covers all U.S. and Canadian models Escort, EXP, Tempo, Lynx, LN-7 and Topaz | |
| **Ford/Mercury/Lincoln 1968-85** | 6842 |
| Covers all U.S. and Canadian models of FORD Country Sedan, Country Squire, Crown Victoria, Custom, Custom 500, Galaxie 500, LTD through 1982, Ranch Wagon, and XL; MERCURY Colony Park, Commuter, Marquis through 1982, Gran Marquis, Monterey and Park Lane; LINCOLN Continental and Towne Car | |
| **Ford/Mercury/Lincoln Mid-Size 1971-85** | 6696 |
| Covers all U.S. and Canadian models of FORD Elite, 1983-85 LTD, 1977-79 LTD II, Ranchero, Torino, Gran Torino, 1977-85 Thunderbird; MERCURY 1972-85 Cougar, | |

continued on next page

| RTUG Title | Part No. | RTUG Title | Part No. |
|---|---|---|---|
| 1983-85 Marquis, Montego, 1980-85 XR-7; LINCOLN 1982-85 Continental, 1984-85 Mark VII, 1978-80 Versailles | | Mercedes-Benz 1974-84 Covers all U.S. and Canadian models | 6809 |
| **Ford Pick-Ups 1965-86** Covers all $^1/_2$, $^3/_4$ and 1 ton, 2- and 4-wheel drive U.S. and Canadian pick-up, chassis cab and camper models, including diesel engines | 6913 | **Mitsubishi, Cordia, Tredia, Starion, Galant 1983-85** Covers all U.S. and Canadian models | 7583 |
| | | **MG 1961-81** Covers all U.S. and Canadian models | 6780 |
| **Ford Pick-Ups 1965-82 Spanish** | 7469 | **Mustang/Capri/Merkur 1979-85** Covers all U.S. and Canadian models | 6963 |
| **Ford Ranger 1983-84** Covers all U.S. and Canadian models | 7338 | **Mustang/Cougar 1965-73** Covers all U.S. and Canadian models | 6542 |
| **Ford Vans 1961-86** Covers all U.S. and Canadian $^1/_2$, $^3/_4$ and 1 ton van and cutaway chassis models, including diesel engines | 6849 | **Mustang II 1974-78** Covers all U.S. and Canadian models | 6812 |
| | | **Omni/Horizon/Rampage 1978-84** Covers all U.S. and Canadian models of DODGE omni, Miser, 024, Charger 2.2; PLYMOUTH Horizon, Miser, TC3, TC3 Tourismo; Rampage | 6845 |
| **GM A-Body 1982-85** Covers all front wheel drive U.S. and Canadian models of BUICK Century, CHEVROLET Celebrity, OLDSMOBILE Cutlass Ciera and PONTIAC 6000 | 7309 | | |
| | | **Opel 1971-75** Covers all U.S. and Canadian models | 6575 |
| **GM C-Body 1985** Covers all front wheel drive U.S. and Canadian models of BUICK Electra Park Avenue and Electra T-Type, CADILLAC Fleetwood and deVille, OLDSMOBILE 98 Regency and Regency Brougham | 7587 | **Peugeot 1970-74** Covers all U.S. and Canadian models | 5982 |
| | | **Pinto/Bobcat 1971-80** Covers all U.S. and Canadian models | 7027 |
| | | **Plymouth 1968-76** Covers all U.S. and Canadian models | 6552 |
| **GM J-Car 1982-85** Covers all U.S. and Canadian models of BUICK Skyhawk, CHEVROLET Cavalier, CADILLAC Cimarron, OLDSMOBILE Firenza and PONTIAC 2000 and Sunbird | 7059 | **Pontiac Fiero 1984-85** Covers all U.S. and Canadian models | 7571 |
| | | **Pontiac Mid-Size 1974-83** Covers all U.S. and Canadian models of Ventura, Grand Am, LeMans, Grand LeMans, GTO, Phoenix, and Grand Prix | 7346 |
| **GM N-Body 1985-86** Covers all U.S. and Canadian models of front wheel drive BUICK Somerset and Skylark, OLDSMOBILE Calais, and PONTIAC Grand Am | 7657 | **Porsche 924/928 1976-81** Covers all U.S. and Canadian models | 7048 |
| | | **Renault 1975-85** Covers all U.S. and Canadian models | 7165 |
| **GM X-Body 1980-85** Covers all U.S. and Canadian models of BUICK Skylark, CHEVROLET Citation, OLDSMOBILE Omega and PONTIAC Phoenix | 7049 | **Roadrunner/Satellite/Belvedere/GTX 1968-73** Covers all U.S. and Canadian models | 5821 |
| | | **RX-7 1979-81** Covers all U.S. and Canadian models | 7031 |
| **GM Subcompact 1971-80** Covers all U.S. and Canadian models of BUICK Skyhawk (1975-80), CHEVROLET Vega and Monza, OLDSMOBILE Starfire, and PONTIAC Astre and 1975-80 Sunbird | 6935 | **SAAB 99 1969-75** Covers all U.S. and Canadian models | 5988 |
| | | **SAAB 900 1979-85** Covers all U.S. and Canadian models | 7572 |
| **Granada/Monarch 1975-82** Covers all U.S. and Canadian models | 6937 | **Snowmobiles 1976-80** Covers Arctic Cat, John Deere, Kawasaki, Polaris, Ski-Doo and Yamaha | 6978 |
| **Honda 1973-84** Covers all U.S. and Canadian models | 6980 | **Subaru 1970-84** Covers all U.S. and Canadian models | 6982 |
| **International Scout 1967-73** Covers all U.S. and Canadian models | 5912 | **Tempest/GTO/LeMans 1968-73** Covers all U.S. and Canadian models | 5905 |
| **Jeep 1945-87** Covers all U.S. and Canadian CJ-2A, CJ-3A, CJ-3B, CJ-5, CJ-6, CJ-7, Scrambler and Wrangler models | 6817 | **Toyota 1966-70** Covers all U.S. and Canadian models of Corona, MkII, Corolla, Crown, Land Cruiser, Stout and Hi-Lux | 5795 |
| **Jeep Wagoneer, Commando, Cherokee, Truck 1957-86** Covers all U.S. and Canadian models of Wagoneer, Cherokee, Grand Wagoneer, Jeepster, Jeepster Commando, J-100, J-200, J-300, J-10, J20, FC-150 and FC-170 | 6739 | **Toyota 1970-79 Spanish** | 7467 |
| | | **Toyota Celica/Supra 1971-85** Covers all U.S. and Canadian models | 7043 |
| | | **Toyota Trucks 1970-85** Covers all U.S. and Canadian models of pickups, Land Cruiser and 4Runner | 7035 |
| **Laser/Daytona 1984-85** Covers all U.S. and Canadian models | 7563 | **Valiant/Duster 1968-76** Covers all U.S. and Canadian models | 6326 |
| **Maverick/Comet 1970-77** Covers all U.S. and Canadian models | 6634 | **Volvo 1956-69** Covers all U.S. and Canadian models | 6529 |
| **Mazda 1971-84** Covers all U.S. and Canadian models of RX-2, RX-3, RX-4, 808, 1300, 1600, Cosmo, GLC and 626 | 6981 | **Volvo 1970-83** Covers all U.S. and Canadian models | 7040 |
| | | **VW Front Wheel Drive 1974-85** Covers all U.S. and Canadian models | 6962 |
| **Mazda Pick-Ups 1972-86** Covers all U.S. and Canadian models | 7659 | **VW 1949-71** Covers all U.S. and Canadian models | 5796 |
| **Mercedes-Benz 1959-70** Covers all U.S. and Canadian models | 6065 | **VW 1970-79 Spanish** | 7081 |
| **Merceds-Benz 1968-73** Covers all U.S. and Canadian models | 5907 | **VW 1970-81** Covers all U.S. and Canadian Beetles, Karmann Ghia, Fastback, Squareback, Vans, 411 and 412 | 6837 |

Chilton's Repair Manuals are available at your local retailer or by mailing a check or money order for **$14.95** per book plus **$3.50** for 1st book and **$.50** for each additional book to cover postage and handling to:

**Chilton Book Company**
**Dept. DM**
**Radnor, PA 19089**

**NOTE: When ordering be sure to include your name & address, book part No. & title.**